A REGIONAL CONTEMPORARY

A REGIONAL CONTEMPORARY

ART EXHIBITIONS, POPULAR CULTURE, ASIA

C. J. W.-L. WEE

The MIT Press
Cambridge, Massachusetts
London, England

The MIT Press would like to thank the anonymous peer reviewers who provided comments on drafts of this book. The generous work of academic experts is essential for establishing the authority and quality of our publications. We acknowledge with gratitude the contributions of these otherwise uncredited readers.

This book was set in Minion and Neue Haas Grotesk by Westchester Publishing Services. Printed and bound in the United States of America.

Library of Congress Cataloging-in-Publication Data

Names: Wee, C. J. Wan-ling, author.
Title: A regional contemporary : art exhibitions, popular culture, Asia / C.J.W.-L. Wee.
Description: Cambridge, Massachusetts : The MIT Press, [2025] | Includes bibliographical
   references and index.
Identifiers: LCCN 2024017288 (print) | LCCN 2024017289 (ebook) | ISBN 9780262552257
   (paperback) | ISBN 9780262382946 (epub) | ISBN 9780262383202 (pdf)
Subjects: LCSH: Arts and society—East Asia—History—20th century. |
   Arts—Economic aspects—East Asia—History—20th century. |
   East Asia—Economic conditions—20th century.
Classification: LCC NX180.S6 W44 2025 (print) | LCC NX180.S6 (ebook) |
   DDC 701/.03095—dc23/eng/20240620
LC record available at https://lccn.loc.gov/2024017288
LC ebook record available at https://lccn.loc.gov/2024017289

10 9 8 7 6 5 4 3 2 1

EU product safety and compliance information contact is: mitp-eu-gpsr@mit.edu

CONTENTS

ACKNOWLEDGMENTS

This book has taken more years to be completed than either desired or expected. Inevitably, it is the result of innumerable conversations, often in supportive and intellectually conducive institutional environments, and so there truly is a need to acknowledge the many who have supported the uneven attempts to explore, reflect, and write.

Much generosity has been offered by various institutions. Caroline Turner helped initiate the research with a visiting fellowship at the Humanities Research Centre at the Australian National University—and offered ongoing and patient assistance in the years after; Ashley Carruthers made Canberra especially comfortable. Brett de Bary's reigning beneficence and intellectual presence during a visiting fellowship at Cornell's Society for the Humanities were incalculably enabling. The Society's 2007–2008 fellows were superbly collegial and generous, and I do need to mention Charlie Kronengold in particular. Cornell faculty and a number of its (then) postgraduate students across many departments—Shirley Samuels, Petrus Liu, Naoki Sakai, Grant Farred, Dominick LaCapra, Nakamori Yasufumi, and Tsitsi Jaji, among others—were welcoming, and I particularly benefited from time spent with Iftikhar Dadi. A sabbatical taken at Duke University was supported intellectually and otherwise beyond all reasonable levels by Leo T. S. Ching; Rey Chow offered her critical thoughts on my work for a presentation as a short-term resident at Duke's Franklin Humanities Institute; and Guo-Juin Hong graciously allowed me the use of his office during my stay. Cambridge's Centre for Research in the Arts, Social Sciences, and Humanities, under Mary Jacobus's directorship, offered a respite for mental endeavor in the summer of 2009. Substantial effort toward completing the manuscript was facilitated by a Luce Fellowship at the National Humanities Center (NHC) in 2020, where Shuang Shen, another fellow, was an essential interlocutor. Lynn and John Hand, as always, made any stay in the Research Triangle area marvelous. COVID-19 disrupted the NHC sojourn but did not rob it of its importance.

I am grateful for the research leave to take up the Luce Fellowship granted by the Nanyang Technological University (NTU), where my colleague Neil Murphy has indefatigably supported humanities research under challenging circumstances. Chua Beng Huat consistently offered general and practical support, such as office space as an associate of the Asia Research Institute, National University of Singapore, during part of a sabbatical leave. Lee Weng Choy has been not only a friend but also a solid cultural-intellectual ally, given his knowledge and participation in some of the artistic events discussed in *A Regional Contemporary*. The general support of Philip J. Holden has always been present.

Elizabeth K. Helsinger has been outstanding as an advisor for umpteen seasons. Patrick D. Flores has offered pivotal insights over many years vital to the cultural-theoretical framework of the book. Much of the popular music content semi-wrote itself with the extensive knowledge gleaned from Mōri Yoshitaka, Anthony Fung, and Shin Hyunjoon. Michael Bourdaghs's knowledge of Japanese popular music contributed too. Uchino Tadashi assisted with many artistic-cultural matters Japanese. Joan Kee's responses and thoughts have always challenged me. Norma Field, Igarashi Akio, and Honda Shiro helped launch my interest in Japanese popular culture ages ago. I learned from T. K. Sabapathy's thinking—as both critic and participant in key exhibition events!

Kuroda Raiji enabled a research trip to the Fukuoka Asian Art Museum and offered his valuable knowledge to me. Vishaka N. Desai shared her experience of when she was director of the Asia Society Museum. The late Tan Boon Hui, director of the Asia Society Museum from 2015 to 2020, gave me access to the Society's archive for work on the exhibition *Contemporary Art in Asia: Traditions/Tensions*. Queensland Art Gallery/Gallery of Modern Art in Brisbane, Australia, allowed me access to extensive archival material related to the Asia-Pacific Triennial of Contemporary Art. Furuichi Yasuko, formerly at the Japan Foundation Asia Center (JFAC), both shared her thoughts on the regional art scene and arranged for vital documentation and material to be sent to me. The students in SHUM419 Imagining Contemporary Asia at Cornell are to be thanked, along with the NTU students in my HL4009 and HL7114 modules over a number of years, for their thoughts as "native informants" on inter-Asian popular and other cultures.

I have also benefited from a wider range of interactions with various scholars, curators, artists, and knowledgeable arts participants on matters the book addresses, and I thank them: Ahmad Mashadi, Chen Kuan-Hsing, Bruce Robbins, Wang Hui, Peter Schoppert, Roger Nelson, Jini Kim Watson, Russell Storer, Tang Da Wu, Kwok Kian Chow, Ray Langenbach, Takiguchi Ken, Ushiroshōji Masahiro, Tomii Reiko, Lee Wen, Amanda Heng, Victor P. H. Li, Chương-Đài Võ, Pauline Yao, Kataoka Mami, Jean Comaroff, Heman Chong, Iwabuchi Kōichi, Helena Grehan, the late Willian S. W. Lim, Note Osamu, Stephen Teo, Takahashi Yūichirō, Meaghan Morris, Elaine Ho, Joshua Comaroff, Rob Wilson, Mandy Thomas, Liew Kai Khuin, Oscar Ho, Carol Vernullis, Sun Jung, Xiao Li, Shim Doobo, Lee Hyunjung, Horikawa Lisa, Roger Nelson, Lee Chor Lin, Shim Doboo, Rob Wilson, John Clark, Stephanie Bailey, Christopher Lee, Thiti Jamkajornkeiat, Loo Zihan, Liz MacLachlan, and Hayashi Michio. *A Regional Contemporary* gained much from three strong anonymous reviews and the insightful editorial work by Victoria Hindley. The production process was detailed and thorough, and I am grateful for the team's work.

Portions of this book are reworked versions of previously published work. Chapter 1 originally appeared as "'We Asians'?: Modernity, Visual Art Exhibitions, and East Asia," *boundary 2* 37, no. 1 (2010): 91–126. © 2010, Duke University Press. All rights reserved. Republished by permission of the publisher. Chapter 3 is a revision of "Discoursing Asia: The Present and Historical Fracture in the Japan Foundation Asia Center Symposia on Contemporary Asian Art, 1997–2002," *Interventions: International Journal of Postcolonial Studies* 25, no. 3 (2023): 306–328, special issue on "Infrastructure as Inter-Asian Method," ed. Xiao Liu and Shuang Shen. Reprinted by permission of the publisher, Taylor & Francis Ltd. Chapter 4 is a substantially expanded rendition of "Imagining the Fractured East Asian Modern: Commonality and Difference in Mass Cultural Production," *Criticism: A Quarterly for Literature and the Arts* 54, no. 2 (2012): 197–225. Chapter 5 first appeared as "East Asian Pop Music and an Incomplete Regional Contemporary," in *Sound Alignments: Popular Music in Asia's Cold Wars*, ed. Michael Bourdaghs, Paola Iovene, and Kaley Mason, 93–127. © 2021, Duke University Press. All rights reserved. Republished by permission of the publisher.

Every reasonable attempt has been made to identify owners of song lyrics copyrights. Errors and omissions notified to the publisher will be corrected in a subsequent edition.

A note on names in the book. As the reader will know, names from the region have diverse forms and often do not match a "first" and "last" names cultural format. By and large, I have used the form of the names as they appear in my primary and secondary sources. However, when a person has an accepted form of his or her name within an artistic or other type of community within Northeast or Southeast Asia and Australia, I will use that form consistently in the main body of the book, regardless of the shape it may take in the published sources.

> *Ubi sunt gaudia?*
> Nirgend mehr denn da,
> da die Engel singen
> *nova cantica*
> und die Schellen klingen
> *in regis curia.*
> Eia, wärn wir da!

INTRODUCTION: A REGIONAL CONTEMPORARY

In the early 1990s, television production in Japan increased in sophistication. The type of dramas that featured urban young people's experiences in love, friendship, and work became more story oriented with better organized plots, had more discriminating use of music, and offered effective sympathetic treatment of their protagonists. Hitherto, such dramas seemed more committed to the representation of fashionable consumerist trends.

In April 1996, Fuji Television released the drama series *Long Vacation* (*Rongu bakēshon*), which became hugely successful. The series implied that even in post–bubble economy Japan, the young can do better than to secure a temporary job. A pianist in Tokyo, Sena Hidetoshi, is unable to live up to his actual talent level and ends up giving music lessons at a local piano company. He meets the perky Hayama Minami, a not-quite-successful model, when his apartment mate jilts her on their wedding day—she very dramatically turns up at Sena's doorstep in her wedding dress. Sena kindly allows Hayama to move into the apartment, as she foolishly gave all her money to her fiancé; this kindness (naturally) marks the start of a romance. However, they are (inevitably) distracted by other romances, and it takes a while for them to sort matters out. Hayama's *ganbaru* attitude—an optimistic, never-say-die commitment to tenaciousness—inspires Sena, and he wins an international piano competition, giving him a scholarship to Boston. He then picks up the courage to propose, and she goes with him to the United States. The long vacation has ended.

Long Vacation became popular in the expanding media markets in East and Southeast Asia, even though this was not Fuji Television's primary intent. Part of the cause, no doubt, was that Sena was played by the charismatic pop singer Kimura Takuya, arguably the best-known member of the boy band SMAP, at a point when what was called "J-Pop" music was spreading in the region as well.[1] And in 1999, Kimura, who was by then a seemingly fixed face in Japanese television, becomes the first Asian brand ambassador of Levi's jeans. The company, presumably, was drawing upon his region-wide celebrity.[2] The other probable reason for its popularity was that the 1990s Tokyo put on display in the drama resonated with diverse regional aspirations. For example, a Taiwanese communications scholar found that for some Taiwanese fans of idol dramas, "the imagery of 'Tokyo' is a *visual place* that mediates between reality and dreams"—despite it being the capital of Taiwan's former colonizers.[3] A perception of Japan as metropolitan could influence the region's imagining of the modern, it seemed.

If Japan, as it were, went out to the larger region, how did the latter make an impact on Japan? We can see one result in an ambitious, three-year exhibition project titled *Under Construction: New Dimensions in Asian Art*. That was the name given to the final exhibition in Tokyo in December 2002 that drew upon seven curators' earlier and locally organized exhibitions in Mumbai, Bangkok, Bandung, Manila, Beijing, Seoul, and Ashiya, a small Japanese city. The larger region's relevance was perceived by the exhibition's organizers through economic globalization, which had led to an increased interdependence that affected societies and cultures. Discussing Asia in Japan, however, remained an awkward subject, given that Japanese colonialism and the war that followed were not quite resolved issues. Nevertheless, the interlinking of economies led the Japan Foundation Asia Center, in conjunction with the Tokyo Opera City Cultural Foundation, to see if, by trial and error, some sense of the dynamic present-day identity of Asia could be collaboratively captured by younger Asian curators who shared a sensibility of a globalized and mediatized world.

Of course, even the Japanese curators' reactions to the curatorial challenge varied. Yamamoto Atsuo, a curator from the Ashiya City Museum of Art and History, was hesitant but open-minded, writing in the exhibition catalogue that he had not much prior "awareness of . . . belonging to Asia . . . [but that as a result of the project, he had] begun to wonder about Japan's strange lack of awareness of her own Asianness."[4] In contrast, independent curator Kamiya Yukie, who cocurated two of the local shows in Seoul and Beijing, directly affirmed the layered dialogues she had experienced: "It is time to change from an Asia being looked at to an Asia where we ourselves are doing the looking."[5]

A Regional Contemporary is an inquiry into how we might think through the tensions, contradictions, and possibilities in the aesthetic- and popular-cultural imagining of a contemporary Asia. Covering the period 1979 to about 2008, with the 1990s as the core of this period, this book is both an account and investigation of a dramatic increase in cultural expression—biennial-style art exhibitions, new discourses in modern and contemporary art, and the production and circulation of debordered popular culture—that, in relation to expanded capitalist energies, performatively projected a fictive but shared contemporary regional identity onto disjunctive spatial standpoints in Northeast and Southeast Asia, collectively taken as East Asia. Various cultural formations of this regional contemporary were able to traverse, although not overcome, uneven national economies, the memory of Japanese empire, and the geopolitical rifts of post–Cold War nationalisms.

The magnitude of the argument is in the foregrounding of not only new cultural expressions but also the novel economic conditions that enabled culture. The latter bolstered a more confident postcolonial questioning of Western metropolitan modernity's dominance and enhanced the capability for intra-regional dialogue in the bid to overcome the legacies of colonial-era modernity—even as those legacies were simultaneously understood to be absorbed into the region. The book also serves to document the voices behind cultural creativity that emerged from the 1990s and to indicate that, indeed, the subaltern, as it were, does speak back to the metropole not only in conjunction with but also *independently* from the liberal sections of the Anglo-American academy and culture.[6]

By the 1990s, a cartographic reimagining of an old cultural entity, Asia, had taken place, in which Southeast Asia became a subdivision of an enlarged East Asia. Quite dissimilar politicians took this position. In 1995, Dr. Mahathir Mohamad—Malaysia's prime minister and a self-styled champion for the Global South—wrote, "We must commit ourselves to ensuring that the history of East Asia will be made in East Asia, for East Asia, and by East Asians"; and the nationalistic Ishihara Shintarō—soon to become governor of Tokyo—pronounced, "During the Cold War Japan was part of the western camp, an anomalous position wholly attributable to the polarized East-West confrontation over communism. Geographically and spiritually, Japan belongs to Asia."[7] Ishihara, of course, was aware of Japan's long-standing ambivalence at being part of a larger notion of a less-developed Asia and the historical legacy of the Greater East Asia Co-Prosperity Sphere. The contemporary moment of a putative "New Asia" is, in Fredric Jameson's term, a "synchronic heterogeneity" in which disparate economic development levels and temporalities (the inevitable need to confront the dyad of the "traditional" vs. "modern" in societies), along with culturally disjunctive entities and national histories, could be coordinated into a *contemporary* regional space.[8] This is in defiance of modern social science's binary logic of advanced and backward, rational and irrational/nonrational, with it being better to eliminate any lingering vestige of the past. The New Asian turn also offered novel possibilities for cultural expression. The context for change was the region's participation in an expansive globalizing capitalism, leading the Asia-Pacific to grow by 9.4 percent in 1988, when the world average was 4.1 percent, as Mahathir noted.[9] In 1993, the World Bank recognized this economic dynamism with the epithet the "East Asian miracle."[10]

The subjects of exploration are, first, art exhibitions mainly in Japan and Australia but also in New York City and parts of Western Europe—visible sites in which New Asia and its modern and contemporary art were curated into "being"—and second, 1990s multilingual Hong Kong film, Japanese pop music (specifically J-Pop), and, from around 2000, Korean pop music (specifically K-Pop) that crossed national boundaries. The 1990s to about the mid-2000s form the central period, as, arguably, it was from the 1990s that the global process of capital accumulation reached a level critical enough such that the region's postcolonial and Cold War–era nationalisms were partially but noticeably reworked, with implications for cultural expression. There was experimentation with newer knowledge frameworks to understand and exhibit the region's modern and contemporary artistic cultures better amid the increased regional economic interdependency. Unsurprisingly, discursive production was prominent as an approach to working out what can be characterized as "a regional contemporary"; discursive material therefore occupies a consequential position in my study. There was also the growth of urbanizing centers and an increased new middle class, which embraced the potentialities of an inter-Asian popular culture. In the process, a flexible synchronization took place that allowed the yoking of tradition, in creative tension with the present, to artistic- and popular-cultural experience of the urban present, all subsumed under the abstraction that was and is New Asia.

This study could have taken other fruitful directions in understanding the circulation of culture. One may have been to see how popular culture with capitalist origins journeyed the region inconsistently, transgressing Cold War–dictated national frontiers, "neither entirely determined by the socialist states nor fully integrated within a capitalist mode or production," resulting in cultural heterogeneities engendered by economic reform.[11] That could yield further insight into the persistent contradictions in mainland China after market reforms, even as it maintained ties with North Korea. Or it could have followed art historian Joan Kee's injunction to forsake the examination of cultural routes or aesthetic-intellectual affiliations and to anticipate the "formation of a new global majority," an "Afro Asia" that could be based on "the proliferation and circulation of feelings, cognitions, and sensations capable of holding their own against various lines of division."[12] Instead, *A Regional Contemporary* has chosen to examine a putative contemporary identity formation that is paradoxically predicated on capitalist incorporation precisely to fathom and historicize the affiliations and cultural circulation better that transpired in the 1980s–2000s.

Even though the region's contemporary moment unavoidably engaged with older ideas of exotic and traditional Asia from the colonial era, the effective result of new forms of cultural understanding was the rejection (if not always deliberately or planned) of essentialist cultural perceptions of the region. While there were variable assertions of synchronicity with both the advanced West and with countries within the region, the book project also reflects upon the discrepancies in imagining a contemporary Asia when ongoing tensions with origins from the nineteenth century—with Japan's modern emanation with the Meiji Restoration (1868) and the First Sino-Japanese War (1894–1895)—to the Pacific War, and then the Cold War, seem more pronounced than ever. No new ideology congruent with economic integration has come about, and regionalizing (if not quite regional) museum and curatorial practices and popular culture are, arguably, the *positive cultural aspects of a fraught contemporary moment* in which culture, intertwined with development, has engaged with older modernist ideologies in ways not previously conceivable. That is, while the enlarged East Asia has seen "a volatilization of temporality," there has been neither the "abolition, [n]or [even] at least the repression of historicity" that we might expect when the regional contemporary becomes a part of the "new global culture corresponding to [the substructure of] globalization."[13] The term "regional contemporary" designates both an analytical category, where the past is overhauled or exceeded to serve present-day cultural projects, and a substantive category, referring to the circulation of cultural practices assisting the signification of the contemporary in the region. *A Regional Contemporary*, then, is also a study of the temporally and geographically "less" modern.

Producing Contemporary Asia after the Postwar Arc of Development

Rapid economic growth in the 1980s–1990s saw a revivification of the idea of Asia, now taken as less backward. This rapid growth, with Japan at the forefront, triggered both discourses on the supposed Asian or, alternatively, Confucian values that underlay dynamic economic growth in East Asia (with Southeast Asia as part of that cartographic imaginary) and a startling increase in artistic-cultural reflection and cultural production.[14] The latter, which formally or informally sought to define inter-Asian multicultures and consumers, appeared in both high and popular formats.

The regionalization of production was particularly stimulated by Japanese capital from the mid-1980s that brought South Korea, Taiwan, Hong Kong, and Singapore and other Southeast Asian countries into "a de facto East Asian economic region."[15] These developments were, at the least, a longer-term, partial, and unexpected consequence of postwar American attempts to bring Cold War Asia back to "normality" through the fostering of regional economic exchange, which also took Japanese economic influence back into Northeast and Southeast Asia, after its defeat in the Asia-Pacific War. Certainly, an inclusive "East Asia" was a better term for conceiving the region than the older, Eurocentric "Far East," which was problematized by the American historians Edwin O. Reischauer and John K. Fairbank as far back as 1960. The latter term registered how "Europeans traveled far to the east to reach Cathay, Japan and the Indies"; Americans who reached the same area via the Pacific could, "with equal logic, have called that area the 'Far West.'" However, for people who live in that part of the world, a "more generally acceptable term for the area is 'East Asia,' which is geographically more precise and does not imply the outdated notion that Europe is the center of the civilized world."[16] Another term for this inclusive East Asia might be historian Arif Dirlik's "Eastern Asia." He succinctly but critically describes the collective postwar developmental weight: "Following WWII, especially from the 1960s, these regimes achieved rapid development under a combination of political authoritarianism (or dictatorship) and sub-contractual economic development, beginning with the creation of export zones, that would serve as the pioneering moments in the emergence of 'a new international division of labor,' neo-liberal assaults on national economic boundaries and, ultimately, what has come to be known as globalization."[17] Eastern Asian success set the context for development in the People's Republic of China (PRC), inspiring their reform and opening-up processes.

The rationale of the link between Southeast Asia and, above all, Japan in Northeast Asia comes about with US policymakers who saw them as major sectors of a "great crescent" to contain communism imagined as a distended arc from the Kurile Islands to the borders of Afghanistan: "Among the many planners and agencies concerned with charting the future of Japan after 1945, the fate of Southeast Asia stands out as a central issue around which they constructed a regional policy."[18] A pervasive concern in the late 1940s was that Japanese economic recovery would be blocked by communist control of most of Northeast Asia, given China's civil war and the political upheaval in the areas that adjoined Republican China. A "southern strategy" was the solution, given the sometimes overlooked economic importance of, say, Malayan tin and rubber to the world economy.[19] While there was tension between the US Defense and State Departments as to how communism should be combatted—either by supporting the weak Chiang Kai Shek regime or by preventing the spread of the menace to Southeast Asia by fostering an economic partnership with Japan—the State Department's position prevailed. Hence, ironically, Japan was to be encouraged to integrate economically with the Southeast Asia they had been kicked out of, and this would serve to provide stability in the aftermath of the impending European imperial sunset. General Omar Bradley, chairman of the Joint Chiefs of Staff, told President Harry Truman in a June 26, 1950, memorandum that "Korea, Japan, Okinawa, Formosa [Taiwan], the Philippines and Southeast Asia are all part of the same problem."[20] Southeast Asia's link with Northeast Asia continues to this day and thus forms the version of Asia that *A Regional Contemporary* examines.

The results of the postwar arc of development enabled parts of the region to feel less behind the thrust of history: "we Asians" live in the coeval moment of the present as much as the advanced West—but an issue remained as to whether coevality might apply to the region in a cohesive way, when development was still uneven. Also, while there was (and is) widespread recognition that the term "Asia" was vague and suffered from the fact of being an empty category defined in binary terms against the category "the West," the term of course continues to be popularly used, despite severe intellectual critiques.[21]

A Regional Contemporary ranges from 1979 to the mid-2000s, as I indicated earlier, as it is during this period that the increasingly global process of capital accumulation reached a level critical enough such that the region's postcolonial nationalisms were reworked, with implications for cultural expression and production. The 1980s onward are less a *late-capitalist* moment for Asia than a *high-capitalist* point in which East Asia becomes part of the *heterogeneous* energies necessary for capitalist reproduction and subsumption. This case was already acutely made by Slavoj Žižek in 1997: "With the direct multinational functioning of Capital, we are no longer dealing with the standard opposition between metropolis and colonized countries; a global company as it were cuts its umbilical cord with its mother-nation and treats its country of origins as simply another territory to be colonized."[22] The "self-referential turn" in capitalism, as Žižek saw it, assisted the revisioning of the formerly colonized and semicolonized zones into aspirational metropolitan zones. The new economic configurations and the middle classes they generated in turn allowed an expansion of cultural markets, one in which "Asianness" could become multiple cultural commodities and—at least for the more economically advanced—undergird a new museum and exhibition culture.[23] There is no static binary of high art versus the market and popular culture here: the market can both contribute to the appreciation of high culture and subject it to the pressures of cultural consumption.

It was no accident that the pioneering journal *Inter-Asia Cultural Studies* materialized in 2000 as a reaction to economic globalization and the transitions in Cold War structures that also gave rise to triumphalist elements in the region, even as new prospects for cultural and knowledge production were created. The coeditors, Kuan-Hsing Chen and Chua Beng Huat, write in the first issue, "Since the 1980s, a pervasive rhetoric of the 'rise of Asia' has come . . . to constitute a structure of feeling that is ubiquitous, yet unambiguously felt, throughout Asia . . . [and resulted in] a need to question and critique the rhetorical unities of both the 'rise' and of 'Asia.'"[24] The new journal as a project, they hold, "has emerged as part of a movement for the ongoing construction and reconstruction of critical Inter-Asian subjectivities."[25] While the journal is a more intellectually centered capacity-building project than the multipronged curatorial agendas to be encountered in this book, and while the popular cultural productions of course entailed money-making intentions, both the latter cultural phenomena were centrally part and parcel of "this potentially generative moment"—a decolonial turn, if you will, in which knowledge production must be geographically grounded—that Chen and Chua ascertained marked the 1980s onward.[26]

There were, without doubt, both several intellectual and other related impulses by 2000 that supported the need for knowledge production outside the bounds of Euro-American cultural and academic institutions. Claims were made regarding the purported cultural exceptionalism of non-Western and "Asian" capitalisms. It should be noted, however, that the claims for cultural exceptionalism were being produced not only by (presumably) obscurantist apologists from a triumphant, rising Asia. Historian Harry Harootunian writes of how, after the Berlin Wall fell, "the mercurial speed with which new economies emerged in China, India, Brazil, and South Korea, trumpeting the triumph of a globalized neoliberalism," were accompanied "by appeals to cultural exceptionalism as explanations for the success of these newer capitalist economies, a strategy pioneered years earlier by Japan."[27] His finger-pointing comment needs to be qualified, as it leaves out important commentary from the United States itself, even before the Berlin Wall fell, that discussed Japanese exceptionalism, especially Ezra Vogel's influential *Japan as Number One* (1979).[28] In that volume, Vogel brought up a Japanese "communitarian vision" and an "aggregation of interests" for Americans to learn—and 450,000 copies of the Japanese translation sold in Japan by a year after its US publication.[29] Asian cultural and capitalist exceptionalism was mutually constructed by actors in both the West and the rest in the 1980s as it is now, in the politico-economic contestation between the United States and China that became more intense during the Donald Trump presidency (2017–2021).

In terms of knowledge production, Edward Said in his *Orientalism* (1978) had already written that "the Arab and Islamic world remains a second-order power in terms of the production of culture, knowledge, and scholarship."[30] That sentiment applied to other less-metropolitan regions too—the *Inter-Asia Cultural Studies* journal project effectively takes up Said's challenge to produce scholarly knowledge. The 1990s is part of this book's particular focus, for it witnessed the issue of producing culture and knowledge, attaining some prominence in both artistic-intellectual and popular-cultural terms. It must be clarified that such cultural-production processes and their results, by and large, did *not* make claims to be part of a supposed "alternative modernity"—to be part of an "unmediated absolute difference."[31] There were questions of how previous cultures continue into the present, but that is different from essentialist appeals to native theories untouched by the longue durée of regional modernizing processes.

High and Popular in the Expanded Field of New Asia

A Regional Contemporary begins by examining significant visual art exhibitions, one of the most visible cultural sites in which ideas of New Asia are curated into being, given the need for major institutions to facilitate inter-Asian artistic networks. Beginning in 1979, and becoming particularly noticeable by the 1990s, select Japanese museums started to document and interpret the historical emergence of modern and contemporary art in Asia—terms not well defined in the 1970s in relation to the region. The 1990s also witnessed the start of notable biennial-type museum events in Australia and Singapore and the appearance of "global" curators from the region undertaking exhibitions on Asian art amid the metropolitan West. The book scrutinizes art exhibitions and the exhibitionary or curatorial imagination rather than the body of work of Asian contemporary art. Although they are related, such a wide scope is not practicable.[32]

The central issues addressed are: first, the ability to represent art from the semiperiphery; second, the capacity of this semiperiphery to define for itself what innovative visual art might be; and third, the usage of the exhibition as a vehicle for new knowledge production, debate, and discourse creation. The three issues taken together led to a broad curatorial rejection of an artistic "high modernism" as a self-sufficient and accepted universal high culture that separated high from low, the aesthetic from the everyday. This logic, when transposed into non-Western contexts, also meant separating the modern from the traditional as part of the everyday. The exhibitions appropriated and modified the historical avant-garde and postwar neo-avant-garde attack on modernism's autonomy aesthetic in the name of an Asia that now should—and increasingly did—possess a contemporary art. The biennial format as "temporary spaces of [cultural] mediation" suited the purpose of reworking the idea of Asian culture(s) as such spaces that offer "interfaces between art and larger publics—publics which are at once local and global, resident and nomadic, non-specialist and art worldly."[33]

One crucial matter of interest for the region's curators regarded attitudes in the 1990s that non-Western modernisms were, in any case, probably either not universal or later derivatives of Western work. As art historian James Elkins has put it, "Any account of modern art that tries to keep itself connected to existing narratives in art history will need to acknowledge the belatedness of many [non-Western] modernist practices in relation to western Europe and North America. Belatedness is a prickly concept: it . . . trails a string of problematic concepts with normative implications, including the avant-garde, influence, originality, and precedence."[34] The questions of belatedness and temporality are major matters related to and emerging from how we regard the standing of the formation of modern and contemporary Asian culture, broadly conceived.

The increased knowledge-creation capacity to conceive critically of a cosmopolitan-multicultural contemporary Asia with some transnationalizing capacity was enabled by both the economically integrating and communicative functions of globalization.[35] Such shared knowledge creation vitally came to pass with the establishment of forums and what can be called "curatorial and cultural-infrastructural networks" on Asian contemporary art that were organized from the 1990s, especially by the Japan Foundation Asia Center in Tokyo. Regional institutions made it a point to feature regional as well as "international" speakers. However, curators were acutely aware that the region's cultural diversity and histories of political fractures from the modern colonial era, Japanese colonialism and the Pacific War, and the Cold War that followed made transnational endeavors difficult. One chief starting point for curation in the late 1980s to the mid-1990s was this question: How *inclusive* was the contemporary, in any case, as it simultaneously was a designation of time and sufflated the theory that informed curation? Younger artists from Southeast Asia, it seemed, exceeded the postwar international style by using newer formats such as installation art that could incorporate material that could mark the local and the traditional. Could tradition in the form of folk art or craft have a place in present-day art and art forms, so that its presence was not simply a sign of times past? Indeed, the question of the status of craft as rural art separate from urban art was itself a question. What is the "qualitative time," as it could be called, that could assist in flexibly synchronizing heterogeneities ranging from tradition in the present to post-exotic artistic- and popular-cultural urban experiences? Globalizing Asia became both the context for and vexed theme in East Asian cultural regionalization.

Acting as a bridge to the inter-Asian popular culture of the same period were art exhibitions with the theme of dynamically expanding and unstable Asian cities. It has been asserted that "the major sites of cultural globalization in the twenty-first century are the emerging megacities of what used to be called the Third World."[36] What are the new imaginative geographies that may be materializing? In this regard, a key event was the traveling exhibition *Cities on the Move* (1997–1999; Vienna Secession and the CAPC–Musée d'art contemporain, Bordeaux), cocurated by Hou Hanru, originally from China. The 1999 incarnation at London's Hayward Gallery carried the subtitle "Urban Chaos and Global Change, East Asian Art, Architecture and Film Now," revealing that ongoing regional attempts to display, frame, or otherwise capture the more-globalized Asia was a multidisciplinary artistic endeavor. While criticized as an updated and even overreaching version of the chaotic East, *Cities* was also acknowledged to be trying to capture distinctive cultural expression in present-day Asia, within which tradition had a less noticeable role.

The urban theme allows the transition to multilingual Hong Kong film from around 2000, J-Pop in Japan from the late 1980s, and K-Pop in South Korea from about 2000. These were products with a polish that led to or facilitated new cultural consumption patterns associated with the very acceleration of urbanization.[37] The latter two pop-cultural forms surprisingly crossed national boundaries in ways that only Taiwanese and Hong Kong pop music and television dramas and Hong Kong film had before, among ethnic Chinese in the region—indeed, they exceeded the reach of these earlier cultural productions.

Significantly, neither J-Pop nor K-Pop were targeted in the first instance at regional audiences. The spread of Japanese TV dramas and J-Pop in the 1990s had surprised many. Televisual producers and cultural industry leaders had tended to produce for national audiences, but newer communicative capabilities (cable and satellite television) and technologies (VHS tapes that could be pirated and the cheap video compact disc) allowed new routes of circulation.[38] Hong Kong cinema after the 1997 Asian economic crisis fared less well than it had in previous years, and to compensate, they pioneered efforts to capture this new market that now watched Japanese anime and dramas and listened to Cantopop (Cantonese-Chinese pop music) and Mandopop (Mandarin-Chinese pop music). Northeast and Southeast Asia's more-established and newer aspirational middle classes both manifested desires to consume not only popular culture in the globally hegemonic language, English, but also foreign-language cultures requiring subtitling or translated lyrics—cultural practices previously restricted to self-consciously high-cultural art formats. Perhaps unsurprisingly, forms of popular culture displayed the effects of increased regional economic exchange and interdependency more than art exhibitions.[39] Popular culture constituted (and still constitutes) a cultural spectacle that is broadly comfortable with the predispositions of mobile capital, and in which there was a tentative debordering of East Asian film and, more firmly, of the national-linguistic spaces of J-Pop and (more intensively) K-Pop.

Culture and art—even in its commodified popular-cultural forms, in which art is not a refuge from business—have historico-aesthetic associations with the affective structure of subjectivity and the experience of temporal form. The curatorial capacity to exhibit contemporary art and a popular culture with inter-Asian mobility jointly point out something of the regional contemporary as lived experience. Art historian Thomas Crow has pointed out that although the fields of high and mass or popular culture are not always conjoined, the theorists linked to both matters were the same—Theodor Adorno, Walter Benjamin, and Clement Greenberg: "The theory of one was the theory of the other. And in that identity was the realization, occasionally manifest and always latent, that the two were in no fundamental way separable. Culture under the conditions of developed capitalism displays both moments of negation and an ultimately overwhelming tendency toward accommodation."[40] One indicative quotation from Greenberg (1909–1994) directly bears out Crow's observation: "Where there is an avant-garde, generally we also find a rear-guard. True enough—simultaneously with the entrance of the avant-garde, a second new cultural phenomenon appeared in the industrial West: that thing to which the Germans give the wonderful name of *Kitsch*: popular, commercial art and literature with their chromeotypes, magazine covers, illustrations, ads, slick and pulp fiction, comics, Tin Pan Alley music, tap dancing, Hollywood movies, etc., etc."[41]

However, a "tendency toward accommodation" does not mean exhibition events cannot help to shape new sociocultural relations. *A Regional Contemporary* argues that the exhibition of Asian contemporary art in the 1990s to the 2000s captured this capacity for "negation" before regional governments fully comprehended how jagged contemporary art has a place in the biennial-exhibition format that official art agencies could sponsor, as the biennial has become a component part of the global-city configuration that supports tourism and functions as a lure for roving capital. And a revamped "contemporariness" led museums and curators to grapple with the politics of constructed postcolonial national cultures that co-opted the local as a fixed cultural past: "exotic" tradition should not be held hostage by newer national states any more than it should by Western art institutions. In terms of negation, popular cultural producers were at times cautious of national politics and its inclination toward what is now described as "nation branding," as such cultural politics were not necessarily positive for transnational sales. Inter-Asian pop music in fact could have more direct political impact. In 2014 and 2015, literary-cultural critic Leo Ching tells us, the region's popular culture fosters sociopolitical relationships by "providing a common grammar for regional interlocution and interreferencing" among student protesters in Hong Kong, Taiwan, and Japan.[42] In both high and popular, the congruity of socioeconomic relations with cultural expression occurred, even if in the case of popular culture, such relations were more apparent. But for both, the force of independent creative agency and the energy of cross-border cultural interaction were also apparent, as was the force of historical contingency.

In place of the old clichéd and static binary between high art and the market, or high and low more generally, we see the liaison between the two in semiperipheral societies via a sense of connectedness in the difference that is New Asia. This does not imply that there is no longer any differentiation between the two, whether in Euro-America or in Asia. It is more that "what used to be a vertical divide has become . . . a horizontal borderland of exchanges and pillagings."[43] The curator Okwi Enwezor goes further to say he "use[s] the term *culture industry* to denote the mass phenomenon that seems currently to be overtaking museological presentation of art in the form traveling-exhibition blockbusters . . . [that] can have both a legitimate mass appeal and a specialized appeal."[44] As for popular culture itself, as Stuart Hall sharply observed decades ago, it should be taken neither in any "'pure' sense" to be resistance politics, nor as "the [commercial] forms which are superimposed on and over them. It is [instead] the ground on which the transformations [regarding entitlement and power] are worked."[45] What can now be presupposed is that complexity is not the sole property of high culture—and we can also register that the pop-cultural components of celebrity and youth, apart from consumption, are also infused into high culture.

A logic of cultural circulation emboldened by economic success informed both cultural forms, although art museums—even via the oftentimes spectacularized biennial format—arguably still serve a sort of civic humanism in an expanded capacity to encompass and rethink the status of art from Asia.

The exhibitionary imagination possessed an Enlightenment aspect to it, as there really seemed something new to be learned and then displayed. High and low come together, if unevenly, and as Andreas Huyssen remarks, "We should pay attention to the ways in which cultural practices and products are linked to the discourses of the political and social in specific local and national constellations"—here reconfigured into a regional cultural imaginary regarding the contemporary.[46]

Discontinuous Temporal Structure in Contemporary Asia

If modernity was the temporal mode of colonial-era capitalism and continued to be so during the post-Second World War decolonization that took place within the context of the Cold War and the dominance of a teleological modernization theory, within which semiperipheral or rapidly developing Asia was behind the curve of history and the temporality of the new, then contemporaneity is the temporal structure of rapid regional development that articulates (at least the fiction of) a global unity. Modernity's temporal structure was a part of a world with supposedly clear centers and peripheries. Such a clear division did not function well: even in the 1960s, Singapore, Hong Kong, and South Korea cannot be described as the peripheries of a global geography of capitalism. Immanuel Wallerstein in 1974 gives us the concept of the "semiperiphery" as "a necessary structural element in a world economy" between core and periphery.[47] As Sandro Mezzadra and Brett Neilson contend, "This [term] works as a kind of compensation chamber that articulates and mediates the more brutal relationships of domination and dependency between core and periphery" that only shows how binary divisions such as "core" and "periphery" were already under pressure before transnational theory and notions of hybridity made their presence felt in the 1990s.[48]

In contrast to modernity, contemporaneity's temporal structure allows the projection of unity onto the differential totality of the times that are at least potentially present to each other under the conditions of the deregulation of capital markets. Therefore, despite the recognition of "Asia" as a colonial-era construct, the historical complications of Japanese imperial history and the Greater East Asia Co-Prosperity Sphere, and the charged political choices to be made in postcolonial economic development, given Cold War politics, the term is revamped into a productive differential concept in which Asia does not need to be "one" but still can pragmatically and performatively connect plural locales—and even contribute to the creation of what on the surface might seem to be oppositional creative forms of the high cultural and the popular cultural.

However, there is no simple replacement of the logic of the modern by the contemporary: the latter exists because of the spatial expansion of the former from the modern-colonial West. Thus, in the 1980s to the early 1990s, amid the fear that Japan's economy would eclipse the US economy, what possibly was obscured was that "it had long been [postwar] U.S. policy to encourage Japan to orient itself toward East Asian markets and to build up in that region a peaceful variation of the 'Greater East Asia Co-Prosperity Sphere.'"[49] Examples of "wakeup call books" from that period include Dan Burstein's melodramatically titled *Yen! Japan's New Financial Empire and Its Threat to America* (1990) and Michael Crichton's 1992 novel, *Rising Sun*, invoking fear over Japanese investment in the US high-tech sector—made into a 1993 film starring Sean Connery. As has been posited, "'Contemporaneity' is the temporality of global unity, the temporal product of globalization."[50] Spatial expansion permits contemporaneity.

The contemporary, then, is *both* a critical (or postcolonial) modernity that embraces notions of multiculturalism for (re)thinking Asia *and* a fractured modernity that does *not* quite manage to be "a break from modern history," as art historian Patrick Flores suggests.[51] The voices of "other" cultural elites and producers struggle to define what "our" historic artistic modernism was and what "our" contemporary is or could be, if not viewed only as Westernized cultural imitations. This is a reflexivity posed as a modernity facilitated by the contradictory cultural valences contained in capitalist entrenchment in the semiperiphery. "East Asia" as a conceptual site became ready for reinscription by the 1990s by curators, artists, and popular-culture producers—in fact, ironically, perhaps *because* Asia "doesn't exist except as a geographical and therefore economically and politically connected space. Which is to say it is gradually escaping European definitions by repudiating cultural and civilizational identifications."[52]

While, as Flores points out, "What is Asia?" is always "an unnerving proposition," it is also "a provocation": "Ontologies always provoke, and they also require provocative anthropologies."[53] Such anthropological manifestations can take the forms of artistic cultures as well as everyday-life practices. However, if a globalized and interconnected world means a world in which there is "the disappearance of History as the fundamental element in which human beings exist, and, not least, the end of an essentially modernist field of political struggle in which the great ideologies still had the force and the great authority of the great religions in recent times," then East Asia functions within a necessarily *incomplete contemporary* in which history and a great ideology such as nationalism are only partially superseded.[54] The uneven development and mixed temporalities capitalism produces are more pronounced in the periphery and semiperiphery.[55] As a result, the processes trying to hold together the region's heterogeneity so that the new religion of "growth above all" can be paramount remain tentative.

Perhaps the tentativeness of the contemporary should be expected, given what has been described as "the 'Not Yet' version of history"—the understanding of "history itself as an imaginary waiting room"—in which political and cultural forms of modernity are not conceivable or achievable without traversing the circuitous route through European thought.[56] The relationship between the Not Yet and the Now, though, historian Dipesh Chakrabarty avers, is *not* that of a binary opposition but rather "that of an 'And.' They both exist. That's why historicism exists."[57] The present, then, is discontinuous with itself. *A Regional Contemporary* looks at some of the positives and the contradictions in the aesthetic-cultural and temporal imagining of a contemporary Asia when the Not Yet and the Now came into a creative tension that escaped the predictable, when memories of strain linked with the traumas of Japanese empire and postwar national formations persist, within the reconfiguration of the region under the pressures of the Cold War and global capitalism. Imperialism, nationalism, and economic development are the specifics in the near and immediate past that make their historical presence felt as that which seem unavoidably to affect the contemporary cultural production investigated, sometimes in the background and occasionally more directly.

The first period—the near past—is from the nineteenth century to the Pacific War. From the early days of the Meiji Restoration, Japanese imperialism was justified via nationalist imperatives. By the first decades of the twentieth century, Korea, Manchuria, and Mongolia were taken as necessary for the defense of the Japanese nation-state, and by the 1920s, Japanese nationalism had grown resentful against a worldwide system of interstate balance of power seen as unfair to a sovereign Japan. However, this regional belligerence must be set in context of a larger political problematic in which though "the most distinctive feature of nationalist *ideology* in the twentieth century is the peeling away of imperialism from nationalism," nationalism did not "overcome the long practical *history* of the nation-state's association with imperialism in the competition for dominance of the capitalist world."[58] This was a competition to which Japan, in any case, was a latecomer, given that Germany and the United States were already challenging Britain's late-nineteenth-century free-trade imperialism via a more neo-mercantilist and national-economic logic—and never mind the rest of Northeast Asia or mostly colonized Southeast Asia.[59] This meant that Japan's anti-Western imperialist nationalism, with its expansionist tendencies unevenly mixed with developmental goals for its colonies, was inside a single global fold with all the unresolved tensions of the era.

As such, while Japan had risen to pole position in the region, owing to its status as the first modern Asian nation-state, it was only one (if a manifestly compelling) part of a larger transformation of polity, society, and culture in East Asia. Languages and language use, for instance, had to change to be able to express the Western ideas entering the region. One well-known example is the classical Chinese expression *geming*, which addressed the question of legitimate rule and was exported to Japan from China in the eighth century, where it was rendered as *kakumei*. During the late Qing dynasty, the loanword returned to China, and by "the mid-1890s, the phrase *geming* appeared sporadically in Chinese discourse with references to either the Meiji Restoration or the French Revolution, yet classical [Chinese] allusions to dynastic change were not eliminated," even as the term was firmly linked to the modern meaning of *revolution*.[60] This is but one example out of an entire class of paleonyms of re-signified classical Chinese vocabulary.[61] Regional and local political actors selected and reworked older terms with new ideas for altered interpretations of political community.

It is during the early twentieth century that pan-Asianism as an alternative to Western civilization becomes visible. The art critic and historian Okakura Kakuzō (or Tenshin; 1863–1913) made an argument in English in *Ideals of the East* (1903) that Japan is an artistic-cultural museum of a multicultural but conjoined Asia that loves "the Ultimate and the Universal," and which could proffer an alternative to materialistic and aggressive Western civilization—if Asian nations would look to the commonalities in their traditions: "The history of Japanese art becomes thus the history of Asiatic ideals—the beach where each successive wave of Eastern thought has left its sand-ripple as it beat against the national consciousness."[62] After the

Russo-Japanese War of 1904–1905, it became a claim that Japan could head an Asian civilization because of its ability to have mastered Western civilization, although this sentiment cannot be directly attributed to Okakura. *Ideals of the East* took nearly twenty years to be translated into Japanese and was addressed to European readers in the first instance.[63] It must also be kept in view that while Japan's historic imperialism stands out in Northeast and Southeast Asia, nationalist ideologues in both China and Japan sought to give a universalist dimension to their state-building projects.[64] It is therefore unremarkable that the late nineteenth century to the Pacific War years occupy minds in the region's art exhibitions, given the pressing question of how modern Asian culture was formed in the maelstrom of the region under European domination. Given Okakura's awareness of how old and new are folded into a single competitive world, he will make a number of appearances in the chapters to follow in the book.

However, it is the presence of the second period—the postwar years up to the 1980s—that is more consistently felt in both art exhibitions and popular culture. The "'Not Yet' version of history" seems to become weaker in those years. Western leaders decided that both the German and Japanese economies had to be rebuilt if the Cold War world order was to be practicable. Such rebuilding, it was reluctantly concluded, required retaining many of the old order elites and institutions. By 1970, Japan seemed rehabilitated, and this could be counted as a victory for the US or Western capitalist side in the Cold War rivalry. The later growth of the Asian tiger economies, apparent by the 1980s, was "a reflection of the emergence of Japan"—and their economic successes meant that the concept of the Third World lost some of its political gloss: "What has not been lost on other countries in what used to be called the Third World is that the East Asian route to prosperity has led through the world market and that it has worked."[65] So, there was a way out of the imaginary waiting room of history. An exit strategy consisting of discriminating state intervention and export-oriented industrial development existed to get beyond the memories of European and Japanese colonialism. This was a strategy that the soon-to-be second tier of newly industrialized economies such as Indonesia, Thailand, and Malaysia were to adopt, given geographical proximity to the tiger economies in the region.[66]

Literary critic Jini Kim Watson rightly contends that "although we typically think of the Cold War as a spatialized confrontation between blocs, spheres of influence, and curtains—whether iron, bamboo, or color—Third

World *futurity and temporality* is of crucial importance to understanding Cold War decolonization."[67] Whose side would the newly decolonized nation-states take? The choice made may make your people up to date, as it were. Cultural identity was less a concern in the 1960s and 1970s than it is in the 2020s.[68] Heonik Kwon emphasizes that decolonization in the Asia-Pacific was inseparably united with the Cold War.[69] Crucially, for Kwon, while in Western Europe and North America, the Cold War was a "'long peace' distinct from the previous era," for the "many new postcolonial nations elsewhere the onset of the cold war meant entering an epoch of 'unbridled reality' characterized by vicious civil wars and other exceptional forms of political violence" that was the result of a bipolarization of modernity into capitalist and socialist versions.[70] For Kuan-Hsing Chen, the Second World War "divided Asia into capitalist and socialist blocs, and as a result, capitalist East Asia was pressured to avoid conflict with the anticommunist camp."[71] From Asian perspectives, has the Cold War with its side-taking nationalisms ended? "The continued military saber-rattling seen in Korea, Okinawa, and across the Straits of Taiwan calls into question that we are living in a post–Cold War world."[72] The politico-economic choices made during Cold War decolonization endure beyond the fall of the Berlin Wall as, "in Asia, the structure of the Cold War has, to a large extent, been preserved and has developed new derivative forms under new historical conditions."[73] And so, the economic transformations that facilitated a more-contemporary Asia remain part of a modern history not easily forgotten and not superseded.

Does the above mean that the regional contemporary in its tangible cultural production is a failed moment, its incompleteness an indictment of expectations that, in the end, can only be misleading? Giorgio Agamben offers us another layer of complexity to ponder upon when asking, "What is the contemporary?" He writes: "The ones who call themselves contemporary are only those who do not allow themselves to be blinded by the lights of the century, and so manage to get a glimpse of the shadows in those lights, of their intimate obscurity."[74] The genuinely contemporary person cannot and should not be fully of their time, complying with all its demands, for they may miss what the presence of shadows connote, thinking them to be purely obscure. The shadows are the past in the present, the past as origin—the *arkhē* that requires attention: "The origin is not only situated in a chronological past: it is contemporary with historical becoming and does not cease to operate within it, just as . . . the child [is] in the psychic life of the adult."[75] The origin as shadows amid the light of the present may be signifiers for that which may stop us from living fully in the Now: "That which impedes access to the present is precisely the mass of what for some reason (its traumatic character, its excessive nearness) we have not managed to live."[76] To become genuinely contemporary is to be able to pay attention properly to half-light and shadows and to understand them "in relation with other times."[77] This will return us anew to the present in which we can become be a contemporary of both the new moment and the past.

We can perhaps say that the art exhibitions and the popular cultural production reviewed in this book insert themselves into the global present, if unevenly so, for there is awareness that the present is not monolithic, trans-historical, or free from the complications of tenacious fragmentation. And yet, despite the long shadows of imperialism, competitive nationalism, and Cold War economic development, the "Not Yet" version of history is exceeded—and cultural representation and production not previously undertaken have occurred. Tradition and modernity are conjoined. A nonexotic urban Asia is imaginable. Confident and regionalizing pop-cultural industries possessing some global pretensions exist. Such changes seem assuredly contemporary in Agamben's complex sense, for the *arkhē* of these transformations still requires attention, as the 1990s to mid-2000s version of Asia must be adjusted to include the looming presence of the People's Republic of China in the region.

The Chapters

A Regional Contemporary begins by exploring art exhibitions and the cultural infrastructure, as it can be described, that helped support the knowledge creation process for the curation of a mainly Northeast and Southeast Asian modern and contemporary art and then shifts attention to popular culture.

Chapter 1, "'We Asians' in Exhibitions—Under Construction," first reviews curatorial developments and the change in exhibitions from 1979 to 2002. It then proceeds to the examination of the exhibitionary imaginary that commences with what I describe as the international-regional art exhibition of the Fukuoka Art Museum's inaugural show, the two-part *Asian Artists Exhibition* (1979–1980)—the exhibition that helped to set the pace for the 1990s self-representation of Asian art, although it could not think past national boundaries in tracing Asian art's modernization. Chapter 1 ends with a contrasting global-regional art exhibition, *Under Construction: New Dimensions of Asian Art* (2002), co-organized by the Japan Foundation Asia Center and the Tokyo City Opera Gallery. *Under Construction* was the conclusion of a three-year exhibition project that tried to comprehend contemporary Asia as a region within which borders were transgressed. Eight young regional curators first undertook exhibitions in dispersed urban agglomerations of various sizes and then proceeded to a final collaborative event in Tokyo. The hope was to discover empirically from the bottom up what was actually happening in diverse urban environs in terms of shared contemporary artistic currents—an inter-referencing of Asia—instead of being stuck in a center/periphery model of artistic-cultural knowledge production in which the West remained the center. What was "under construction" was a curatorial network in progress that began with examining the geo-cultural framework known as Asia but aimed to move outward to a polycentric global connectivity.

The next chapter, "Showcasing Tradition-in-the-Contemporary and a Post-Exotic Urban Modern," examines select major regional exhibitions and their curatorial strategies in some detail: the *First and Second Asia-Pacific Triennial of Contemporary Art* (Queensland Art Gallery, 1993, 1996) and the *4th Asian Art Show, Fukuoka: Realism as an Attitude* (Fukuoka Art Museum, 1994). Also included are pioneering Asian art exhibitions targeted initially at Western audiences and undertaken by curators from or originally from the region: *Contemporary Art in Asia: Traditions/Tensions* (Asia Society Galleries, 1996—curator Apinan Poshyanda from Thailand) and *Cities on the Move* (Vienna Secession and the CAPC–Musée d'art contemporain, Bordeaux, 1997–1999—curators Hou Hanru, originally from China, and Hans-Ulrich Obrist). The chapter commences by considering issues that appeared in two groundbreaking exhibitions—*Magiciens de la Terre* (1989), which featured Western and non-Western artists placed side by side without any obvious hierarchy, and the Tercera Bienal de La Habana (Third Havana Biennial; 1989), which Cuba used to leverage itself as a Third World cultural leader—and how the 1990s exhibitions on Asia were both similar to and different from these two exhibitions. An essential curatorial-theoretical line of inquiry regarded an expanded sense of the modern elastic enough to retain "tradition." Underlying this response was the rejection of conceptions of self-sufficient high culture that separated high and low, spiritual and material. The exhibitions appropriated the early twentieth century's historical avant-gardist and postwar neo-avant-gardist anti-art attacks on modern art's autonomy aesthetic and demonstrated how the region's installation art, performance art, and conceptualism drew in local materials and cultural traditions in their deliberate referencing of the present-day quotidian world. Chapter 2 concludes with another decisive line of inquiry, as represented by the traveling exhibition *Cities on the Move*, that dealt with intensive regional urbanization and how a post-exotic art attempted to capture the experience of the region's expansive and oftentimes illiberal capitalism. This obviation of the traditional-contemporary, as it might be called, represented a second thread in the understanding of a regional contemporary.

If the 1990s saw art exhibitions and biennials staged in Northeast and Southeast Asia and Australia that sought to represent a more-than-traditional Asia, these events were supported by region-wide fora on Asian contemporary art that promoted and helped authorize the discursive and imaginative capacity to curate this Asia. Chapter 3, "Cultural Infrastructure Networks and the 'Intellectual Mastery' of Knowledge," considers the Japan Foundation Asia Center's contribution to this capacity, building what could be called "cultural infrastructure" networks—their symposia on Asian contemporary art from 1994 to 2008. The Asia Center's approach was to increase and entrench an expanding network of curators and thought leaders who could more firmly ascertain the contemporaneity of present artistic practice. In the process, the symposia revealed that the strengthened capacity to exhibit an Asia that has at least partially arrived economically did not overcome embedded modernizing ideologies that had contributed to the Pacific War. Nevertheless, the symposia did bring about agreement that a regional curatorium should aspire to the conjuncture of diverse regional locales with still disparate development levels and temporalities to produce a fictional totalized present to be projected in exhibitions that strove to rise above national clashes. These may have been *performative* projections of the contemporary, but the chapter emphasizes how the cultural infrastructure to support such possibilities were not hitherto available.

Given that the New Asia imaginary was predicated upon an interconnected capitalist modernization accompanied by urbanization, the question follows, How is the East Asian urban-modern represented in popular culture? From the late 1990s, the potential of a more integrated regional market encouraged cross-border casting, multilingualism, and attempts at coproduction of TV dramas and film. While a number of such productions drew on the Chinese *wuxia* (martial heroes) genre, such productions tended to avoid sensitive issues, unlike productions set in the present. Chapter 4,

"Debordering Hong Kong Film and Commonality/Difference in Urban Spaces," concentrates on Hong Kong cinema at the millennium's end, when its core regional ethnic-Chinese audience was in decline, a situation exacerbated by the 1997 Asian economic crisis. Hong Kong cinema tried recreating itself via multilingual film that mixed Cantonese, Mandarin, Japanese, and English, as that might appeal to a middle class constituted not solely through a homogeneous national culture but also through networks of markets and global cultural-financial flows. The region's built landscapes and environment were essential and constitutive backdrops to these experiments. Three indicative films receive particular attention: Lee Chi-Ngai's *Sleepless Town* (*Fuyajo/ Bu ye cheng*, 1998), a noirish depiction of shifting identities and loyalties in Tokyo's red-light district, Kabukichō, that centers on a low-rung, half-Chinese gangster; Jingle Ma's *Tokyo Raiders* (*Dongjing gonglue*, 2000), a film consonant with the region's libidinization of market modernity; and Johnnie To's *Fulltime Killer* (*Quanzhi shashou*, 2001; co-director Wai Ka-fai), featuring two professional killers from Japan and China competing to be the region's best. The films map the region as one containing urban spaces that are simultaneously not quite national and not quite transnational.

Chapter 5, "J-Pop, K-Pop, and the Partial Negotiation of the National," scrutinizes urbanized J-Pop music from Japan from the late 1980s and K-Pop from South Korea from the late 1990s. Both these pop-cultural phenomena exceeded the regionalizing attempts of Hong Kong film—and yet their regional success was unintended and unexpected, testifying to a progressive translocal change in cultural subjectivity. Even the national emergence of the two pop cultures was highly diverse. They have negotiated, although hardly overcome, the oppositional politics of economic regionalism and the not-quite-post–Cold War nationalisms. The subject of modernity tends to be singular—the nation-state, national culture, both of which presuppose a "we" with some sort of dialectical unity. If art, as it is claimed, is a privileged carrier of the contemporary, as it was of modernity, then pop culture, because it is more ordinary in its claims than high culture, has at least the same capacity to be a carrier of the contemporary and to assist in the imagining of a non-singular subjectivity. This chapter completes the argument that the contemporary juncture manifests an antagonistic unity within which the great modern ideology of nationalism coexists with a vision of a regional market that exceeds the confines of the national—a juncture in which sameness and difference are no longer in an antinomian relationship.

The book ends with a coda on how China partially displaces some of the possibilities for an inclusive Asia envisaged by the book's featured cultural actors, when it becomes a location and a market of regional promise. The Asian financial crisis of 1997, during which the bulk of investment and significant economic weight shifted from Japan and the Association of Southeast Asian Nations (ASEAN) states to China and India, contributed to China's increased centrality in the cultural thinking on Asia. The coda reflects upon China's first international biennale, the Shanghai Biennale (2000), with its theme "Shanghai Spirit," and the Japanese/Chinese coproduced romantic drama-comedy film *The Longest Night in Shanghai* (*Yoru no Shanghai/Ye Shanghai*, 2007) as emanant components in the imaginary of contemporary Asia in the first decade of the new millennium.

1 "WE ASIANS" IN EXHIBITIONS— UNDER CONSTRUCTION

That humans become free is thus part of a free world. . . . This requirement is only thereby fulfilled when what a human being ought to be appears as the external world he makes his own.
—G. W. F. Hegel, *Philosophy of Right* (1817/1818)

The 1980s and 1990s "East Asian miracle" saw a revivification of the idea of "Asia," now no longer taken as backward. Those decades witnessed the emergence of not only triumphalist, state-driven discourses on a contemporary East Asia that had "Asian values" that led to "alternative" Asian modernities, but also a dramatic increase in cultural production that circulated intensely within the region, ranging from visual art exhibitions to bilingual or multilingual film and to pop music straining to see what a multicultural inter-Asian culture (and consumer) looks like.

This chapter examines the visual arts scene in East Asia (with Southeast Asia taken as a part of that cartographic imaginary), one of the most visible sites of cultural interaction in which the idea of contemporary New Asia has been examined and curated into "being," given the necessity of major cultural institutions to facilitate intra-Asian artistic cooperation. This cartographic imaginary is a postwar development. Meiji-era Japanese Asianists, for instance, were generally not interested in areas south of China, and during the 1930s East Asia Co-Prosperity Sphere period, Northeast Asia was the main focus in imagining Asia, as Asianist ideals depended on Confucianism; non-Confucian societies, in contrast, needed "guidance." A certain superior attitude toward Southeast Asia, it has been noted, continued in Japan's postwar "return" to Asia as part of its politics of economic productivity.[1]

The 1980s onward saw Japanese museums start documenting the historical emergence of Asian modernist and contemporary art, and the 1990s saw the establishment of numerous biennale-type events in East Asia and Australia that significantly exhibited Asian artists. A key curatorial goal was the attempt to imagine a cosmopolitan and multicultural Asia able to transcend national boundaries as part of the means of understanding the potentialities of the new, even as there was the awareness that the region's cultural diversity and history of political fractures made this endeavor difficult. Globalized Asia becomes both the context for and vexed theme in East Asian regionalization.

Increasingly, "Asia" as an historical category resulting from an "emanation" model of a universal World History, inspired by G. W. F. Hegel (1770–1831), in which the *fons et origo* of the modern world is Western Europe—the entrenched binary opposition of the modern West counterposed against traditional Asia vital during the era of European colonialism—becomes challenged by visions of a modern(ized) and increasingly urbanized region pursuing capitalist development. This region becomes more able to undertake self-representation so as to put in its claim to its place in the world. Harry Harootunian suggests that when "Marx raised the prospect of the formation of a genuine world history, as an alternative to a Hegelian universalist history, he emphasized the importance of transmuting a purely 'local being' into a 'universal being' that would lead to the universalization of the particular and the localization of the universal."[2] While not explicitly theorized in such a manner, we will see that the curatorial positions examined in this chapter follow the approximate logic that Harootunian sets out. Such positions are shared by both political and cultural actors in similar and divergent forms, and both are inextricably linked to the region's economic transformation.

I primarily argue that the "exhibitionary imaginary," as it may be called, can be understood to be an articulation of a modern culture that represents the contemporary moment of East Asia. Such a representation is accompanied by the inevitable attendant danger of reification and collusion, even if accidental, with highly ideological and suspect claims for a "new Asian hemisphere."[3] However, the exhibitionary processes were disaggregated enough to facilitate quasi-autonomous forms of inquiry and flows of humanistic and artistic ideas, predicated upon a desire to have a comparative understanding of the regional creation of modern culture. As has been argued, "to posit . . . the context from which any form of art emerges is [not] to deny the ability of art and curation to generate their own context. . . . 'Display' or the act of making art visible, therefore, becomes a context . . . because it enables the social practice of art to be a communicable event, to assume sensible sociality."[4]

This quasi-disengagement from state agendas on Asia allowed a multi-lateral curatorial engagement with the contemporary in which cultural actors could try to exceed an older history of the modern. This is the problematic ideational formation of a Greater East Asia associated with Japan's disastrous historical attempts to "leave" backward Asia and modernize—or come under full Western colonial domination. The curatorial representations of a now more thoroughly modernized and interlinked region do not mean that modernity's debilitating "entry" into the region is ignored.

In this regard, the contemporary becomes both a critical or postcolonial modernity that embraces a notion of multiculturalism for "rethinking" Asia and a fractured modernity struggling with its own past. What is recorded in this chapter are the "other" voices of cultural elites as they struggle toward defining what "our" historic artistic modernism was and what "our" contemporary is or could be, if not viewed only as Westernized cultural imitations: this is a reflexivity posed as a modernity facilitated by the contradictory cultural valences contained in capitalist entrenchment in the semiperiphery. "East Asia" as a conceptual site became ready for reinscription because the question as to whether advanced cultural globalization needs necessarily and inevitably be Euro-America-centric at its core becomes more loudly articulated from the 1980s.[5]

One consequence is that the various East Asian international exhibitions that resulted were "conceived primarily for viewers in Asia," where an "Asia-centric paradigm replaced Euro-American centricity," as Thai critic-curator Apinan Poshyananda argues.[6] They have partially decentered a hegemonic cultural history and fostered a cultural agenda that more consistently caters to regional-local concerns. However, one danger is that the capitalist "empowerment" to challenge the exclusion of non-Western modern and contemporary art from the Western narrative of artistic modernism may also mean a prejudice against nonmetropolitan-oriented art and cultural achievement, and against nonurban East Asia. The absorbed metropolitan multiculturalism also faces the challenge of being swallowed by the capitalist modernity to which it is linked.

Two significant curatorial-culturalist moments in the exhibition of Asia receive the main attention here. The first is the Japanese Fukuoka Art Museum's inaugural exhibition, the two-part inaugural *Asian Artists Exhibition*, which comprised *Modern Asian Art—India, China & Japan* (1979) and *Festival: Contemporary Asian Art Show* (1980). The exhibitions sought to think comparatively of the "arrival" of modernist art in the region but were unable to break the frame of national art histories that separately engaged the modern West. Despite this, Fukuoka crucially set the stage for new possibilities. The second is the Japan Foundation's thirtieth-anniversary exhibition, co-organized by their Asia Center and the Tokyo City Opera Art Gallery, *Under Construction: New Dimensions of Asian Art* (2002). This three-year project tried to comprehend contemporary Asia as a region within which borders were transgressed, with the result that curators could look to the region for shared artistic currents instead of being stuck in a center/periphery model of cultural-knowledge production within which the West remained at the center. What might be thought of as the "global-regional" curatorial framework of 2002, versus the "international-regional" framework of 1979–1980, stood for that attempt to think of the potentialities of a critical modernity in the light of a more economically integrated regionalism.

The Voices of the "Others" in the New East Asia

It is important to start by elaborating on how increased economic integration in the 1980s–1990s helped facilitate sometimes triumphalist visions of a modern East Asia. The 1980s was the decade in which East Asia was seen to come into its own. The "flying geese" model of development—with Japan as the leading goose—was an expression first used in 1962 to describe the life cycle of industries amid economic development, during which there is the shifting of industries from more advanced countries to those catching up from behind. One often-given example of this is the shifting of textile production from Japan to the Asian newly industrializing countries and then further to ASEAN countries and China.[7]

Alternative spatial representations of the world appear within which Asian urban centers could claim to represent a major economic region that the old colonial West could not ignore. The emergence in that decade of discourses on Asian democracy and economic rights, rather than human rights, were indicative and assertive self-representational strategies not possible in the 1960s during decolonization.[8] The Asian exhibitionary imaginary functioned in parallel with but not the same as these discourses and their politico-economic practices. This imaginary is a dynamic knowledge production process—facilitated by arts and cultural institutions that supported what could be called "cultural infrastructural networks," as I will address in chapter 3—and discourse enhanced by modernization. These discourses, however, do not have a self-sufficient autonomy because of the extraregional connection with the United States in particular, and also because, intellectually and culturally, it is hard to dislodge the concept of modernity from its Euro-American dimensions.

The evocation of the New Asia via various Asian values and Asia-that-can-say-no discourses was undertaken not only by Lee Kuan Yew from Singapore and Dr. Mahathir Mohamad of Malaysia, the best-known proponents, but also by others, such as Tokyo's governor, Ishihara Shintarō, for sometimes distinctive local purposes. Among other reasons, Lee had dreams of tying Singapore to China's rising star, Mahathir had his postcolonial skirmishes with Britain, and Ishihara had his right-wing nationalist concerns. Their politico-cultural practices can be described as "national culturalisms"—identity politics mobilized at the level of the nation-state.[9]

While such national culturalisms were new, East Asian discourses and their supposed alternative modernities based on Asian values nonetheless were part of "the reconceptualization . . . of modernization [theory from the 1960s] as globalization."[10] Non-Western states flexibly participated in their own (unexpected) version of postmodern, "resistance" identity politics as part of the multicultural logic necessary to maintain national competitiveness.[11] National culturalisms stood for larger late-modern shifts in culture and the economy. The contemporary East Asia proclaimed as the now-indigenized space of globalized modernity was part of the Western modernity being contested.

These culturalist capacities were linked to market-driven regionalization processes that had led to significant economic integration between Japan, the Asian newly industrializing countries, and the ASEAN countries. In terms of institutional links, however, this integration has not led to notable intergovernmental processes of regional institution building—the result of a lack of political, cultural, and religious cohesiveness; a general caution regarding rigid institutions; and the extraregional institutional and trade dependence on the United States.[12] The voices of New Asia could not be said to represent the region in any coherent way. Still, the possession of the new—of intense export-oriented industrial modernization—allowed a complex "resistance" to the West, even as extraregional dependence in trade continued.

The Asian values rhetoric vanished after the 1997 Asian financial crisis led to denouncements of such "values" as corruption, collusion, and nepotism, but this in itself did not disperse the idea of an East Asian modernity.[13] A key version that survived did not claim a common culturalist condition of essentialized and region-wide primordial values. It is true that the idea of a pan-Asia that draws upon "culturalisms, statisms, and theories of civilization," rather than a diverse Asia well aware of intra-regional political and cultural differences, is hard to escape from, even when these approaches have been roundly criticized.[14] Nevertheless, it is arguable that the "new" East Asian-ness that remains is a region predicated upon an increased sense of a shared (if clearly not equal levels of) capitalist modernization and modern culture, manifestly visible in rapid urbanization.[15]

Interest in urban renewal also transpires because of the goal to foster premier world cities as assets in capitalist development. In general, there is a pertinent relationship between modernization and urbanization, and in 2020, the World Bank indicated that 61 percent of East Asia and the Pacific—some 1.4 billion people—lived in urban areas.[16] Tokyo, Hong Kong, Seoul, Singapore, and Taipei stand out in a network of aspiring modern Asian metropoles, now joined by Shanghai and Beijing, with Tokyo at the apex as the leading "postindustrial metropolis."[17] Tokyo becomes viewed as a premier world city within an "alpha world city" band, with Singapore and Hong Kong occupying a lower-tier level of that band.[18] That is to say, one major image of the new East Asia vision is a modern-urban and, increasingly, metropolitan one.

It is necessary to recall that region making in the East Asian context is inseparable from the expansion of Euro-American capitalism. Contrary to what one might expect, the economic developments described as globalization produced greater regional relations via trade.[19] Indeed, the very emergence of the little-tiger economies of South Korea, Taiwan, Hong Kong, and Singapore—forgotten at times—was used to abet and justify the potential of neoliberal or free market economics, and to argue that export-oriented growth and integration into the world economy was superior to development outside world markets.[20]

Also forgotten—perhaps because of the bouts of fear regarding a more competitive new Asia—is that it was long-standing US foreign policy starting from the 1960s, with the Kennedy administration, "to encourage Japan to orient itself toward East Asian markets and to build up in that region a peaceful variation of the 'Greater East Asia Co-Prosperity Sphere' that Japan had earlier sought to impose by force."[21] "East Asia" in the 1980s was the result of a political, economic, and military order part of—in historian James Cronin's words—"the world the Cold War made," one in which the advanced industrial Western nations and Japan enrolled anti-communist alliance states. That China with its now-transformed second-world modernity, historically at odds with Japan, is now part of this economically enhanced region is one of those twists of history. Even a prominent politico-historical commentator such as historian Timothy Garton Ash forgets his Asian history and "others" the consolidating modernities of the "rise of the rest" as that which raises their threat level above that of normative great power rivalry: "The opening ceremony of the [2008] Beijing Olympics, like the skyscrapers of Shanghai, show us how authoritarian capitalism already stakes that claim [to be liberal capitalism's alternative]."[22]

While the basic pattern for economic cooperation in the postwar "return" to Asia was set in the late 1950s by then–prime minister Kishi Nobosuke (1957–1960), the serious process of regionalization—the integration of markets across national borders within a macro region for labor, capital, services, and goods—started after the 1985 Plaza Accord among the G-5 countries. That saw the revaluation of the yen upward and led to an outflow of foreign direct investment—"outsourcing," as it is called now—into ASEAN countries. Korean and Taiwanese manufacturers followed suit, as their currencies too had appreciated. By 1992, China also began to draw in foreign direct investment, thereby competing with ASEAN countries. This led to an accumulation of regional manufacturing capacity marked by both collaboration and competition.[23] The region "exists," but still competes internally.

Japan's regional investments resulted in an unprecedented focus on commercial land in Tokyo's central wards, as the infrastructure and physical environment to turn Tokyo into a center for finance and transnational production and trade had to be built.[24] The city's population has expanded continuously since then, and now "Tokyo has all the lineaments of the postindustrial city . . . and arguably serves as a reliable guide to what other cities in the region could experience," given that the recent evolution of other potential postindustrial regional urban centers resemble Tokyo in the 1970s and 1980s in retaining manufacturing in outlying urban zones, even as services become more significant in the core urban areas.[25]

The "contagion" of the 1997 Asian financial crisis, which started in Thailand in July, dramatically illustrated how truly interdependent the region had become. The perception of the International Monetary Fund as an extension of US global economic policy—owing to the restrictive conditions in the bailout packages offered to Indonesia and Thailand—combined with the loss of regional confidence in the Asian "miracle" encouraged institutionalization through, for example, a greater openness to making various free trade agreements. China was relatively stable throughout the crisis and used the opportunity to show regional responsibility by not devaluing the renminbi. Indeed, the crisis boosted Beijing's confidence in trying to shape the region. Aware of the anxiety in ASEAN over the competition that China posed, premier Zhu Rongji in 2000 proposed that China and ASEAN explore possible discussions on free trade agreements. China's sharp diplomacy suggested a shift in the regional balance of power, given an economically stagnant Japan, which had led the way in regionalization, and a United States mired in the so-called war on terror. Nevertheless, "Japan remains a major force in East Asia, and together with the United States, China, and other polities, offers a broad range of [political] alternatives."[26] While this last statement was made in 2006, and China overtook Japan in 2010 to become the world's second-largest economy in terms of GDP to gain a more pronounced regional presence, the assertion remains broadly valid, even if globalization processes by 2021 are seen to be weaker.[27]

Fredric Jameson sees that the "outmoded . . . concept of modernity . . . is in fact back in business all over the world."[28] He criticizes the desire for a supposedly superior Western modernity by already modern countries as "an optical illusion nourished by envy and hope, by inferiority feelings and the need for emulation. Alongside all other paradoxes built into this strange concept, this one is the most fatal: that modernity is always a concept of otherness."[29] His insight here is strangely not accompanied by an understanding of the attractiveness for the modernity that seems greener on the Euro-American side of the fence. The refurbished "new" itself has become a key—if not *the* key—commonality for the different states with their contrasting multicultures in the region.

This latest version of the new and the metamorphosis of postwar modernization theory into "globalization" theory, along with the identity politics that accompanied it, do not mean that the move from the older internationalism to globalism and regionalism is easily attained, given East Asia's difficulty in finding an ideational foundation for regional institutions.[30] Nor does it mean that old histories are forgotten. Japan's nineteenth-century entry into the modern era was an attempt both to take the place of and to gain autonomy from China's long-standing regional dominance and to confront the West: it tried "shedding Asia" (*Datsu-A Ron*), an infamous phrase from 1885 formulated by Meiji Enlightenment intellectual Fukuzawa Yukichi (1835–1901). *Datsu-A Ron* was an editorial first published in the newspaper *Jiji Shimpo* on March 16, 1885, and this expression has been variously translated as "shedding Asia," "escape from Asia," and "disassociation from Asia." Fukuzawa likened the modernizing process to a disease, brought about by the dominant presence of the Western colonial powers in East Asia: "There can be no other policy than to move on with the rest of the world and join them [i.e., 'Western man'] in dipping into the sea of civilization, . . . and joining them in the pains and joys of civilization. Civilization is like an epidemic of measles."[31]

Asia itself was a region that, in historicist thinking drawn from German idealism, was traditional, despotic, and agrarian and lacked nation-states, even if it was the starting point of world history.[32] Historically, the "new" was a dividing factor in the region. Ideologically, Japan located its position via the idea of Asia, in a triangulation of itself, China, and the colonial-modern West, a process that actually *broke apart* the Asia–West/traditional–modern binary opposition. China is therefore the "hidden resource" for modern Asian thinking.[33] The attempt to break the Asia–West binary led to the Greater East Asian War, more commonly referred to as the Pacific War. However, the implications inherent in the former formulation should not be missed. Thus, Sun Ge notes that "the question of Asia must not merely be pursued within the framework defined by the dichotomy of East versus West, but also be considered as dealing with the internal problems in the Asian region."[34]

The regional contemporary is a modernity aware of its colonized past, although how the mobile term "Asia" currently functions has a continuity with but is not quite the same as in the late nineteenth century. East Asian state and also semi-disengaged state and non-state actors, as we will see, participated in that de-territorialized locale, East Asia, which now exists with operational sets of logic. Subjectivity and identity politics from the 1980s were able to encompass this region for political and other purposes in new imaginative formats. The grand narrative of spirit as the story of unfolding progress is brought "home" to East Asia, which is new in its economically enhanced ability to claim possession of the justifying civilizational myth of modernity, even as East Asia remains linked to Western markets.

There is general agreement that Asian art—contemporary art, primarily—drew noticeable international interest in the 1990s by its appearance in both the more established international and increasing East Asian exhibitions witnessed that decade. The greater metropolitan openness to contemporary Asian art was assisted by the regional economic integration that had enabled the politico-cultural discourses on an Asian counter-modernity. However, that metropolitan openness and the Asian exhibitionary imaginary of the curatorial and museum intelligentsia itself also gained intellectual stimuli from—broadly speaking—cultural and postcolonial theory and Euro-American multiculturalism, forms of knowledge generally critical of neoliberal economics and colonialism. These forms of knowledge have helped to drive the reconfiguration of a diverse and fractious East Asia into a multicultural East Asia—at least as a goal to work toward.

By and large, the exhibitions and biennales that resulted have also furnished opportunities to attempt a comparative understanding of the regional (if not transborder) creation of modern culture, however fractured, and the later appearance of contemporary art practices. Further, the art events "fostered a new sense of regional contemporary art identity" by the creation of "spaces in which [regional] artists . . . could meet, [and] see each other's art."[35] That is to say, contemporary Asian art identity is one in which a singular center/periphery model of cultural knowledge production is being abjured. To be sure, a slippage into triumphal pronouncements on Asia's "arrival" can occur culturally, as it did politically—but this probably is to be expected, as contemporary art culture is critical of the colonial modern history to which it is related. The more consistent constraint on critical art discourse is the ongoing co-optation of culture as a resource for postindustrial economic development.[36]

Kobena Mercer argues that "the shifts brought about by identity politics in the 1980s, and global trends in the 1990s, have affected the art world just as all other areas of cultural and social life have been affected."[37] The result: a "global turn" in art programming with an interest in curating and representing non-Western and minority artists in the metropolitan art world, and attempts to decenter art criticism and loosen the canon of modernism. As art historian Julian Stallabrass (drolly but accurately) observes, "The shift [toward the multicultural-postcolonial] was prepared for by postmodern critique which, in a complex series of theoretical moves, affirmed what the market had slowly sanctioned, unveiling the white male 'genius' skulking behind the universalist façade of high culture."[38] The market and governments have been relatively quick to understand that heterogeneity and even "resistance" can be converted into the new, cutting-edge standardization that seems at ease with the neoliberal.

The curator Jean-Hubert Martin declared his *Magiciens de la Terre* (1989), held at the Centre Georges Pompidou and at La Villette in Paris, to be "the first worldwide [and therefore multicultural] exhibition of contemporary art."[39] While there were criticisms that the show still exoticized Third World artists, it was the first *metropolitan* show that used a "global" or "planetary" framework in which the West/non-West dualism and hierarchy were avoided—arguably, the first Global South event that utilized a similar framework was the Bienal de La Habana, which started in 1984.[40] Martin conceived of the global multiplication of artistic images as "des symptômes du resserrement de la communications et des liens, médiatiques et personnels, entre des hommes sur la planète" (symptoms of the greater communication and ties, both mediated and personal, between the people of the planet).[41] While he never used the term "multiculturalism," Martin criticized the arrogance of "our" culture, and presented the work of the "magicians" not as primitive but as contemporaneous and thus contemporary art, and their works were not hung or displayed separately from the Western contemporary art on show.

Art critic and curator Tatehata Akira has commented that despite the existence of exhibitions held outside the West, it was Martin's exhibition that, up to the early 2000s, offered the most effective "post-colonial point of view" on art: "Multiculturalism in art was first advocated most clearly in Europe (there are no regular large-scale international exhibitions in the United States, except for the Carnegie International in Pittsburgh), and this approach spread and influenced[, even if indirectly,] . . . the establishment of international exhibitions outside the West."[42] In contrast with *Magiciens*, Tatehata brings up *Primitivism in the 20th Century*, mounted at the temple of American modernism, the Museum of Modern Art in New York City, five years earlier in 1984. *Primitivism* demonstrated how tribal art and ancient ruins had informed Western modernism from Cubism to earthworks—and ended up reiterating the modernist logic of "treat[ing] things that actually existed in the same time frame as having a temporal distance from each other."[43]

Primitivism could not inspire non-Western art exhibitions, while *Magiciens* was "an epoch-making exhibition in terms of promoting globalism in art that rejects a Western-centered approach."[44]

What is missing in the accounts by critics such as Kobena Mercer of the multicultural-postcolonial that arose and artistic margins coming into representation (as instanced by *Magiciens*) is the *non*-Euro-metropolitan multiculturalist and decolonial representations of their own modernist and contemporary art. The first biennale exhibition in East and South Asia was the India Triennale in New Delhi (1968).[45] More recently, public museums and state-sponsored cultural institutions chiefly in Japan and Australia and, from 1996, in Singapore—with the founding of the Singapore Art Museum— facilitated the emerging infrastructure of contemporary regional art in the 1990s. Under prime minister Paul Keating (1991–1996), Australian visual art exchanges with Asia started truly to transpire, and visual arts organizations also wished to engage within the region. As for Japan, curator and arts manager Alison Carroll is of the opinion that both Japan and Australia, "through the '90s, [ran] a parallel program of activities with the rest of the region. . . . There was a similar sense of positioning, both aware of the need to be more proactive culturally within the region" while treading carefully—Japan because of its Pacific War history and Australia because of its "white Western, non-Asian cuckoo-in-the-nest status."[46]

The shifts in the thinking of art coincided with East Asian economic integration from the mid-1980s and increasing talk of the "Asian century." Among the significant East Asian locales, the Fukuoka Art Museum stands out because it was arguably the inaugural 1979–1980 *Asian Artists Exhibition* that set the pace for the 1990s regional self-representation of Asian art. This exhibition became the Fukuoka Triennial in 1999, when the Fukuoka Asian Art Museum was opened. Other prominent international biennale exhibitions inaugurated from the 1990s onward include the Taipei Biennale (1992; this became an international exhibition in 1998); the First Asia-Pacific Triennial of Contemporary Art (APT), Brisbane, Australia (1993); the Gwangju Biennale (1995); the Shanghai Biennale (1996; this became an international exhibition in 2000); and the Yokohama Triennale (2001).

Alongside the new biennales and exhibitions was also an increase in art writing that began to go beyond "the confines of national readership and interests," Singaporean curator Ahmad Mashadi observes, which assisted the comparative cultural reflection that went into the new art events: "Broadly, the writings that emerged over the period of the early 1990s allowed a prospecting into modernities, their emergence and ways they were understood, cultural contexts through which they may be received and advanced, decolonization and nationalism that at once particularise and universalize [*sic*] responses."[47] Art writing is part of the new forms of cultural knowledge that enabled the comparative dimensions in the Singapore Art Museum's inaugural exhibition *Modernity and Beyond: Themes in Southeast Asian Art* (1996).

The Japan Foundation (Kokusai Kōryū Kikin) too played a prominent enabling role through its Asia Center, which introduced Asian visual and performing arts to its home constituents and supported collaborative work in inter-Asian theater. It also facilitated intellectual exchange through symposia on the contemporary arts. The Asia Center symposia brought to Tokyo notable art critical figures and also cultural intellectuals from the region, including Australia.[48] The Japan Foundation was created in 1972 by then–foreign minister Fukuda Takeo as a special institution under the foreign affairs ministry to promote cultural exchange. Under the pressure of Cold War fears of the 1970s and also in reaction to the anti-Japanese riot that greeted prime minister Tanaka Kakuei's visit to Jakarta in 1974, Fukuda, when he became prime minister, felt that cultural diplomacy had to accompany ongoing economic cooperation to strengthen the "special relationship" with Southeast Asia. After Fukuda's visit to ASEAN countries in 1977, the acronym "ASEAN" replaced "Southeast Asia" in official terminology.[49] In 1990, the Japan Foundation established the ASEAN Culture Center, which was then reorganized as the Japan Foundation Asia Center in 1995, with a remit to include more of Asia in the Center's work. In East Asia, the Japan Foundation and the Singapore Art Museum have the greatest number of exhibitions "investigating modernity and contemporary art."[50]

Japanese diplomacy in the cultural realm indubitably would have aroused suspicion, even if that was a charm offensive to ease the memory of the Pacific War. However, the Japan Foundation's investment in resources and the programming results have been substantial. The JFAC and its predecessor, the ASEAN Culture Center, regularly mounted not only exhibitions on individual ASEAN and (on one occasion) Northeast Asian countries and artists (e.g., *Heri Dono: Dancing Demons and Drunken Deities* [2000] and *Lee Bul: Monster: Asian Contemporary Artist Solo Exhibition Series III* [2003]) but also exhibitions on the region's modern and contemporary art (e.g., *Asian Modernism: Diverse Development in Indonesia, the Philippines, and Thailand* [1995], which traveled to all three countries mentioned in the show's title). Such events were ways of expanding the scope and participation in a putative Asian curatorium—the *Heri Dono* exhibition on an Indonesian contemporary artist was curated by the Thai curator-critic Apinan Poshyananda. Kishi Sayaka has noted how the Foundation's 1992 exhibition, *New Art from Southeast Asia*, featuring new work by seventeen artists and co-organized with the Fukuoka Art Museum and the Hiroshima City Museum of Contemporary Art, broke away from the customary financial support and know-how of newspapers and appeal of established artwork, showing that public art institutions could function "as the authorizing body, . . . conferring artistic value upon artists and networks by way of reciprocal interaction with the art market."[51] While, in the end, she also writes that the preexisting system was not easy to overturn and that forming a larger Asian contemporary art market was limited by stronger interests in China and India, nevertheless a petrified conception of Asia was subjected to scrutiny.

A point that needs to be registered is that the world of Japanese art elites, like any other grouping, is non-monolithic. There are circles in the elite national center of Tokyo that still see Japan as "outside" Asia and more akin to the Euro-American West in possessing an advanced modern culture—as befitting the first modern Asian nation-state. The Japan Foundation's Visual Arts Program seemed able to move beyond the most obvious aspects of this pride in modernity and try to place Japan *inside* a multicultural Asia. As for the Fukuoka Art Museum, part of its adventurousness may stem from its provincial location in Kyushu and therefore in being removed from the cultural assumptions of the two major urban centers, Osaka and Tokyo.

In general, it is perhaps unsurprising that it is sections of the Japanese curatorium who have initiated intra-regional artistic dialogue, given Japan's uneasy cultural engagement with the modern West. This encounter—certainly in relation to the rest of the region—is also manifested in publications such as the bilingual (Japanese and English) review *ART iT*, which started in 2005 and examines global art developments with the region's varied perspectives in mind. A special issue on the East Asian presence at the 2007 Venice Biennale offered readers "A Short Chronology of Modernism in East Asia," which outlined the virtually enforced creation of modern visual-arts culture. The French Revolution is the first date given, presumably as their chosen starting point of the modern West. This is followed by dates pertaining to the Western "opening up" of Asia between 1840 and 1860: the Opium Wars (1840–1842),

Commodore Perry's visit to Japan (1853), and India coming under direct rule from London (1858). Then, for 1860–1900, developments in the institutionalization of a modern art culture are noted: "Japan participates in the Vienna Exposition officially for the first time (1873)," "Tokyo Fine Arts School (now Tokyo University of Fine Arts and Music) opens (1867)," and "Japan participates unofficially in the (2nd) Venice Biennale (1897)."[52] The Vienna Expo is a vital moment in literal and cultural translation, for it is there that the term for "art" in its Western sense is rendered into being by the Japanese Secretariat as *bijutsu*. The same Kanji characters will soon be used for *meishu* in Chinese and *misul* in Korean.[53] The historic Western engagement is presented through a postcolonial mental set firmly aware of the recuperative capacities of the center/periphery model of knowledge and modern cultural production, even in an era in which such dichotomies are supposed to have been shattered.

Given this recuperative resilience, the region's art institutions are important, as they have more of a stake in attending to what modernism was in Asia and to the presence of regional contemporary art than would the more "international" institutions in the metropolitan West. The emergence of East Asian biennales and museum exhibitions showcasing Asian modern and contemporary art indicates that self-reflexive investigations have emerged on how "the rest of the world" produced and still produces its modern culture out of related quasi- or directly colonized experiences, even if the ability to investigate such questions are hamstrung generally by a lack of funding and other institutional capacities to support committed cultural work. Still, as Rasheed Araeen, the British-Asian artist and critic, has bluntly exhorted, "It would be naïve to expect that this job [of representing the others] should have been done by the West's own critics or historians. How could they, without not only disturbing their perception of the other but also demolishing their very philosophical framework of Eurocentric modern art history on which their power is based?"[54]

The gaining of representation is an ambiguous and contradictory process. The modern-urban vision of New Asia is now perhaps inevitably part of the cultural capital that governments in the region can use to boost their credentials as possessing the metropolitan culture that complements their desired world city status. The inaugural Singapore Biennale of 2006, for example, was inextricably connected with the Singapore state's developmental goals to forge a competitive and creatively "innovative" world city.[55] However, art historian and artist Iftikhar Dadi has asked, "Are we really willing to trade the globalized art world for the pre-biennial nationalist era, [even] if such were possible?"[56] The contradictions entailed in a "globalized" modernity means that there are possibilities of self-representation and new artistic imaginaries that can contest capitalist logics within the very cultural institutions that newly wealthy states seek to forge for the sake of becoming "global."

More recently, the expression "contemporary Asian art" has been criticized as "a very problematic rubric, a default term . . . [by] exhibition-makers . . . [that] oftentimes has obscured the actual works and artists." Nevertheless, curator Doryun Chong also adds that such exhibition making "did bring a lot of artists in the region across national borders. . . . I think it formed *relations*."[57] The challenge to imagine culture across borders continues.

Struggling from the Older to the Present Moment of the New

With the above, we arrive at the pre-biennial and still-national (if not quite nationalistic) moment of the Fukuoka Art Museum's inaugural *Asian Artists Exhibition* of 1979–1980 and then proceed to the contrasting "global-regional" exhibition as manifested in JFAC's and Tokyo City Opera Gallery's 2002 exhibition *Under Construction: New Dimensions of Asian Art*. Despite the stated goals of the organizers, the Fukuoka shows finally were not able to think comparatively of modern art's emergence from the colonial and immediate post-independence cultural-intellectual contact zones being established. The curators found it hard to think past national boundaries and art-historical narratives that defined cultural identities mainly against modern Western culture rather than in relation to other cultures around them. The 1979 part of the exhibition, *Modern Asian Art—India, China & Japan*, in particular, became mired in considering what common cultural essence(s) could "genuinely" have defined Asia. Fukuoka remained caught in the transition from the older moment of the new in East Asia.

By 2002, outsourcing from the advanced Western economies and outflows of Japanese capital that helped induce intensive regional economic integration meant that fresh attempts could be made to breach national frameworks of cultural thinking. This did not mean that the older traumas of the new were transcended—Japan has never firmly come to terms with its wartime past, as we know. Still, regional transformation did assist in the imagining of a global-regional curatorial framework for presenting the contemporary moment as a defective but nevertheless postcolonial East Asian modern. What is also revealing of the change are the different Japanese intellectuals appealed to and the uses to which they are put in 1979 and 2002.

The "International-Regional" Exhibition

The intent of Fukuoka's *Asian Artists Exhibition* was twofold, as set out in the catalogue for *Modern Asian Art*. Kennoki Toshihiro, the museum's director, wrote that the exhibition would "trace the modernization of Asian art in these three nations by clarifying how traditional and modern art have interacted and how these nations have been able to maintain and develop their own national characteristics while undergoing modernization and a transfiguration of their art."[58] The first goal is to see how older cultural identities have been kept within the newer modern art forms that arose with the (post)colonial adaptation to the Western nation-state model of political modernity and socio-industrial transformation. Shinto Kazuma, the city's mayor, offers us the second goal: "to promote friendly relations between these Asian countries and to deepen their mutual understanding."[59] This is a version of liberal international solidarity.

Fukuoka's city government often emphasizes its historic status as a gateway of "imported" culture from China and Korea and thus as a regional contact zone.[60] The founding of the art museum—with the extensive programming in Asian art, uncommon both internationally and in Japan—was the mark of the city leadership's wish for fostering regional cross-cultural dialogue and to try to think of Japan's commonality with Asia. In fact, the inaugural exhibition was meant to focus on twentieth-century American art, but Yasunaga Kōichi, a member of the *Asian Artists Exhibition* curatorial team, told *Newsweek* that mayor Shinto overturned that plan for an Asian art show.[61]

The *Modern Asian Art* catalogue has four essays: a framing essay and three separate national essays on India, China, and Japan. The region "Asia" includes not only the two major states of East Asia but also India, and these "big" three front the first exhibition. In keeping with what Kennoki had written, the essays offer national outlines of the impact of Western artistic culture during the high-colonial era on traditional art and some evaluation of how previous art categories and work were mediated by newer contexts but, in the final analysis, only limited gestures to intra-regional interaction between the three countries.

Given its stated goals, Fukuoka's initial shows can be described as "international-regional" exhibitions. "International" implies mapped, distinct, and organized entities that *had* to relate to each other across boundaries. The existence of the Cold War, along with the intense postwar nationalism that accompanied India's decolonization on August 15, 1947, made connecting across boundaries more difficult, given larger international alliances required in yet another dichotomous cartographic splitting of the world into East and West. Boundaries were reinforced by the realities of national economies. India, for instance, practiced economic autarchy—closed economic planning—in the 1960s.

Yet, in the late 1970s, the time the exhibitions were organized, an internationalization of financial markets was taking place via market deregulation, and a so-called flexible regime of accumulation was developing, versus nationally rooted mass production. Then, East Asian regionalization intensified from the mid-1980s. It is therefore no surprise that at the start of the next century, by the time of *Under Construction*, we had "global-regional" rather than "international-regional" art exhibitions.

The term "global," in contrast to "international," implies the transgressive (that which can cross national and cultural borders, that which could be hybrid), the more creative, and (in terms of the arts) the less-formalist and plural "postmodern," which would not have modernism's obsession with newness and innovation in form. Regional artists in this context could now look to each other, without conceptions of (sometimes essentialized) national culture hampering them, for artistic inspiration and concerns, instead of looking only or primarily to the West, and in terms of the circulation, Asian art could increasingly be received by audiences within the region, regardless of whether the established metropolitan centers were interested in such art. Caroline Jones submits that with "the turning from 'the international' and 'the world' to 'the transnational' and 'the global,' there is also a shift from legislated orders to dynamism, from vertical hierarchies to horizontal spread."[62] Certainly, the understanding of a global-regional contemporary Asia is a form of resistance to the West, although there is still clear interest in US and Western European recognition of the Asian modern in art and culture: *inclusion* remains one of the stakes at hand—the two impulses are not mutually exclusive. But we must keep in mind that the "global" also implies deregulated free markets and transgressive capital flows, leading to the valorization of specific art forms amenable to the global art world's hierarchy of marketable art. I shall return to this later.

The point now is that, despite the politico-economic situation of the late 1970s, Fukuoka's opening shows—arguably in an interregnum between the international and the global—still could not see past center/periphery and national-modern models of culture. The three essays in the catalogue for *Modern Asian Art* are mainly national accounts of art development.

The essay on India is by the late Dr. Laxmi Prasad Sihare, then–director of the National Gallery of Modern Art, New Delhi. He offers a now-established art narrative. Sihare writes that the British had "degraded Indian aesthetic norms," and it was Abanindranath Tagore (1871–1951), the nephew of Rabindranath Tagore (1861–1940)—"partly exhorted by [the Japanese critic and curator] Kakuzo Okakura [(1862–1913), who had visited India and knew both the Tagores]"—who initiated a "new school of national art" in the early twentieth century. This allowed a revival of "ancient literary themes and the transformations of blending of various oriental techniques[, primarily 'the technique of Japanese water color painting']."[63] He concludes by arguing that, first, the "evolution and development of Modern art in India is unlike that in the West," as it was the inorganically introduced academic oil-painting style that had initiated "modern" development, and second, while the "modern International style" was now dominant, "the issue of evolving its own cultural identity has always been the concern of Indian artists."[64] A sense of national incompletion inheres Sihare's national-cultural imaginary.

The essay on Japan by the then–director of the National Museum of Modern Art, Kyoto, Michiaki Kawakita, stresses how the entry of Western art upset an earlier cultural ability to absorb the "Asian artistic currents [that have] entered Japan from ancient times."[65] Here, too, is a sense of loss linked with the impact of modern Western culture. He also cites Okakura Kakuzō and furnishes a quotation from his *Ideals of the East* (1903)—written in English by the bilingual Okakura: "Japan is at once a museum of Asian arts [in the way many remnants of such art could be found] and also more than that."[66] Kawakita later reminds the reader that Okakura, along with his mentor, the American Ernest Fenollosa (1853–1908), worked to revivify traditional visual culture. Fenollosa had entered Japan in 1878 and, in 1886, was appointed as an Imperial Commissioner of Fine Arts in Japan. In the end, Western art forms and the "revived Japanese-style painting . . . began to coexist as two powerful forces in Japanese art of the 20th Century."[67] The invocation of Okakura, as discussed in the Introduction, becomes inextricably linked to the traumatic incursion of colonial modernity that haunts the postcolonial construction of national-cultural history.

Of the three, the Chinese essay has the least sense of loss and is the most "official" (it is attributed to "The Exhibition Organization") and propagandistic, smug in an apparently stable and happy Second World modernity free from the fractures of (post)colonized cultures. The years 1840–1919 saw the destruction of "feudalistic and conservative art ideology" by "an art with a new rhythmical style . . . [achieved by] energetically enhancing the best of traditionally based art of the former ages"—that is, this art was iconoclastically modern partially in the way the retrograde past has been tamed.[68] Artistic renderings of post-1949 communist control were drawn from many country sources, and the visual arts became so popular that "industrial and agricultural workers also paint."[69] The Chinese piece proclaims a self-satisfied modern national culture purged of the earlier trauma of the new and the manifestations of capitalist decadence—it is unaware of (or possibly chooses to ignore) how the 1978 "open door" economic policy was encouraging experimentation in artistic formalism and sociopolitical critique in 1979 in Shanghai and in Beijing, although the transition into "contemporary art" did not take place until the early 1980s.[70]

The framing essay is by Shinji Koike, the subcommittee chairman for part I of the *Asian Artists Exhibition*—curator Yasunaga Kōichi confirms that Koike was the chief project officer for the curatorial process and that it was he who realized the importance of Okakura's artistic ideas on Asia.[71] Koike's essay revealingly indicates how the older experience of the new has hampered the exhibition's aims. He commences by expatiating upon how Fukuoka's history of receiving foreign culture has become transformed into "a[n exhibition] theme based on international exchange of Asian art."[72] And then, as in Kawakita's essay and to a lesser extent in Sihare's essay, Okakura (here Okakura Tenshin, the pseudonym by which he is also known) is conjured up for the idea of Asia: "Tenshin Okakura was a man who had a great influence on Japanese modern art. After his study tour of Western art as well as his travels to India and China, he said: 'Asia is oen' [*sic*]. Can Asian art be thought of as a unit like Western art? Do all Asian countries have common aesthetic sources or values? Or, is the Asian art world today in such a chaotic state characterized by a diversity of styles unrelated to each other? The planning for this 'Asian Artists Exhibition' stemmed from such honest enquiries."[73]

These seem genuine rather than rhetorical questions. The problem is that they constitute neither curatorial aims nor a brief. The three countries, he does suggest, have "a historically deep relation through Buddhism," a position that Okakura would have agreed with.[74] Apart from that vague commonality, the common reference point is the colonial West: "Representative works of the last one hundred years were chosen to compare the artistic reactions of each of these countries and to research how their art was influenced by Western art."[75]

The repeated summoning of the controversial Okakura as an intellectual authority for ecumenical cultural-regional relations tells us how a crisis-driven period of the modern pertaining to the colonial-modern Western powers and Japan–China competition interferes with the postwar wish to analyze critically the region's modern cultures. Okakura, a founder of the Tokyo Fine Arts School cited in *ART iT*'s chronology of Japanese-Asian modernist moments, had reacted with related concern to the Western presence in East Asia that Fukuzawa Yukichi had, slightly earlier. He famously wrote in 1903:

> Asia is one. The Himalayas divide, only to accentuate, two mighty civilizations, the Chinese with its communism of Confucius, and the Indian with its individualism of the Vedas. But not even the snowy barriers can interrupt for one moment that broad expanse of love for the Ultimate and Universal, which is the common thought-inheritance of every Asiatic race, enabling them to produce all the great religions of the world, and distinguishing them from those maritime peoples of the Mediterranean and the Baltic, who love to dwell on the Particular, and to search out the means, not the end, of life.[76]

Although Okakura believed that the modernizing of Japan was necessary, he formulated a contradictory nativist-spiritual response against instrumental civilization. He argued in *Ideals of the East* that the origins of Japanese art, as it is seen in temples in the forms of, say, bronzes or carvings, was impossible to understand without knowing how the expanding force of Buddhism in all its variety was pushed into Japan via the Korean peninsula and China. Japan's island status allowed this variety to be conserved from the ravages of war that mainland Asia suffered—and thus Japan could be seen as a relatively unsullied "museum" of Asia. One of Okakura's arguments was for a restoration of this Buddhistic Asia that could be seen in Japan. The search for native connections across the region riven by the great colonial powers led to this culturalist elevation of Buddhism as an historical commonality.

Okakura's romantic version of art is a counterpoint against the new commercial-industrial modernity. He tells a US audience in a talk, "You should remember, however, that our wholesale adoption of your methods of life and culture was not purely a matter of choice but of necessity. The word 'modernization' means the occidentalization of the world. The map of Asia will reveal the dismal fate of the ancient civilizations that have succumbed to the spell of industrialism, commercialism, imperialism, and what not, which the modern spirit has cast over them."[77] While in some respects he seemed out of touch in the Meiji era he hailed from, the proclamation "Asia is one" was later co-opted by the wartime machine to validate the Pacific War as a cultural war vented against the colonial-modern West. Although Okakura is controversial, both Koike and Kawakita feel he must be cited amid their economically successful late 1970s, as his intellectual status was still an emblem for the dislocating processes in Japan's nineteenth-century modernization.

The inability to transcend or obviate the older moment of the modern; a lack of an incisive intellectual framework by which to curate a show that could exceed the boundaries put in place by decolonization and the Cold War; the absence of a defining theme per se; and—although the catalogue never tells us how works were selected between the museum and the country representatives—what may have been a lack of enough curatorial intervention in the artwork selected all lead to an incoherent framework for a comparative exhibition. The common ground of Western art of the colonial period does not allow for the exceeding of a fundamental Asian country/West dichotomy and orientation—regional connection is desired but not quite expressible.

If *Modern Asian Art* and the "heavyweight" three were Asia Major in historical relief, then part II in 1980, *Festival: Contemporary Asian Arts Show*, included both Asia Major and Minor, with largely contemporary artists—in the sense that the artists presented were mainly younger artists—from thirteen countries on display. Apart from China, India, and Japan, there were Sri Lanka, Nepal, Thailand, Malaysia, Bangladesh, Indonesia, Korea, Singapore, Pakistan, and the Philippines. There was also a symposium held on the topic "What must be done for the future of Asian tradition and art which have been changed under the influence of Western art?" Part II moves a step closer to a "global regionalism" simply because more countries are represented and because it presented present-day artwork.

The goal to facilitate a better understanding of contemporary culture in various regional locations is better articulated in the *Festival* catalogue than in the *Modern Asian Art* catalogue. Aoki Shigeru, the exhibition chairman, writes that the new museum with "its young curatorial staff is accepting the challenge of doing something which has never been tried at any other museum in Japan": curating a show in which an Asian country looks exclusively at Asia.[78] The "pipe-line" that now opens up between "the Japanese art world and the art worlds of Asian countries . . . may be a thin pipe-line but it is a very valuable one."[79] While Japanese economic activity in the region had increased contacts, "in the sphere of culture and art, the Japanese people's knowledge and understanding of these Asian countries is probably shallow, certainly if compared with their knowledge of that of the West."[80] The Fukuoka Art Museum, however, did bring both the history of regional modernism and contemporary artists to Japan and into direct contact with each other in a single venue, directly enabling the increased possibility of rethinking in a comparative way "region" and artistic modernity's regional impact.

Yasunaga Kōichi, a member of the original nine-member curatorial team for the *Asian Artists Exhibition* and later a director of the Fukuoka Asian Art Museum, recalls that the team did not have any knowledge of Asian modern or contemporary art, save for China. He understood that the inaugural show would be a one-off event. Instead, various countries involved requested that the museum continue with displaying Asia, and Fukuoka's younger curators were keen to organize more such exhibitions.[81] The museum's *3rd Asian Art Show* in 1989, unlike the *Asian Artists Exhibition*, would have the theme "Symbolic Visions in Contemporary Asian Life," and with that, the museum's firmer comparative approach to the region's modern and contemporary art commenced.

The "Global-Regional" Exhibition—Now Under Construction

The JFAC's and the Tokyo City Opera Art Gallery's 2002 exhibition *Under Construction* was different from Fukuoka in that the intellectual-curatorial framework and the final exhibition produced in Tokyo more effectively functioned as a global-regional exhibition that sought, first, to enhance art and cultural links between countries within a region and, second, to articulate that region as a globalized space. Efforts were made to obviate the national as a defining (and confining or essentialized) identity category—no discussion of what was truly unique about, say, Korean or Filipino cultures occurred.

The shared contemporary and contemporaneity of Asia instead was projected to be a common sense of extraordinary modernization most visibly expressed in intense urbanization and multilayered urban cultures with which visual art interacts. India, in a spirit of inclusiveness (as was the case in Fukuoka), is in the exhibition as a part of Asia, but the intellectual framework that underlies the "Asia" to be constructed in this exhibitionary imaginary has a strong East Asian provenance. The reorganization of the Japan Foundation ASEAN Culture Center into the Asia Center was one key reason for the larger scope of Asia for *Under Construction*, and part of that change, as art historian Kajiya Kenji tells us, meant that "the Center adopted a new policy to promote multilateral cultural exchanges and collaboration works within the Asia region in addition to the development of understanding Asian art in Japan"—and when we reach the 2000s, the interest in collaborative approaches to presenting contemporary art occurs among professionals in the region as well.[82] While the contemporary that was enunciated was critically postcolonial in its wish to bypass the center/periphery view of the world, the older clash between Japan and the rest of East Asia was still addressed.

The exhibition catalogue has two framing essays by Furuichi Yasuko, the project program director, and Kataoka Mami, then–chief curator of the Tokyo Opera City Art Gallery and the collective exhibition cocurator.[83] There were eight other curators, and each had their own essay, save for the Thai curator, Gridthiya ("Jeap") Gaweewong, who featured transcripts of discussions she held with artists and critics. The other seven curators hailed from India (Ranjit Hoskote, art critic), the Philippines (Patrick Flores, art historian), South Korea (Kim Sunjung, curator), Indonesia (Asmudjo Jono Irianto, college art history lecturer), mainland China (Pi Li, researcher), and Japan (Kamiya Yukie, independent curator, and Yamamoto Atsuo, curator).

A central goal of the exhibition, Furuichi tells the reader, was the collaborative curatorial effort to come to terms with actual contemporary art practice after manifold regional economic developments over the past fifteen years—hence the representative range of Asian curators. Despite a decade of Japan Foundation efforts to introduce Asian art to the Japanese and to foster the understanding of Asian art through exhibitions and symposia, changes in the art environment had outstripped their work. Attaining a fresher understanding entailed trying to avoid using preconceived Western ideas of "Asian art," as the mutual cultural conceptions held by those in East and South Asia may be filtered through inherited colonial-era lenses: "Asia will be defined by Asians, instead of just being a[n] historical concept rooted in memories, and this task is one that only we who live in the same age and space are able to do."[84] As such, the exhibition is not interested in any "historical . . . [or] abstract sense" of Asia, by which Furuichi means clichéd ideas of "traditional" Asia, along with Asia merely defined as being the "non-West," which is a non-category.[85] Understanding the different inflections of the "contemporary" in different locales was the way forward. Although "little was known about the art of neighboring countries, the [artistic] exchange that took place from the 1990s within the region gradually strengthened peer-to-peer relationships."[86] The scope for exchange had to be broadened.

Collaboration required curators to understand the layered socioeconomic environments of the contemporary region. In her essay, Kataoka observes that "the shift in interest by the international art scene towards non-Western nations, including Asia, is creating a change in the artists' working environment. . . . In addition, [the curators need to see that] rapid economic and social changes have created a situation where the hybrid and multi-leveled environment found in the gap that lies between traditional and modern society and between urbanization and rural life has become the norm. This has resulted in more natural demand for the particular everyday environments that form the identity of each individual."[87] Kataoka offers a concretization of what is significant in the contemporary in Asia: intense urbanization, urban life, and the increased gap between rural and urban life, with the complex impact these make on subjectivity and individual identity. This larger world—which now includes the metropolitan art world—was part of the multifaceted, fragmented, but also vibrant daily urban environments that artists have to deal with and which curators must address. Many of the artists selected were born in the 1960s and 1970s, as were a number of the curators. This selection of those who saw firsthand the emergence of the East Asian modern as young adults in the 1980s is deliberate: they would collectively share the experience of the new urbanism.

Under Construction had exhibitions in dispersed regional urban agglomerations of various sizes—from the immense Beijing (about fifteen million) and Mumbai (about thirteen million), decreasing to Seoul (about ten million), Bangkok (about nine million), Bandung (about two million), Manila (about 1.6 million), and Ashiya (in Hyogo, between Osaka and Kobe, about ninety thousand)—that addressed local art concerns in a less hierarchical manner. Then, finally, it moved to Tokyo for a single, collective exhibition. Furuichi explains, "The project was to plot multiple dots of equally borderless values that exist at the same level, but for the multiple dots, at the same time, to create a single space. The keyword for linking these multiple 'dots' can be 'Asia' as a function."[88] With regard to that odd, technicist word "function"—to which I shall return—she goes on to add that "art in Asia is not 'something that lies within a system,' but a function in a living relationship with society."[89] The use of the word "function" indicates the avoidance of culturalism in the "bad" or nativist sense. The hope was to discover empirically from the bottom up what in reality was happening and to see directly the shared sense of daily life in diverse urban environs.

If "Asia" is the keyword for Furuichi to be thought through, Kataoka tells us that the curators collectively parsed that term and came up with critical keywords that would work for that cartographic term based upon their investigations of the various local art scenes of the cities of the pre-Tokyo exhibition. The terms chosen resonate with the present multicultural-postcolonial global art lexicon:

- Daily life/Habitation/Subculture/Place/Working with Community
- Hybrid/Process of Exchanging/Transforming/Economy/Mobility/Here & There/Sea
- Memory/Enigma/Fantasy/Dream[90]

Kataoka thinks that what is important is the "respect [not only] for the equality of individuals, but also for the differences in the historical and cultural backgrounds that shape each individual."[91] That is, she looks beyond the values of the now-suspicious transcendent modern and the values attached to it—with its link between colonialism and the human seen as universal, along with the possible suggestion of Japan's superiority to the region—to the plural or multicultural values of the latest new.

The curatorial process therefore required firsthand visits to different cities by the curators in smaller teams. Some curators had actually never visited other countries in the region. Kataoka adds that one of the very themes of the exhibition was "beyond the boundaries of curation," but this was not revealed to exhibition visitors as it was professional in its orientation. However, it did indicate another part of what was under construction: "a [curatorial] network-in-progress, transcending the geographical framework known as 'Asia' and continuing to expand on a global scale."[92] Expanding a multicultural Asian curatorium itself was a step toward polycentric global connectivity.

Unsurprisingly, the curators were dismayed that the final Tokyo exhibition required some dismantling of the initial local contexts and the themes generated to come up with some overall sense of the Asia under construction. The frustrations Kataoka took to be salutary in the procedure of curating the collective exhibition from "below" to seeing "the image of the new generation of Asian art that would be curated by remixing and reconstructing the whole."[93] The three-year process consumed many resources—financial and otherwise. The final "compendium show" has been described in a review as "slightly disjointed," given that a definitive exhibition or display of Asia was less the goal than the "experiment in intellectually crossbreeding young Asian curators . . . to give them a reason and a means to think together about Asian art."[94]

The major intellectual authority invoked in *Under Construction* is the sinologist, Takeuchi Yoshimi (1910–1977), author of the important essay, "Asia as Method" ("Hoho to Shite no Ajia," 1961). Takeuchi wrote:

> Today, in order to solve the region's common problems which have increased as a result of the rapid formation of an interdependent structure, the Asian countries have had to transcend the confines of nation and state to jointly address particularly urgent issues. And, in order to address this reality, what is required is not so much an Asia defined in a historical and abstract sense, but "Asia as a method" or "Asia as a function." This does not mean an Asia that functions for the benefit of an individual nation, as Japan did before the war. Rather, the expectations are for an Asia to function as part of the process in which people in the region question their own identity or acquire new identity.[95]

If in 1979, in Fukuoka, Okakura's invocation implied how an older, crisis-driven moment of the new was carried into a postwar attempt to imagine Asia, Takeuchi is used by Furuichi to argue in 2002 that the reimagining of an increasingly interdependent region must not be stuck in the bad old days. However, there is no forgetting the regional costs paid for Japan's early formation as a modern nation-state.

Takeuchi had argued that modernizing Asia must not be understood only in relation to the advanced West but also in relation to the ways in which the modern had been engaged *within* the region. China, like Japan, had become modern too, even if China in 1919 was seen by the League of Nations to lack even "the requisite unity to qualify as a nation-state."[96] For Takeuchi, the qualitative difference in the two modernizations was that Japan was modernized from the top down; this was not the case with China. The oppressive

Twenty-One Demands of 1915 by Japan led to the May Fourth Movement in 1919. He affirmed that movement to be "the first victory on the part of the people's movement in China."[97] The explosion of the modern spirit came from "below" in China, and it is that which gives it a greater potential than Japan's modernity, at least in Takeuchi's assessment. This notion of modernization from the bottom up was also clearly picked up for *Under Construction*.

What was at the crux of this understanding of comparative "arrival" of the modern for Takeuchi?

> I realized that we must not always compare Japan's case with that of the advanced nations of the West, as had traditionally been done. This way of thinking could be seen among scholars and laymen alike. Politicians and businessmen, for example, compare Japanese political institutions with those in England, just as Japanese art would simply be compared with French art. We had to cease such comparisons, for these were inadequate to the task of grasping our own position. It was then that I realized the importance of conceiving of Japan's modernization trilaterally by reference to different types of modernization [in the region], such as, for example, that of China or India. . . . It was at this time that I realized the importance of conceiving of modernization on the basis of a more complex framework than that of simple binary oppositions.[98]

He did not reject the need to understand the Western origins of the modern but rather called for a greater knowledge of what has transpired in the surrounding countries if we are to escape the ignorance of how the modern was established all around Japan, an ignorance wrought by a West-centered binarism. While Takeuchi made his arguments more than four decades ago, it seems that his theoretical purchase comes now, when a congeries of Asian others work to represent themselves culturally and have the institutional capacity through which to do so.

Takeuchi saw Japan as being "part of the Orient," although he knew other Japanese intellectuals argued against this.[99] He did think that, despite mutual cultural exchange between Japan and China, "it is yet extremely difficult to see them (as well as India) collectively as one cultural entity outside of their resistance to Europe"; this was perhaps also a swipe taken at Okakura.[100] The Asia and the "Asian principles" and values that Takeuchi sought to help create through intra-regional dialogue have to do with the diverse but connected modernizing processes: "Perhaps these values do not already exist, in substantive form. Rather I suspect that they are possible as method, that is to say, as the process of the subject's self-formation. This I have called 'Asia as method,' and yet it is impossible to definitively state what this might mean."[101]

Under Construction drew from but also tried to exceed Takeuchi's arguments. What is at stake in an Asia under construction is the formation of a mutual subjectivity that will encompass the now-existent transformations of the region since the impact of colonial-era modernity. While Takeuchi's modern values were still to a great extent the great values of equality and freedom from the older modern period, when man was thought to exist, Furuichi and *Under Construction* in general transposed "Asia as Method" to a multicultural New Asia register where cultural difference was appreciated.

A profile of the newest new in Asia—a combination of a vibrant everyday urbanism and cultural complexity—is found in the essays of Kamiya Yukie, Kim Sunjung, and Pi Li, who curated the local shows for Seoul and Beijing, collectively entitled "Fantasia." Each curator has a slightly different interpretation of that term, according to Kim: Kamiya sees it as the fantasy that surpasses daily life; Pi Li sees the sociopolitical elements in it; and Kim sees the way reality is channeled into works of art. The new urban spaces of globalization are hubs of dynamic clashes, and what Pi Li has to say seems both truism and cliché in imag(in)ing life in the constantly morphing Asian built environment, in cities apparently without geometry.[102] At the "macro level," Pi Li says, we see the free market living side by side with state economic control, and individualistic consumerism with collectivism; at the micro level, the demands of daily life accelerate the "emptying and sanitation of the imagination": daily life in East Asia may be collective and individualistic, contradictory in its own distinctive manner, as other urban centers are also contradictory, but it is not the exotic of the Western colonial imagination. All three seem to argue, in Pi Li's words, that "the Asianesque imagination" for artists rejects "the concept of everyday life as insipid and monotonous"—the predations of everyday life need to be confronted artistically, in spite of and, in fact, because of the capitalist "emptying . . . of the imagination."[103]

In a way, Kamiya is the most upbeat of the three: she regards Hong Kong film *auteur*-director Wong Kar-wai as a prime example of the imaginative engagement with the everyday. In particular, she holds up his iconic *Chungking Express* (1994), set in Hong Kong, as a paramount example of productive-fragmented artistic creativity. That city's depicted urbanism becomes the embodiment of a noirish and frenetic vision of New Asia:

> The movie captured everyday life in a contemporary Asia, conveying the atmosphere of its speed. . . . He turns his gaze to the nitty-gritty of the urban landscape, such as convenience stores . . . and to sights from everyday life where elements of culture from domestic and foreign are all mixed up. . . . What emerges from it all is the reality and the fantasy that belong to all Asians in an age where things, information, and people are all moving. . . . The gaze of new-generation artists onto their everyday lives overlaps with that revealed in the movie of Wong Karwai, in which he is inspired by urban daily life.[104]

This is the almost clichéd rhetoric of the global postmodern—a blurry rush of images to signify the transnational, the cultural hybridity of high and mass culture, social fractures caused by the circulation of capital and people. But yet just to say this flatly without qualification is also to be unfair to the *actual* intensified nature of daily life and the circulation of culture and capital not only from the advanced West into the region, but—in a pronounced way from the 1980s—*within* the region itself. Kamiya argues that younger Asian artists "need to create a platform where they can express themselves and go out to public places to increase their interaction with the public": this is where contemporary cultural critique must be directed.[105]

Asmudjo Jono Irianto's ironically titled essay "Asia Now: Under Construction?" foregrounds not so much only the urban preferences of the exhibitionary imaginary on display, given that his own local exhibition—*Dream Project: Under Construction*—is in Bandung, a city of some two million, but rather its *metropolitan* bias. The metropolitan West is challenged, it would appear, so that modern-urban Asia too can become culturally metropolitan. While *Under Construction* was for "ourselves" and not for the "them" of the Western metropole, Asmudjo notes that "Asian identity is certainly [still] not free from the shadow of classic sentiments regarding East-West relations."[106] The extra-regional connection with the former colonial West remains, not only in terms of trade but also in terms of cultural ambition.

There is another Asia, Asmudjo points out, that does not participate in the rapid development that makes parts of Asia no longer "identical with the East [of the colonial era]"; this other Asia has "tendencies of self-destruction, through intra-national conflicts and internal conflicts . . . , or in different terms, a difference of identities."[107] Cultural difference and diversity within a national setting are not always matters for celebration, for difference cannot easily become cosmopolitan multiculturalism. This sobering reminder covers Indonesia as well, which experienced authoritarian development, becoming a second-tier newly industrializing economy under president Suharto (1921–2008). It was very much set back during the 1997 Asian economic crisis and when the Suharto regime fell and the country experienced severe interethnic tensions.

Asmudjo also brings up the role of art in relation to the varied development levels of Asia. *Under Construction* itself was possible because Tokyo had both the institutional structures and larger public support for high-cultural events: "Development in the era of globalization has more or less resulted in a metropolitan society that is also cosmopolitan," and so "the theme Under Construction can be seen as a critical and reflective attitude toward whether its 'existence' has already become part of a common identity with similar features in Asian societies."[108] Indonesia's contemporary art is in the lurch, for it lacks strong public support and the physical and institutional structures for staging the contemporary. Asmudjo quotes art historian Hans Belting: "Contemporary art would not only be homeless without the museum, it would be voiceless and invisible," and with that he concludes, "Contemporary art is an identity absent in the large cities of Indonesia."[109]

This leads one to ask how we might locate the Indonesian artists who may *not* be able to circulate internationally at the biennales because their artwork is incompatible with the globally favored formats of contemporary art. Such artists' work is "actually better known and supported by the local public."[110] Do we ignore such work because of a desire to be metropolitan—to be global in our regional outlook? The chaotically creative "Fantasia" theme of the Seoul-Beijing exhibition modulates into the hopeful "Dream" theme of the Bandung exhibition. Fittingly, one of the distinctive artworks for "Dream Project" is *Fabriek* (Dutch: factory) *Gallery*, by Jakarta-based artist-designer Sofwan, a semi-permanent building that actually housed the exhibition, made of a corrugated metal roof and plywood—material often associated with the makeshift housing of squatters—and with scaffolding deliberately surrounding the entire structure. The local *Under Construction* exhibition he curated was undertaken "in the hope that the existence and support of contemporary art practices will become an important aspect of the identity of society in Indonesia's bigger cities."[111]

Asmudjo's critique and queries, combined with the *Under Construction* project taken as a whole, express a hope, a wish that the New Asia, with better economic circumstances to support it, will now be able to nurture a metropolitan-urban and inclusive multiculture, one that is genuinely able to capture truly the heterogeneity of cultural practice. The multilateral Asian art exhibition, with all the challenges that face it, seems to have obtained enough institutional and cultural-intellectual capacity to think through how a critical East Asian contemporary could be imagined—but it is a contemporary that still struggles with its own modern history and present-day differences.

The 1990s saw the desire to create and curate the "authentically" new in the region, and to conceive of the region as new, in the wake of postwar economic changes. This new modernity, though, cannot fully go beyond the older modernity—the "inauthentically" new—with its oppressive features that are not desirable: the regional strife over becoming modern nation-states and the war it gave rise to; the repressiveness linked to the old European colonial powers; and the teleology of their cultural aesthetic as it moved on, in triumph, from the new to the newer to the newest, all the while trampling upon and consuming the (invented) cultural-aesthetic "traditionalism" of Asia.

Thus, the present versions of New Asia in its free-market-dependent/neoliberal yet (quasi-)authoritarian forms have not entirely escaped the older presences of the new. Indeed, neither can the most innovative versions of the new afford do away with *all* of the essentially modernist categories of the old new: ongoing modernization in the region still requires the teleology of "progress"—or else crafting effective political or even aesthetic-curatorial-cultural programs will be difficult if history truly has ended. The model of the modern used by the members of the East Asian curatorium for *Under Construction* is a complex mix of an "authentic" progress that seeks to supersede the region's past that is combined with aspects of postmodernism's well-known rhetoric of the decentered, the multiple, and the heterogeneous is ambiguous and even contradictory. It is, arguably, a potentially productive ambiguity-contradiction in a revamped version of modernity in which the new fetish of difference is (uneasily) conjoined to the older fetish of the new. During the 1990s and the 2000s, during which modernity had become reduced to a universal, free-market order, letting such contradictions speak facilitated other critical possibilities.

I conclude with a reflection by Kamiya Yukie, the director of the Japan Society Gallery in New York City since 2015. She has reaffirmed that *Under Construction* should be thought of as one illustrative component of how collaborative curatorial practice may work: "It is important to not only introduce current art scenes and emerging artists, but also to continuously engage in discussions on how to approach Asia as a whole, what that would entail and what needs to be said about Asia now. . . . [A]rt can be a medium for transnational dialogue, rather than an object of exploitation by the privileged nations, and confirm the importance for the future of platforms for professional development that can encourage flows of talent across Asia, as well as building of systems that do not limit such talent flows."[112]

2 SHOWCASING TRADITION-IN-THE-CONTEMPORARY AND A POST-EXOTIC URBAN MODERN

The first chapter looked at the overall trajectory of regional art exhibition development with the increasing importance of representation by regional institutions of art in or proximate to Northeast and Southeast Asia and the change of the focus from the international-regional exhibition at the start of the 1980s in Japan to the global-regional art exhibition by 2002. This chapter focuses on a selection of key representative exhibitions from the end of the 1980s, surging into the 1990s, during which New Asia and its modern and contemporary art were curated into being, so to speak. They are the *3rd Asian Art Show, Fukuoka* (1989) and the *4th Asian Art Show, Fukuoka: Realism as an Attitude* (1994); *Contemporary Art in Asia: Traditions/Tensions* (1996); the *Second Asia-Pacific Triennial of Contemporary Art, Brisbane, Australia* (1996), with its "integrating concept" of "Present Encounter"; and the traveling exhibition *Cities on the Move* (1997–1999).

These exhibitions from the region, next to the region, or with curatorial expertise from the region to varying degrees articulate flexible intimations of the global-regional in contemporary art—an art able to synchronize the heterogeneities of tradition and what can be called the post-exotic urban modern into an inclusive understanding of Asian contemporary art and in which the exhibition itself is an inseparable part of new knowledge production. How should art now be presented as contemporary if freed from the West/Rest binary, did not have to reject the presence of the traditional, and did not have to conform to paradigmatic painting and sculptural practices linked with a postwar "high modernism" that privileged abstract expressionism and proclaimed itself as universal? Such were the issues and questions reviewed in the 1990s.

The exhibitions particularly address the questions of tradition, cultural encounter, and cultural change in contemporary art. But while, expectedly, the legacy of colonialism persists, the overall thrust is to set art in the everyday context of rapid modernization and urbanization in the wake of Cold War–era nation building and to examine the art enabled by the weakening of modernism and its preoccupation with the formal characteristics of artwork and separation from daily life. The curatorial approaches examined in this chapter represent clear moves away from the privileging of abstraction and other forms of modernism for a distinct understanding of how contemporary art is linked to social, political, and cultural realities in the region. In this regard, given the dramatic economic changes since the decolonizing 1950s and 1960s, unqualified notions of the Third World or the postcolonial as applied to the region did not seem entirely relevant, given the dynamic change most recently seen in China's burgeoning post-1978 illiberal capitalism.

This chapter argues that the curatorial and theoretical responses to the latest new in the region are twofold. First, there is an expanding sense of the modern elastic enough to retain "tradition" as part of a present-day life that, additionally, might exceed the cultural essentialisms of post-independence nation building. Second, an examination takes place of an urban cultural modernity that was unsettled or unstable because of the rapid speed of urban development in Northeast and Southeast Asia—this is a facet of daily life that cannot be quite characterized as traditional or exotic.

Underlying both responses, it could be said, is the rejection of high-modernist conceptions of self-sufficient high culture that separated high and low, spiritual and material. The exhibitions appropriate and modify the early twentieth-century historical avant-garde's and postwar neo-avant-garde's anti-art attacks on modernism's autonomy aesthetic in the *paradoxical* appreciation of how installation art, performance art, and conceptualism that seemed able to draw in local materials and cultural traditions now should be recognized *institutionally* as part of the practice of a regional contemporary art.[1] The overall exhibitionary direction examined in this chapter is to correlate both tradition and post-exotic art increasingly with urban dimensions as part of the positive engagement with the present. As Matei Calinescu has pointed out, the European "avantgarde, despite its various and contradictory claims, tends to be regarded as the most extreme form of artistic negativism—art itself being the first victim."[2] But art developments and history do not move in a linear manner; that is a key position of the exhibitions. The historical avant-garde attack on cultural institutions was in a European context in which high art legitimized establishment claims to aesthetic knowledge.[3]

That is less the case for East Asian art museums, given that few countries in the region possessed major visual arts establishments in the 1990s. The institutions that existed boosted regional representation in global art.

However, art exhibitions did not necessarily encompass or present both inscriptions of the contemporary—that of tradition-in-the-contemporary and a post-exotic urban modernity—at the same time, although these components did overlap. The chapter further argues, then, that the 1990s manifest a synchronized heterogeneity in which there is the yoking together of contrasting perceptions of the present. The exhibitions from the early to mid-1990s attested more to tradition and its tensions, along with the transformations and juxtapositions of contemporary and traditional artistic formats associated with rapid sociocultural change, and the late 1990s witnessed exhibitions more directly concerned with urbanization and change. The first version of *Cities on the Move* (1997) took motivation from the region's own postwar urbanism and design, including the Japanese architects who, in 1960, worked through an earlier disorientation of meteoric economic growth by way of a commitment to rational planning that drew inspiration from manifestly less-modernist cultural notions of the regenerative. The manifesto on city design and architecture, *Metabolism 1960: The Proposals for New Urbanism*, for instance, emphasized the growth of cities like a living organism with "metabolic" cycles.[4] The results of both exhibitionary inscriptions of the contemporary, such as the exhibitions in chapter 1, are inevitably uneven, but these efforts to authenticate an Asian contemporary art made their mark.

It is important to register that while there was some discussion regarding what Asia might "truly" be said to be, that term was by and large deliberated on as a *problematic* category that yet *could not* be released from both general and artistic-cultural usage. Iftikhar Dadi notes, "Asia is undoubtedly on one level the emptiest of categories and a juicy target for deconstruction, but I believe we must nevertheless continue to wrestle with its connotations—if only because it is an established social fact—and to repurpose its meanings towards more equitable and just significations."[5] Asia, then, in the exhibitions from Fukuoka Art Museum's initial 1980s experiments with Asian contemporary art to *Cities on the Move* is a heuristic device, an approach taken to problem solving, discovery, or attempts at cultural signification that employ practical curatorial methods and theoretical questions that may not be optimal but which remain sufficient for the immediate goals to rethink recent artistic formations in the region. While the conjoining of Asia, art, and the contemporary, as curator Doryun Chong has argued, can result in a cultural category such as "contemporary Asian art" that can become a "problematic [and generalized] rubric . . . [that] often times [*sic*] has obscured the actual works and artists, . . . it did bring a lot of artists in the region across national boundaries."[6]

The Modernity/Tradition Dyad and the Global Art Exhibition

To gain a firmer sense of the distinctiveness of the art exhibitions' trajectories in this chapter, initial comparison and contrast can be made with two widely recognized exhibitions in 1989 said to herald the advent of the global art exhibition. They are *Magiciens de la Terre* (Magicians of the Earth), curated by Jean-Hubert Martin and held at the Halle de la Villette and the Centre Pompidou in Paris from May 18 to August 14—featuring mainly new work by 104 artists from more than fifty countries, selected equally from the Euro-American West and the non-West—and the Tercera Bienal de La Habana from October 27 to December 31, with its theme of *tradición y contemporaneidad* (tradition and contemporaneity)—featuring the large participation of about three hundred artists from forty-one countries.[7]

Both of these exhibitions, and those that followed in East Asia in the 1990s, might be said principally to iterate the need for the other both to gain representation and to be free from mirroring developments parallel with Western artistic movements to possess consequence. To escape that trap is to escape the valuation of being either a belated modern culture or poor copies of more authentic modern or contemporary artwork or both. And with that, the pejorative and intractable modernity/tradition binary—that, in turn, seemed irredeemably tied in with the Western/non-Western dyad—might be weakened, so that the traditional need not be understood as the exotic from a past time. However, Havana's effort also to be a discursive event if alternative knowledge forms of cultural assessment were to come about gave it more criticality than *Magiciens*. The East Asian exhibitions follow in entrenching reflexivity in the process of making and discussing representation. This impulse, though, was already surfacing in the Fukuoka Art Museum's exhibitions in the 1980s and was not a singular invention by Havana. It should be noted that Havana, *Magiciens*, and Fukuoka were all distinctive opposites of the inaugural Bienal de São Paulo of 1951, the first large-scale exhibition outside the Euro-American cultural centers. São Paulo curated concrete art and thus abstraction as an early claim to artistic globality, refusing figuration and marks of difference in the attempt to stake out a Third World or "southern" claim for artistic possibilities in an earlier period of the Cold War.[8] Difference is an issue not refused by Havana, *Magiciens*, or Fukuoka.

Magiciens was briefly discussed in chapter 1, which offered curator Tatehata Akira's assessment of it as "an epoch-making exhibition in terms of promoting globalism in art that rejects a [hierarchical] Western-centered approach."[9] Promoting globalism, though, does not in itself address the significance of locality within it. Curator Pablo Lafuente, citing anthropologist Benoît de L'Estoile, remarks that "the history of museography can be read as the history of two models of museum: the museum of the self, and the museum of the other."[10] *Magiciens* attempted both representations as coetaneous or coexistent art. Art writer Sean O'Toole notes, "The exhibition was non-hierarchical in the sense that it juxtaposed established artists such as Marina Abramovic . . . with a broad constituency of [living] non-Western folk artists, crafters, shamans, [and] priests [invited to produce *in situ* works]."[11] This extended diversity led to the criticism that the basis upon which the art is compared is not made clear—the local then becomes stranded. When "the present state of religious and popular art beyond the West" is juxtaposed with "works with pieces by western artists working in western contemporary art circles, Jean-Hubert Martin established a manner of implicit and problematic comparison."[12] In Martin's own words, *Magiciens* displayed "objects with aura."[13] An inclusivity that extended the application of romantic genius to folk art and craft actually "glossed over the colonial residues . . . in the imagining of non-euro-American [*sic*] artists as magicians."[14]

Nevertheless, displaying artwork in recognizably contemporary formats from Asia in *Magiciens* mattered. This included *Reptiles* (1989), a serpent-shaped papier-mâché installation made from newspaper pulp by the then–emerging artist Huang Yong Ping (1954–2019), one of three from China, who benefited by being set among established artists such as On Kawara (1932–2014) and Nam June Paik (1932–2006)—who by then were seen as *global* rather than presumably *Asian* artists. Apinan Poshyananda situates *Magiciens* as one of several major exhibitions that exposed contemporary Chinese artists to a Western metropolitan audience: "Participation by Chinese artists in 'Magiciens de la Terre' (Magicians of the Earth) in Paris, France, the 45th Venice Biennale (1993), in Venice, Italy, 'Silent Energy' (1993) at the Museum of Modern Art, Oxford, England, individual shows by Gu Wenda and Xu Bing aroused critical attention among Western audience[s]."[15] Also vital was the usage of local information for the choice of artists.[16] Curator Hou Hanru concedes that while the show "present[ed] the quasi-absolute equality between Western and non-Western artists in a[n admittedly] mechanically egalitarian way," "eventually, one could sense . . . the end of the hegemony of Western modernity and its entire ideological positions, aesthetic canons, and institutional systems."[17] While this is hyperbole, the point that cultural decentering was taking place can be accepted.

The power imbalances in the art world that hobbled equitable representation that *Magiciens* grappled with is also present in the third iteration of the Bienal de La Habana. The first was held in 1984, and art critic Marian Pastor Roces argues that the commitment to challenge art-world norms made it the first alternative biennial.[18] Havana in 1989 is similar to *Magiciens* in that it deliberately confused the divergence between art and popular craft in its display of Mexican dolls, wooden effigies of Simón Bolívar, and African wire toys with the work of experimental contemporary artists such as photographer Sebastián Salgado (Brazil) and sculptor Roberto Feleo (Philippines).[19] This diversity was more effectively held together, compared with *Magiciens*, by the theme of tradition and contemporaneity, suggesting that popular or rural art was not ahistorical, compared with the assertion that all artists are similar in being like (premodern) magicians. Indeed, the integration of a major conference, "Tradition and Contemporaneity in the Art of the Third World," "into the Bienal's structure represents a decisive step towards conceiving of biennials as discursive events, in which the actual display of artworks is part of a much broader project of research and knowledge production."[20]

One result of the conjoined categories, *tradition* with *contemporaneity*, is the undercutting of the conservative understanding of tradition in Third World cultures, such that tradition could (co)exist in the present moment of artistic production and be represented as such: "Traditions, in other words, were a living force that could be articulated in a contemporary (international) idiom, and they were important because they made manifest the complicated history of cultural encounters within the colonial and postcolonial process."[21] Context is essential for both terms, as Caroline Turner would put it in 1993: "People and nations bring their past with them into the future, and the historical context is fundamental to an understanding of contemporary art."[22] Havana's reorientation toward the representation of tradition and contemporaneity will be parsed extensively in the Asian Art Shows (the third edition actually also takes place in 1989), in both the first and second editions of the Asia-Pacific Triennial, and in *Traditions/Tensions*.

The 1990s East Asian exhibitions also manifest an engagement with alternative discourse and knowledge creation relating to culture and art as vital features of exhibition construction, and this aspect of the exhibition creating process will be addressed more in the next chapter. The discursive component, however, was initially diffuse in the work of the Fukuoka Art Museum in the 1980s, despite the holding of symposia, but their exhibitions by the 1990s become part of the region's larger discourse on art. Each new art show also had previous exhibitions as reference points to draw upon as the delineation of contemporary art from the region continued apace. What is unique for the 1990s for the region and Australia, though, is the consistency of the development of critical discourse, continuing into the 2000s. The APT, for instance, with a stable curatorial core that invited in other curators could widen the range of critical exploration (critics allege problematically) from the first triennial in 1993 to the third in 1999. As with *Magiciens*, this was also part of the development of a transnational project-based curation process.[23] The printed matter that accompanied the exhibitions is vital in informing our understanding of the art on display.

A crucial difference with Havana is that the Third World as a category is invoked less in the region's exhibitions, given that a number of countries in the region were open to capitalist investment even before the revolutions of 1989 and communism's collapse, with some being recipients of first American and then European and Japanese outsourcing from the 1960s.[24] The early versions of the Bienal de La Habana, which first went on in 1984, focused on Latin America, the Caribbean, and the Third World. Lilian Llanes Godoy, director of the 1986–1997 editions, while admitting that the last category was problematic, said it was used to establish "a common interest among countries which . . . faced serious problems . . . arising from the system of relations imposed by the highly industrialized countries in the aftermath of colonialism; that is, the underdevelopment and economic dependence of neocolonialism."[25] While all Southeast Asian nations (save Thailand) emerged "in the aftermath of colonialism," four of them, along with four Northeast Asian nations—Singapore, Malaysia, Indonesia, and Thailand, with Japan, South Korea, Taiwan, and Hong Kong—had a real per capita GDP that rose twice as fast as in any other regional identification between 1965 and 1990.[26] The 1989 revolutions did make an appearance in Havana: Rachel Weiss comments that a conference attendee introduced the term "post-communism," which "broke the insular spell of the event, which was, after all, taking place at the very moment when European communism was falling apart."[27] No such "insularity" was allowed to exist in the various frameworks deployed by the 1990s exhibitions on Asia.

This is not to say that there were no attempts to locate Southeast Asian nations, for instance, as part of a Third Worldist projection of the tradition-and-contemporary theme. In 1995, the Indonesian artist-curator Jim Supangkat—who was involved with both the APT and *Traditions/Tensions*—led the curation of *Contemporary Art from the Non-Aligned Countries*, held from April 28 to June 30, 1995, in Jakarta, Indonesia, featuring a massive four hundred works from forty-two developing nations, capaciously and eclectically ranging from Benin, China, Croatia, Egypt, India, Indonesia, Madagascar, Malaysia, Singapore, Thailand, Yemen, to Zambia. The national curators of the participating countries selected the works—so the nation-states' interests were maintained—but a diverse international curatorial board, including the Nigerian curator Emmanuel Arinze (1945–2005), the Indian artist Gulammohammed Sheikh, and Singaporean art historian T. K. Sabapathy, was convened to categorize the works. In the catalogue's introduction, the board members write:

> Though it is undeniable that the development of contemporary art in general is not related anymore to rigid international standards, the development of the contemporary art in the Northern countries (the mainstream) can be said to remain in conformity with the homogenous development. By contrast, the development of contemporary art in Southern countries in some ways can be seen as heterogenous since it is related to a cultural diversity.
>
> Emerging from previous forms, Southern contemporary art show expressions related to an indigenous ethos and symbol-making of the local traditions. This phenomenon has never been considered as important in international art discourse.[28]

Despite the decentering of contemporary art, the "Northern . . . mainstream" still holds sway. The existence of diverse "indigenous ethos and symbol-making artefacts" that are part of "local traditions" get in the way of equitable representation, possibly as such artifacts still connote the sacred or the theological. How, then, can they be part of contemporary culture and its secular artistic idiom?

Supangkat's nonaligned alternative contemporaneity (as it may be called) therefore is linked with Havana's Third Worldism that is at least partly predicated upon dependency theory and its key idea that resources flow from the underdeveloped states to a core of wealthy states. It might be noted that by the 1990s, dependency theory was less prominent than in the 1970s, although the 1990s saw those arguing for its continued relevance, despite the increased prominence of theories of globalization.[29] The exhibition received criticism in the Indonesian media, Supangkat notes, for being anti-West and for not offering a definition of either a "'Non-Aligned Movement visual art' or '. . . a Southern visual art.'"[30] He rejects the charge of incoherence but agrees that there was no preconceived theoretical position, "for ideas and concepts are complex contrivances that intend to change reality," but *Contemporary Art from Non-Aligned Countries* undertook a "radical empiricism" to be "a study of reality" of the Global South: the "curatorial team" scrutinized the submitted works and then worked out the categories for the artwork, choosing "Confrontation, Questions, Quests, Tradition or Convention, Sign-Symbol-Script, Body, [and] Space-Land-People."[31]

There is a problem in that the curatorial board has to trust the aesthetic-political judgments of the national curators for artwork selection. So, the range constituting "reality" depicted is already preselected. That aside, we must still examine the basis on which Supangkat rejects the need for a theoretical position. He writes that the collapse of the Soviet Union, the fact of China becoming "a capitalist nation," and Japan in 1995 being "a world economic power" meant that the trajectory of a progressive history dominated by the West has been tripped up, and, as a consequence, "sanctions against [Euro-America-centric] modernism [as a universal art] have emerged," and we now can get "an understanding of the truth of pluralism."[32] Given that "these strange changes occur in a barrage and without pattern," a chaotic empirical reality therefore abjures the need for theory.[33] But yet what he is also pointing out is that in this pattern-free reality, some less well-off Asian nations now embrace capitalism and at least parts of the liberal cultural globalization associated with it. The decentered West, in this case, also means a decentered capitalism that benefits parts of the Global South represented in the exhibition, such as China, Indonesia, and Malaysia—if not quite Benin and Yemen. This is a phenomenon that Supangkat acknowledges but does not sort out enough. The exhibition is an extension of the critical framework set out in Havana in 1989, attempting a comprehensive "emancipatory internationalism" for "subaltern subjectivities" but without a firm epistemological or theoretical intervention.[34] What Supangkat also misses is that, as historian Vijay Prashad has argued, the very rise of the Asian "miracle" economies "dampened the enthusiasm for the Third World's exertions to transform the world order."[35]

From Tradition-from-Yesterday into Tradition-in-the-Contemporary

When we come to the Fukuoka Art Museum's Asian Art Shows, from 1979/1980 to 1994, we witness incremental and persistent attempts to address tradition against the backdrop of regional economic development and its multifarious sociocultural impacts gaining increasing relevance as that which affects both artistic content and form. Tradition and indigenous cultural pluralism are found to have coordinates in the present's everyday life.

As discussed in chapter 1, Fukuoka's inaugural show in 1979 begins with the issue of "the problem of tradition vis-à-vis [the] present age in Asian art," and until the *3rd Asian Art Show, Fukuoka*, their survey-style shows do not exceed being indefinite regional tracings of modernist and contemporary art.[36] The lack of a curatorial framework meant that catalogue essays by regional contributors were not marshaled into any larger critical whole. In any case, curatorial investigations could not exist, as the artwork was selected solely by various national art agencies, given a wish to affirm the embodiment of older cultural identities in recent art forms—not unexpected, given post-independence nation-building imperatives. The main reason, according to Mikio Soejima, the acting director for Fukuoka during the 1985 second art show, for the exhibition procedure taken was a commitment to two resolutions. One was passed by a UNESCO organization, the International Association of Art, in 1973, "encouraging [the] protection of cultural identity possessed by each country," and the other by the "Cultural Ministers' Conference held also in 1973 in Jogjakarta, Indonesia, . . . [dedicated] to promoting international exchange . . . and vitalization of every cultural originality."[37]

Jim Supangkat's *Contemporary Art from the Non-Aligned Countries* is but a late version of this exhibition dilemma. The laissez-faire curatorial situation added to the challenge to detect any obvious pattern in the region's artistic styles, given asynchronous art-historical circumstances. Soejima wrote in his 1985 Asian Art Show catalogue essay, "Cultural Traditions in Asian Art," that "artistic expression in Asia is literally in a conglomerative state of confusion with employment of all the different styles that appeared after the War, ranging from the Informel style of the fifties to the Conceptual Art in the seventies. Unlike the unified universalized situation of contemporary art in the West[,] . . . its Asian equivalent indeed poses a chaotic picture."[38]

How, then, might curation be undertaken? The modernism of Art Informel coexisted alongside contemporary art's conceptualism. This condition is further complicated, he found, by exceptions in Northeast Asia—unlike Southeast and South Asia, generally speaking—that did not have reservations with *either* the modern *or* the traditional, and so were more in sync with the "universalized . . . West": young Japanese artists were free from "old stagnant aesthetic values" and Korean Dansaekhwa (monochromatic painting) used white as "their national traditional color" in minimalistic painting as responses to Western modes of abstraction.[39] The impediment in 1985 to reimagining Asia is actually Soejima's need to discover the "*genuine essence* of Asian art" (my emphasis).[40] This lingering Orientalist search for a single and authentic cultural nucleus will weaken within a decade.

What assisted the pioneering reconstitution of tradition by the *4th Asian Art Show* was the willingness to allow "what" tradition might be to change, given that artists interacted with different historical moments in varied ways. This freed tradition from, first, a fixed location within the progressive telos of modern Euro-American art—with tradition trapped in the past by the binary tradition/modernity framework of Oriental exoticism—and, second, from possible national-cultural abstractions developed after decolonization (or after European influence weakened, for societies not directly colonized), a thought to be developed more fully in *Traditions/Tensions*. Additionally, comparison or inter-Asian referencing may release tradition from the arbitrary colonial borders that became the new national borders and allow more regional perspectives on shared cultural components. The *4th Asian Art Show* makes the case that contemporary art formats such as installation, performance art, and objets trouvés assisted creativity by permitting artists to incorporate the local in a nonexotic way—aiding "interaction with everyday reality"—which was harder to do with modernist art's formats and commitment to autonomy from the quotidian.[41] The Fukuoka events before the *4th Asian Art Show*, it can be said, suffered from an inability to transcend an international-regional and liberal-internationalist perspective on culture in which national-cultural heritage was distinct but still should possess universal dimensions.

By and large, the early exhibitions also did not much benefit from a critical discursive component. Although the museum did organize symposia as part of their Asian art shows, they did not seem to be part of a larger strategy of knowledge production. The meetings for the *3rd Asian Art Show* and the *4th Asian Art Show*, unlike the symposia for the inaugural *Asian Art Show* and *2nd Asian Art Show*, were practical preparatory conferences with official representatives from official art agencies from the participating countries held before the exhibitions. Obviously, there were no incisive improvements made. The negatively phrased title of the one-day symposium held during *Festival: Contemporary Asian Art Show* (1980), part II of their inaugural *Asian Artists Exhibition*, suggested handwringing rather than a serious search for the resolution of the question put forward: "What must be done for the future of Asian tradition and art which have been changed under the influence of Western art?" Most (although not all) of the panelists were members of national art agencies, and so there must be some burden to represent the nation and national identity. The moderator, print artist and Western-style painter Masuda Yoshinobu (1905–1990), summarized the overall discussion at the end of the symposium thus: "Asia has to create the Asian arts with the national consciousness or identity that requires closer cooperation."[42] That captures one type of response. For example, the Pakistani delegate, modern landscape painter Ghulam Rasul (1942–2009), contended that by the end of the 1970s, Pakistani artists had "matured sufficiently to be able to assimilate all the significant [modern] trends from all over the world without losing their own identity," and so "Pakistani art, while remaining distinctly national, will also have a universal appeal."[43] There was no general anti-Western attitude in the symposium—mainly cautious stances on modern Western art's impact on local identity and heritage.

However, there were intimations of how heritage and the present could be sorted out so that modern culture need not be perceived as a threat that were not picked up until the third show in 1989. For example, Raymundo Albano (1947–1985), the Filipino artist-curator whose own work ranged from abstract expressionism to installation and performance, firmly argued in his presentation that "borrowing" is a creative act and not part of a (neo) colonized mental set:

It is a fact that sometimes our colonial mentalities forget this [creativity] matter and we feel that borrowing is such a grievous, unrewarding or even traitorous but [yet] inevitable act. But the '80s in the Philippine art will have to remove this bias and adopt new processes and materials from the [local] environment—even if it will entail a re-definition of art itself. In the end, paint on canvas may not be important for us. Installations as what you saw in the slides [I used] might be closer to our lives. . . . [A]nd what a more meaningful experience would it be if part of our preserving our tradition is the recognition that its scope of presence is world-wide.[44]

It is a prescient indication of how the regional curatorium will present tradition-in-the-contemporary by the mid-1990s. Setting aside colonial-era inhibitions and using contemporary artforms such as installation art may not only outstrip modernist art formats such as paint, but also offer a new art practice that both hews close to its locality—thus "preserving our tradition"— and expands the comprehension of what, using a term not available in 1980, a comprehensive "global art" might be. The Indonesian painter Mochtar Apin (1923–1994) ends the panelists' discussion session by urging all present to work toward recognizing "our own Asian art movement": "I want to stress on the authority [of] and the confidence [in the future of art in Asia] very much depend on ourselves. Until now, the development of the art in the East, you can see, can accept, as the same what happened in the West. . . . It's a kind of [Eurocentric] domination in [our region's] acceptance of the artists. That's why I propose that we have to recognize our own artists independently of the West."[45] Recognition and the road to global representation must begin with we Asians and not only follow from Western recognition of Asian artists: that is how to come into our own—and the third show would take one step toward recognizing "our own artists independently of the West."

The *3rd Asian Art Show* in 1989, unlike the first two editions, was given a theme: "Symbolic Visions in Contemporary Asian Life." Mikio Soejima, by then the confirmed director of the Fukuoka Art Museum, presented his curators' brief in the catalogue essay "In Pursuit of a Genuinely Asian World." In keeping with a more centered exhibition modus operandi, the artwork selection now required the national selectors to make their preliminary choices based on a curatorial brief, and the Fukuoka selection committee would have a strong say in the final selection. Still, the process was unwieldy. China, Nepal, the Philippines, Brunei, Korea, and Japan allowed the museum's selection committee to make the final decision; Thailand, Singapore, Indonesia, Bangladesh, Pakistan, Malaysia, Sri Lanka, and India made their final decisions based on the committee's recommendations, and Mongolia, as a fresh participating country, was allowed to make its own selection.[46] The Japanese museum system, even in the late 1980s, seems hierarchical in its collective leadership, as the catalogue suggests that the museum curators—as in the previous Asian art shows—were not involved with the final artwork selection, since they are not listed as members of the selection committee.

As regards a "genuinely Asian world," Soejima also writes that the museum had looked at Asian difference via "European models [of art] as universal standards," resulting in a self-inflicted, Western Orientalist point of view on Asian cultural production. Japan instead should "look at Asia from inside as fellow Asians, and place more emphasis on the intrinsic and unique characteristics of each Asian country."[47] It should inter-reference art and culture from a vantage point *inside* the region. From that point of identification, a theme is assessed: "We have positively recognized 'tradition' as something still living in 'the modern age' and continuing to stimulate us today," and because of this, Soejima added, we will be able to understand how even varied "traditional elements" may function, and we can stop "abstractly discussing 'tradition' in contemporary Asian art."[48]

However, was there any commonality in this Asia with vastly differing "traditional elements"? Soejima argued that there was: a collective "'Asian sensitivity,' manifesting itself in Asian images."[49] This sensitivity was seen in the "symbolic visions" in Asian contemporary art that uses "iconographic symbols (such as Mandala or Tantric symbols) which can be traced back to 'tradition'" but yet either do not repeat "dead iconography" or do not manifest "'symbolic visions in everyday life' which have been revived today after having gone through the ordeals of modernization."[50] Symbolic visions are *repurposed* symbols—and therefore not a simplistic "uncritical repetition of dead iconography"—that told us something about present-day social or economic tribulations.[51] The *3rd Asian Art Show* reconstituted tradition, relocating it in the quotidian realm where history was made. However, Soejima brought up one further matter—one that tripped up the entire enterprise: "We Asians have a mental structure which lets us find gods, or the marvels of nature or a unique view of the cosmos in the environment of our everyday life."[52] And with that pronouncement on a unique, pan-Asian "mental structure," unfortunately, we Asians reenter the zone of the clichéd authentic Asian cultural nucleus that was also an ahistorical zone out of "everyday life."

If Soejima's essay could not quite hold together Asian artistic heterogeneity, the cause seemed a difficulty he previously brought up in the 1985 catalogue, mentioned at the start of this section, regarding the lack of discernable pattern of modern and contemporary art production in the region. The *3rd Asian Art Show* concentrates on younger artists not previously exhibited so as to see their potential "to contribute to the development of 'new Asian art,' departing from imitation of the West" and to discern the cohesion in this new art.[53] In Japan, there is a concrete understanding of contemporary art as "works embodying avant-garde, experimental and radical forms of expression."[54] Arguably, this "concrete understanding" has been present since at least the Tokyo Biennale: Between Man and Matter (1970), curated by the art critic Nakahara Yūsuke—now a member of the third show's selection committee of participating artists. Art historian Reiko Tomii contends that the 1970 event "almost single-handedly made visible the state of international contemporaneity for a Japanese audience."[55] Like the Tokyo Biennale, the *3rd Asian Art Show* featured mainly young artists so as to showcase the newest new, but 1970 "emphasized what can be generally characterized as post-minimalism and conceptualism [as the new], both of which embodied a clear break from conventional painting and sculpture."[56] Soejima's view is that while Japan shared common artistic bases with the metropolitan West in relation to modern and contemporary art, the "social role and position of art in Asia differ widely . . . [and so, for now,] we may have no other alternatives [*sic*] than to define 'contemporary Asian art' to be art produced by contemporary Asians."[57] This was a tautology, not a definition: it was an excuse, as was the "mental structure" position, for an uncertain opinion on Asian *contemporary* art.

One of Soejima's curators, Kuroda Raiji, wrote a catalogue essay on the exhibition's Japanese selection that, unintentionally, adumbrated on how Japan connected with the region via an economic reality, "Symbols Transgressing the Border," on how disparateness can be synchronized into a Asian contemporary art in the context of rapid economic development.[58] He began by bluntly asserting that "in contemporary Japanese art, [there are] few works, if any, in which 'tradition' is deliberately represented [to] deserve positive appraisal."[59] Indeed, Japan, being proud of its economic success and having accepted things Western, may have less need for solidarity either with Asia, contra the West, or with the uniqueness of Asian culture, but rather "has now begun to consume Asia, both materially and spiritually, form [*sic*] the standpoint the West once took. The 'ethnic (Asian in this context) taste' which is now conspicuous in the preference of the Japanese . . . [has been] accelerated by the strong yen."[60] But, in turn, he was aware that Japan was also similarly consumed by the West in a similar way, as wealth can confer the pleasurable consumption of cultural otherness.

For Kuroda, the dichotomies or dualisms such consumption was predicated upon—East versus West, spiritual versus material culture—were false, given that Japan was committed to modern material culture, as were other Asian nations. One cogent aim of creating exhibitions, therefore, "should [be to] reveal to one another the realities of culture and life which 'the modern age' of each [country] is producing, and this should be done without [any] idealization or mystification [of cultural purity]."[61] Kuroda thus averred the need to avoid both the exoticized consumption of tradition in Asia and representing our cultures as completely unique, as such cultural constructions follow only from accepting the modern/traditional dyad as foundational reality. But what might now be reconsidered was why the consumption of Asia did *not* mean that Japan had less of a part in the larger East Asian sphere. This capacity to consume had been facilitated by the 1985 Plaza Accord, when the Japanese yen appreciated substantially against the US dollar. The revalued yen led not only to Japanese tourism in the larger region "to consume Asia, both materially and spiritually," but also to the offshoring of Japanese industrial facilities, with Southeast Asia as a key recipient zone, increasing regional economic integration. The mid-1980s saw the "repositioning [of] the country within [a larger] East Asia after so many years 'outside' the region under the cozy embrace of an American patron."[62] Intentionally or otherwise, both the staging of the Asian art shows *and* Japan's material-spiritual consumption of Asia were part of what has been called "Japan's 1980s return to Asia."[63] Kuroda's economic logic reappeared in the *4th Asian Art Show*. It is arguable that the Asian art shows operate broadly within what historian Simon Avenell describes as a "Japan in Asia" trajectory, in which he writes, quoting the political scientist Takashi Shiraishi, the aims "should be 'to harmonize internationalism and Asianism,' and to create 'a stable Asian regional order,' along with 'expanding and deepening exchange' through 'economic cooperation, cultural cooperation, intellectual cooperation [and] technological cooperation.'"[64]

The 1994 *4th Asian Art Show* was the breakthrough in characterizing Asian contemporary art. The theme this time was "Realism as an Attitude." The selection process was more stringent than was the case for the third show: the participating countries still made their selections based on the theme, but Fukuoka curators also nominated artists (with the national agencies' permission), and final decisions were made by Fukuoka's selection committee. Similar to the third show, art was featured from Northeast Asia (China, Mongolia, South Korea, Japan), Southeast Asia (Thailand, Singapore, Indonesia, Philippines, Malaysia, Brunei, Vietnam), and South Asia (Nepal, India, Pakistan, Bangladesh). The catalogue from the third show had pictures of the artwork arranged by country, while the fourth show significantly arranged the artwork illustrations by the themes.

The exhibition's dense framing essay was by Ushiroshōji Masahiro, a pioneer Japanese curator for Southeast Asian art.[65] "Realism as an Attitude: Asian Art in the Nineties" argued that the art in the fourth show can be defined as Asian contemporary art because new artistic form and content emerged in relation with definitive *regional* and not only global events in the 1980s—crucial, as "global" is often a euphemism for "Euro-America."

To begin with, Ushiroshōji used "realism" in a restricted manner:

> Since the end of the late 1980s, a common outlook has been widely noticed in Asian art: namely an extremely realistic attitude. For instance, some works are based on an awareness of social problems . . . [such as] the suppression of human rights by a political or social system. The advent of urbanization, industrialization, and a consumer society in the wake of economic development is changing people's lifestyles, while traditional values that form the basis of village communities are being lost. . . . Another group of works focuses on everyday events that are close to the artist. . . . [T]his group of works probes the changing face of society through changes in everyday reality.[66]

"Realism" did not refer to illusionistic realism in visual art but rather to the artist's stance toward the "everyday reality" of political-economic events that may destabilize societies. Those two components in the adjective seemed inseparable in Ushiroshōji's essay. He begins with the political—with the fall of the Berlin Wall in 1989, but then proceeds to the regional: "In Asia, several political systems have changed and the democracy movement has led to bloody incidents. Even countries that rigidly cling to socialism have actively pushed economic reforms and liberalization. The member states of the Association of Southeast Asian Nations have followed on the heels of the 'four dragons'—South Korea, Taiwan, Hong Kong, and Singapore which achieved dazzling economic growth in the 1980s. In the 1990s the economy of China is booming."[67]

The indirect reference to the massacre during the June 4, 1989, Tiananmen Square protests as one of the "bloody incidents" would have been inescapable in 1994, and this was followed by China's increased prosperity after the suppression by a socialist regime. And China is not alone in the pursuit of economic growth. The success of the mini-dragon economies is accompanied by the rise of Southeast Asian nations, including socialist Vietnam, with its *Đổi Mới* (renovation) economic reforms in 1986. Socialist transitions into not-quite-capitalist transformations, rapid urbanization, and industrialization in essentially agricultural societies, Ushiroshōji remarked, "seemed to have confused and distorted people's minds."[68] But all the above is still context and does not explain how the new artistic "realism" arrives, one that references political, economic, and social transmutations.

Ushiroshōji examines two artistic conundrums that motivated artistic change and offers a comment on regenerative possibilities offered by new formats in art. The first concerns the issue of identity that he had previously written about in a 1992 Southeast Asian art show on "the often contradictory goal of establishing a non-Western identity while learning [art] from the West itself, [even as] Asian artists until the 1980s [also] relied on indigenous Asian traditions as a source of identity or unique expression."[69] One common solution he saw was the depiction of non-Western subjects such as Asian landscapes or traditional life, including religious life, by applying "Western [art] methods—for example, perspective and modeling . . . —to traditional art forms and techniques."[70] The second conundrum was the call and demand of the national to have Asian themes, styles, and subjects for post-independence art that, ironically, could lead to the reusing of clichéd images of Asia: "Serious attempts to discover an Asian type of aesthetic awareness in tradition are inseparable from an inner sort of Orientalism."[71] Either way, the artist lost his individuality—which is exacerbated by the postwar domination of modernism, for "Western-style modern art has discarded [issues of intense personal concern] in the quest for impersonal artistic expression and the independent value of colour and form."[72]

Ushiroshōji contends that the *4th Asian Art Show* takes place "in the aftermath of modernism," going beyond dilemma-stricken "basic framework of modern Asian art" for two reasons.[73] The first is that artists have access to new formats and media such as "installations and performances, and there is a noticeable increase in the use of personal everyday objects" for "undertaking a new subject such as one about society demanded the use of a new of representation."[74] The third show had showcased some anti-formalist tendencies, and the fourth show picked up from there. The second is that "the term 'Asia' . . . encompasses different social circumstances resulting from different economic conditions and political systems," and so, depending on how open or closed countries are to the latest imperatives to develop economically, both artistic content and form will morph.[75] This does not mean that the traditional disappeared, but rather that, freed from the constraints of modernist formats and the burden of being "national," artworks now convey more individual messages through the free use of local resources: "Using as a base the traditional forms used in *Wayang*, Java's shadow [puppet] theatre, Dadang Christanto (Indonesia) wryly protests against mass murder."[76] Ushiroshōji effects a definition of Asian contemporary art in which the late 1980s becomes a moment of rupture with the postwar legacy of modernism, in which the postcolonial/post-independence demands to be "national" were weakened and when vanguard art practices could be used in conjunction with local cultural resources and heritage. Reiko Tomii remarks: "In English, 'contemporary art' . . . shed its genuine meaning of 'today's art' to become a critically loaded concept: it followed 'postmodern art' of the 1980s and 1990s before it came into frequent use in the 21st century and began to invoke the discourse of 'the contemporary' and 'contemporaneity.'"[77] In comparison, Ushiroshōji's Asian contemporary art marks a moment in the mid-1990s when it becomes more conceivable to invoke cultural heterogeneity so as to position it in horizontal conjunction with the contemporary and contemporaneity.

The exhibition categorizes the artwork into six themes, which follow from Ushiroshōji's understanding of the "aftermath of modernism": society as reality; nation, nationalism, and history; the city and consumption; images of communities; the natural environment; and intimations of violence. The artwork selected for images of communities seems idyllic in its presentation of the rural, although its purpose is to assert the coexistence of the urban-modern and rural-traditional "pre-modern life for the majority embodies the reality of Asia today"—there is here the danger of slipping back into the binary modes he has been critiquing.[78] "The City and Consumption" will be part of the core concerns in *Cities on the Move*. The *4th Asian Art Show*'s central curatorial reconstitution of tradition-from-yesterday into tradition-in-the-contemporary was work in progress that continued into *Contemporary Art in Asia: Traditions/Tensions*, the second APT, and *Cities*.

The Tensions of Synchronizing Tradition-in-the-Contemporary

In an essay for the *Second Asia-Pacific Triennial of Contemporary Art* catalogue, curator Julie Ewington credited the *4th Asian Art Show* with removing "the lingering sense that the archetypal experiments in modern art belong to the canonical figures in the West."[79] By registering that Asian artists effected genuine artistic innovation, Fukuoka curators struck a contestatory theoretical stance: "'Realism as an Attitude' was a bold attempt to outfox the exhausted dichotomies: East/West, past/present, timelessness/history, in favour of a focus on what [literary-cultural critic] Homi Bhabha calls 'the enunciative present.'"[80] We move away from fixed cultural identification to the performative synchronization of heterogeneity into a present-day Asia. Ewington recognized Fukuoka's contribution to a regional intellectual mastery of the artistic present. The insight on "exhausted dichotomies" gains elaboration in two high-profile 1996 exhibitions: the Asia Society's *Contemporary Art in Asia: Traditions/Tensions* and the Queensland Art Gallery's (QAG) second APT.

Patrick Flores, writing about critiques of the universalized Western norm as applied to Southeast Asian art from the 2000s, offers us an array of the subjects problematized in the 1990s: "This critique is the negation of the West and simultaneously the negation of the Orientalist gesture to idealize, exoticize, marginalize, provincialize, nationalize, internationalize, regionalize and globalize. At the same time, the impulses of this negation—the ideal, the exotic, the marginal, the provincial, the national, the international, the regional and the global—are turned into the premises on which to politicize or radicalize these same impulses."[81]

These "impulses" were part of expanding exhibitionary trajectories that coordinated tradition and indigenous pluralism with everyday life. *Traditions/Tensions* featured artwork from Indonesia, Thailand, India, Philippines, and South Korea and radicalized the exotic-traditional in ways that impugned hierarchical or state-driven national(istic) usage of tradition. While the exhibition organized by the Asia Society in New York City was in the first instance for an American audience, the then-director of the society's galleries says, aiming "to give [a] sense of dazzling quality and diversity [and] to get them away from some [limitations of] 'Asianness,'" the guest curator selected was Thai curator and artist Apinan Poshyananda, who was recognized to have global-curatorial star potential.[82] Apinan notes that a roundtable in New York in 1992 of critics, scholars, and curators that "helped to form the core and the rationale of the exhibition" agreed "that instead of American curators with particular conceptions to select art and artists from Asia, an Asian guest curator would be responsible for working with advisers from the five Asian countries represented in the show."[83] Among those present at the roundtable were well-known American critics and curators, including Robert Storr and Alexandra Munroe. Others present from Asia, Australia, Canada, and Britain were Gao Minglu, T. K. Sabapathy, Jim Supangkat, Kuroda Raiji, Gulammohammed Sheikh, John Clark, and David Elliot—that is, both an Asian curator and less fixed or "particular conceptions" of a varied contemporary exotic-traditional Asian art were to be displayed.[84] The Korean art in *Traditions/Tensions*, though, led to an unintended tension in which the national commitment to modernization and then globalization, in contrast with the other works presented, rendered tradition into a lingering memory of socio-economic change. I will return to this later.

The second APT had a wider art selection than *Traditions/Tensions*, grouped in loose geographical clusters of East, South, and Southeast Asia, but it is harder to pin down its thematic foci because of the QAG's preference for "integrating concepts" rather than themes—"Tradition and Change" for the first APT and "Present Encounters" for the second. The inclusive concepts went hand in glove with a costly cocuratorship model for the Triennial's first three iterations, incorporating participation by regional curators, artists, and advisors, with more opinions coming in via the largest international art conference ever convened in Australia up to 1996, making the Triennial a considerable discursive event in thinking Asia. This served to further network a burgeoning regional visual-arts scene. The second APT had fifteen teams comprising forty-two Australian and foreign curators and featured Apinan as the curatorial coordinator for Australian art. His appointment helped ward off criticisms of cultural imperialism, but also drew the criticism that the Australian art selected should have had "a stronger profile."[85]

The curatorial decisions, artist-critic Pat Hoffie explains, served "to offer an understanding of the contemporary in a way . . . that sought for a gradual, slow, collaborative and consultative understanding that made way for [productive] disagreements and 'failed dialectics.'"[86] With no thematic remit to assess, we are then left to reflect upon sometimes disjunctive images of the region on display—but as curator Caroline Turner sets it out, "There is no sense of a homogenous regional identity yet there are common themes which emerge. . . . Perhaps the most significant factor that does emerge from the region is a sense of dynamic change."[87]

Unsurprisingly, the QAG's curatorial approach was criticized—Ushiroshōji Masahiro wrote that the second APT "lacked coherence."[88] The other view was that a "real and actual engagement of the region according to many different terms of reference [transpired]."[89] The curatorial latitude made the second APT an expanded display of the tension in *Traditions/Tensions* between arguments, on one hand, for the exotic-traditional to be reconceived as the contemporary desire for traditions and, on the other hand, for the de facto commandeering of the global—re-signified so that it is no longer a covert sign of Western cultural hegemony—and "dynamic change" in which a metropolitanizing of Asian art, in critic Geeta Kapur's words, forsook the "delight . . . of plenitude via tradition."[90] Caroline Turner, then–deputy director of the QAG, told the conference during the opening weekend that the second APT was focused "on the issues of the present" given "that there is no immutable sameness about Asia-Pacific art"—and so, "definitions of traditional and contemporary art need review."[91] Both exhibitions ran almost simultaneously, with the Triennial opening on September 22 and *Traditions/Tensions* on October 4, 1996. Despite the differences in scale between the two events, their curatorial experimentation with newer knowledge frameworks resulted in the flexible synchronization of contrasting views on the contemporary into an inclusive present. I now examine *Traditions/Tensions* in more detail.

In the preface to the catalogue, Apinan sets up the context for *Traditions/ Tensions*. The millennium's end saw "the whirlwinds of political, economic, and cultural change" in East Asia, with one result being that "decentered megacities in distant corners of the globe" are now unwilling to be "disconnected zones of silence."[92] The demand for artistic-cultural voice and representation in the wake of economic globalization becomes de rigueur for exhibitions after Fukuoka's *4th Asian Art Show*. The five countries in the exhibition, though, offer only indicative understandings of "long Asian traditions which are now experiencing stages of intense transition," given that "in contemporary Asia, tradition extends across such vast heterogeneities and cultural differences."[93] In the catalogue's introduction, "Roaring Tigers, Desperate Dragons in Transition," Apinan contends that the post-Cold War new world order should have offered an "an unprecedented free play of pluralism and heterogeneity" of the burgeoning visual art of New Asia, but this was not the case.[94] One difficulty was that new artistic cultures remain subordinated, as the West does not give up its metropolitan artistic status easily, even though "centers with rich traditional histories, such as Bangkok, Manila, Bombay, and Jakarta, are fast becoming alternative spaces of exchange and dialogue in contemporary art and culture."[95] However, this matter is not truly examined in *Traditions/Tensions* and becomes more the content of *Cities on the Move*. The other difficulty is that of tensions within Asian societies and postcolonial states' authoritarian control: "Cultural diversity and national identity tend to arouse fictive versions of art and culture enclosed within homogeneous wholes of exotic, tranquil, [and] timeless Asia."[96] Supposedly postcolonial nation-states are quite capable of deploying essentialized identities to support internal colonization. This concern had a central space in *Traditions/Tensions*.

The exhibition displayed contemporary artists whose work "include fragments of tradition that serve to question nationalistic aesthetics and bigotry."[97] One representative example for Apinan is the Indian artist N. N. Rimzon's installation sculpture, *The Inner Voice* (1992), which featured a contemplative standing nude made of resin fiberglass, derived from a Jain deity, surrounded by cast-iron swords arranged in a semi-circle, with the swords' sharp ends facing the nude—a symbol of nonviolence under threat. The installation was Rimzon's comment on the destruction of the Babri mosque in Ayodhya on December 6, 1992, by Hindu activists. Another example was Korean artist Soo-Ja Kim, who used fabric and textile in conjunction with traditional handicraft techniques to signify a feminine aesthetic. Apinan's own catalogue essay, "Contemporary Thai Art: Nationalism and Sexuality à la Thai," excoriates what he calls "neotraditional Thai art"—"a consensus art, [possessing] nonthreatening styles of art used to illustrate subject matters that revere Buddhism and Thai consciousness" that supported "the spectacular promotion of Nation, Religion, and Monarchy—the three pillars of nation-state ideology."[98] A burgeoning business climate in point of fact encouraged neotraditional display via commissioned murals in hotels and corporate headquarters. Confronted by Thai-centric art, Apinan expounded, "radical Thai artists" have resorted to contemporary art formats such as conceptualism and installation, "though they have drawn inspiration for their site-specific installations from local rituals, practices, and spaces, . . . [and used i]ndigenous materials . . . [in] pursuing the theme of Thainess in transition. . . . Installation art . . . is now central to this [identity] project because it signifies both Thainess and internationalism."[99] Installation was not a Western influence that impaired Thai identity but allowed a rethink of indigenous identity in transition and within more globalized socioeconomic circumstances.

Catalogue essays by Geeta Kapur from India, Marian Pastor Roces from the Philippines, and Jim Supangkat from Indonesia promote inter-Asian referencing for readers in which shared histories of European colonialism were not seen to constrain contemporary cultural formations. Kapur's and Pastor Roces's essays are the most cogent, and I will concentrate on them. Kapur's "Dismantling the Norm" examines "nationalist cultural discourse" in art: "Until recently, the identity of the Indian artist was [male,] modern and secular."[100] While qualifying that "the norm of an integrated Indian identity was honorable, . . . what most needs unmasking is the civilizational profile that cultural practitioners in India, artists among them, have hith-erto adopted," a profile within which the sectarian (tribals, Dalits, women), the religious, and popular visual culture are suppressed via the primitivist trope where "traditional" cultural praxis is placed.[101] At the same time, she also contends that a celebration of the eclectic and the hybrid cannot be the replacement for the nationalist monolith. Instead, a "space for [present-day, suppressed] contradictions has to be opened within the national/modern paradigm so that there is a real (battle) ground for cultural difference" as "postmodern notions of hybridity" will not create that ground.[102] Kapur pushes back against the hybridity argument deployed by Desai and Apinan in the catalogue. Postmodernism's ahistoricism blunts the diachronic reality of marginalized cultures and does not aid the dialectical synthesis that Kapur's Marxist culturalism requires. An Asian avant-garde and contemporary art will "open out the sacred and the self-incorporating secret with which objects in the world and in art are imbued . . . [and] recode them for present cul-tural purposes."[103] It is arguable that the power of the installation work seen in *Traditions/Tensions*, as Kapur piercingly argues, arose from "a relationship to materials and skills that is quite different from that known in the West. We must remember that, in Asia, the material is also connected with artisanal practice and there are artisans in transitional cultural stages within a village and urban market economy who have traditional skills."[104] This judgment on a still-existing artisanal practice for the contemporary artist to draw upon applied in approximate ways to work in the exhibition from India, Indonesia, and the Philippines, but less so to South Korea. I will return to this later. Kapur effectively affirms that the Asian contemporary artist was *not* Jean-Hubert Martin's magician of the Earth but rather a person who acquires an artistic language that exceeded tradition "while respecting the material conditions of artisanal practice."[105] She hopes that such renditions of the avant-garde will challenge hegemonic Euro-American versions, given that Asia "also promises to be [Euro-America's] economic rival and ultimate nemesis!"[106] Kapur establishes in direct horizontal conjunction the exotic-traditional, the contemporary avant-garde, and economic New Asia.

Marian Pastor Roces's "Bodies of Fiction, Bodies of Desire" is aligned with Kapur's position. She is critical of tendencies to "reduce peasants, nomads, tribal people, and the poor—in other words, the majority of the Philippine people—to the [heroic] 'folk'" and use ahistorical ideas of traditional art to insist that responsible contemporary artists must "imbue traditional art with life, . . . [and] greater resplendence" rather than allow "intermixing" of format and content in contemporary art practice.[107] Tradition has always coped with the tension of intermixing, or otherwise, she posits, "it would not be a tradition, a structure of continuity, distinctively configured but never in isolation."[108] The undertaking instead should be to make contemporary art an effective fiction-making technology that challenged the other cultural fictions one might think suspicious: "For fiction—liberating, repressive, questioning, mourning—is the only potential for contemporary art making, which can claim neither the quintessentially Other nor the utterly universal."[109] She acerbically (and efficaciously) remarks that while "white colonial reveries" are a problem, more alarming are essentialized emancipatory agendas: "Certainly, it may be someday demonstrated that an unknown society in the Philippine archipelago celebrated life and was one with nature and was unfettered and so forth in ways that do not reiterate the European daydream of the noble savage."[110] Contemporary culture in Asia is neither the other or the same. Apinan had spoken of "fictive versions of [national] art," but Pastor Roces here makes positive the potentiality of such fictionality.

All three writers recuperate the exotic-traditional from a position embedded in the past in their versions of an Asian contemporary avant-garde. Jim Supangkat's essay, "Multiculturalism/Multimodernism," is in broad accord with them, as he argued that the transition to the contemporary came from

Indonesian artists' use of marginalized local materials, rebuffing their status as "low art" in Indonesia's artistic significations. However, the general orientation of the radicalized exotic-traditional against nationalistic tradition did not apply to the South Korean essay by curator and art historian Jae-Ryung Roe, "Encountering the World: The Past and the Present." Her argument is that the Korean artists selected for *Traditions/Tensions* had artwork shaped by "the consequences of the nation's past—the history of modernity, the burden of assimilating and catching up, the lingering memories of tradition, and the tensions created in the process of change."[111] The signal difference lies in the *lingering* memories of tradition after feeling to have "caught up" with the advanced West (and presumably Japan, the erstwhile colonial power) in (secure) economic and (less secure) artistic terms. To begin with, the reception of Western art had been one of a "paradoxical unity of ambiguity and anguish" and not simply anguish per se.[112] Western art came about in the eighteenth century and became more prominent under the Japanese occupation of Korea (1910–1945). While a division between *suh'yang hwa* (Western painting) and *dong'yang hwa* (Oriental or traditional ink painting) subsequently developed, the discomfort with modern painting was "also [because] it was brought to Korea by the [more modern] colonizer."[113] By the 1970s, there was a more comfortable assimilation of modernism through a monochromatic and minimalist painting linked to "spirituality in East Asian art and distinctively Korean aesthetics," although the 1980s Minjoong art (or people's art) movement still saw this as Western mimicry.[114] However, the real game changer was the 1994 national policy on globalization, or *segehwa*: for a ruptured art community, "the discourse about becoming globally competitive and about gaining international recognition for Korean contemporary art is the one unifying element on the [artistic] agenda."[115] In this version of Asia, there was not much tension between a national contemporary art and any idea of the exotic-traditional.

The forsaking of a positive tension between tradition-in-the-contemporary and a post-exotic modern in South Korea looms into broader relief in the exhibitionary and discursive contours of the second APT, to which I now proceed. In the *Present Encounters* conference that accompanied the Triennial, Korean curator Soyeon Ahn—who helped select the APT's Korean artists—echoes elements of Roe's argument: "From the end to the 1950s, Korean art has kept pace with world art movements through the various practices and reflections of art and its own identity during the last forty years. . . . Moreover, . . . Koreans have become aware of the importance of global exchanges and [are] proud of our potential to make a contribution to global culture."[116] The weakening in Korea of the dichotomies of East/West and past/present followed from an incremental relationship with international contemporaneity that led to a revamped relation between national and global culture: "When we emphasise only our own national or regional identity, I think our art will decline and be seen as exotic or folk art, which satisfies the Western taste for anthropological appropriation."[117] There is thus no need to rehabilitate the exotic-traditional. Another question then arises here: should industrialized Asian societies be directly compared with the less-developed parts of Southeast Asia? Korea's particular presence within *Traditions/Tensions* and now the Triennial demonstrates how globalizing Asia was both the context for and tense subject matter in the ongoing reimagining of Asia.

Modernization and cultural change in urbanized Asian centers is a topic that Apinan had brought up but did not actively pursue in *Traditions/Tensions*. In contrast, this topic appears in the Triennial's catalogue as it applied not only to Korea but also to Japan, given its longer modernizing history. Curator Nanjo Fumio writes in "The Present Situation of Japanese Art" about futuristic images of society, even as "customs, habits, ways of living and systems handed down . . . are still functioning": "These new cultural and social conditions are emerging conspicuously today in Hong Kong, Taiwan, Korea, Singapore, Thailand, and Malaysia, but Japan was the pioneer in taking this direction. Following World War II, Japan was forced to abandon a large part of its heritage because of defeat in war, and it also [chose] to give up many of its traditional values" to foster an advanced economy.[118] Nanjo here does not make a distinction between Northeast and Southeast Asia, given his understanding of a shared desire for development in the larger region. The newer Japanese art from the second half of the 1980s, as Nanjo outlines it, engaged with what might be described as "local metropolitan elements": "comic books, consumer society, pervasive commercial and cultural signs, multiculturalism, Japanese taste, body theory, urban theory, and technology."[119] Some art did adopt what Nanjo calls *Japonisme*, one example being the work of Nakahashi Katsushige (b. 1955), who has used images of Sumo wrestlers as a traditional symbol. Revealingly, he adds that such contemporary work appeared exotic to the Japanese young.

If post-exotic sociocultural transformation came into unimpeded view in the second APT, what also occurs is that Geeta Kapur's tradition-in-the-contemporary standpoint is radicalized beyond what we saw in *Traditions/ Tensions* in another incisive essay, "Two or Three Things About Ourselves." She arrived in Australia after the United States and the struggle (said only semi-jocularly) to speak of Asian art to Americans, and pronounced that the APT's sympathy to Asia's contemporary cultures affords "an occasion to chart a [conceptual] topography that is geographical, civilisational, and [that] draws out the Asian Now."[120] Kapur does not intend a weakly presentist pan-Asian commonality, but—as she did in her essay for *Traditions/Tensions*—asserts that an active predilection still existed for the classical traditions. India's hinterland held living artisanal and vernacular traditions that could be reinterpreted for the present. While she does not suggest that unmediated cultural history is just "there" for the taking, she stresses that an Asia Now need not be metropolitan in its outlook, whether Western or Asian, which we could say seemed the assumption in Nanjo's essay. Kapur provocatively queries, "It is worth asking why the civilisational frame [for contemporary art] should have to shrink to the size of the global metropolis—is that the only recognized site for art today? It is also necessary to develop, within the framed *mise en scéne* of the past, stylistics of being that suits the historically conscious contemporary."[121] We need not recode artisanal materials only for indigenous Asian avant-gardes, as she argues for *Traditions/Tensions*, but can think about the fundamental "existential continuity in the creative act itself" if the modern artist lives in a country with "a culturally rich and materially pauperised hinterland": might the artist not consider practicing an art offering "a generosity which can encompass and contain the loss of 'superseded' culture"?[122] Civilizational memory and still-living folk aesthetics have a place in the composition of a present-day national selfhood.

Kapur's views had perhaps been modified after the May 1996 Indian general election, as she believed the "electorate has voted with such cunning" that the long-ruling Indian National Congress was thrown off its roost, "forcing an encounter between the right-wing Hindu nationalist party[, the Bharatiya Janata Party (BJP),] with a broad alliance of secular forces. With regional Dalit and minority aspirations riding high, a new federalism is on the cards in which the communist parties [in India], by modifying their rigid forms of sectarianism, can play a key role."[123] How such equivalent possibilities existed for other societies in this version of contemporary Asia occupied Kapur's mind as the hope for the regional. Her political expectation for the first-ever BJP government, led by Atal Bihari Vajpayee, only lasted all of thir-teen days as he failed to gain the necessary parliamentary majority.

Kapur's civilizational-aesthetic framework makes her own previous argu-ment for distinctive and non-Eurocentric avant-garde emergences that came out of the dialectical tradition look like privileged advancements ignoring economically uneven societies. And, certainly, it was observed by the novel-ist Nicholas Jose in a review of the Triennial: "There is a correlation between the size of a country's economic clout and the acceptance of its contemporary art."[124] But the need for a contemporary avant-garde that Kapur had sanc-tioned is reinforced in curator David Elliott's catalogue essay, "A Short Walk in the Hindu Kush." The radical art that arose in Europe and Russia in the nineteenth and early twentieth centuries, he wrote, gained "ironical over-tones" after "reductivism, conceptualism and dematerialisation" become part of the advanced, neo-avant-gardist art of the 1970s, as this politically charged art was "superseded by the anything goes, free market aesthetics of the 1980s, in which a vacuous [pseudo-]historicism and eclecticism replaced the positivistic progressions of earlier decades."[125] And so, the historical-traditional becomes reinterpreted into kitsch. What also happens is that progressive, class-based politics become replaced by ecological, identity, and gender issues. While he certainly does not dismiss the new cultural politics, what Elliott has in mind in contrast to such politics and postmodern kitsch is artwork that appeared, for example, in the *China/Avant-Garde Exhibition* held in Beijing in February 1989, which displayed "artists who had tried to exorcise the ghosts of Mao's Cultural Revolution, not only by re-establishing the idea of artistic autonomy but also by envisioning and agitating for new forms of democratic government."[126] His contention is that it is in China, Indonesia, Taiwan, and "to some extent" also in Singapore and South Korea that "the mix of economic development, artistic discourse, modernity and political power was radically different from that of the West, [and] that the concept of an avant-garde seemed valid."[127] The pointedly contrasting con-ceptual topographies of Asia that Kapur and Elliott represent acknowledge the uneven impact of rapid economic development in the region, resulting in differing yet synchronized understandings of radicalized artistic possibilities in the second APT.

The Post-Exotic Urban Modern and the Art of Heterotopic Urbanism

David Elliot's conceptual topography of Asia that combined economic modernization with politically aware art within which the theory "of an avant-garde seemed valid," further mixed in with the newer politics of ecology and urban identity, takes the limelight in Hou Hanru and Hans Ulrich Obrist's *Cities on the Move*. The first incarnation of the traveling exhibition in 1997 was at the Vienna Secession, and the exhibition connects a vision of art and everyday life with the Secession's artistic modernist motto hung over the pavilion's entrance: *Der Zeit ihre Kunst. Der Kunst ihre Freiheit* (To every age its art. To every art its freedom). Did New Asia's desire for global cities lead to art and freedom? Or are artistic experimentation and freedom restrained by some of the region's paternal if pro-capitalist regimes and the consumerism that development fosters? *Cities* suggested both occurred.

The exhibition diverges from the others examined thus far, not only with its urban-presentist bias but also with how this bias gave rise to the unequivocal commitment to design the exhibition space, which changed with each version of *Cities*.[128] The Succession's gallery space was reworked by the Beijing-based architect Yung Ho Chang (b. 1956). More than a hundred works were densely installed around a central space functioning as a sort of city square, surrounded by bi-level metal scaffolding with platforms. The scaffolding, resembling that common in regional building sites, was covered with translucent curtains with holes that allowed the audience to view the artwork from both a higher level and with different perspectives. The design and installation, Hou has noted, challenged the modernist, meditative white-cube aesthetic that saw art as separate from daily life and—implicitly—historical time.[129] As the participating Malaysian contemporary artist Wong Hoy Cheong (b. 1960) recalls, "Works conversed and clashed with each other in a cacophony of forms, sounds, and sensations[, given that film, video art, architectural maquettes, and installation sculptures were involved].... Navigating through the exhibition became a heightened sensorial and physical experience, not unlike negotiating many a city in Asia, particularly one with 'post-planning' developments, as postulated by [Hou] Hanru some years earlier in a conference in Shenzhen, China."[130] By "post-planning," Hou meant that speedy urban construction in a country such as China led to some details of a new building messily hammered out while being put up, rather than being neatly planned in advance. Unsurprisingly,

Hou and Obrist's exhibition strategies had a mixed reception. Curator Douglas Fogle observes, "'Cities on the Move' was as much an experiment in the architectonic construction of an art exhibition as it was an investigation of the contemporary urban landscape of Asia. . . . While this might be seen as problematic coming from the perspective of either the architectural or visual arts communities respectively, it is the parallels between this curatorial displacement and the counter-modernist development of the Asian supercities that made this exhibition so provocative."[131]

As the above hints, *Cities on the Move* is exercised not by the tensions of tradition and the contemporary, but more by a post-exotic urban modernity and the art, architecture, and urban planning that engages with intense urbanization. While the exhibition's sprawling themes are inexactly pieced together and theorized, a compelling set of associated concerns, nevertheless, are discernible, held together in the 1997 catalogue by a breathless and oftentimes hyperbolic prose that becomes part of the representation of rapid and unsettling change.[132] The theme of speed permeates the cocurators' catalogue discourse on the "pervasive expansion and explosion of urban space and metropolitanization" in which the negotiation between older sociopolitical structures and liberal capitalist flows invited in by regional governments turns their major cities into zones of both new oppressions and capabilities.[133] Asian cities, even without a unitary vision of modernization, rushed into the future as a way of catching up with the Western metropolitan present. If the other exhibitions to date displayed a synchronized heterogeneity of the contemporary that yoked together perceptions of the present and tradition, *Cities* examines how the region's critical and experimental art must face social control exerted via tamed, consumerist-oriented cultural production and how its varied urbanism and architectural practitioners can adapt traditional ideas as enabling inter-Asian fictions to address new problems, such as the increasing environmental issues that are the legacy of Western modernity's separation of man and nature. Asian cities become Foucauldian heterotopias—as loosely interpreted by the cocurators—that are deviations from the liberal Western metropolis, even as both the governments and societies of these cities are complicit with Western capitalist imperatives that lead to a corrosive comfort. This is the double logic of heterotopias in which capitalist "normalcy" is both sustained and interrogated.

Hou and Obrist's starting point is that the number of rising economies beyond the initial successes of Japan and the mini-dragon economies has led to an East Asia in which "the impulsive and almost fanatical pursuit of economic and monetary power becomes the ultimate goal of development" and that given the competitiveness of these pursuits, there can be "no such thing as a collective Asian identity."[134] Burgeoning cities must deal with the consequences of regional governments' belief in the "pragmatic . . . co-operation between Asian lifestyles and social orders and a globalising liberal consumer society."[135] The cocurators recognized that although the 1990s was a decade that linked globalization and democratization positively, they choose to refer to parts of the region loosely as comprising "post-totalitarian" local governments and multinational corporations not keen on enabling the freedom to oppose development.[136] One statist containment strategy was to allow or actually foster "spectacularly aseptic entertaining [*sic*] through music videos or soap operas" for an "almost 'comfortable' censorship and deliberated [*sic*] reduction of spaces for non-commercial cultural activities"—that is, for critical artwork.[137] In reaction, visual art practitioners have created "non-institutional 'artist-run-spaces'" that offered "a kind of 'emptiness' . . . in the very centre of construction turbulence."[138] Artists could further resist sterilized cultural consumption via transdisciplinary dialogues with architecture and film to gain new synergies within the frenzied city, and to keep the city creatively animated—exactly what *Cities* hoped to achieve.

Most of the curatorial essay, however, is dedicated less to art than to architecture and urbanism. If art was forced to come to grips with an unstable urbanization that left established cultural modes disintegrating, Asian architecture and urbanism—the art of the built environment—should reject functionalist architecture as the model for Asian cities, given "Western Modernism's separation between Man and Nature" and the resulting danger of environmental degradation.[139] Here, the cocurators prescribe a different post-exotic direction than those offered for art: they deliberate upon how "the pursuit of a harmonious relationship between man and Nature has always been a part of Eastern tradition" and that the concept of Feng Shui, "usually translated as 'geomancy,'" could be repositioned as "a 'tentative fiction' designed to deconstruct the dominance of the West."[140] The traditional was to be tactically and nominally utilized as a "local" cultural component that had corresponding versions in regional cultures—as opposed to Marian Pastor-Roces's usage of "fiction" in *Traditions/Tensions* to signify how contemporary art could be a mix of older and newer formats and content.

Hou and Obrist indeed suggest that models that bridge ideas of "linear growth and 'irrational' intuition" and subvert "the established [Westernized] 'universal' order" already existed in postwar Asia—to be found in Hong Kong, Malaysia, Singapore, India, and Japan.[141] For example, Malaysian "Ken Yeang has developed [*sic*] 'Bioclimatic Skyscrapers' to respond to the necessity of environmental considerations."[142] However, the cocurators throughout the essay are consistently short on explanatory details, which obscures the significance of the exhibition. They do not mention that Yeang's pioneering work began in the 1970s: knowing that the newly decolonized countries would inevitably build tall buildings to appear "developed," he argued for designs that could respond to their site's climatic conditions, such as the incorporation of vertical gardens, sky courts, vegetation, and natural ventilation for a tropical architecture.[143] The curatorial essay, in particular, highlights the Japanese architects connected with the Metabolism movement as "the first to acknowledge the relevance of Asia's [own] urbanism."[144] As with Yeang's notable work, the essay does not give the reader the core of what should be appreciated. The context for Metabolism is important: from 1953 to 1970, Japan's high-growth era, postwar economic recovery and industrialization took place that witnessed annual GNP increases of about 10 percent, much of it concentrated in the corridor connecting Fukuoka, Osaka, and Tokyo. A young generation of architects in 1960 tried to address the problems often associated with growth, such as inflexible city planning and inadequately planned urban infrastructure. The foundational precept as set forth in the manifesto *Metabolism 1960: The Proposals for New Urbanism* was that "architecture and the city should not be conceived as permanent but that architects and urban planners should design the city and the buildings in such a way as to remain open to the processes of growth, decline, and transformation."[145] Metabolism embodied a more organicist conception of city planning, in keeping with Hou and Obrist's elevation of Feng Shui, and the Japanese architects are, in fact, arguing that the new high-growth era should learn from Asia's earlier experiments in architectural design and urbanism.

The art, architecture, and urbanism surveyed in *Cities* are "Utopian projects . . . based on a consideration of reality, and confrontation with the chaotic, disordered nature of our [globalizing] world" in which East and West encounter each other. However, Hou and Obrist then confusingly add that the projects can also be thought of as dystopian, as they offer alternative visions of the future city in which harmony with nature and "the global Cyber-network" might be linked.[146] It is not apparent why such urban futures would be dystopian, given that the urbanism offered could help avoid the environmental apocalypse or how the utopian becomes the dystopian. Then, rapidly, citing the thinking of Japanese architect Arata Isozaki (b. 1931), who had been an early Metabolist, two more terms appear: "'Another Utopia,' or 'heterotopia,'" the latter being Michel Foucault's expression.[147] While disorienting, what the coauthors struggle to allude to is that while utopias, as Foucault explained, "are sites with no real place," heterotopias might be thought of as "something like counter-sites, a kind of effectively enacted utopia in which the real sites that can be found . . . are simultaneously represented, contested, and inverted."[148] While Foucault's usage of heterotopia has its provisional aspects, Hou and Obrist deploy it in two ways: to indicate that regional art and architecture draw upon but simultaneously deviate from globally circulating ideas and practices with origins in advanced Western metropolitan development.[149] A double logic of heterotopias—in this case, one that both sustains and undermines the "normalcy" of Western urbanism—is apparent in the curatorial essay, as heterotopias do not exist except in relation to other spaces, here the spaces of the West.

Hou and Obrist reckon that a number of the region's urbanist practices could be models viable for larger adaptation. Therefore, they planned their catalogue not as "an extension of the exhibition" but rather as "a heterogeneous reader of different city concepts, ideas and practices," assembled in alphabetical order and in the form originally submitted to the cocurators.[150] Two examples illustrate their plan to present both new oppressions and cultural capabilities. The first art project presented after the introductory essay is by Arahmaiani (b. 1961), the Indonesian performance and multidisciplinary artist-activist. On the top of the first page of her project description is handwritten: "City life, city life / Living in a box of ideas / possibilities → for sale." The second page has a drawing of a woman in a coffin-like box, with this text above it: "Culture Box of Coke Age (To be consumed in the mid of chaotic traffic)." On the left of the coffin box is written: "myself=agent of change / producer of culture / to be consumed."[151] In the midst of the "chaotic" city very open to foreign influences and filled with consumerist opportunities as represented by the Coke bottle, a central signifier for cultural imperialism in Arahmaini's art, she asserted that activist art and the artist can offer means to counter globalized cultural imperialism, especially in its American variant, and thus becomes one example of artwork aware of the dangers of "a globalising liberal consumer society."[152]

The second example is the third project in the catalogue, "A Cosmic Dragon: The Feng Shui Project for Mito," by the United States–based Chinese artist Cai Guo-Qiang (b. 1957), and it is one illustration of Feng Shui used as a "tentative fiction" to loosen the grip of Western urbanism. Cai becomes an example of intraregional cultural cooperation—"a model for post-nationality"—to rethink urban order.[153] The project was originally commissioned for the "Mito Annual '94: Open System," organized by the Contemporary Art Center, Art Tower Mito, in the capital city of Japan's Ibaraki Prefecture. Cai at that point was a Japanese resident, having moved there in 1986: there is no nationalistic Chineseness here. The artist proposes some ways by which Mito can have stronger flows of energy to benefit its citizens with greater natural harmony. A computer-manipulated print spans the center of the first two pages of Cai's proposal, in which an image of a dragon is imposed on an aerial shot of Mito.[154] On the top of the two pages is handwritten text, informing us that Mito "was built on plateaus and in the shape and essence of a dragon. . . . [However, a] railroad literally decapitates the dragon's head from its body," disrupting energy flow, and "to appease this situation, a stone lion is erected at the northern point of the railroad. Its gruesome face looks northerly, fending off evil energy from that direction."[155] The rest of the catalogue proceeds in the above vein and ends with fifteen reflective essays by a wide range of critics, architects, and artists on the theme of urban culture—including sociologist Saskia Sassen, Japanese comedian and actor Kitano "Beat" Takeshi (b. 1947), and Singaporean theatre practitioner Kuo Pao Kun (1939–2002). The catalogue ends as eclectically as it began.

As is the larger contention of this book, the 1990s was a decade in which the global process of accumulation reached a level sufficient that the region's postcolonial and Cold War–era nationalism were partially but noticeably reworked, with implications for cultural production. In the art exhibitions investigated, we witness the attempted coordination of disparate economic development levels and temporalities—including the need to confront the inevitable dyad of the "traditional" and the "modern"—with a post-exotic urban modernity into a regional contemporary. The resulting variety of cultural expression is in defiance of modern social sciences binary logic of advanced and backward, rational and irrational/nonrational, with it being better to eliminate any vestige of the past.

As art historian Joan Kee acutely and cogently observes, "If [the idea of] contemporary Asian art was partly meant to be a socio-political intervention, [then] one of its main concerns was to construct a platform on which to consider cultural difference without reiterating modernist distinctions pitting the authentic against the derivative."[156] While Kee goes on to contend that by the mid-2000s, the contemporary art rubric has become so inclusive that "it verges on the point where the idea ceases to have any real meaning," what is more immediately pertinent to the argument now is a related question of the *platforms* on which the knowledge of contemporary Asian culture is constructed. The exhibitions were supported by region-wide fora that promoted the discursive capacity to curate contemporary cultural Asia, a capacity building that can be called cultural infrastructural networks. It is this topic that the next chapter will examine.

3 CULTURAL INFRASTRUCTURE NETWORKS AND THE "INTELLECTUAL MASTERY" OF KNOWLEDGE

His ideas took the form of aphorisms: *Location is irrelevant: what matters is not where something is, but rather where it leads. . . . What are objects? Bundle of relations. . . .*
—Tom McCarthy, *Satin Island* (2015)

The 1990s exhibitions in chapter 2 that navigated their ways through both a rethinking and coordination of tradition-in-the-contemporary and the post-exotic urban modern demonstrated an enlarged curatorial and theoretical capacity to rework and interact with cultural Asia as a medium beyond levels possible in the 1980s. In particular, the chapter looked at the burgeoning institutional capabilities of the Fukuoka Art Museum and the Queensland Art Gallery in relation to a so-called rising Asia. In 1996, the opening of the Singapore Art Museum meant that the city-state was trying to join Australia and Japan as a regional arts player, although as arts manager Hoashi Aki notes, the latter two countries' "longer duration of modernization . . . have enabled them to build cultural infrastructures, such as museums and cultural policy" beyond Singapore's mid-1990s level.[1] Still, the pertinent point remains that the economic and political climate of the decade encouraged the expansion of cultural institutions and exchange.

This chapter inquires what sort of capacity building in regional art knowledge based on art-critical and historical approaches accompanied the physical and institutionalized cultural enlargement. Okakura Kakuzō, associated with the agonistic relation of colonial modernity and Japanese art, perhaps unsurprisingly, is once again of use—here to offer an historical starting point—or even precedent—to reflect upon the 1990s building of what can be called "cultural infrastructure networks" that helped assist a regional representational facility to ascertain the contemporaneity of present-day artistic practice. Erecting buildings is one thing, but how is the intellectual-cultural capacity to be built up, especially if a region-wide knowledge of artistic endeavor is required. Often, the story of cultural knowledge, like that of the story of the Internet network, is that of it spreading monolithically outward from a Euro-American center. This chapter, in contrast, is a story of a network spreading within primarily, if not exclusively, within Northeast and Southeast Asia and Australia that concentrated on the imaginaries of the modern and the contemporary. In 1993, curator Caroline Turner asserted, perhaps over-confidently, that "the authority of the compelling image of empire [that once overtook] . . . so many procedures of intellectual mastery [of the colonized] has been left behind in the new societies of the Asia-Pacific region."[2] While "left behind" may be too strong an assertion, it was discernible that colonial-era and Euro-American modernist "procedures of intellectual mastery" were, minimally, not so "compelling" in the 1990s East Asian world, so dramatically was it changed from the decolonizing 1950s and 1960s.

In *The Awakening of Japan* (1904), Okakura complains of the Western colonial powers and the modern industrial and communication structures they had forced upon the world: "It is the rapid development of mechanical invention which has created the present era of locomotion and speculation, a development which is working itself out into various expressions of commercialism and industrialism, accompanied by a tendency toward the universal occidentalization of etiquette and language."[3] The progress such industrial and infrastructural development represented had its origins in the Enlightenment idea of a world in movement, open to the flows of goods, ideas, and even culture—and with that, change in the cultures of Asia was also fomented.[4] Such "restlessness," Okakura adds, which "constantly moves its home from the steamer to the hotel, . . . has brought about the possibility of a[n enforced] cosmopolitan culture" that was "inimical to Eastern art . . . because the cheap is [now] worshiped in place of the beautiful."[5] Colonial infrastructure systems, it can be said, were not only technical, but also transmitted ideas and culture in the form of an exclusionary yet transformative cosmopolitanism with mass-cultural effects—fascinating for some, revolting for others, or for him, it would seem, both at the same time.

Okakura, though, did not simply reject technology, a hegemonic and supposedly "universal occidentalization" of culture, infrastructural advancement, and the associated evolutionary thinking that accompanied these phenomena. *The Awakening of Japan* was written in 1904, during the

Russo-Japanese War, when, with the assistance of advanced warships, Japan gained freedom from the Russian threat: "We fought not only for our motherland, but for the ideals of the recent [1868 Meiji] restoration [and its modernizing impulses], for the noble heritage of classic culture, and for . . . a glorious rebirth for all Asia."[6] Becoming modern led to the need to rethink the regeneration of heritage culture not only for Japan but "for all Asia"—an ominous association when read back from the perspective of the 1937–1945 Second Sino-Japanese and Pacific Wars. Colonial modernity saw Okakura locked into charged views: colonial infrastructure may not have directly aided inter-Asian classical cultural advancement, but affirmation was given for Japan's national hopes to be part of a contemporaneous modernity that promoted industrialism and repeated warlike acts as a model from elsewhere—which in turn might capacitate cultural renewal.

Nearly a century later, in a period that witnessed the 1990s recognition of the so-called Asian miracle economies, the now assimilated "commercialism and industrialism" and the newer industrial, trading, and financial infrastructure that consequently was created have undergirded the creation of knowledge infrastructure platforms—visual-art and culture-oriented conferences—for the comprehension of contemporary art and a diverse reimagining of Asia. The interest was to enhance a regional representational capacity that could facilitate the boosting of the sound art-critical and historical approaches and help ascertain the contemporaneity of current artistic practice. The discourse on present-day cultural production helped, in turn, to establish a relational approach to temporality to work through the recognition that contemporary artistic formations occupied a coeval time zone with contemporary Western art. The 1904 wish for a contemporaneous modernity manifested in the 1990s within greater claims for at least a putative postcolonial cultural equality.

The emergence of infrastructural platforms for representing artistic Asia included what could be described not only as the technical (the artwork and the exhibitions themselves) but also the discursive (discourses revolving around and generated by the exhibitions). A network of artists, art professionals, and academics addressed regionally shared art-historical and cultural questions by reworking and contextually rehistoricizing Euro-American cultural-theoretical discourses. As Caroline Turner has noted:

The Asian region has continued to develop its own forums for art and creative dialogue between artists, curators, and scholars. The 1990s witnessed a rethinking of cultural frameworks and hegemonies, and critiques of what then was often referred to as the "Euro-American paradigm." Over the next decade and into the new century new definitions of "contemporary" Asian art were tested in various fora, including conferences, symposia, exhibitions and publications, in the region and beyond. The Japan Foundation has been a leader in these debates, as has the New York-based Asia Society.[7]

The increase in meetings accompanied the expansion of cultural markets and a rising museum and gallery culture. The newly bolstered technical capacity also mandated an expansion of the discursive, so that effective curation could consider regional-local specificities for exhibition halls. Many of the exhibitions that chapters 1 and 2 take stock of therefore loosely run parallel with the conferences and fora, functioning in mutual reinforcement. We can see this in the related themes and concerns that both exhibitions and fora address.

The Japan Foundation Asia Center takes the spotlight here, as their ambitious symposia were the most sustained of the conferences that Turner mentions, bringing in speakers from Northeast and Southeast Asia, India, the United States, and Britain from 1994 until 2008. The JFAC's chosen locution in their symposia—Asian contemporary art rather than contemporary Asian art—was their attempt to avoid invoking essentialist assumptions regarding a region of elusive identity or possibly even nonidentity. It is for this reason that *A Regional Contemporary* adopts their lexical decision. The Asia Center's commitment to the discursive was the infrastructural means through which ideas were directed and exchanged, thereby assisting the definition and coordination of the very space traversed by artwork, curators, and intellectuals so as to escape "Euro-American paradigm[s]." The outcomes and confusions of each symposium were systematically ported into the next one. The JFAC managed what might be called "cultural logistics."

Despite the contestatory aspects of the dialogues, there was no disposition to separate exhibitions from a global exhibitionary order, only from the colonial-era modern infrastructural knowledge order that preceded it—but it was unrealistic to think that an acute division might separate the two. The burdensome notion of temporality affiliated with colonial modernity as manifested in Okakura's ambivalence toward becoming modern—the gains in industrial modernity and progress versus the simultaneous fear of the loss of distinctive identities being lost and "the universal occidentalization of etiquette and culture"—was not easily obviated. Is modernity always and only a *Western* modernity that, by definition, is unattainable? It will be apparent that the difficulty of transcending a fractured modernity marks this chapter, as it does the preceding chapters.

An embedded Hegelian teleology of progress was transmitted to the contemporary discursive art infrastructure via postwar modernization theory, as instanced in W. W. Rostow's *The Stages of Economic Growth: A Non-Communist Manifesto* (1960). The teleology of developmental time persisted, despite the miracle economies' apparent announcement that the future had arrived. Anthropologist Hannah Appel contends, "Though the staged theories in which infrastructure was mobilized have now been rejected as valid scientific description, anthropologists have often noted that modernization theory still hangs out ethnographically. People around the world talk in terms of developmental time, progress and relapse, of being behind and needing to catch up."[8] A key area examined in the challenge for intellectual mastery is the question of temporality—"developmental time, progress and relapse"—in societies with the kind of GDP figures and the increasing physical and cultural infrastructure to think that they have caught up with the advanced West.

In the final analysis, the JFAC's symposia did not sufficiently address the United States' postwar economic agenda of fostering regional economic exchange, driven by a revived Japanese economy that, arguably, assisted in the questioning of national boundaries and thereby abetted the debordering of artistic-cultural exhibitions and symposia in tandem with the predispositions of globalizing capital.[9] To comprehend this debordering requires seeing that, as Sandro Mezzadra and Brett Neilson propose, "borders sit at the center of a number of global processes of transition, which are as much economic and cultural, social and political."[10] This lacuna in comprehending "global processes of transition" indicated how the new infrastructural capacity that supported self-representation in the context of contemporaneous cultural production functioned in tension with older modernizing ideologies linked with the competitive, identity-driven era that marked Japan's emergence as a nation-state. Sedimented histories of older knowledge forms lingered. In the 1990s, arguments were made that history had ended—that a freed capitalism and the construction of global supply chains had achieved a state of perfection.[11] The JFAC's symposia attested to the delusion that was, even then, and the selected symposia examined here also read as representative texts of the rocky road to becoming contemporary.

The Japan Foundation Asia Center and Facilitating Asia

As was discussed in chapter 1, the institution that had substantially supported the building of the knowledge infrastructure platforms for Turner's "rethinking of cultural frameworks and hegemonies" had to navigate past its wartime legacy before positive cultural work could be undertaken—but that work started by the mid-1970s. The Japan Foundation initiated the Asian Traditional Performing Arts exchange program in 1976.[12] Their inaugural film festival, A Panorama of South Asian Films, was held in 1982, and in the years that ensued, series featuring Thai, Hong Kong, and mainland Chinese films, among various regional locales, occurred.[13] The Foundation established the ASEAN Culture Center in 1990. With the establishment of the ASEAN Culture Center, specialized art exhibition staff were added to the existing staff in theater and film, and the result was that art exhibitions and symposia were organized for the Japanese public. That Center was reorganized as the Japan Foundation Asia Center in 1995, with an expanded scope of target countries. The JFAC was closed in 2004, although the arts and cultural exchange programs continued. The "rise of China" had started to divert "Japanese attention from ASEAN[, even before its closure, as had] increasing contact between Japan and South Korea[, combined with] declining financial support from public and private sectors in Japan for this relationship."[14] The financial repercussions from the Japanese asset price bubble burst in 1992 took its toll, as did changed directions in foreign policy under the Koizumi Junichirō government (2001–2006).

As Singaporean curator Ahmad Mashadi has pointed out, encouraging "regionality also requires a currency of exchange. Culture offers itself as a currency that is often seen to be particularly neutral, pliant to the needs of bilateral or multilateral interests."[15] At the same time, cultural exchange is not a zero-sum game. As art historian Kajiya Kenji cautiously advances, "cultural interest is creative and diverse, and not just a facilitator for developing economic and political relations."[16] Kajiya goes on to add that the Japanese interest in Southeast Asia is because it "has been valued as a target of economic expansion and as a counterweight to China, and . . . because it was thought it would also reinforce the building of relations on economic and political levels."[17] So, while culture, economics, and politics may be in tension, they are not mutually exclusive interests in the cultural infrastructure the ASEAN Culture Center and then the Asia Center created. Art historian

Kishi Sayaka explains that the Foundation's programs exceeded a "'one way' public diplomacy predicated on national interest," as "excluding statements and expressions that could be considered critical by the Japanese government and its counterparts" would actually thwart "the building of mutual trust and respect through academic and artistic fairness and neutrality [that in the final analysis] contributed to the broader national interest."[18] As one example, the exhibition *New Art from Southeast Asia* (1992) that the Japan Foundation co-organized with the Fukuoka Art Museum and the Hiroshima City Museum of Contemporary Art featured Malaysian contemporary artist Wong Hoy Cheong's *Sook Ching* (1989; Chinese: "purge through cleansing"), a work that examined the Japanese Army's wartime violence against ethnic Chinese in British Malaya.[19] However, Kishi also tells us that in 1994, on the forty-ninth anniversary of the Pacific War, the JFAC exhibition *Works of Japanese Traditional Craft* in Seoul met with protests—political tensions are not easily avoided and, in terms of the JFAC symposia, can be generative.[20]

Although the JFAC was closed in 2004, its arts and cultural exchange programs continued on a reduced scale, and when the Asia Center was revived in 2014, it was to produce "a new[er] generation of actors for connecting Japan and Southeast Asia and developing art and culture across Asia."[21] Furuichi Yasuko, the JFAC's exhibition coordinator from 1990 until 2020, noted that, in the 1990s, the Center "implemented numerous projects for exhibiting contemporary art" so as to promote an "understanding of the social and cultural contexts informing that art," with the latter being an issue prominent in the symposia to be examined.[22] In the 2000s, the JFAC's remit expanded to "fostering common values and building networks in Asia. The first of these collaborative projects was 'Under Construction,' led by nine [young and] emerging curators from seven Asian countries. Comprising both local exhibitions [in assorted regional venues] and a final comprehensive exhibition [in Tokyo], this was an Asia-based collaborative/process-oriented project that sought to approach contemporary Asia from multiple perspectives through extensive dialogue and research, guided by the main theme, 'What is Asia?'"[23]

The collaborative project is the exhibition *Under Construction: New Dimensions in Asian Art* (2002), co-organized by the JFAC and the Tokyo Opera City Gallery that is examined at the end of chapter 1. The infrastructural platforms the JFAC offered were hence both technical—organized and co-organized art shows—and discursive—organized symposia that assisted knowledge advancement for curation. The 2002 symposium "Asia in

Transition: Representation and Identity" was planned in conjunction with *Under Construction* and registered how the Center's interest in representation and curation functioned in conjunction with a question more accurately phrased as "What can Asia be *now*?" A knowledge of "contemporary Asia" had to come in dialogue with various "local" understandings of culture and art.

The JFAC symposia of 1997, 1999, and 2002 are examined here for their (self-consciously qualified) capacity to ease along shared definitions of the region's sense of the contemporary, and for foregrounding how difficult it was to have a fully cogent discussion of how a New Asia that produced art might be established. Nevertheless, the Asia Center's support for an Asia-wide network and even beyond—with symposia participants from Northeast to Maritime Southeast Asia, but also with Australian, Indian, British, and US participants—strengthened regional engagement with thorny issues. The 1997 symposium "Asian Contemporary Art Reconsidered" and the 1999 symposium "Asian Art: Prospects for the Future" contended with what representing the region's contemporary art meant, given the attempts of various 1990s exhibitions to claim temporal coevality with the metropolitan time of the West's artistic culture.

In general, that nebulous word "Asia" was indispensable. In the 1999 symposium, in particular, the question of how Asia and its cultures were reshaped under Western colonial dominance came to the fore. This question, along with the issue of Japan's struggle to become a great power that resulted in Japanese Empire, was taken up in the 2002 "Asia in Transition" symposium. Perversely, despite the term "transition," that symposium unfortunately only partially engaged with Cold War economic conditions that helped sustain the cultural representations of a New Asia that drove the symposia in the first place. The term "Asia" could not be released from general usage, resulting in a curatorial-intellectual thrust toward reimagining an entity that might feasibly eclipse an Asia of only national identities. Thus, *Asians* produce *Asia*, despite the conundrum that *it* does not quite exist.

Asia therefore was the central component in the JFAC's discursive infrastructure, coming with historical baggage: the entrenched colonial-era dyad of the modern West and traditional Asia that underlay Okakura's fears of an occidental cosmopolitanism that was "inimical to Eastern art."[24] Knowledge that was part of colonial-era commercial and industrial infrastructure could not be fully precluded. Nevertheless, the 1990s had a region—challengingly including less modernized rural areas, for the symposiasts were conscious of urban/rural divides—that envisaged itself as entering into what the philosopher Peter Osborne describes as the "global contemporary," which "functions as if the speculative horizon of the unity of human history has been reached. . . . It is a productive act of the imagination to the extent to which it projects an *actual* conjunction of all present times."[25] The limited confrontation of contemporary economic Asia—that, in the first place, helped stimulate aesthetic-intellectual engagement—did restrict the symposia's ability to project "an *actual* conjunction of all present times." However, to backtrack too much into the national realm may have stymied any new vistas for commonality.

The 1990s was the time for the region's art professionals to stop waiting for Euro-American art institutions to include them and move forward with their own self-representational commitments. The emergence of curators from Asia with a metropolitan reach coincided with the Center's infrastructure building. From the early 1970s, curation in general started to exceed the display of discrete artworks and began "framing those exhibition-making activities through [a] series of principles and possibilities," requiring new or revised knowledge structures to frame artwork.[26] The 1980s saw a "new global curator" who "set out from a notion of cultural pluralism based on random difference and an ethnographic approach toward the 'other,' to acknowledge the impossibility of representing a total world view within a single exhibition. Instead, postcolonial and collaborative approaches were encouraged, which had the effect of changing the position from which the artistic canon could be read."[27] The 1990s importantly marked the appearance of "new global curator[s]" from Asia who could "authentically" represent the other and fulfill the postcolonial urge to rework "the artistic canon." Crucial emergent curators such as Apinan Poshyananda (b. 1956), Nanjo Fumio (b. 1949), and Lee Yong Woo (b. 1947) participated in the JFAC symposia. The Center's discursive infrastructure, despite limitations, helped reinforce the regional curatorial capacity for self-representation. The warp and woof of what were intellectual but not academically finished presentations in the symposia must be seen with their nuances and uncertainties, for it was only in the process of reflection and disagreement that the core stumbling blocks to self-representation became manifest.

Scene Setting in 1994: How to Speak of Japan *and* Asia?

Before we commence with the 1997 symposium, the inaugural symposium requires preliminary attention. The difficulties in initiating a cultural infrastructure network on dialogue concerning contemporary cultural Asia were instructive in seeing how cultural affairs could have relative autonomy from the political or diplomatic spheres. The Japan Foundation symposium in Tokyo in 1994, "The Potential of Asian Thought," aimed at bringing in Southeast Asian involvement. The ASEAN Culture Center's agenda was queried by both some Japanese participants and, above all, Thai curator Apinan Poshyananda. Given the history of Japanese intellectual thought on Asia in relation to its wartime history, could Japan even conceive of itself as part of Asia? During the symposium, curator Shimizu Toshio observed that the "countries of Asia were forced to become Western colonies and then were invaded by Japan, a country which had been modernized on the model of the West." Now, with Asia rising, "the Western model[, including the model of modern art,] which Asians were forced to accept is losing its effectiveness."[28] What were the implications of this change? Could a more comparative and genuinely open inter-Asian framework of thought result from a possible weakening of the West centrism in Japanese cultural thinking? The sometimes-jagged queries seemed verily to strengthen the openness to a post–Cold War agenda for a networked regional discussion on the formation of modern regional culture.

The symposium commenced with art critic Nakamura Hideki, who chaired the first session and gave the opening paper, "Suggestions for the Symposium."[29] He offered his personal views on the phrase "Asian thought" in the event's title. That had been the ASEAN Culture Center's translation of *Ajia shicho*, used in the Japanese title. Initially, the Center rendered the term as "Asian spirit" but changed the translation, presumably because "thought" escaped the murky essentialist connotations of "spirit." Nakamura stressed that the Japanese term entailed neither "a rejection of Western ways of thinking" (it was not anti-Western) nor "refer[red] to some existential reality which must eventually be recognized" (it did not invoke a "true" Asia): "Ultimately, [even] confirming differences is also an achievement of a sort. What is important is to gain knowledge of the facts."[30] His explanation of the symposium's thrust is deliberately ambiguous as to whether it was to find commonality, differences, or both, within and without Asia, and his slightly defensive posture also reflected the precariousness of the knowledge enterprise being undertaken.

The symposium's sensitive character remained at the fore when Nakamura later mentioned a cultural-policy article he had recently written highlighting key concerns pertaining to the holding of Asian art exhibitions. These included the questions "What does Asian mean?" and "Is Japan a part of Asia?"[31] While both the symposium and he welcomed open regional dialogue on such matters, he understood that the event could be interpreted as part of a Japanese assertion of cultural hegemony. This, in fact, was a charge leveled by Apinan Poshyananda that Nakamura's article revealed "a Japanese sense of superiority."[32] This, Nakamura said, was a miscontextualization of his (arguably already unclear) statement: "In the future, Southeast Asians will probably become conscious of themselves as Asians."[33] Despite this defense, he emphasized that Apinan's criticism should be heard in the name of frank and effective cultural exchange.

Apinan functioned as the major intellectual gadfly in the symposium, a role continued in later JFAC symposia. The provocations in his paper "Asian Art in the Posthegemonic World," however, were intended as inducements toward right action. Nevertheless, he was the only 1994 regional participant whose formal paper delivered extended acerbic critiques of questionable assumptions that might underly the symposium's agenda. He approved of the technical infrastructural platform that the ASEAN Culture Center provided with the "'New Art from Southeast Asia 1992' exhibition [as it] was probably one of the few in depth attempts by Japanese curators to seriously interpret contemporary art by their Southeast Asian neighbours"—and that surprised him, as in the late 1980s and early 1990s, the Japanese were distracted by mainly (and, implicitly, insecurely) promoting their art in the United States to show that "not only has Japan caught up in economy but also in art and culture."[34] This qualified approval is further circumscribed with the assertion that while *New Art from Southeast Asia* possessed "commitment, dedication, and professionalism," its organization and art selection was entirely Japanese: this "intervention in contemporary art" would be "more plausible [if] a better understanding in art infrastructure between these countries [exhibited] and Japan."[35] While it is good that Japan now appreciated contemporary art from Asia and perhaps hoped to lead the region in art and culture, apart from economics and politics, had they missed the boat? This exhibitionary intervention occurred in a Japan weakened by the equity and real-estate bubble burst that started in the autumn of 1989. In contrast, Australia's larger-scale *First Asia-Pacific Triennial of Contemporary Art* (1993) "gave a rare lesson for the

Japanese as well as other Asian participants" for, whatever its flaws, it was "one of the most ambitious and enlightening art exhibitions ever organized in the Asia-Pacific region."[36]

Apinan then went on to more admonishment: "Japan should be reminded that to many Asians, the Japanese still remain very much the Other."[37] One cause of this was the insistence on cultural uniqueness, and the other was an overly fixated gaze at Euro-America: "Is Japan a member of the Western contemporary art scene or does she envision herself as being Asian? Can she be both?"[38] Given both issues, might cultural exchange become a subtle exercise in cultural hegemony? One solution was that—even if better late than never—the ASEAN Culture Center should make symposia "such as this one" into regularly scheduled meetings with speakers going beyond the familiar ASEAN countries and Northeast Asia and who can speak "openly about artists dealing with problems at [extended numbers of] particular nodal points within Asia" such as Pakistan or Tibet.[39] That is, the Center should *entrench* and *extend* its new discursive infrastructure platform for an expansive management of cultural logistics and arts leadership with a wider and more democratic edge for Asia's complexity to be made manifest.

Fukuoka Art Museum curator Kuroda Raiji picked up, expanded, and inflected Apinan's contention regarding Japan's fractious connections with the region at large. His critique is the most outspoken of the Japanese participants: "While I am happy to see a growing interest in recent Asian art in Japan, . . . I am very much afraid that a Japan-centered view of Asia is being presented here. The Japanese respond psychologically to Asians, I believe, as *familiar others*."[40] By this, Kuroda mainly meant that, first, the contemporary artists from "the Korean peninsula, the Chinese mainland, and Taiwan who live in Japan are thought to be more *familiar* than *other* because of similar racial characteristics," ignoring the politico-historical realities of Japan's colonial past that effectively still interpellated them to as *others* in Japan; and second, Southeast Asia art that has examined the Japanese invasion or "the destruction of the natural environment and communities in Asia by Japanese business . . . [is] appreciated only as the 'culture' with a history unrelated to Japan"—that is, in contrast with Northeast Asians, Southeast Asians are made more *other* than *familiar* despite interrelated histories.[41] Kuroda, like Apinan, welcomed the symposium's discursive potential but wanted cultural blind spots exposed in Japan's rethinking of its relation to Asia.

Art critic Tani Arata's presentation "History: Steps Towards the Present," which opened the session of the same title, set up the comparative possibilities for the session—which in turn arguably contributed to comparative, inter-Asian possibilities in symposia to come.[42] He started off, as had Kuroda, by noting the limited number of even the Southeast Asian nations represented in the symposium, given that they had to be ASEAN members, and that "Asia" itself was not a self-obvious category, but he thought these issues could be addressed in future symposia. He then proceeded to the session's comparativist question. Western modernism in visual art has made an impact in Asia, and examining this matter must progress to "studying the structure and characteristics of the thinking of the people of Asia."[43] Let us get away from thinking that the region's art must be national entities "characterized simply as being opposed to Western art" and instead "focus on what the Western modernism meant to Asia and the special characteristics in Asian artistic expression to which it led."[44] That is, as Sinologist Takeuchi Yoshimi postulated in 1961, the point would be that instead of always comparing individual national cultures against the West, try instead to think of Asia as the "formation of an interdependent structure" and then to compare one Asian society with another, giving rise to "'Asia as a method' or 'Asia as a function,'" with "an Asia [able] to function as part of the process in which people in the region question their own identity or acquire new identity."[45] Takeuchi is discussed in chapter 1 and invoked by Furuichi Yasuko in relation to the 2002 exhibition *Under Construction*—the discursive framework haltingly addressed in 1994 arguably had some fruition in the later technical execution of exhibitions.

The very tensions generated during the 1994 symposium served to clarify what questions might be consequential for a discursive infrastructural platform. Could Japan be reconceptualized as a part of Asia, given the region's colonial-era, wartime, and Cold War histories? Can Asia effectively be conceived as an inter-Asia struggling with the formation of modern cultures with differing levels, as a zone not to be compared only with the West? What are the imaginative prospects of the abstraction Asia in the contemporary moment when of increased levels of economic development? The hesitant outcomes in 1994 define the future space to be traversed by artwork, curators, and intellectuals to help escape Euro-American paradigms of artistic culture.

Increased Technical Achievements and Metacritical Assessments

The 1997 symposium "Asian Contemporary Art Reconsidered" followed from "The Potential of Asian Thought." The ASEAN Culture Center had in the meantime become the Asia Center, with an expanded remit on Asia beyond the ASEAN countries. In contrast to 1994, Furuichi Yasuko wrote in 1997 that there were "more exhibitions of contemporary Asian art" being staged, and "information on the art of this region [was] more available."[46] The foreword to the published proceedings by the JFAC's managing director at the time stated that the Center's goal was "to investigate [the] issues that had developed during the process of incorporating Asian art into the art system of exhibitions and museums and to 'reconsider' the current situation of Asian contemporary art."[47] The Center's agenda supported the contestation of the larger visual-art system so as to *enter into* it rather than dethrone it.

We might say that "Asian Contemporary Art Reconsidered" manifested a broad consensus that a denationalized but still Asia-centric approach to Asian contemporary art exhibitions necessitated, freeing present-day art from singular stereotypes of traditional-yet-transcendent Asia. Multiculturalism as a liberal Western cultural-theoretical program served to validate artistic work from "elsewhere." However, Asia was not a monolithic entity, even if, simultaneously, presenting art bound too tightly within narrow and national contexts in the name of multiculturalism should also be avoided. Thematic approaches to the region could assist in seeing the similarities, differences, and tensions at play in art shaped by contemporaneous and interconnected economic and sociocultural forces in the region. What remained imperative was that the capacity for regional self-representation must continue to expand. After 1994, the agenda for a networked regional discussion for a contemporary Asia had become more settled and ambitious. The theoretical stakes were significantly increased—and part of the cause was that specific exhibitions could be and were referred to in 1997. "Asia" would not be an anti-Western category, but attention must be prioritized for the various points of view from inside the region, and whatever the convolution, "contemporary Asia" would be another prioritized thematic to benefit the already bolstered technical capacity for mounting regional exhibitions.

Appropriately, with regional self-representation in mind, the symposium started with Vishakha N. Desai speaking on *Contemporary Art from Asia: Traditions/Tensions* and Caroline Turner speaking on the first two Asia-Pacific

Triennials in 1993 and 1996, among the major exhibitions on Asia up to 1997. The issue of representing a contemporary but non-monolithic Asia was immediately brought up. Session I moderator Apinan Poshyananda polemically pronounced, "The history of representation of contemporary Asian art is relatively new both within and without Asia. Here, the role of cultural arbiters or taste-setters must be considered from the simultaneous perspective of inside/outside."[48] Representation needed "cultural arbiters" familiar with or from the region to be "innovators and agents of change" in projecting suitable interpretations of art both inside and outside the region.[49] Apinan, with a PhD in art history from Cornell University, was one such regional cultural arbiter—who held the promise of attaining global curator status—and was invited to be the guest curator by Desai.

Desai, herself the first Asian director of the Asia Society Museum, emphasized the challenges of representing Asian art as contemporary and not traditional in "East in the West: Presentations of Contemporary Asian Art in the US." To begin with, the range of Asia in *Traditions/Tensions* was restricted to India, Indonesia, Thailand, the Philippines, and South Korea. If that conglomeration "sounds somewhat arbitrary," the purpose was simply a low-level "debunk[ing of] the notions of monolithic Asia."[50] Desai noted that up to the early 1990s, there had been only two Asian contemporary art shows in the United States, both on Japanese art. She agreed with Apinan that the remit of *Traditions/Tensions* would be restricted to artists examining "perceived notions of traditions in their respective cultures in the context of dynamically changing, globalizing trends that are evident in all parts of Asia"—hence the oblique stroke in the show's subtitle between "traditions" and "tensions."[51] She remarked that while premodern Asian art is easier for American audiences to absorb, the exhibitions would at least allow the audience to see shared cultural concerns in countries different from each other.

It might be noted that the 1990s level of cultural ignorance of "Asians," and even "Asian Americans," was not exaggerated. Witness the felt need by American studies scholar Lisa Lowe for a basic qualification for the category "Asian American" in 1991 for academic North American readers: "I begin my article with these particular examples drawn from Asian American cultural texts in order to observe that what is referred to as 'Asian America' is clearly a heterogeneous entity. From the perspective of the majority culture, Asian Americans may very well be constructed as different from, and other than, Euro-Americans."[52]

Desai particularly brought up the mixed audience response to the prominent contemporary installation artworks in the exhibition. These are large-scale, mixed-media constructions, often temporary, which became a major strand of contemporary art from the 1960s. She made reference to the Indonesian artist Dadang Christanto (b. 1957) and his *Kekerasan* (1995; Indonesian: "violence"), a pyramid of terracotta heads set on a base of bricks, with their mouths agape in possibly a collective prayer or a grimace of pain, or both. Desai remarked that "the traditional art audiences . . . would immediately react to it's [*sic*] seemingly traditional quality" and not comprehend that the contemporary did not require the erasure of "local" specificities.[53] There were conflicting comments on the installation art: they seemed "too Western. Or too Asian. Or too little of one or the other."[54] Art professionals, she said, had to make clear that contemporary Asian art possessed what sociologist Saskia Sassen called "'strategic geographies': places and projects where one functions in a language that is at once transnational and locally specific."[55] Contemporary art from Asia is contemporary art that is *also* Asian. Desai's contribution to thinking Asia was to articulate that the disparate components in it can be and are part of transnational contemporary art.

If Desai laid out tradition as a major stumbling block to representing contemporary artistic-cultural production across a range of Asias, Caroline Turner's presentation on the APT, "Enriching Encounters," defined effective cultural arbitrage and regional self-representation to include the systemic multilateral curatorial collaboration between Australian curators and curators from the region. This had enabled curatorial capacity building and allowed regional collaboration in the final selection of the artworks for the Triennials. The economic dynamism of New Asia was at least part of what drove the Queensland Art Gallery to commence arranging their own interregional infrastructural platforms from 1987, starting with the Museum of Modern Art in Saitama, Japan. Turner suggested that Australians' "geographical position and future lie within the Asia Pacific."[56] Like Desai, she recognized that while contemporary Asia is not one, there was value in approaching the region with a comparative framework by arranging the artwork by themes. This allowed for the display of "overlapping territories, displacements, [and] the need to expose difference, marginality and even tensions" in a dynamic Asia with multicultures, for "the changing nature of the world at the end of the 20th century has certainly forced a new appraisal of the art of the region."[57]

If Desai and Turner argued for contemporary art representation within the framework of a non-monolithic yet interconnected Asia learned from their respective exhibitions, Fukuoka Art Museum curator Ushiroshōji Masahiro, in "Emergence of Asian Art Gallery," emphasized the role of temporality when interpreting Asian art. He remarked that during the early Fukuoka Asian Art Shows in the 1980s, Fukuoka Art Museum was asked, as *Traditions/Tensions* was, "Is there such a thing as contemporary art in Asia?"[58] The inaugural 1979 and 1980 shows and the *2nd Asian Art Show, Fukuoka*, in 1985, were fairly large-scale events. The last show featured 264 artists from thirteen countries, with their works chosen by art museums or state agencies in the participating countries, as had been the case with the inaugural shows. In fact, Fukuoka Art Museum "was then rather skeptical about the quality of Asian art."[59] However, the *3rd Asian Art Show, Fukuoka* (1989) had a theme, "Symbolic Visions in Contemporary Asian Life," and became a museum-curated exhibition that went beyond traditionalism and exoticism "to see the contemporary art of Asia as the direct expression of people living in the present age."[60] Euro-America centrism and Japan's pride in possessing an advanced modernity had to be breached for the particularity of Asian contemporary art's modernity to be granted, so as to "look at Asian art, not in the context of Western discourse, but in the Asian cultural context."[61] We can say that for Desai, Turner, and Ushiroshōji, revising the accepted culture of curating led to the more effective projection of unity and coeval times in Asia and the genuine curation of culture(s).

As the symposium continued to Session II, "Issues for Critics and Artists," voices were heard qualifying that Asia must not be taken as *too* distinct. Discussions based on specific exhibitions now proceeded to more metacritical assessments. Tatehata Akira, a curator-academic and advisor for the symposium, said that while he was in favor of multiculturalism as a space-clearing device for Asia's emergence, he cautioned in "A Trap in Multiculturalism" that *indigeneity* could lead also to the essentialization of culture: "The claims of multiculturalism as applied to Asia and the Third World . . . make indigeneity an inviolable essence with absolutist and religious overtones. This view tends to make the cultural differences between Asia and the West absolute and runs the risk of fabricating differences that do not exist. Unfortunately, this sanctification of indigenous qualities is in a sense very easy to accept because it appeals to a naïve sense of justice."[62]

The clear implication is that we should still think of *art* as a shared cultural construction with the West. Art museums must "provide the necessary information end educational programs" to create respect for original Asian contexts, but indigeneity must be thought of as relative and not become a reductive postcolonial gesture, a blunt anti-Westernism that is the result of "appeals to a naïve sense of justice."[63] In Session III, the plenary session, the well-respected Nakahara Yusuke, curator of the 1970 Tokyo Biennale, pushed back against even that, declaring, "'Asian art' is not a valid concept."[64]

In the end, the symposiasts seemed to decide that it was necessary for self-representation to increase. In "Cultural Sentinels at the Crossroads," Apinan Poshyananda did not disagree with Tatehata's cautionary counsel on essentialized indigeneity, for the repudiation of the Euro-American paradigm as being universal has become too simplistic in this theoretically postcolonial and multicultural moment. Nevertheless, he unapologetically contended for the need for a corporate and strategic representation of the region's art by the region: "I'm sorry but I feel that we have to look at things in Asian-centric terms at the moment. . . . It is a competition. I am saying that within the region, we have very enriching projects and we've come a long way within the past decade in Singapore, Brisbane, elsewhere. . . . If we look at it in a very Asian, smiling, lethargic way, we will still be left behind and misinterpreted."[65]

Even with the increased technical achievements in exhibitions that Desai, Turner, and Ushiroshōji spoke of, the globalized moment remained a competitive one in which the overcoming of developmental time was not guaranteed. An (ironically phrased) "Asian, smiling, lethargic" attitude was no good. We must not return to a Hegelian *Weltgeschichte*—a world history—in which Asia will once again lag behind the present and potentially lose the voice to represent itself.

Investigating the Urban Present and the Shadow of the Past

If the 1997 symposium investigated the increased capacity for representing the regional contemporary via the qualified repositioning of tradition, indigeneity, temporality, and the pluralism of Asia, the 1999 symposium "Asian Art: Prospects for the Future," rather than appraising where the curation of exhibitions could go from there, ended up reevaluating the relationship between the contemporary and an older colonial-era modernity. The symposium's spotlight was shone on the most recent curatorial strategies taken in Hou Hanru and Hans-Ulrich Obrist's *Cities on the Move* that presented a post-exotic, unstable, modernizing, and urbanizing Asia. Were such curatorial strategies possibly conforming to older Eurocentric historical clichés of chaotic Asia? And what of rural Asia? Could not that zone be contemporary? In addition, the capitalist-connected global art system, despite the commitment to contemporaneity, could still reduce the Asian contemporary art exhibition into entertainment that had associations with the exotic. The attention paid to context in 1997 led to an interest in history that took the symposium back to the problematic formation of modern art in the maelstrom that was colonial-modern Asia. That is, former histories part of an older, colonial-era infrastructural knowledge started to be conspicuous. The 1999 expansion of the discursive infrastructure, intended to investigate the "further development of Asian art in the twenty-first century," did not overcome developmental time.[66]

Curator David Elliott's presentation "'Asia': Enduring Stereotype or Black Hole?" placed the issue of contemporary Asian identity at the symposium's center. For Elliott, although he was not against its topical usage, Asia was "a eurocentric construct of ancient Greek cartographers—rather than based on any social, political, economic or cultural coherence."[67] Although factually wrong about the region's economic incoherence, he succinctly went through a series of negative Eurocentric historical associations of Asia, and additionally contended that "no good art exhibition can seriously claim to take the continent in which its inhabitants live as a central theme," for artworks should be selected for their outstanding qualities even while they are "rooted in specific, real feelings and experience" of their time.[68] Geography was not a curatorial theme. As for the exhibitions in Fukuoka, New York, and Brisbane, their various "definitions of what constitutes Asia . . . have differed wildly."[69] In essence, Elliott rubbished parts of what were constructed in the 1997 symposium.

What, then, of *the* most recent major attempt to represent the "real feelings and experience" of an ultra-modernizing and urbanizing Asia? This, for Elliott, was Hou and Obrist's traveling exhibition spectacle *Cities on the Move*, with its celebration of "the contemporary East Asian urban condition as shifting, expanding, modernizing, unstable and exciting."[70] The 1999 London version at the Hayward Gallery featured 107 artists, with the multidisciplinary artwork—installation art, architects' maquettes, recent film—inserted into a gallery designed by the architect and urban theorist Rem Koolhaas: "Walking around it is a physical, chaotic and noisy experience, and is intended to be rather like that of passing through an Asian city."[71] For Elliott, this was more an updated version of the older chaotic East and not enough art "from the perspective of what artists are actually doing and thinking in East Asia."[72] And yet, by the symposium's end, he had changed his mind: "I think the only exhibition [in Europe] that has taken on the issue of [representing a contemporary] Asianness has been 'Cities on the Move.'"[73] What emerged was partially a question of temporality, as Ushiroshōji Masahiro had raised in 1997: How did an exhibition imaginatively capture dynamic Asia given an underdeveloped cultural interpretation of the Asian present?

During the discussion for Session II, "Examining Asian Contemporary Art of the 1990s, Part 2: Perspectives of the Presenters," the moderator—independent curator Nanjo Fumio—agreed with Elliott that clichéd notions of Asia in curation must be avoided and that regional contexts mattered, for "if you do not know the cultural background of a country, it can be difficult to understand the meaning of the [art]work."[74] Apinan Poshyananda concurred that it is "difficult to . . . display [art] in a foreign space," and *Cities on the Move*, while trying to avoid the exoticism of the traditional, had a "mini-festival" quality that gave it the air of "an anthropological survey" that could be perceived as updated clichés of chaotic Asia.[75] Elliott responded to qualify his position: he felt that Asia as a term could be used, but that more particularity was required to say "what kind of Asia we are referring to." For him, when curators say that today's "Asia is all about 'Cities on the Move,'" he would say that Asia is "mostly agricultural rural land."[76] Despite the relative success in exhibiting regional art in the 1990s, there now needs to be more curatorial exactitude in demarcating the contexts that mark the diversity of Asia. Significantly, Nanjo's reaction to the discussion was to link the need for contexts of contemporary Asian identity or identities to history. His post-symposium reflection was instructive: "In order to be honest to history and the facts it is necessary to accept the diversity of Asia, taking the [almost contradictory] attitude that chaotic conditions making strict definitions impossible is a cultural [and therefore curatorial] asset."[77] The "chaotic conditions" of the region's general history—and therefore also of its art history—cannot be ignored for thinking contemporary Asia.

Apinan's own presentation in Session III, "Asian Art and the New Millennium: From Glocalism to Techno-Shamanism," despite its futuristic title, did not remain in the present and effectively continued discussing the region's historic "chaotic conditions." He commented on the dangers of homogenizing global cultural forces. The cultural and socioeconomic practices of "the Global Village and [the] New World Order attempt to [homogenize cultures and] make the world become one," given that Western "cultural hegemony and the [older] 'othering' discourse that relates closely with [colonial] 'civilizing' missions and [the] display of the 'exotic'" have transmuted into forms befitting globalized desires to consume and be entertained.[78] The international expositions in Europe and the United States in the nineteenth century, Apinan continued, "displayed [the] strangeness of the ethnic people" from Asia and the Middle East.[79] If art is used as a transnational "lubricant" for economic exchange, is this exchange the old exposition model transformed into the "art extravaganzas . . . of the post-industrial age"?[80] Still, globalized culture does enable Asian contemporary artists to be polycentric, with less of the older pressure "to produce heritage-related arts that continue . . . purist roots" to celebrate essentialized traditional national or regional identities.[81] But while informational globalization has created new artistic options, we must still be careful of the "new rules of [economic] globalization"—and their impact on cultural production—as the Asian miracle economies had been hammered by "turbo-capitalism" during the 1997 Asian financial crisis.[82] Noticeably, Apinan was the only symposiast to advise engagement with present economic conditions.

The shades of the past then led Apinan to argue that Asia-centric exhibitions thus far really had not challenged *enough* Western conceptions of Asia. *Traditions/Tensions* and *Cities on the Move*, which sought to demystify "exotic" and "eccentric" Asia, were *still* received in the West as "derivative and inauthentic"—as art that seemed without a cutting edge and creative modern capacity.[83] One solution to this dilemma was that cultural leadership in Asia was needed, and that leadership had to be truly multilateral and democratic, and not dominate Asia's multicultures: "Leading Asian countries such as China, Japan and South Korea [that have the financial clout for regional art leadership] must be careful in their construction of Asianness or 'Asia as One.'"[84] "Asia as One," as we can recall from chapter 1, is an indirect quotation from Okakura Kakuzō's *Ideals of the East* (1903)—and in making this indirect citation, Apinan also surfaced a danger in leadership associated with an older modernizing ideology of Asia co-opted by the Japanese military in the 1930s to justify colonial expansion.

It can be seen from the above that seemingly disparate areas of thought were drawing the symposium back into the colonial era. Perhaps unexpectedly, the tipping point for that era to come fully to the fore was David Elliott's attempt to include nonurban art in order to gain a fuller understanding of contemporary art's pluralism. He asked if to be contemporary meant to be urban and then answered himself: "You don't really have to be in a city to be contemporary."[85] That prejudice was learnt from the Western metropole. Despite the fact that Elliott was endeavoring to open up the idea of the contemporary, the general discussion thereafter retreated to history and the problem of art in a world dominated by the great Western powers.

Tani Arata, director of the Utsunomiya Museum of Art, later in the discussion session called attention to the fact that the very Japanese terms for craft (*kogei*) and painting (*kaiga*) were "created after modernization began in [the] Meiji era and did not exist before then." The Meiji Restoration government's modernizing impetus resulted in an arts policy that followed "what Westerners considered to be 'art,'" with craft not being part of that definition.[86] We are brought to another negative moment during the colonial era—the creation of the idea of modern art and its converse, traditional art, in the region was part of the traumatic encounters with the modern and colonial West. We can say that while craft was invented as a category to be part of industry's "other" during the industrial revolution, it became an artistic category that traveled to Asia. In that regard, the question of craft and nonurban art and whether we can think of them as contemporary art made no sense without the question, "What was Asia?" Asia in the colonial modern period and the artistic culture(s) produced were intertwined issues.

Recent art-historical work has sought to theorize and historicize craft as a modern cultural category.[87] As the first editions of the Bienal de La Habana from the mid-1980s attempted to examine the difference between art and craft, as was discussed in chapter 2, so the symposiasts in Tokyo in 1999 had to ruminate upon artwork and craft objects and the relationship between urban and rural cultural production. The discussion returns the symposiasts to Immanuel Kant's famous distinction between art as a pure and free beauty and craft—whether within or without Europe—as cultural production that adheres to predetermined ends, as set out in his *The Critique of the Power of Judgment* (1790).

Independent curator Shimizu Toshio responded to the above questions by bringing up Japan's troubled historical relationship with Asia itself: "Even to me, someone who lives in Asia, Asia was the 'other' until a certain time in my life. In the case of Japan, we needed to establish an identity [as a modern, colonizing nation-state] in counterbalancing the Western powers. The identity of Japan and of Asia led us to war."[88] As the very idea of a backward Asia was introduced by the Western powers, he added, "we [in the region] were forced into defining it [that is, various Asian 'selves'] through the encounter with the West."[89] In his post-symposium summary of the discussion, Mizusawa Tsutomu, chief curator at the Museum of Modern Art, Kamakura, suggested that "it is impossible to understand the nature of contemporary art as anything more than fashion without a keen awareness of art's historicity."[90] The symposium ceased ruminating on the future prospects for contemporary art when the parlous formation of modern Asian cultures during the high colonial era made its appearance.

Perhaps this tripping up over history is unsurprising and even salutary. The 1999 symposium reveals the situation of the contemporary person who is forced, as Giorgio Agamben has suggested, "to read history in unforeseen ways, to 'cite it' according to a necessity that does not arise in any way from his will, but from the exigency to which he cannot not respond . . . [for] his historical investigations of the past are only the shadow cast by his theoretical investigation of the present."[91] With parts of East and Southeast Asia being in better economic circumstances than before to think through contemporaneity, the JFAC and the regional curatorium had, without option, to confront dark historical fractures from the nineteenth century to the Cold War as a constitutive action through which the 1990s components of emerging exhibitionary production might continue to be coordinated into moments of performative contemporary identity.

From Fractured Colonial-Modern Asia to Contemporary Structures of Cultural Difference

As a consequence of the direction that the 1999 symposium had taken, the 2002 meeting, "Asia in Transition: Representation and Identity," included not just art professionals but also academics in the humanities, who offered reflections on the historical meanings of Asia. However, the objective in 2002 was also to "initiate a dialogue that transcends nationality to define a new identity of Asia and relationships within the region," given that brisk economic growth had led to an increasing knowledge network of "interdependent relationships within the region [through which] the different societies and cultures of Asia are influencing each other in deeper and broader ways [than in the past]."[92]

The result was less "a dialogue" than a lurch from an older Asia of binary oppositions and in a transitional historical stage to an Asia that, through the example of curator Lee Yong Woo for the 1995 Gwangju Biennale, could be coordinated, as it were, into an historical present—one in which the regional-local was carefully associated with circulating visual culture. The 2002 symposium in its entirety, not despite of but because of its shuddering gaps, enacted a *synchronic heterogeneity* in which disparate economic development levels, temporalities, and culturally disjunctive entities could be coordinated into a contemporary regional space.[93] While the infrastructural knowledge supporting the conceiving of a newer Asia could not be separated from the knowledge structure that preceded it, nevertheless, a discursive network that had spread—however unevenly—now existed as part of the "interdependent relationships within the region."

In his opening remarks as moderator of the first session, Mizusawa Tsutomu recalled that the 1999 symposium ended up "not being able to say anything about [contemporary] Asia" because of history: "Nationalism and Asian self-awareness came together over a century ago and, as it were, caught fire, leading to the formation of many theories of the identity of Asia. The existence of these theories, besides raising the question of what Asia is in real terms, demonstrates the historical fact that Asia has been a form of discourse. . . . [As a consequence,] we wanted to take a closer look at the history and the essential qualities of Asia this time."[94]

Mizusawa, an advisor for the symposium, expressed his support for incorporating an investigation of the colonial-modern discursive construction of identity—and it is appropriate that the JFAC's discursive platform was the means for this examination. In contrast to 1999, though, the changes wrought by economic success were now consciously factored into the examination. Sociologist Yoshimi Shunya observed during the second session that given a more economically interdependent Asia, it was necessary also to "speak of [culture] going over the borders in the context of globalization, political economy, and the direction of power and capital, [for] money is what takes us over the borders—cash and multinational financial capital."[95] In the end, the symposium only partially engaged with what can be described as the disjunctive postcolonial unity of Asian cultural-artistic multicultures functioning within the still-increasing ambit of the global capitalist system. This limitation was apparent from the outset.

In his keynote address, literary-cultural critic Naoki Sakai asserted that all geopolitical identities are ambiguous. Like David Elliott in 1997, Sakai rightly reminded the audience that the term "Asia" was European and was a result of "co-figuration, the working of a schema thanks to which the figure of 'us' is constituted in the projective imagining of the figure of 'them.'"[96] This binarism was still a hazard: "Asia arrived at its self-consciousness thanks to the West's or Europe's colonization. The historical colonization . . . is not something accidental to the essence of Asia; it is essential to the possibility called Asia."[97] This "historical colonization" could be seen in how the Japanese understood their identity as former colonizers, for "seeing things from the civilizing positionality" is not something "accidental . . . to Japanese subjecthood."[98] The internalized former colonial West is also a "mytheme" that supported an ongoing distinction between Asia and a coherent West that did not exist.[99] This distinction gave reprehensible credence to arguments of developmental over human rights in the name of Asian values, allowing excuses "for not submitting things Asian to the same analytical fields of investigation as things modern and Western."[100] Sakai was criticizing the highly ideological "Asian values" discourse of Lee Kuan Yew and Dr. Mahathir Mohamad in the 1990s. While shards of the region's "historical legacies" still featured in the present—the 2002 symposium was proof of that—what was missing from Sakai's examination was the symposia's collective curatorial discussions on the representation of Asia in art exhibitions in all the symposia.[101] Whatever the constraints, they already had drawn consistently upon self-differentiating analytical capacities *different* from those that drove the colonial modern era, and that capitalist development no longer foreign to Asia.

Like Sakai's keynote, literary-historical scholar's Wang Hui's "Imagining Asia: A Genealogical Analysis" scrutinized Asia as a derivative discourse that "provided a framework [not only for] European intellectuals, [but also for] Asian revolutionaries and reformists, and historians to represent world history and Asian societies."[102] He offered a reconstructed perception of world history within which "multipl[e] worlds of history communicate and fight with each other, permeate into each other, and mould each other," markedly diminishing the importance of the binary identities.[103] The European characterization of Asia from the nineteenth century questioned Asia's relation to modernity's fundamental temporal concepts—progress, revolution, *Neuzeit*. Asia, with its multiethnic empire and agrarian mode of production, was a political form in opposition to the European nation-state and a social form in opposition to European capitalism and the worldwide spread of the market system. As such, it was taken to be in a transitional zone between an unhistorical stage and an historical stage.

Although Wang Hui accentuated the question of Asia and its historically weak link to capitalism, this did not lead to any discussion of their relevance to the present. David Elliott commented after the symposium's end that "culture should [have been] integrated more into this wider discussion [of economics] which is not only cultural in itself but also provides a framework within which culture may develop."[104] Some consideration for the economic did occur, but solely in Lee Yong Woo's subsequent presentation. Sakai's and Wang Hui's presentations led to an indeterminate hope for Asia to transcend the past. As moderator Mizusawa later remarked, "Asia may be described as a child who was hurt at birth."[105] Despite this, Asia as a category was still relevant for him for "we can see from history that people in different cultural regions are looking for something."[106] That "something" included a flexible Asian identity that might eclipse the competitive nation-state system that the region had adopted as part of anti-colonial outcomes.

As the moderator for Session II, "Asia That Is Exhibited/Asia That Is Not Exhibited," Yoshimi Shunya brought the question of Asia to the present: "Asia is a concept that is constructed, made, and multiplied within the process known as globalization, which [also, like colonial modernity,] contains contradiction, division, and repression."[107] If the process of capital accumulation has become inherent in the New Asia, can contemporary structures of cultural difference and its related artistic production be the same as those of colonial modernity? This question was taken up in some measure only by Korean curator, Lee Yong Woo, in his presentation "Globalism and the Vanity of Its System." Lee suggested that circulating global culture, the global biennial system, and local and regional cultures could be brought into conjuncture through prudent calibration and coordination. The symposium offered Lee the opportunity to share how he had rethought the "cultural frameworks and hegemonies" allied with the "Euro-American paradigm," as Caroline Turner has put it.[108]

Lee was the artistic director of the first Gwangju Biennale in 1995. Titled "Beyond the Borders," it featured art from fifty-eight countries and commemorated the 1980 pro-democracy protest and massacre now known as the Gwangju Uprising. Students peacefully protested the inauguration of military strongman Chun Doo-hwan as president after Park Chung-hee's assassination, with tragic results: civilians were killed and tortured by the military. We will see that for Lee as a curator, the *practical possibilities* of staging theoretical postcolonial contemporary thinking effectively mattered as much as fully-fledged intellectual ripostes against the global culture system. He aimed to tie circulating culture in its biennial form to regional and local cultures, here involving both Gwangju's history and its citizenry's possible response to contemporary art.

Lee complained that a central fantasy of capital was the cultural unification of the global, a process not necessarily in East Asia's favor. The globalized language of art "erases memories of the original language of each region and offers a linguistic foundation for a new language. In this way, the biennial presumes to present something like a new standard time that rectifies regional inaccuracies."[109] This is both a charge of cultural erasure and a fake coeval temporality attained via the hegemonic correction of regional clocks not in sync with the artistic time of the metropolitan centers. However, a positive was that the biennial seemed to be "acclaimed by the general public" in East Asia "for bridging the cultural and historical gap between the East and the West."[110] A major step toward rehabilitating the biennial would be to insist that the region's culture in its particularistic daily and national senses *was* part of art's global language and standard time. A next step was to return to the original purpose of the biennial, with its "separation from the oppressive and categorical walls of the museum," to be a place "where spectators from all walks of life come together, where pluralism is the overriding theme, and where a uniquely democratic aesthetic takes over."[111] This was a refusal of organized art-institutional collusion with capital, of what Yoshimi had earlier referred to as "money [that] . . . takes us over the borders."[112]

Gwangju was far away from the art world, and this made it a good venue for "attack[ing] the political center and loud global [artistic] themes."[113] The city lagged behind in development because of its anti-government history, but this history offered "both . . . a strategy and an ideological foundation" for creating the art event.[114] So, "a separate ground was designated as a place for the souls of the martyred patriots who . . . became symbols of the struggle for democracy in Korea."[115] Despite protracted debates over the biennial's organization, "the citizens of Gwangju . . . liked the fact that here, in the cradle of the movement for Korean democracy, an innovative art biennial was also in the process of gestation."[116]

If the above is how Lee tackled the local and the national, what then of the regional and a more genuine global pluralism? A short history of the Gwangju Biennale tells us that "the theme Beyond the Borders conveyed a message of global citizenship that transcended divisions between ideologies, territories, religion, race, culture, humanity, and the arts. Aesthetically, it manifested itself in art's ability to overcome meaningless pluralism [found in the multicultural vocabulary of globalization] and intended to establish new orders and relationships between the arts and mankind."[117] Forty percent of the artists were from Asia—that took care of the region. Lee also instructed his supporting curators in the name of a more indubitable pluralism to select new or emerging art by "young, lesser known artists who had yet to enter into the biennial circuit" and "artworks of value that inspire the public's participation and provide it with [sufficient] information."[118] He sought to avoid the superficial application of metropolitan theories of the plural and the repeated exhibition of celebrity global artists. An "aesthetic of populism" offered a global event that purposefully elevated Gwangju's citizens into a conjunction with new art of the present time.[119]

Did Lee's actions avoid the vision of a world market, as Fredric Jameson once provocatively put it, that can lead to "increasing [singular] identity . . . [and to] the rapid assimilation of hitherto autonomous national markets and productive zones into a single sphere"?[120] As Peter Osborne has contended, though, "global networks of communicative action are more radically denationalizing and de- and re-culturing than the idea of global culture[, including artistic culture,] can sustain," and the contemporary "is a productive act of imagination to the extent that it performatively projects a non-existent unity onto the disjunctive relations between coeval times."[121] The 2002 symposium and those that preceded it testify positively to both of Osborne's stands. The JFAC was keen to foster a regional network of visual-art professionals so as to denationalize artistic-cultural discourse for the benefit of an Asia that might outstrip narrow interests, even as it affirmed a multicultural Asia that is *not* "one," and also as speakers from past symposia asserted that Asian contemporary art—a contemporary art that is *also* Asian, rather than fully autonomously Asian—is not completely distinct from a larger global practice of art. The Asia Center symposia provided a cultural-logistical platform for the expansive facilitation of curatorial capacity building with regard to

Asian artistic identities-in-progress from the colonial era to the present day of intensive modernization.

Thus, Asia is used and reused—an Asia no longer traditional and exotic, but an Asia that represented a desire to rise above inter-Asian national clashes. The Asian contemporary art exhibitions and the curatorial imagination that supported them brought into relationship qualitatively incommensurate cultural, local-national, and historical components, turning them into a fictional totalized present. But this does not mean that the "bad" modernity from the historical modern period has dissipated: it coexisted in a tense relationship with the regional contemporary. New infrastructure has not quite superseded old infrastructure.

4 DEBORDERING HONG KONG FILM AND COMMONALITY/DIFFERENCE IN URBAN SPACES

Henri Lefebvre remarks that the "opposition of center and periphery goes a long way, since it stretches from the great capitals and world cities to the most miserable, so-called 'undeveloped' regions and countries," and that the "domination of centers . . . guarantees the homogeneous character of space [for i]t exercises control at all . . . points of view over peripheries that are both dominated and broken apart."[1] What happens, though, when areas produced as semiperipheral capitalist spaces assert an increased economic centrality in the ongoing formation of a world market—and not only produce "things in space" but also start to be producers of their own representational space, culturally and artistically?[2] When there is some resistance against the "dominant form of [capitalist] space . . . [that] endeavours to mould the spaces it dominates"?[3] If one prefers, this question is about the transformation of *place*, in Michel de Certeau's sense of a previously designed and stable locale, into a *space*, a locale that is now made polysemic and polyvalent.[4]

The 1980s and the 1990s witnessed the intensified cultural innovation in and circulation of the visual arts, as thus far argued, and—even more prominently and the focal point of this and the next chapter—popular culture from the 1990s within Northeast Asia and Southeast Asia. Mass-consumed culture took the form of televisual programs, film, and pop music from Japan, Taiwan, South Korea, and Hong Kong, plus Japanese anime. Using two indicative Hong Kong cinema productions and one Japanese-Hong Kong coproduction, I will maintain that post-1980s East Asia media and cultural industry production contributed to a shared vision of a New Asia as a region predicated upon an interconnected capitalist modernization, modern culture, and—vital for visual-media producers—a potentially more cosmopolitan, middle-class audience. This shared vision emboldened cross-border casting and the use of multilingualism. A defining feature of this vision of

Asia was an intense urbanizing process. In general, such cultural productions were functionally an extension of the urban-directed, post-exotic art curated in the late-1990s traveling exhibition *Cities on the Move* examined in chapter 2. Exotic Asianness or cultural essentialisms of the sort formulated during the colonial era become less critical in this creative zone.

To "spatialize," as historian Harry Harootunian notes, is to side with the modernization process, and an urban design critic such as Peter Rowe has found "a fascination with the sheer scale, rate and bold newness of [regional] modernization and consequent changes to built environments."[5] Contemporary East Asia is located inside capitalist modernity and therefore shares the "homogeneous character of space" of the Western metropolitan centers, but the "points of view" that arise are also those of the transitioning semiperiphery and reflect their characteristic histories of the modern. There is an underlying totality here, but one that "unfurls violently," even if at a broad level modernity is "an incessant production of difference as the same."[6] The spatialization practices in culture are part of "the global dominance of capital" as it becomes "more and more disentangled from a world order centered on the primacy of Europe and the West (as the current forms of capitalist development in East Asia surely attest)."[7]

The presence of difference, though, does not mean that East Asia appears as a decentered, intercultural urban festival. The regional contemporary that is coming into view, as I have sought to demonstrate, is fractured. What can be called "inter-Asian cinematic productions" evocatively recognize *both* the historic ideational and militarily enforced formation of a Greater East Asia, associated with Japan's past attempts to leave "backward" Asia and modernize, *and* the shared postwar possibilities for a desired First World East Asia. The region's media and culture industries do not escape the specters of modernity's debilitating "entry" into the region.[8] At the same time, as film critic Stephanie DeBoer contends, Northeast Asian cinematic coproductions from the 1960s "have been closely tied to the desires for progress and development that have accompanied the region's construction and reconstruction in the infrastructures of the Cold War . . . and the intensities of transnational capital."[9] The combined tensions and upbeat possibilities of Cold War developmental opportunities can be extended to non-coproduced film and the region's media and culture industries taken more inclusively.

Specifically, this chapter will examine the increased dimensions of a New Asian regional identity through thinking of how cinema in the late 1990s and at the start of the twenty-first century attempted to deborder national limits so as to rework itself in terms of a fractured but modern New Asia. I particularly examine three films indicative of the cultural productiveness at stake. The first is the Japanese-Hong Kong coproduced *Sleepless Town* (*Fuyajo*/*Bu ye cheng*, 1998), directed by Hong Kong's Lee Chi-Ngai. The next is Jingle Ma's *Tokyo Raiders* (*Dongjing gonglue*, 2000), a film consonant with what might be said to be the libidinization of market modernity in the region. The third is *auteur*-director Johnnie To's *Fulltime Killer* (*Quanzhi shashou*, 2001; co-director Wai Ka-fai). Lee's *Sleepless Town* examines a biracial Japanese/Chinese gangster's struggle to survive when held accountable for the murder of a senior Shanghainese gang member by his friend, the culturally disenfranchised son of Japanese returnees who lived in wartime, Japanese-controlled Manchuria. Ma's film was one of the most popular in Hong Kong in 2000 and is distinct in being a Hong Kong film set mainly in Tokyo, in having extensive dialogue in Japanese, and having a Sino-Japanese detective hero untroubled by his biracialism. To's even more multilingual film, one that also draws its artistic resources from the region's popular culture, unintentionally but also unavoidably becomes an allegory of the core East Asian states competing: two professional killers from Japan and China struggle to see who will be recognized as the region's best.

The question of the *circulation* of culture and cultural products within the region is inextricably tied up with the questions of both *commonalities* and *differences*. The three concerns are not only conjoined but even thematized in cultural innovation. The central commonality is the ongoing growth of urban-modern lifestyles—understandable because cities are major spaces for transnational and national capital investment. The differences are not only linguistic and national-cultural differences, but also the differences of the politico-historical struggles to become modern in the first place. Finally, the very circulation of cultural products by its producers and intermediaries suggests that the *foregrounding* of the common and the different are that which, paradoxically, media critic Kōichi Iwabuchi proposes, can generate a "cultural economy of . . . resonance" that crosses borders.[10] However, *how exactly* translation (subtitling of dramas or pop songs incorporating more than one language) or how "cultural translation" (that which comes about when the viewer feels that there is "cultural proximity" between the televisual or filmic program he/she is watching and his/her own urban context) lead to the creation of regional cultural "resonance" is not apparent. This chapter clearly attempts to think through this question of "resonance." Commonality-in-difference becomes suitable for deployment by the region's media and culture industries, and the urban-modern becomes that contemporary nodal point through which it can be narrativized and represented. Resonance may come in the form of audience identification with the glossy representations of modernity in cultural products (as exemplified by *Tokyo Raiders*) or, alternatively, cultural products may reflect or otherwise mediate the region's cultural and political concerns (as exemplified by *Sleepless Town* and *Fulltime Killer*).

The three films map the contemporary region as one containing urban spaces and cultures that are simultaneously not quite national and not quite transregional: *East Asia* is a contingent but yet still structured cultural subjectivity and imaginary, a response to economic growth still semantically only partially emergent. The fundamental frame for inter-Asian cultural production, arguably, is less the resurgence of local realities in the First World parts of the former Third World, but more the complexity of "region" in the still-changing profile of successful but interdependent national economies and their new middle classes.[11] Until recently, the world could be spatialized and represented as East or West, communist or non-/anti-communist. Such representation is less suitable now, as witnessed perhaps above all by the phantasmatic entity of an authoritarian-capitalist Communist Party of China fostering its own world cities in the People's Republic of China.

While the regionalizing attempts of Hong Kong film tailed off by the mid-2000s, it did offer within the region the "cultural productivity" that (re)produces a shared or a desired vision of everyday urban life—even as the tensions in the region are showcased in artistic-cultural productions.[12]

Circulation, Commonality/Difference, and the Urban-Modern

In considering the matter of an increase in the production of popular culture in the region, it is necessary to start with postwar economic growth that sees the renewal of Asia as a deployable idea and what might be described as an urban-modern vision of development. The latter is the central component of the commonality that helped bridge historical fissures and cultural differences. An enlarged middle class is part of this shared commonality.

As it has been noted, East Asian growth was "most rapid during the last half of the twentieth century, [and] so it is then that social groups, cultures, and lifestyles [linked with urban transformation and consumerism] have probably changed most rapidly from a global perspective."[13] Economic and industrial development hastened urbanization in what the World Bank once described as "HPAEs"—High Performing Asian Economies—and such development helped advance a more consumerist lifestyle for an enlarged middle class.[14] The HPAEs primarily referred to the little-tiger economies that to some extent all followed, along with key second-tier economies such as Thailand, Malaysia, and Indonesia, in Japan's footsteps. Henri Lefebvre has referred to the city as "designed space," as that place where a "formidable force of homogenization exerts itself on a worldwide scale, producing a space whose every part is inter-changeable (quantified, without qualities)."[15] The expansion of Seoul, Hong Kong, and Taipei, and, more recently, Beijing-Tianjin and Shanghai has been "accompanied by more rapid economic growth, resulting in a[n urbanization] pattern . . . [similar] to that of Japan."[16] Shared characteristics appeared in the new cities and their newer urban populations in the region.

There is a direct connection between rapid growth and shared concep-tions of consumption: "the increasing speed of circulation of the 'new middle classes' throughout the region means a degree of cultural homogenization, for which Japan [once again] provided many of the critical models."[17] This new cultural homogenization is hence inseparable from the region's indus-trializing and urbanizing imperatives. The growth of these new middle classes also led to a new horizontal solidarity in political and cultural expression that may be dependent upon but not limited by their respective states. As Takashi Shiraishi argues, "Because the middle classes are consti-tuted not solely through a homogeneous national culture but rather through networks of markets and global cultural and financial flows, middle-class consciousness is fostered through interactions between national govern-ments and domestic and transnational markets. . . . The emergent region-wide middle classes are a crucial engine of East Asian region-making [as they constitute the expanding regional consumer market]."[18] Shiraishi also does go on to point out that, "far from being defined solely by their capac-ity to consume, the East Asian middle classes have also been constituted as political subjects . . . [with] important political consequences in reshap-ing their states and articulating new nationalisms."[19] That is, new identities simultaneously and additionally can also generate new nationalist tensions. We will see this simultaneity in the films to be explored.

In terms of the urban-modern commonalities in an inter-Asia imagi-nary, Japan's regional investments also led to an unprecedented focus on commercial land in Tokyo's central wards in the 1980s, as the infrastructure to turn it into a center for finance and transnational production and trade had to be built.[20] As has already been suggested, Tokyo becomes a model for emulation—in a number of ways. The city's population has expanded continuously since, and now this "postindustrial city . . . arguably serves as a reliable guide to what other cities in the region could experience," given that the recent evolving of other potential postindustrial regional urban centers resemble Tokyo in the 1970s and 1980s in retaining manufacturing in outlying urban zones, even as services become more significant in the core urban areas.[21] More recently, urban redevelopment also transpires because of the goal to foster premier world cities as assets in drawing in and retaining the flows of capital.

All this is not to suggest that there exists a general phenomenon called the "East Asian city," for putative world cities in the region are sites where politico-economic and social processes that are common to other capitalist-urban centers in the metropolitan West manifest themselves.[22] Nevertheless, there are palpable connections in the region's cities to do with the relatively sustained nature of economic growth—Japan in the 1950s–1970s, the tiger economies thereafter, followed by China, leading to cityscapes morphing at an unsettling pace beyond that experienced in advanced Western cities—and historical regional relations, certainly in terms of popular-cultural production and mass consumption. In this regard, one "distinctive, although not unique feature, has been the step-by-step emulation by one nation of the practices of others in the region that were slightly better off," facilitated by centralized governments from the top down.[23] Revealingly, the defining moments of East Asian cities that tell us the "time" when most building took place is not the nineteenth century of many European cities, nor the early twentieth century of New York City, but the postwar years that were initially charged with the communist question: the 1960s and 1970s for Tokyo and Seoul; the 1970s and the 1980s for Taipei, Singapore, and Hong Kong; and the 1990s for Shanghai.[24] The speed of regional urban development itself has long been commented upon, such as by the Dutch architect-theorist Rem Koolhaas: "Singapore is an apotheosis of urban renewal, a built answer to the shift from country to city which was thought, 30 years ago, to force Asia to construct in 20 years the same amount of urban substance as the whole of Western Europe."[25]

The "contagion" of the 1997 Asian financial crisis, precipitated by the Thai baht's devaluation, dramatically showed how interdependent the region's economy had become—with implications for middle-class consumption. The PRC used the opportunity to display regional responsibility by not devaluing the renminbi. The crisis boosted Beijing's confidence in trying to shape the region. Its market power since the late 1990s has already affected the production and consumption related to regional media and culture industries, including the Hong Kong film industry—which, in the 1990s, was losing status as a media capital and had started to rely on the PRC market.[26] China's growth substantially affects the idea of Asian modernities, as its looming presence diminishes the prior attempts to construct East Asia discursively as a geopolitical and economic space comprised centrally of Japan, the tiger economies, and ASEAN countries.[27] In any case, regardless of the vicissitudes of post-financial crisis life, the urban-modern vision of development seems fairly entrenched. The refurbished "new" that development has wrought has become a key—if not *the* key—commonality for the different nation-states with their multicultures.

The increasing export and circulation of culture within the region has become a part of the means of generating a contemporary Asian way of life that, in turn, is inextricably linked to the a lifestyle consumerism that part of the is the US economic system exported through American media products.[28] However, as we might expect, East Asian media and culture industries have adapted the "American way of life" in their cultural productions to the region's cultural pluralism and differing states of development levels in their direct or indirect support of aspirations to First World living standards. But more than adaptation, they also draw upon local or regional ways of life and the region's own history of modern popular-cultural production. "Americanization"—or "cultural globalization" as a synonym for that term—facilitates not only US hegemony but also other cultural-economic transformations. By the 1990s, there was already a history of popular-cultural production that was neither simple nor simplistic imitations of US material.[29]

The creation and circulation of culture and cultural products within the region therefore is tied up, necessarily, with the concerns of both commonalities and differences, past and present. Conceptions of urban-modern Asia serve as a major node for and of the expression of a shared commonality-in-difference. They offer points of transnational connection within the region and a means of generating the circulation and sale of cultural products that can negotiate the zones of national-cultural differences and old political disputes, with this negotiation sometimes foregrounding difference.[30]

Unsurprisingly, the urbanizing-industrializing practices related to the East Asian economic success in the 1980s, resulting in possibilities (and difficulties) of new ways of being-in-the-world, would be enmeshed with 1990s cultural production. The new regional middle classes would be the beneficiaries of such new modes of being.[31] Film and, it might be added, televisual dramas are aesthetic media technologies well suited for the representation and narrativizing of social worlds—here worlds related to a putative regional system. Narrative figurations, Fredric Jameson has contended, have a "structure [that] encourages a soaking up of whatever ideas in the air. . . . [Film as] narrative [text] today conflates ontology with geography and endlessly processes images of the unmappable [world capitalist] system."[32] A needed qualification to Jameson's assertion is that film and the media and culture industries in general from the transforming East Asian economic semiperiphery are concerned not only with the region's relationship to the world system, but also with the region's shifting centers and fractious ethno-cultural, national, and other identities within that system. Thus, if only obliquely, Hong Kong cultural production at the end of the twentieth century must refer to the monumental event of the British colony's "return" to China in 1997, with its implications for the city's ongoing experience of the new, and regional cultural production must also make reference to the newest economic current—the PRC's gradual overtaking of Japan as Asia's largest economy. This does not occur in the timeframe that *A Regional Contemporary* covers, but the PRC comes second behind the United States in GDP terms in 2010, although we should keep in mind that Japan's per capita GDP remained some ten times that of China's in that year.

Andreas Huyssen has previously argued that when we think of commercial culture, we should not assume that corporate goals regarding exchange value completely decimate any use value: "Culture industry, after all, does fulfill public functions; it satisfies and legitimizes cultural needs which are not all per se false or only retroactive; it articulates social contradictions [if only at times] in order to [try to] homogenize them."[33] Modern "'high art' has been amply documented," and that the same documentation and analytical procedures should be applied to popular culture.[34] The multiple processes of popular culture's articulation—certainly in the regional context this chapter is concerned with—occur vis-à-vis the uneven postwar modernization of many lifeworlds, with all the contradictions to be expected, and merit exploration. Devon Powers has acutely discerned that if *popular* is made to denominate "a particular type of consumption practice," and *popularity* the process when culture is put to work to make connection, the "politics [that do] emerge . . . [are] not a[n obvious] function of popularity per se."[35]

To begin with, we must flag that border-crossing popular culture existed before the 1990s. Much of the prior transnational-regional cultural circulation was composed of Chinese-language film, televisual, and music productions in Mandarin-, Cantonese-, and Hokkien-Chinese (or *minnan hua*) from Hong Kong and Taiwan that went out to ethnic Chinese communities in Southeast Asia.[36] Then, in the 1990s, Japanese televisual dramas and J-Pop gained popularity, becoming "a centering force around which regional ways of knowing and affiliating cohere and compete."[37] In retrospect, it was clear by the late 1990s that "mass-cultural Asianism" was part and parcel of changes in the ways Asia was perceived in a larger regional and not only Japanese imaginary.[38] Difference may be a commodity, but it is a commodity form that contributes toward the regional resonance of popular-cultural production. Many of the products circulate primarily within East Asia, although South Korea's culture industries, notably, have made attempts from the mid-2000s to try to get their music stars into the United States.[39]

Singapore already received Japanese TV programs in the 1960s and 1980s, expanding in the 1990s, and Hong Kong, during the 1970s–1980s, took up to 30 percent of Japanese TV programs.[40] The differences between this earlier period and the 1990s is that the later surge of non-Chinese-language products rested on a much broader consumer base than had existed before and, surprisingly, seemed able to break through national-linguistic barriers substantially. There was, first, the Japanese wave in the early 1990s that exceeded an earlier minor wave in the 1980s. The appearance of postwar Japanese capital in Southeast Asia may have raised the awareness of local populations to Japanese culture and ameliorated the negative perceptions of the Japanese engendered by the Pacific War. A lifestyle development that occurred in Singapore, for instance, that may have further paved the way for the increased popular-cultural presence to come was the opening of department stores by Japanese retailers Isetan in 1972 and Yaohan in 1974.[41] Nevertheless, it remains hard to generalize the conditions that assisted the Japanese popular-cultural arrival in a region as diverse as East Asia.[42] The Japanese government itself responded to rather than was directly involved with the Japanese cultural waves. The possibility of promoting popular culture as a form of "soft power" seemed to come about only after the publication of American journalist Douglas McGray's influential 2002 article "Japanese Gross National Cool."[43] From the late 1990s, there was the Korean wave, led initially by film and then by televisual dramas and pop music (K-Pop), as South Korean political and cultural life was liberalized.[44] Chapter 5 will return to the question of circulating popular culture, especially pop music.

Postwar coproductions in East Asian media and film—effectively early inter-Asian or pan-Asian media—also played their roles in the pre-1990s circulation of culture, and go back to the Japanese Daiei Film's and the Hong Kong-based Shaw Brothers' 1955 *Princess Yang Kwei Fei* (*Yōkihi*/*Joeng Gwaifei*), directed by Mizoguchi Kenji, "the first picture to bear the common name of a 'Hong Kong-Japan co-production.'"[45] In the 1950s and 1960s, Hong Kong filmmakers had looked up to Japan for its advanced technical and creative capacities. The Japanese, for instance, then had the only postproduction facility in the region, and there is the often-cited loaning of a Japanese director, Inoue Umetsugu, to the Shaw Brothers in 1965 to help them internationalize in terms of both technology transfer and expanded modes and formats in film genres. Political changes also facilitated later coproduction across formerly taboo national lines.

In 1972, diplomatic relations between China and Japan were normalized, allowing film and media coproductions that could address wartime violence and Cold War disconnection, as seen in the TV drama series *A Son of the Good Earth* (*Daichi no Ko*) in 1995, produced by the national broadcasters Nippon Hōsō Kyōkai (NHK) and China Central Television (CCTV).[46] The year 1995 marked the fiftieth anniversary of the end of the war. The drama featured a war orphan, Isshin Riku, who is left behind in China in the chaos of Japan's Pacific War retreat. A supportive Chinese family takes him in, and he is given the name "Lu Yixin," but he later suffers the privations of the Cultural Revolution. The drama was based on a 1991 novel published by Yamazaki Toyoko, and it was made in celebration of seventy years of broadcasting in Japan. Earlier, in 1992, NHK had broadcast the earlier NHK-CCTV coproduced drama *Back to the Steppes* to commemorate the twentieth years of normalized Japan–China diplomacy. Similar to *A Son of the Good Earth*, the program tells the story of a Japanese orphan left behind in Mongolia.[47] For Stephanie DeBoer, such coproductions crucially served as "areas of negotiated meaning . . . and uneven assemblages concerned with producing a sense of Asian place"—they are reflections on the potential meaning of Asia itself amid the shifting Cold War politico-cultural terrain.[48] Thus, film and media coproductions also engage with the region's simultaneously competing yet cooperating cultural identities and shifting media centers.

Even the combination of circulation, commonality, and difference via a bilingual screenplay is not without precedent. The thematization of difference in Japanese–Hong Kong film is to be found in the 1971 coproduction by Katsu Production Company and Wing Luen (Yonglian) Movie Film Company of Yasuda Kimiyoshi's and Hsu Chen-hung's *Zatōichi Meets the One Armed Swordsman* (*Shin Zatōichi: Yabure! Tōjin-ken/Mangxia dazhan Dubei dao*), which cultural critic Meaghan Morris takes to be "a fine symbolic starting point" for East Asia–based but globally marketed action film.[49] The twenty-second installment of the popular Zatōichi film series has the blind masseur-swordsman Zatōichi (played by Katsu Shintarō) meet the popular hero of the Hong Kong director Chang Cheh's *The One-Armed Swordsman* (*Dubei dao*, 1967), Wang Kong (Jimmy Wang Yu).[50] The Chinese swordsman rescues a young boy from marauding samurais while visiting Japan and becomes an outlaw. Zatōichi sees the mortally wounded father of the boy, whose last wish is that the former take care of his son. There is a deadly showdown between the two because of mutual linguistic incomprehension—despite the fact that both are similarly constructed "good heroes." What is distinctive is not only that the studios took into account the different markets they were aiming at, but also the *way* this occurred, given the historical enmity between the two polities. The film has both Mandarin-Chinese and Japanese, and the ending for the Japanese audience has Wang Kong dying, while the version for Chinese-language markets has Zatōichi dying. National-cultural and linguistic differences—and indeed, racial and nationalistic prejudice—are exploited. To ensure circulation, differentiated unhappy endings are *required* and can be taken as "two different strategies for engaging with the Cold War regional landscape."[51] Even in 1971, circulation, commonality, and difference could "happily" come together.

An instructive understanding of how commonality-in-difference could be deployed by the late 1990s to about the mid-2000s, when inter-Asian cinematic production starts to decline, can be found by examining select Hong Kong films. While these cinematic experiments came up against a glass ceiling of possibilities, it remains important to understand the strategies adopted to breach literal and cultural borders and, in chapter 5, to see how the imagined audience does apparently surge into existence. The heyday of Hong Kong cinema had been the 1980s–1990s, and the late 1990s saw it in difficult times, with pressure on it to rethink what a regional market meant in terms of creative productions. The Asian economic crisis of 1997 heavily weakened the Southeast Asian markets that Hong Kong cinema had relied on to consume its products.[52] The countries that are especially important are Singapore, Malaysia, Indonesia, the Philippines, and Vietnam, where there is the presence of ethnic Chinese citizens. With the understanding that the Hong Kong market and its previous markets may now be unable to sustain its cinema in a time of crisis, new strategies had to be found to reinvent Hong Kong film. The incorporation of Japanese popular culture—significant in Hong Kong and in much of the region, as already noted—had started earlier in the 1990s with the use of Japanese motifs and stars in televisual and film production. Other distinct developments in Hong Kong inter-Asian cinema become noticeable: by the late 1990s, Hong Kong cinema had cross-border casting, with mainland Chinese and Korean actors, and was paying more attention to new markets, including China.

What resulted has been described as "a strange cosmopolitan fantasy" with "pan-Asian" casting, as seen in director Benny Chan's *Gen-X Cops* (*Te jing xin ren lei*, 1999), a fluffy but well-choreographed action thriller with renegade young male cops with "attitude" dealing with a vicious punk and a Japanese arms dealer. In such films, the "multicultural ensembles . . . flawlessly switch from Cantonese to English or Japanese as they jet around the region."[53] Other films in the same "cosmopolitan fantasy" action mode include *Purple Storm* (*Chi yue feng bou*, 1999) and *2000AD* (*Gong yuan 2000AD*, 2000). The latter film was co-produced by Hong Kong's Media Asia Films and People's Production Limited, and Singapore's MediaCorp Raintree Pictures. It was shot on location in both cities, and while it was not as financially successful as expected, it is also another urban-oriented, regional coproduction strategy. While we have seen some precedent for bilingual inter-Asian film, monolingual film had remained the norm in Hong Kong. The use of multilingualism to bridge regional differences was striking, as the subtitling required was more associated with arthouse cinema.[54] If linguistic and ethno-national differences pose continual challenges to mass circulation, a shared aspirational desire for a common urban-modern lifestyle offered a newer means by which to narrativize and spatially express the commonality-in-difference of the New Asia, assisted, when necessary, by a multilingual cosmopolitanism.[55] Tokyo and Hong Kong become the noteworthy urban exemplifications of contemporary Asia, as they arguably are among the two most instantly recognizable of regional cities.

The dramatic difference between the 1990s and 2000s representation of a cosmopolitan urban Asia and that of a not-so-distant past becomes apparent when we consider a famous Western image from seventy years ago: the charmingly decrepit Hong Kong as captured in Ray Stark's production of Richard Quine's *The World of Suzie Wong* (1960), which premiered in Hong Kong in March 1961. While the film is a sort of a travelogue with an accompanying "exotic" melodrama, the bar girls in the film are sympathetically represented as dignified beings, although, in the end, Suzie (Nancy Kwan) needs the Great American Hero Robert Lomax (William Holden) to save her. The quality of the depiction of Hong Kong street life—Central's banking district, the markets of Yaumatei and Wan Chai, Wan Chai's waterfront, Wan Chai's bars with American soldiers—is crucial to the film's appeal.[56] But the uncertain 1950s transit port city has been replaced by a financial center, Wan Chai's waterfront is now composed of tall buildings, and Fenwick Harbour has become reclaimed land, with the Hong Kong Academy of Performing Arts "sitting" on top of it. An exotic, down-at-heel urban modernity has been supplanted by a less-exotic modernity. While, of course, oriented toward the West, such urban images were important to the region at large, if nothing else then as now retrograde images that need to be eradicated via developmental agendas.

When we jump to the 1990s, we have regional popular-cultural products emphasizing lustrous urban lifestyles that offered a progressive environment of personal freedom. That was depicted in Japanese TV dramas, which increased in sophistication from the early 1990s. Fuji TV's *Tokyo Love Story* (*Tōkyō Rabusutōrī*, 1991) was the drama that helped lead the revivified Japanese cultural wave in televisual programs in the 1990s. Its heroine was presented as unhesitating in her choice of the man she wanted, even if she does not win him in the end from his more socially acceptable former high-school classmate. On display was an emancipated attitude that contrasted with Suzie Wong's dependent attitude. It was a surprise hit in Taiwan, Hong Kong, and also, in 1997, China, translated as *Dongjing ai qing gushi*.[57] Tokyo itself, as the foremost East Asian metropolis, seemed a key part of the serial's popularity.[58] The city could be and was depicted as a glistening center that potentially can spread liberal attitudes through its media industry products.

The increased speed of life in regional cities can either indicate the open horizons of the "new" or unsettle though. They are part of the continuum of shared images of everyday life as generated and circulated by East Asian media and culture industries. The image of Hong Kong entrenched in *auteur*-director Wong Kar-wai's iconic arthouse film *Chungking Express* (*Chongqing senlin*, 1994) offers us the more fragmented and therefore complementary urban counterpart to Tokyo's gloss. Wong's film revolves around two parallel stories of cops (played by Kaneshiro Takeshi and Tony Leung Chiu Wai) and their attempts to find love. Kaneshiro himself, as a leading man in film and television productions in Taiwan, Hong Kong, Japan, and China, embodies transregional elements. Of Japanese-Taiwanese parentage, he speaks English, Mandarin-Chinese, Cantonese, Taiwanese-Hokkien, and Japanese.[59] The protagonists live alone in small rental flats. They do not interconnect yet occupy the same urban spaces; both experience unrequited love. Time is important to both cops, but time slips by, offering the feeling that Hong Kong is too fast paced. The city becomes a blur, and "space becomes ambiguous, things and objects around the foreground and background merge and blend with each other."[60] The locations—a déclassé and culturally diverse Kowloon district, a snack shop in the Central District with its unique escalator climbing up the crowded slopes to Mid-Levels Hong Kong Island—become urban characters in their own right. A notable building in the film is the Chungking Mansions, located at 36–44 Nathan Road in Tsim Sha Tsui. It famously draws in South Asians, Middle Easterners, and Nigerians to its vicinity.[61]

Chungking Express is a compelling component part of a larger urban-oriented cultural production. A curator in the 2002 multicity set of Asian visual art exhibitions *Under Construction*, discussed in chapter 1, holds up Wong's film as a paramount example of a ragged commonality and creativity for more than Hong Kong's denizens: "The movie captured everyday life in a contemporary Asia, conveying the atmosphere of its speed. . . . [Wong] turns his gaze . . . to sights from everyday life where elements of culture from domestic and foreign are all mixed up. . . . The gaze of new-generation artists onto their everyday lives overlaps with that revealed in the movie . . . which . . . is inspired by urban daily life."[62] This is the perhaps clichéd rhetoric of the global postmodern: a rush of images signifying the transnational, cultural hybridity, and social fractures. Nevertheless, to say this without qualification is to dismiss the signifying capacity of the commonality-in-difference of the East Asian urban-modern.

Hong Kong cinema, in its attempts to reinvent itself in the 1990s and early 2000s, and some regional cinematic coproductions offer mixed depictions of the urban-modern as a transgressed borderscape of global and regional processes of transition that are as much cultural and social, or even political. How borders are actually rendered matter, as Étienne Balibar cautions us: "The theorist who attempts to define what a border is in danger of going round in circles, as the very representation of the border is the precondition of any definition."[63] And what we see represented is the contemporary juxtaposition of the newest of the new against versions of the "old" new that still dog the present.

The Double-Edged Affectability of Memory in Networked Tokyo

Lee Chi-Ngai's romantic crime thriller *Sleepless Town*, released in 1998, and Jingle Ma's lighthearted detective thriller *Tokyo Raiders*, released in 2000, offer indicative and instructive insights into how the regional affectability of memory associated with imperial/colonial and Cold War pasts becomes a double-edged dynamic in the transnational/cosmopolitan but yet not quite representation of metropolitan-urban Asia, here Tokyo. *Sleepless Town* is more tangentially interested in globalized development—chiefly in suggesting how existing Chinese crime networks may take on a more intense form of criminal globalization—and remains more emotionally invested in an older colonial-era modernity that includes Japan's empire and its invasion of China. This earlier formation of the modern leads to internal sociocultural and racialized/racist borders within Tokyo that are hard to cross. *Tokyo Raiders*, in contrast, redirects but also palliates over older interconnections for the more contemporaneous and apparently less fraught cross-border flows of capital and culture at the century's end. The networked city is enacted in both films, but with clear emphases on different sections of Tokyo, with *Tokyo Raiders* appearing to be fascinated with the (oftentimes literally) brighter and also newer components of the built environment, versus the night-time half-world of *Sleepless Town*, and those who cannot sleep well within it.

Both films feature cross-border casting and multilingual screenplays. *Sleepless Town* has actors from Hong Kong, Japan, and Taiwan, with the multilingual Kaneshiro Takeshi as the young, biracial Japanese-Taiwanese narrator/protagonist Ryū Kenichi/Liu Jianyi who makes a living trafficking in stolen goods. He is a member of a Taiwanese gang headed by his father,

Yang Weimin (Lung Sihung). Despite his lineage, Kenichi is a small-time player caught within a larger gangland game. The action largely takes place in Kabukichō, the (in)famous red-light entertainment district in Tokyo's Shinjuku ward filled with host and hostess clubs, love hotels, and bars—the film's "sleepless town." The plot is truly rife with the required double and triple crosses, creating a protracted, baroque, and confusing narrative that led to the criticism that while the film is beautifully shot, it remained a standard crime thriller.[64]

In terms of the film's urbanscape, it is said that the Japanese funding of the film led to Hong Kong director Lee's imaging of Kabukichō as virtually a cliché of decayed "Asian" urban environs: "Hong Kong was remapped onto an imagined and exoticized section of Shinjuku with the same orientalist lens through which Ridley Scott saw Japan in [in his 1982 film] *Blade Runner*."[65] However, it has also been argued that the ensuing Orientalism for "advanced" Asians has a twofold result: Kabukichō may become a fantasy of Asia for the Japanese, but it is also effectively deterritorialized and reinvented into a new-style "exotic spot" for both Japanese and Hong Kong audiences, "only a stop in a borderless world where the exiled, the marginal, or the diasporic drift and wander along."[66] The film commences with a spectacular tracking shot of some four minutes of Kenichi walking through Kabukichō's streets, going through a brothel, encountering Japanese acquaintances and culturally diverse South Asian and black people. As film critic Shelly Kraicer writes in his review, "Following our first view of him, in the prologue, scorned and feared as an outsider by Tokyo cops, the [tracking] shot refutes it and substitutes the continuous image of his character knitted into the fabric of an integrated community."[67] Kabukichō is a demi-monde composed of those some would call the Chinese mafia (*Chūgoku mafuia*) with affiliations to Taiwan, Beijing, Shanghai, and Fujian, all part of the film's play with dual natures, problematic parentage, and blended origins that are a part of Japan. This twofold depiction of a reinvented exotic Kabukichō—with its gangland habitués amid its nighttime and neon-lit garishness—and plot specificities to do with war history that are central to the labyrinthine storyline together warrant attention so as to recognize the trauma lodged at the film's heart that makes *Sleepless Town* more than a standard thriller, despite the presence of a number of clichés.

The plot concerns Kenichi's former partner and friend, Wu Fu-chun/Sakamoto Tomio (Shiina Kippei), who has killed the right-hand man of the Shanghainese gang leader, Yuan Chenggui (Hong Konger Eric Tsang), and has now returned to Tokyo from Nagoya. Yuan goes after Kenichi and gives him three days to draw Fu-chun in—up to the symbolic Chinese New Year's Eve for a new start, and the period the film covers—or else he becomes the scapegoat. Kenichi then comes up against the femme fatale, Satō Natsumi, aka Xiao Lian or "little" Lian (Yamamoto Mirai). Both of them become yoked romantically and by a deeply shared understanding of marginality, even as we learn that she is Fu-chun's woman. In keeping with the theme of cross-border identities, the names in the film move back and forth from Japanese to Chinese forms.

Kenichi's brother, Tien Wen, a restaurant owner, pleads with him to give up the gang business. Both their father and Cui Hu, the violent-tempered boss of the Beijing faction, he says, are living in the past, still too local in their outlooks on crime. "Everyone's going global," Tien Wen says, as the Yokohama gang and Fujian gang linked with Ikebukuro, another Tokyo district, are smuggling drugs, weapons, and girls into Japan on a large scale. However, he knows that their father is trying to upscale their Taiwanese group's activities. This is the tangential appearance of the global-regional in *Sleepless Town*. Predictably, Tien Wen is almost misogynistically emphatic that Kenichi stay away from the woman, fearing the worst.

We get to learn that Fu-chun is the son of a Japanese wartime orphan whose family returned from Jilin in China in 1984. He grew up in Chiba, east of Tokyo, and was picked on by the local born. Fu-chun started a gang called—as might be expected, given the local rejection of his Sinicized Japanese identity—the Dragons. Yuan Chenggui's murdered right-hand man had taught his youth gang how to fight. And now, Fu-chun is in Tokyo both to do Yuan in and to locate Xiao Lian. Kenichi has commissioned an investigation on her and proceeds to confront Xiao Lian with what he learns: she is actually Wu Fu-lian, Fu-chun's sister, and possibly even more lethal than him. She had been in a youth gang that abused her, and she subsequently maneuvered her older brother into killing three gang members, and he ends up in prison. Xiao Lian tearfully responds with information that intensifies the incest component. Her younger brother Fu-chun, after the murders, had raped her. She escaped to Nagoya, but he traced her, and she then fled to Tokyo. The historical trauma at the film's heart, along with the consequences of dysfunction that follow, are now revealed. The siblings are violently disruptive and peripatetic figures who, because of personal histories caught up in the region's politics, end up in Kabukichō looking for some resolution.

As *Sleepless Town* moves toward its denouement, Xiao Lian's deep skills in manipulation are further revealed: Fu-chun and she had stolen six hundred million yen from the Yokohama group, and she is after the money. To save himself in the final violent denouement, Kenichi has to kill her, shooting her while holding her within his arms on a small wharf by Tokyo Bay. Then, snow flurries appear, and all is covered by snow, recalling Xiao Lian's wish for snow in their earlier romantic idyll at a mountain hot springs. When Kenichi had first met her, he had quizzically asked, "War orphan's daughter?" Naturally catching the innuendo, her rejoinder is, "So what?" Kenichi is from Taiwan—which had, of course, been a Japanese colony from 1895 to 1945. They are joint members of a mixed world of ethnic outsiders associated with still-unresolved inter-Asia histories in which varieties of Chineseness are not foreign either to or in Japan.

In the closing sequences, we learn that it is Yang Weimin who has been the ultimate manipulator par excellence, aiming all along to dominate every Chinese gang. Tien Wen was wrong: their father *had* worked out a contemporary business objective. The film concludes with Kenichi seeing his car magically fill with symbolic snow as he exits it for a glass-fronted office tower, a structure that is in stark contrast to Kabukichō's lower-rise profile and less salubrious urban environs that opened the film. He is poised to kill his father, but the vision of snowflakes makes him smile as he steps out. The present manifests shards of the past but also somewhat uncomfortably looks to a coming future.

Sleepless Town is inseparable from and resonates with 1990s media productions that reflected on ethnonational tensions in the China–Japan relationship. We can recall the NHK-CCTV coproduction of the TV drama *A Son of the Good Earth* that had been made only a few years earlier in 1995, which, while not dealing with war orphans, did examine the larger wartime trauma for abandoned young Japanese. The pronounced multilingualism in a noir setting was not without local Japanese precedent. For example, director Miike Takashi had released his first film made for release in cinemas (as opposed to the direct-to-video market) in 1995, *Shinjuku Triad Society* (*Shinjuku kuroshakai: Chaina mafia sensō*, or "Shinjuku underworld: Chinese mafia war"), which used Japanese, Mandarin-Chinese, and Taiwanese-Hokkien.[68] Miike's film featured a conflict between a Sino-Japanese detective, Kiriya (Shiina Kippei, who plays Fu-chun in *Sleepless Town*), and Wang, the homosexual Taiwanese head of the Dragon's

Claw Triad—we witness again the theme of cultural identity–related alienation from Japanese society but enhanced with a gender dimension. The productions, of course, were engaging with a larger sociopolitical context. In 2000, for instance, Tokyo's governor, Ishihara Shintarō, famously pronounced that Japan's supposedly declining public-safety levels could be blamed on "violent crimes by *sangokujin*," a pejorative wartime expression for mainland Chinese, Korean, and Taiwanese nationals.[69] What separates *Sleepless Town* from the productions and national context above is the more recently conceived New Asia audience being targeted for this coproduced film expressing shared commonalities-in-difference—despite and perhaps *because* of the marked presence and critique of Japanese ethnonational elements.

When we come to Jingle Ma's *Tokyo Raiders*, we get a notable example of the urbanized "cosmopolitan fantasy" strain in inter-Asian Hong Kong cinema, with cross-border casting featuring, from Hong Kong, Tony Leung Chiu Wai, Ekin Cheng, and Kelly Chen and, from Japan, leading man Nakamura Toru, supported by Abe Hiroshi. Ma was a successful cinematographer who became a director with his first film in 1998, the futuristic action thriller *Hot War* (*Huanying tegong*, or "phantom strike"). *Tokyo Raiders*, for which he was both director and cinematographer, was Hong Kong's top-grossing film in 2000.[70] Showcasing New Asia and thinking of an expanded regional market for this film requires bilingual cultural production in which Japanese and Cantonese are used, along with the passing use of Mandarin-Chinese and English. *Tokyo Raiders* is a sparkling and humorous spy thriller spoof and pastiche in which surface, style, and verbal repartee are everything in its gleaming and urbane depiction of an East Asian urban-modern—the built environment on display is akin to the fancy tower block and plaza space at the end of *Sleepless Town* but featured in the daytime. No angst-causing historical fragments or depth are allowed. No red-light districts appear. And yet uncomfortable matters are raised, if momentarily, and ignored.

Tokyo Raiders draws upon James Bond 007 as an intertext, in the line of other related Hong Kong action film since the 1960s.[71] It is worth noting that the early Hong Kong Bond look-alikes were directed by Japanese contract directors who were themselves using Japanese film models that utilized the Bond motif.[72] *Tokyo Raiders* draws inspiration not only from Anglo-American popular culture but references its own inter-Asian popular-cultural history in its public show of a Tokyo that is a part of the region.

Contemporary Tokyo—evoked with its most sleek built environment on display and as a world city with recognizable urban architectural icons—becomes one of the film's stars in this upbeat depiction of commonality-in-difference. The storyline, while less intractably complicated than *Sleepless Town*, is a little knotted. However, humor, clever fight-and-chase sequences (including one on motorized skateboards), and Ma's light directorial touch propel *Tokyo Raiders* along. There are also plot twists that gesture to a new orientation toward (supposed) common regional interests, even if we are not to take the plot too seriously, as well as a leading man who turns out to be biracial and bicultural—a Sino-Japanese character who can represent both Hong Kong's and Japan's interests in a neutral fashion, without any wartime history getting in the way. Plot detail is important, for we see that putting forth the happy-clappy face of New Asia requires a suppression of older dissensions.

The heroine, Macy (Chen), multilingual in Japanese, Cantonese, Mandarin, and English, is left at the altar in Las Vegas by her Japanese fiancé Takahashi Yūji (Nakamura), who heads a US investment firm in Tokyo. The United States–West is rapidly left behind as she returns to Hong Kong to look for him. There, she learns he has gone to Tokyo and meets an interior designer, Yung (Cheng), who just happens to be a martial-arts expert, and to whom her boyfriend owes a large sum of money. Yung trails her to Tokyo, and they link up with an impossibly cool private investigator, the transplanted Hong Konger Lam Kwai-yan (played with droll panache by Leung, with many spy gadgets), and his team of four *Charlie's Angels*-type assistants. A Japanese *yakuza* boss, Itō Takeshi (Abe), leader of the Kobe gang, is after Takahashi, as he has run off with his woman.

The plot's major twists unfold for us: first, that Takahashi is a CIA agent tasked to flood Japan with counterfeit yen when he became distracted with the gangster boss's woman; second, that Lam is really an officer of Sino-Japanese descent in the internal division of the Japanese ministry of defense, gone undercover to foil the dastardly American plot; and, finally, that Yung is a private bodyguard sent by Macy's rich banker father to protect her—her father had objected to Macy's liaison with a Japanese man. The implicit interethnic discomfiture is rapidly buried, becoming a suppressed moment of ethno-national difference. Unlike *Sleepless Town*, all can be resolved in the end, after a speedboat chase sequence in Tokyo Bay and the waterways of the Sumida River, the film's major set piece.

What is noteworthy is the way "cool" is evoked—clever dialogue and slick action sequences aside—via urban images from the start in *Tokyo Raiders*. The opening sequence is representative. We first get a bird's-eye view of Tokyo and are shown the iconic Tokyo Tower in Shiba Park, with its white and international orange air-safety colors, taller than the Eiffel Tower and built in 1958 to symbolize Tokyo's postwar rebirth. Then, we see the Sumida River, and the camera proceeds to zoom in on the commercial, urban-transit, and public-administrative hub that is Shinjuku, a special ward of the city. The towers of west Shinjuku, with the metal-clad new Tokyo City Hall complex, designed by the late modernist architect Tange Kenzo (1913–2005), stand out. The camera then settles down near the south entrance of Shinjuku station, where we see the suited office crowds and young women wearing the youth fashions that emerged from the mid-1990s—platform boots (particularly highlighted) and designer accessories—that exerted so much influence over the young in the region. The density of Tokyo's street life becomes apparent. There is no need to "explain" the architectural icons or the city's fashionableness and Shinjuku's stylishness—although the camera does momentarily rest on a stainless-steel sign in *kanji* (Chinese characters) that proclaims "Shinjuku"—any more than it is necessary to "explain" London's West End.

After the initial swoop, the camera moves to a Shinjuku back lane, where Lam—with stylish and stylishly camp moves—fights off villains sent by the *yakuza* with an umbrella, assorted gadgets, and martial-arts skills, to the accompaniment of spirited Latin music—presumably signifying "sophistication"—by Hong Kong composer Peter Kam. We have combined here the extended starting action sequence of every Bond film combined with the American Western. This approach signals the director's self-reflexive, wink-wink-nod-nod stance throughout the film. Although *Tokyo Raiders* is lightweight, Ma, using his honed skills as a cinematographer, delivers a high-gloss visual style that captures Tokyo's daytime sheen with a lifestyle magazine's precision. This multilingual thriller implies and thus helps reinforce the idea of a shared, urban "us-ness" for Hong Kong and Japan, a world far removed from Suzie Wong's exotic Oriental urbanism—and even from the neon-lit and reworked contemporary or neo-exotic section of Shinjuku that Kenichi is immersed in.

The lead characters are comfortable members of this cosmopolitan world. Macy's fluency in Japanese and clear comfort with Tokyo makes her "a Hong Kong character well and truly at home in the world. The worldliness of her world is enhanced with a Japanese setting and characters."[73] Lam's sophisticated biculturalism is literalized, and he is made to be *miscegenated*, biracial. This allows him to be in an easy position to be a sociopolitical and cultural interstitial, occupying an embodied third space between the Hong Kong Special Administrative Region (SAR) that is now a part of the PRC—no longer a British colony—and Japan, *even while* he is an agent of the Japanese government. Any discomfort with Lam's position between and betwixt the two core states of East Asia is papered over by the plot that makes the United States the ultimate villain in the story: for some unexplained reason, it wants to damage its most important East Asian ally through weakening its currency. While we should not take the film's gestures too seriously, it is nevertheless suggestive that a Sino-Japanese Asia can even be imaginatively constructed in the first place to share a commonality that places it at odds with the US hegemon. Commonality trumps differences, and regional blemishes are powdered over in the positive face of urban-modern Asia.

Texts, whether filmic or literary, are capable of carrying varied and even contradictory significations, as *Sleepless Town* and *Tokyo Raiders* attest. Film is "a cultural form [that is] permeated at every level by the practices and paradoxes of marketing—a postmodern practice that oscillates between the passive reproduction and the active remodelling of audiences."[74] *Sleepless Town* embodies a more passive reproduction of audience expectations of a fractured modernity, while in *Tokyo Raiders*, culture acts out its own commodification in an attempt to have a post-national product that may be able to breach national and linguistic boundaries for the new middle classes "out there," waiting to be reached. *Fulltime Killer*'s more experimental artistic nature, we will see, works to allow the contradictory to move out more firmly into the transnational-regional foreground.

Competitive Border Crossings

Fulltime Killer directly exhibits older regional differences reconstituted into an allegory of the two core East Asian states competing not only in the cosmopolitan Asian city—here, Hong Kong—but also in other Northeast and Southeast Asian territories where there may be new middle-class audiences for putative inter-Asian film. As with the earlier attempts at inter-Asian media production, the acknowledgment and thematization of ethnonational and racial difference, rather than the direct resolution of whether the Japanese or the mainland Chinese killer is the best, may be enough to assist regional identification and thus also product circulation. Hong Kong *auteur*-director Johnnie To and co-director's Wai Ka-fai's *Fulltime Killer* offers a more reflexive and multitiered cultural reflection than both *Sleepless Town* and *Tokyo Raiders* on the ideological and historical tensions between national-cultural identities and languages and of the challenges of the "active remodelling" of an East Asian audience.

Johnnie To is a versatile filmmaker who has directed comedies, action movies, and crime movies. Despite the different genres, To's themes often focus on friendship and the changes in Hong Kong society. *Fulltime Killer* is consistent with the second of the themes, relating as it does to the return of Hong Kong to the mainland in 1997. He has reflected directly on the difficulty on envisioning what an "Asian" film at the start of the millennium for the region's new middle-class audiences may look like:

> Suppose we think of this movie [*Fulltime Killer*] as an "Asian" movie. . . . For international audiences, the language of the dialogue—whether it is Chinese, Japanese, or Korean—doesn't really matter. Hong Kong audiences may experience something new by having to pay close attention to subtitles when watching a Hong Kong film, but for Westerners, they probably won't notice a difference. If there's a Hong Kong movie that can be called an "Asian movie," I think something has changed then in Hong Kong cinema. . . . Of course I do hope it can be accepted by audiences in Asia, but it's not easy.[75]

Linguistic differences are real, and he wonders if the viewing practices of a cosmopolitan, if mainly Western, arthouse audience can be re-created among the mainstream of East Asian moviegoers less used to reading subtitles. Can the representation of linguistic-cultural differences be overcome in the representation of East Asia? To try to achieve this would then result in the exceeding of Hong Kong film's achievement thus far and gesture to a way forward for Hong Kong cinema amid market challenges.

Fulltime Killer—a deconstructivist, anti-"killer" genre film and psychodrama that obliquely critiques the John Woo/Ringo Lam-type gangster film genre of the 1980s—features, first, an emotionally inward-looking and deliberately unnamed monolingual Japanese hitman, known only as "O" (Sorimachi Takashi); second, his mainland-Chinese competitor, Tok (Andy Lau), a self-dramatizing and showy cinephile who wants to exceed O's reputation and to become a legend in his own time; and third, a Mandarin-, Japanese-, Cantonese-, and English-speaking Taiwanese woman—a character from a nationally uncertain "Chinese" area—working in a Japanese video rental, Chin (Kelly Lin), who also cleans O's flat. She is confused, personally and culturally, and seems to be looking for adventure and self-fulfillment that the two rivals can offer her. As with *Sleepless Town* and *Tokyo Raiders*, plot details matter.

The film is one of To's more stylistically experimental films, and he himself has said, "It's not a movie that a lot of people will like."[76] The psychological accounts offered of the two professional killers are somewhat opaque in the film's narrative: it is not clear why O lives in Hong Kong or why he is a loner, and while we are shown Tok's failure as an Olympic athlete, it is not clear why this failure should lead him to professional killing as a form of alternative achievement. These opacities and mangled subjectivities combined become an *excess* in the film that generates the allegory of the two core East Asian states competing. The battles take place mainly in Hong Kong SAR, the regional stage on which diverse East Asians can meet. Hong Kong's ambiguous national status as a "mainland-Chinese" city uncomfortable in being such makes it a suitable stage for the action. The film also functions largely in Japanese and then English, but it also features Cantonese and Mandarin; subtitles abound in this Hong Kong-"Chinese" film attempting to become an "Asian movie."[77]

Tok (real name Lok Tak-wah) was a failed shooting participant in the 1992 Olympic Games. He is epileptic, and his fits undermined his attempts to be the first mainland Chinese to take a gold medal in the event and even his lovemaking attempts with Chin. Tok's older brother had a similar problem in the 1984 Olympics—there seems to be a lot to prove in the competition. There is also an English-speaking Interpol cop from Singapore, Albert Lee (Simon Yam), who, obsessed by the titanic clash, cathartically turns to writing about the pair.

O only slowly realizes the challenge Tok poses. The latter knows that Chin works for O, and courts her to get in touch with O. A huge debacle for O occurs in Macau, where Tok undermines O's assassination assignment, and Chin and O end up on the run from both the police and mobsters. Toward the film's end, Chin meets now ex-Inspector Lee in a café: he has become so dysfunctional that he has fallen out of police service. Chin recounts to him a fatal showdown between the two professionals in a warehouse with hidden weapons, and says that Tok had finished off O. As she leaves, the penny drops, and he dashes out to see Chin leaving in a Mercedes with O: he understands that O has retired as the reigning killer for love and private life and has given the arriviste Chinese killer the legendary status he wants. Indeed, the pair obtained what they wanted: O a way out of the profession, and Tok legendary status. In reality, though, the fireworks that had been set off accidentally in the warehouse had also set off another of Tok's epileptic fits. Lee decides that he will entrench the version that Chin had offered him.

A violent cartographic imaginary of the New Asia is immediately put on show in the film. *Fulltime Killer* begins by literalizing the flow of competitive difference. While the film is set primarily in Hong Kong, the first ten minutes rush into stunning overkill. There are bravura set pieces of killings by the two: first, O doing the necessary in the train station in Kuala Lumpur, Malaysia; then, Tok in a police station near the River Kwai, Thailand, in a typically showy manner, riding a bike, using a shotgun hidden under a bouquet of flowers and hand grenades.[78] The contrasting styles provide the understanding we are to have of them. A confrontation follows between Tok and Fat Ice, the crime boss who hired him, in Harry's Bar at Boat Quay, Singapore. Finally, O meets with his agent in Busan, South Korea. This mapping of Eastern Asia has Southeast Asia as a subsidiary realm to Northeast Asia, a mapping apropos for the post-1997 Asian financial crisis Eastern Asia, during which the region's economic center has moved to Northeast Asia and to the PRC in particular. The Southeast Asian-Singaporean Lee is thus a suitable scribe for the Northeast Asians' fight for dominance. From the start, it is difficult *not* to read the film allegorically as being about the heterogeneousness of intra-regional competition for hegemony in New-World-(Dis)Order(ed) Asia. O's and Tok's competition for the culturally confused Taiwanese Chin, with her unsettled linguistic and national identity (given Taiwan's troubled relationship with the PRC), becomes a synecdoche of the larger issues of ego and shifting regional centers of power the film investigates.

To's film, in the first instance, though, draws upon themes investigated in previous films that Wai Ka-fai and he had made for their Milkyway Image film company, which started in 1996. The downturn in Hong Kong filmmaking in the 1990s led Milkyway both to follow and to challenge Hong Kong cinema's masculine tradition, although these films "end up choosing to reproduce [the tradition] instead of creating new male subjects."[79] In these earlier films, the male characters are often insecure and fearful, with hesitant relationships between the men; they also lack the confidence to master the opposite sex. The new development in *Fulltime Killer* lies in the choice for love made by O, and the change shifts *Fulltime Killer* from anti-killer genre movie to inter-Asia allegory. This becomes apparent after O discovers he has been set up by his "Korean" handler—really Tok's brother, Lok Gan-wah. O goes to Busan to confront him and shoots Lok's right hand rather than killing him. Lok says that he had nearly become number 1 in pistol shooting in his 1984 Olympic bid, but—and here there is plot confusion—in the end, O (who has not participated in any Olympic Games) beat both brothers. The scene's overdetermination suggests a displacement from psychological loss to questions of national identity and pride, even if the film never offers a direct explanation of why this displacement takes place.

There is intentionality at play in the film's disjunctures and representation of ruptured regional identities. The main characters have been changed from the original Chinese-language novel, *Full Time Hitman* (1999) by Edmond Pang, upon which the film is based. In the novel, O is a Chinese assassin, and Tok is Eurasian.[80] The change in ethnic composition is suggestive. But *Fulltime Killer* is more than an adaptation of Pang's novel. The presence of many filmic intertexts manifest a self-reflexive craftsmanship at work, and the presence of two Japanese intertexts—one a film, the other a comic—reveals the film to be a careful exploration of contemporary regional tensions that appropriately uses the region's own modern artistic-cultural resources.[81] The vital intertexts embed regional ethno-national difference at the film's heart.

The first intertext is maverick Japanese director Suzuki Seijun's absurdist and self-mocking *yakuza* thriller *Branded to Kill* (*Koroshi no rakuin*, 1967), now a cult classic. A third-ranked hitman, Hanada Goro (Shishido Jō), with a fetish for boiling rice, fumbles one of his jobs and has the legendary but nameless Number One Killer (Nanbara Kōji) sent as retribution for this mistake. The egotistic Number One toys with Hanada but ends up being shot by him in a boxing arena and dies—but not before returning the favor. As Number Three himself dies, he mutters that he is a champion and instinctively but accidentally shoots the woman he loves when she enters the arena. To adapts the *yakuza* urban myth, transforming the Hanada character who has learned to love into the Number One O, who then forsakes the top ranking for love, although not for death. The lower-ranked Chinese Tok, much more than Hanada Goro as Number Three, becomes the aspirant who gains the top rank and becomes a legend—but a dead legend. To's transformations are almost moralistic in its condemnation of self-seeking glorification.

The second Japanese intertext is even more vital and is disclosed via a Hollywood reference. Tok had been visiting Chin at the video shop wearing a Bill Clinton mask, in a reprise of a scene from Kathryn Bigelow's *Point Break* (1991). At a café where Chin meets O monthly, Tok reveals his face and addresses her in Cantonese. Thus far, he deliberately has only spoken in Japanese. He tells her that he is Chinese and wants to kill a Japanese assassin—possibly trying to draw sympathy for his cause based on ethnic or racial solidarity. Then, he says that she is like Emu in *Crying Freeman*, a quiet girl transformed into a sexy woman after she meets an assassin, presumably referring to himself.

This cryptic one-off reference is to a Japanese manga (or comic), *Crying Freeman* (*Kuraingu Furīman*), written by Koike Kazuo and with artwork by Ikegami Ryōichi, that originally appeared in *Weekly Big Comic Spirits* between 1986 and 1988.[82] *Fulltime Killer*'s intertextuality encompasses non-filmic East Asian texts, indicating that even the genre boundaries of different regional cultural texts are porous. The comic series was about an assassin, Hinomura Yō, a Japanese potter. He is kidnapped by the 108 Dragons, a Chinese gang who have him hypnotized and turned him into a killer, sardonically giving him the name Freeman. He remains a sensitive soul and cries after every killing. One murder is witnessed by Hino Emu, a lonely artist. Instead of killing her, Hinomura falls in love and finally marries her. Finally, the heads of the 108 Dragons recognize Hinomura's talent and name him as the heir to take over the organization. New Chinese names are bestowed on Hino and Hinomura, Hu Qing-lan (tiger pure orchid) and Long Tai-yang (dragon sun), respectively. The second name is resonant with the gang's name. The two "become" honorary Chinese in Japan, gaining a central place among the racially marginal in Japanese society, a marginal group that, through violence, has reordered their sociocultural identity.

As with the *Branded to Kill* intertext, *Crying Freeman* is a significant structuring device. O is clearly the sensitive Freeman: at the start of the film, O had mourned the death of his previous cleaner, killed for not divulging information about him. Tok is professional but not sensitive, and he is using Chin. The film also shows him unable to complete the lovemaking act with her, making the fits that occur to him a metaphor for a larger weakness:

overweening ambition, the desire not only to emerge as Number One but also to become apotheosized into a legend.

The exact transposition of the manga story to *Fulltime Killer* is therefore complex. O and Chin are crowned—but they do not and do not *want* to take charge. Although *Crying Freeman* displays stereotyped views of Chinese gangsters in Japan, this is not directly repudiated but instead translated into a larger field of competitive ethno-national differences in which there is some narrative repetition, if inverted, from the manga (a Japanese assassin is accepted the way Freeman is, and the love stories both have fruition), and some deliberate disconnections (the Chinese killer Tok, unlike the Chinese gang, is unable to really take charge through violence). There is no attempt to resolve the problem of difference. The contradictions at the heart of *Fulltime Killer* are acknowledged by the Ancient Mariner figure in the film, ex-inspector Lee. To the arriviste Chinese killer goes the glory and the creation of the triumphant killer legend; the rest will take a quieter life. What are the implications generated for a China rising and its role in contemporary Asia? The memory of past violence and the reframed context of the history of old Sino-Japanese animosities and current intra-regional politico-economic situations muddy up the ending of the film. *Fulltime Killer* as an "Asian movie" persistently displays and then contains the contradictions in the not quite mainland Chinese city of Hong Kong.

Although *East Asia* remains an elusive cultural space, if taken in strict ideational-ideological terms, there has been enough shared or similar economic development that it has become "real" enough to create popular artistic representations to try to cater to "it." If East Asia has changed by working fervently to participate in the "trancelike moods of contemporary consumer culture," as cultural critic Paul Gilroy acutely phrases it, that change is part of the context that some recent inter-Asian media and films take into consideration.[83] What Johnnie To understands to be part of the new are the expanded middle classes who have been the beneficiaries of an urbanizing and contemporary but fragmented Asia: "Only a few years ago, many movies in Hong Kong were, for example, films with a lot of dirty jokes or stories about gangsters. But now Hong Kong has changed very much, and in Asia I think something has changed too. . . . There has been a recent wave of Korean films, all alternative in a way because of their emphasis on a middle class setting. And in Japan, the films show more and more of the middle class, because of the economic changes there. The people have changed, and so movies have to change."[84]

To's remarks and film should lead us to reflect upon not only the relationship of "that most industrialized zone of a former Third World now called the Pacific Rim" to the global or world system, but also the fractured yet interrelated region itself, and especially at the moment when China from the 2000s—and with its 2001 accession into the World Trade Organization (WTO)—can start to assert its centrality in Eastern Asian space. Once, the PRC vigorously resisted the capitalist mode of production. Once, it at least could be argued that "only the [mainland] Chinese way entails the effort to secure the (active) participation of an entire people in a dual process: the creation of wealth and of social life—and the production, in space, of space as a whole."[85] But no more. At the same time, a socialist-capitalist China does not as yet quite have the imaginative popular-cultural capacity to create images of an East Asia that can resonate fully in the region. Government censorship and insufficient investment capital in the first decade of the twenty-first century made it difficult for innovative cultural forms to arise, though, in terms of cinema production, joint and coproductions have offered some relief for the latter difficulty.[86]

China's "return" to Asia reminds us that the ghosts of the earlier rupture caused by a colonial-era capitalist modernity are still with us, enforcing a recognition that "unevenness continues to constitute one of capitalism's principle conditions of reproduction."[87] And this present state of unevenness should lead us to rethink what the "opposition of center and periphery" referred to at the start of this chapter might now mean, given the ongoing valorization of the economic forms that, despite recent economic crises, still reign in the capitalist places of contemporary East Asia.[88]

5 J-POP, K-POP, AND THE PARTIAL NEGOTIATION OF THE NATIONAL

On September 16, 2011, the still-popular Japanese boy band SMAP (Sports, Music Assemble People)—who were born between 1972 and 1977 and debuted in 1988—appeared at the Workers' Stadium in Beijing, their first concert outside Japan, before a crowd of some forty thousand. In the early 1990s, SMAP helped lead a Japanese wave of pop-cultural flows in Northeast and Southeast Asia, including TV dramas and pop music. The most prominent member of the band, arguably, is Kimura Takuya—and he was extensively interviewed by CCTV and other broadcasters such as Phoenix Television (based in Hong Kong) when SMAP went to Beijing.[1]

Mundane enough, given the pop-spectacular world we live in, but astonishingly, the band had been invited in May to perform by none other than the PRC premier Wen Jiabao, after previous attempts by SMAP to appear in China had failed.[2] They had been scheduled to appear in Shanghai in September 2010, but this was canceled by the mainland Chinese organizers because of the political problem of a Chinese trawler detained by the Japanese coast guard, among the most prominent incidents of ongoing internecine clashes between the two major East Asian states over territorial disputes and contentious Japanese history textbooks. The concert's theme—designed to register Japan's thanks to China for assistance rendered after the disastrous March 11, 2011, Japanese earthquake and tsunami—was "Do Your Best Japan, Thank You China, Asia Is One."[3]

The last phrase, one that has echoed through other chapters in *A Regional Contemporary*, was obviously meant to adjure solidarity between Japan and the now-reemergent power of China amid unresolved tensions stretching from before the Second World War to the Cold War. However, it was also provocative in that it was a reference to a much quoted and (in)famous proclamation by art historian Okakura Kakuzō that appeared in his English-language book *Ideals of the East, with Special Reference to the Art of Japan* (1903) that "Asia is one."[4] Apart from the fact that Okakura's thinking on Asia was later co-opted by the Japanese military to justify colonial expansion in Northeast and Southeast Asia, his high-civilizational ideal of Asian oneness, which opposed thought predicated on commercial-industrial instrumentality, becomes transformed with breathtaking if unintended irony into a diplomatic placebo linked to a shared inter-Asian commercial pop culture—a form at odds with Okakura's high-civilizational proclivities. Once again, Okakura signifies, however indirectly, the presence of various crises-driven periods of the modern that inform the present.

This chapter examines the emergence of a regionalizing East Asian pop music as another partial consequence of 1960s American attempts to bring Cold War Asia back to "normality" through the fostering of regional economic exchange, a cultural emergence that eclipsed the possibilities of Hong Kong and Hong Kong coproduced inter-Asian cinematic production investigated in chapter 4. The unexpected spread of Japanese pop culture in Northeast and Southeast Asia in the 1990s and the Korean pop culture that followed in its wake from the late 1990s—both of which, unlike inter-Asian cinema, were ironically *not* aimed at regional audiences in their origins—follow from a progressive and intensified translocal change in cultural subjectivity, even though, like the cinematic productions, these pop-cultural phenomena should not be taken as linked in their entirety with the various Asian developmental states' politico-economic agendas. The images in these pop cultures fall in the category of a glossy urban and bright Asia—not much cultural essentialism or exotic Asia.

Historian Bruce Cumings has stressed the cultural incoherence of post-1960s Asia: "the lingering animosities of colonialism and war, combined with the dominance of American mass culture, tend to override . . . [any supposedly shared] traditional [Confucian] heritage and to make of northeast Asian popular culture a hodgepodge of national constructions united only by American-style pop songs and videos."[5] Cumings, of course, is right about traditional culture and the (still-unresolved) colonial-era fractures that came about with the appearance of the first modern Asian nation-state, Japan, in 1868, and the Second Sino-Japanese War from 1937. The animosities are fixed into place by the American postwar settlement, the "loss" of China in 1949, and the Korean War. Nevertheless, we are arguably witnessing the emergence of a putative contemporary cultural sensibility that not only has long-since absorbed US pop culture but also, particularly, can effectively draw new middle-class youth into the multifaceted consumption of various Asian pop-cultural forms more ready to compete with Anglo-American pop culture. The 1960s economic agenda of fostering regional economic exchange has enabled a cultural spectacle that is comfortable with the predispositions of "globalized" capital and in which we see the strong debordering both of pop music as a medium and of the national-linguistic spaces of pop music and culture. The increased circulation and consumption of a regionalizing inter-Asian pop culture signal how existing national social forms have been transformed by economic exchange relations and interdependency. This pop culture has negotiated—although assuredly not overcome—the seemingly oppositional politics of economic regionalism and of postcolonial, not quite post–Cold War nationalisms.

While there has been recent productive work inspecting a transnational socialist popular of folk and national songs among postwar youth in the 1940s and 1950s, in which the popular is not tied to capitalism, this chapter inquires how we might think through the contradictions of imagining a capitalist New Asia from the 1980s, when tensions with origins ranging from the mid-nineteenth century to the Cold War seem more pronounced than ever in the 2000s.[6] As Wang Hui has perspicaciously noted, the "commonality of Asian imaginaries derives partly from subordinate status under European colonialism, during the Cold War, as well as in the current global order," and that the Cold War nation-state structure "has to a large extent been preserved and even developed new derivative forms under new historical conditions."[7] However, we should register that the "new derivative forms" from "new historical conditions" can be remarkable. While no new ideology congruent with economic integration has genuinely come about, regionalizing (if not quite regional) pop music is a notable component of a now-extensive and expanded inter-Asian popular culture in which cultural production and representation, intertwined as they are with the commitment to economic growth, has engaged with older modernist ideologies and the national borders that resulted in ways that have outpaced the other high and popular cultural phenomena thus far examined.

Security Asia, Economic Asia, and Mass-Consumed Culture

As has been asked of all artistic-cultural production inspected in *A Regional Contemporary*, we now ask if we can speak of an "East Asian pop culture" when it is often said that Asia is so culturally diverse that it does not truly exist.[8] How is this pop culture imagined into contemporary existence? I have consistently argued that it is regional economic development fostered during the Cold War that has created the capacity by which emergent forms of East Asian cultural production have been able to materialize, even as the transitioning Cold War military structure and economic development imperatives have given the region the schizoid makeup of an "Economic Asia" and a "Security Asia," a split identity that indeed has intensified since the Asian financial crisis of 1997–1998. Such is the context to be contemplated in relation to the commercial popular music that this chapter examines—this context is even more firmly a part of the pop-cultural forms than the films in chapter 4 are.

The United States planned for a regional postwar economy driven by a revived Japanese economy with access to markets and raw materials, a goal that complemented its security plan to contain communist expansion by the USSR. However, the "loss" of China to the Communist Party of China in 1949 meant that this hinterland for Japan would have to be Southeast Asia—ironically, given the Pacific War that had recently ended. The mordant fact is that it was the Cold War in the specific manifestation of the Korean War that moved Japan on toward its postwar industrial reemergence, as it benefited from "America's wars to lock in an Asian hinterland for Japan and the 'free world' in Korea and Vietnam."[9]

The 1960s saw stronger regional connections come about: under US pressure, relations between Japan and the Republic of Korea were normalized in 1965, and both Taiwan and South Korea start their export-oriented industrial development, in many cases using obsolescent Japanese technology.[10] As for Southeast Asia, Cumings explains yet another irony regarding Japan and the "rise of Asia" and its 1980s "return" to Asia: "Japan never really developed markets or initiated core-periphery linkages in East and Southeast Asia until the 1960s," when US policy pushed it in that direction—and then more foreign direct investment flowed into Southeast Asia in the 1980s.[11] While Northeast and Southeast Asian economic development in the 1980s and the 1990s was also significantly driven by South Korean, Taiwanese, and so-called overseas Chinese foreign direct investment, Japan was the key country providing the "economic force" in the region since the 1960s. Japan also cautiously (and unsuccessfully) argued by the 1980s for the need to channel resources for industrialization so as to develop an internal market for export, going against the neoliberal dictates of what became known as the "Washington consensus."[12] While Japan has not truly become the regional political leader for reasons to do with its own unresolved nationalistic tendencies and China's increased regional presence after the Asian financial crisis of 1997, more recently, Prime Minister Abe Shinzo (1954–2022) tried to change that status. During his second period in office from 2012 to 2020, for instance, Abe "led the creation of the concept of a 'free and open Indo-Pacific.'"[13]

Despite the changes and developments, "the American cold war military structure still holds down regional security, even as the cold war's abrupt end fades into history."[14] One generally acknowledged result of the US dominance in the postwar settlement is that there were (and are) few multilateral institutions and mechanisms to help settle the nationalistic and increasingly charged disputes in the region. Outstanding issues over access to and control over parts of the South China Sea by Southeast and Northeast Asian claimants (with China making the largest claim), between South Korea and Japan over the Liancourt Rocks in the Sea of Japan (called "Dokdo" by the Koreans and "Takeshima" by the Japanese), and between Japan and China over the Senkaku/Diaoyu islands have come to demand attention.[15] History never seems to go away in these major disputes. For instance, the PRC's more recent claims over the South China Sea are based on their "nine-dash line" map published by the Republican Chinese Ministry of the Interior in 1947: "The map served as the basis for the Declaration on China's Territorial Sea, which was made by the Chinese Government in 1958 and laid territorial claim to a majority of the islands in the South China Sea. Additionally, in 2009 China submitted a diplomatic note to the United Nations Secretary-General, asserting its sovereignty over islands in the South China Sea which was presented with a map of the 'nine-dash line.'" The legality of the supposedly historical nine-dash line map is disputed by all other South China Sea territorial claimants, and "this situation continues in 2014, with China's new map of mid-2014 showing a controversial ten-dash line encompassing the South China Sea and Taiwan."[16] The ten-dash line has since modulated back into nine dashes. ASEAN has tried to take the lead in a neutral fashion to mediate the disputes, but thus far, it has been unsuccessful.

The region is at a point at which "Economic Asia"—"a dynamic, integrated Asia with 53 percent of its trade now being conducted within the region itself, and a US$19 trillion regional economy that has become an engine of global growth" that is increasingly dependent on China and the Chinese market—is in conflict with "Security Asia," which is inclined to be nationalistic and, despite the integrated economies, "tacking hard toward the United States[, which has decreasing trade with the region,] for their security." "Rampant and competing 19th and 20th-century nationalisms," it is contended, "have moved again to the fore as pathologies that seem frozen in time raise the specter of renewed conflict."[17] The Donald Trump administration intensified such tensions, for it increased competition with China, identifying it as a "revisionist power" in late 2017. The result, as one policy paper put it, is that "Southeast Asia has once again become a major arena of Great Power competition."[18]

If a globalized and interconnected world means a world in which there is "the disappearance of History as the fundamental element in which human beings exist, and, not least, the end of an essentially modernist field of political struggle in which the great ideologies still had the force and the great authority of the great religions in recent times," then East Asia functions within an *incomplete contemporary* in which history—one of the "splendors of the modern"—and the great ideology of nationalism have not entirely given way to the blandishments of "the new transnational 'culture-ideology of consumption'" that might be able to conjoin the "different but equally 'present' temporalities or 'times'" in the region.[19] That is to say, the East Asian contemporary is a present in which modernist ideologies are only partially superseded, and as a result, the processes trying to hold together the region's heterogeneity so that the new religion of "growth above all" can be paramount are necessarily tentative.

Nevertheless, the contemporary pop cultures from Japan and Korea that have crossed national, linguistic, and even at least some features of racial boundaries since the 1990s in the region represent what philosopher Peter Osborne describes as a "capitalistic sociality (the grounding of social relations in exchange relations)" that has negotiated the politics of regionalism and nationalism through a combination of global-regional dynamics.[20] Indeed, the (often young) middle class seem to have *desired* the coming together of the different times of the region within the parameters of a common pop-cultural world that manifests if not a multicultural New Asia then at least a more open-minded New Asia possessing multicultures.

As discussed in chapter 4, the inter-Asian flow of popular culture was present before the 1990s, after which it increased by leaps and bounds. In terms of popular music, collaboration between musicians has certainly existed since the 1930s. By the 1920s, Shanghai was known as a center for jazz. The composer Li Jinhui (1899–1967) had the reputation of Sinicizing jazz in that city. The Japanese were also present in Shanghai, and one of the more important cross-cultural encounters involved Hattori Ryōichi (1907–1993), who first went to Shanghai in 1938 and became impressed by Li's work. Hattori "was one of the first Japanese musicians to attempt to translate Japanese and Asian music genres into the jazz vocabulary."[21] His collaborative work continued into the 1960s, when he composed music for Shaw Brothers' musical films, including *King Drummer* (*Qing chun gu wang*, 1967), directed by Japanese director Inoue Umetsugu (1923–2010). That film displayed dueling drummers that alternated between glorious Eastmancolor and a black-and-white TV screen. This portrayal of music, Stephanie DeBoer observes, was to show that Shaw Brothers had become "ever more proximate to the markets potentiated in its achievement of international film standards that were held to be more palatable to a (developed) world."[22] The march to cultural contemporaneity with the advanced West was certainly present there in the 1960s.

Thereafter, much of the pre-1990s transnational-regional cultural circulation was composed of Chinese-language film, televisual, and music productions in Cantonese-, Mandarin-, and Hokkien-Chinese (or *minnan hua*), from Hong Kong and Taiwan, respectively. These circulated primarily to ethnic Chinese communities in Southeast Asia.[23] The Japanese and Korean pop music that arose from the 1990s to a fair extent followed the same routes laid down by various types of Chinese-language pop music in and around the region. According to Chua Beng Huat, "Without the massive and well-established Pop Culture China market and its audience that receives the Japanese and Korean pop cultures via different Chinese languages, flows and exchanges between Japan, Korea and other particular East Asian locations would be merely bilateral rather than regional."[24] If this circulation represents Chineseness, then such an identity is already non-monolithic, as it is not linked to a homeland.

The differences between earlier periods of popular music and the 1990s is that the later surge of non-Chinese-language products rested on a much broader consumer base than had existed before and, unpredictably, seemed able to break through national and ethno-linguistic borders more substantially. There was what I think of as a preliminary Japanese wave in the 1980s that was linked to the enormously popular television drama *Oshin*, dealing with the travails of a woman born at the start of the twentieth century in Meiji Japan; the male pop duo Chage and Aska; the teen female *aidoru* ("idol") singer, Matsuda Seiko (b. 1962); and cutting-edge youth fashion from Tokyo.

Oshin is probably the most cross-generational of these popular forms. It was originally aired on Nippon Hōsō Kyōkai (NHK, Japan Broadcasting Corporation), the national broadcaster, from April 4, 1983, to March 31, 1984. Fifty-three countries broadcasted *Oshin*, fourteen of them in Northeast and Southeast Asia—Singapore was the first in 1984.[25] The major Japanese wave started in the early 1990s, led by televisual dramas and also by pop music (J-Pop), and then from the late 1990s, more spectacularly, the Korean wave (*Hallyu*) developed, led initially by film and television dramas and, from about 2005, mainly by pop music (K-Pop) as South Korean political and cultural life was liberalized.[26] The term *Hallyu* was used from around the late 1990s. There are different accounts as to the origins of the term—either mainland China or Taiwan are cited as sites of its emergence.

How or why do some cultural productions surpass national borders even or especially when there may have been no plans for border transgressions? Despite the studies that have been done on East Asian pop culture, it remains hard to generalize the conditions that assisted the Japanese and later Korean pop-cultural circulation in a region as diverse as Northeast and Southeast Asia. The easy access, say, to translated song lyrics or fansubbing of television dramas online does not itself account for the cultural resonance of any one national pop product with nonspecialized audiences. It is one thing to speak of a "pop culture China," even with three Chinese languages involved, as sociologist Chua Beng Huat has done, but while it has become normalized for East Asian youth to listen to songs in a foreign language other than English, it was a counterintuitive idea when the practice first developed in the 1990s. Regardless, what is vital is that the formation of the middle classes in East Asia is part of the social bases for regionalization. As discussed in chapter 4, this was, of course, the audience to which inter-Asian cinema reached out. The first wave of middle-class formation was apparent in Japan in the early 1970s, and the 1980s saw middle-class formation in the four mini-dragon economies of South Korea, Taiwan, Hong Kong, and Singapore, with Thailand, Malaysia, and Indonesia (to a lesser extent) following suit. The first decade of the twenty-first century saw such class formations in China's cities.[27] As the main consumers of a regional market, they potentially contributed toward new varieties of putative regional cultural commonalities as part of an aspirational lifestyle—the inevitable Americanization is desired, but now, so is some syncretic version of an East Asian modernity. So, for example, in terms of the success of Japanese cultural products, what is relevant is that regional consumers—certainly the youth demographic for pop music—*appropriate* them as part of their own aspirational desires and not, for instance, as the result of later (and belated) Japanese government "soft power" attempts to capitalize on that success.[28]

The increased and increasing circulation of culture within the region, it can be said, became a part of the means of generating a contemporary Asian way of life that is inextricably linked to consumerism.[29] This is a lifestyle form extensively exported through American media products, but by the 1990s, there was already a substantial history of pop-cultural production that was no longer simple or simplistic imitations of US content.[30] The following assessment by Fredric Jameson of (the lack of) Japanese cultural power at the height of the bubble economy underlines the central issue here:

> At any rate, it does seem to me that fresh cultural production and innovation—and this means in the area of mass-consumed culture—are the crucial index of the centrality of a given area and not its wealth or productive power.... [Despite] Sony's acquisition of Columbia Pictures [in 1989] and Matsushita's buyout of MCA [in 1990], ... the Japanese were unable to master the essentially cultural productivity required to secure the globalization process for any given competitor. Whoever says the production of cultures says the production of everyday life—and without that, your economic system can scarcely continue to expand and implant itself.[31]

Jameson, unsurprisingly, was unaware of the Japanese wave occurring at the time of the publication of his book chapter in 1998, and he would have even been less likely to know that a television series broadcast by CCTV in June 1997, *What is Love?* (*Sarangi mwŏgillae*) produced by Korean broadcaster MBC in 1991–1992, became an unexpected hit in China and was broadcast for a second time in 1998—this is the televisual production widely held to have initiated the Korean wave.[32] The cultural productivity that supported regionalization in East Asia was emerging, but just not within a single national locale—although it naturally did not and could not overtake the United States–dominated globalization process.[33]

By the 1960s, the Euro-American West had witnessed the startling outburst of what was then described as "mass culture," in which cultural commodities exceeded the previous centering in television and Hollywood films. In pop music terms, as Jameson himself noted back in 1979, "the social moment of Elvis or rhythm-and-blues—and behind that Black music—unpredictably develops [after the 1950s into] the 'high modernisms' of the Beatles and the Stones, and thereafter into rock postmodernisms of the most appropriately bewildering kinds."[34] The technological changes in the media and culture industries since, with the increasing capital devoted to culture, enabled contemporary pop culture to look like an embodied vision of cultural pluralism rather than the mass culture it once was, and as the Asian miracle economies "take off" (to use a 1960s expression), that "bewildering" vision becomes available for appropriation.[35]

J-Pop as Globo-National Culture, Equal to the West

The key irony regarding the regional emergence of Japanese popular culture from the 1980s is that, arguably, it was a combination of national pride in relation to a wish for global cultural standards that led, first, to new forms of Japanese pop music for domestic consumption and, second, to J-Pop's ability to appeal to a larger regional audience. What has been described as "J-pop nationalism" was thus the startling starting point of debordered pop music going beyond the more-predictable boundaries of circulation set by Chinese-language pop music.[36] The term "J-poppu" first appeared in 1988, by which time popular music created within Japan and targeted at a domestic audience had assimilated Anglo-American modalities, rhythms, instrumentation, harmonies, and even language, admittedly used in idiosyncratic ways, leading to new cultural expressions that, to its producers and consumers, seemed consonant with Japan's more confident presence in international business. The prefix "J" does not refer to the essential(ized) national culture of the nation-state but rather to a Japanese identity erected upon an "intercultural identity, positioned against a dominant Western [largely American] viewpoint."[37] The exotic and the traditional hailing from some colonial-era modernity were not and are not a notable part of the equation in New Asian cultural fantasies within or without Japan—and why should they be? The invention of a globalized Japanese self for home consumption *separate* from the national sociocultural order that was supposedly a mix of tradition with modernity's mass culture was *also* attractive for a rapidly developing region, despite its (literally) postmodern nationalist origins.

The spread of J-Pop was part of a larger diffusion of Japanese popular culture in the region. While it is not possible to articulate a single or singular narrative of the Japanese wave in the region, as different national locales had different contexts (as is the case for the Korean wave), we can say that manga (Japanese comic books) and anime (Japanese animation) were already circulating in the 1970s, but that it was television dramas that led the way in the region from the 1980s, coming to a head in the 1990s and the following decade. One 1995 survey reported that 47.3 percent of Japanese private broadcasters' programming exports went to Asia, compared with 25.7 percent to North America.[38] In 2002, similar figures hold: 46.1 percent of television exports went to Asia, with 27.9 percent to Europe, and 7.6 percent to the United States.[39] Despite these numbers, Japanese cultural producers were not aggressive in their regional marketing, since the domestic market was quite strong on its own, and the bigger markets in East Asia (apart from China), Taiwan and South Korea, were both former Japanese colonies that imposed bans on Japanese cultural imports. The historical fact of former Japanese colonialism, of course, does not stop the circulation of culture. Those bans, however, were lifted in 1993 for Taiwan and progressively from 1998 for Korea. The appearance of low-level digital technology in the form of the video compact disc helped facilitate the widespread illegal distribution of Japanese dramas by the late 1990s in markets such as Hong Kong, China, and Singapore "largely at the initiative of the Asians on the 'receiving end.'"[40] A market manifested itself and made its interest known.

Pop music in the 1980s benefited from the television dramas that increasingly used pop stars to sing the original soundtracks for the programs. This had a knock-on effect, helping Japanese pop to gain prominence in Hong Kong in the mid-1980s, for instance, and the then–Crown colony became at that point the biggest overseas market for Japanese records.[41] By the 1990s, both Taiwan and Hong Kong had become consumption and redistribution centers for television dramas and J-Pop content alike, licensed and pirated. A smaller market such as Singapore, which tended to be behind the curve in trendy inter-Asian consumption, was a beneficiary of Taiwanese and Hong Kong editions of music album CDs and pop magazines, which retailed at cheaper prices than the Japanese versions. The success of J-Pop in Singapore, precisely because it was a less major center of consumption than Taiwan or Hong Kong (or even Bangkok, Thailand), is a testament to J-Pop's regional impact.[42] Following Hong Kong, Japanese pop music experienced a smaller and short-lived boom in the city-state in the 1980s, but by 1999, J-Pop became visible in a pronounced way, with the third album of the dance-pop girl band Speed (stylized as SPEED), *Moment* (1998), a compilation of all their singles to date, becoming the first Japanese album both to break into Singapore's top 10 list and to take the number 1 spot.[43] SPEED was a teenaged, four-girl group from Okinawa that had their label debut in 1996. They disbanded in 2000 and reformed as a group in 2008. In the first three years of their existence, they racked up sales of more than twenty million units.[44]

However, although the spread of J-Pop throughout the region was part of a larger cultural phenomenon, it could not have occurred without the increased confidence and maturity in Japanese pop sounds that transpired in the 1980s. J-Pop does not refer to a single genre of music, although it has been suggested that it applies more to idol singers, whether male or female, individuals or in groups.[45] The term was coined by a Tokyo-based radio station in 1988, J-WAVE 81.3 FM, the first station to use the English "J" to signify a global identity for the Japanese pop music they chose to play, which "often had English and English-like Japanese lyrics, though they were played by Japanese musicians and made in Japan."[46] That musical-linguistic style gained purchase in contemporary J-Pop production—and would also influence K-Pop production. Initially, J-Pop was linked with Shibuya-style (*Shibuya-kei*) music that originated in the late 1980s from the fashionable youth/young-adult hub of the Shibuya shopping district in Tokyo, which aesthetically defined itself against the then–mainstream pop released by the major labels known as *kayōkyoku* (Western-style pop songs that did not deploy stylized pronunciations based on the English language).

Shibuya-kei music, broadly, can be described as a self-consciously internationalist fusion of jazz, synthpop, bossa nova, and retro-pop that gave rise to what became J-Pop.[47] By the 1990s, the Shibuya-kei association was transcended, and the term "J-Pop" was applied to a wide range of young people's music, ranging from female and male idol music (especially the latter during the 1990s), to visual-style (*visual-kei*) rock bands such as X-JAPAN and Glay, to female singers Amuro Namie and Hamasaki Ayumi. It has been noted that J-Pop is used by the Japanese mass media to distinguish such pop artists from other kinds of *hōgaku* (popular music that is created for a Japanese audience) such as *enka* (popular songs drawing from regionalism and with a sentimental orientation).[48] Arguably, 1988–1998 was the golden era for J-Pop, when million-seller artists were not uncommon, and sales of music albums overseas could reach into the hundreds of thousands.[49] J-Pop emerged at a moment when new technologies such as the Internet and the mobile phone enabled marketing strategies not available before, and at present, the term "is widely used by East Asian audiences to describe music from Japan overseas and has so integrated in a wider East Asian consumer market that this terminology has recently been transferred to describe other Asian pop cultures: 'K-*poppu*' . . . is another trend [that draws on the term J-Pop]."[50] The increasing growth in confidence in the postwar Japanese music industry, combined with forms of transmission not available before the 1990s, played significant roles in the regional emergence of J-Pop.

Japan's evolving relationship with the United States is one that needs to be taken into this account of cultural change, from the Allied occupation, which ended in 1952, through the Cold War years to the present. In the years immediately after the Second World War, imported music and Japanese music in the Western modes were predominant, as they (virtually inescapably) signified "modern life."[51] Cultural sociologist Yoshimi Shunya contends that there is a continuity in the presence of American popular culture in Japan from before the war, but that the cultural relationship after the war changed, first, from a love-hate nature to one where, by the 1960s, American products were no longer seen as antithetical to Japanese life and second, by the 1970s, to a relationship in which the United States became a "source of information" as American culture was remade in Japan. Increasing postwar prosperity assisted with this change in cultural relations.[52] In the process, "made in Japan" music became considered music of quality production that both was and was not quite Japanese sounding at the same time.[53]

In the more-confident 1980s, a number of notable socioeconomic transformations occurred that arguably enhanced J-Pop's attractiveness. These included the development of idol culture. While J-Pop is not a single unified genre per se, some critics associate it with *aidoru* or idol culture, as earlier noted, for good reason—because of its inextricable link with consumption. Although the first idols appeared in 1971, the 1980s are thought of as the golden age of idols—Shin Sannin Musume (literally, Three New Young Girls) is considered the first idol group. The 1980s bubble economy—when Japan could be conceived of as number 1—gave rise to new heights of everyday lifestyle consumption that included idol culture, contributing to an alluring image of contemporary Asian lifestyle possibilities. Idols (still) refer to multifaceted performers who sing and are media celebrities, highly groomed, young (or young-looking), male or female, and who perform across a number of genres and media platforms. They are thus a fitting pop-cultural phenomenon to be associated with the bubble economy, and they also contributed to fortifying domestic pop culture against Anglo-American cultural dominance. The ability to develop a sizable "pool of local idols and celebrities helped to center the Japanese media on the domestic market," and, in due course, "the cult of celebrity came to function as a defense against global media flows . . . [and] indigenized television programming by inviting proximity and familiarity through their regular appearances in a variety of different programming and media outlets."[54]

Idol music was part of a "Japanese-made" pop music that started to dominate sales in the domestic market, displacing Western pop music by the late 2000s.[55] The 1980s also saw Sony Corporation's buyout of CBS Records in 1988 and Columbia Pictures in 1989, while in 1990, Matsushita purchased MCA/Universal. That stretch from the 1980s onward therefore saw the Japanese media and creative industries enter the global market, while domestic media companies strengthened their grip on the home market with its own specific tastes.

What of youth attitudes toward the changing cultural production and the valorization of the Anglocentric prefix "J"? If the "old," heavy-duty, modern national identity that drew upon the idea of *Nippon* depended on traditional and/or serious-minded high culture, along with anchored sociocultural points of reference, a *contemporary* globo-national identity, as it might be described, instead leaned upon lighter, lifestyle culture, a trend that continues into the post-bubble 1990s. Drawing upon the work of the postmodern critic Asada Akira and the psychoanalyst Kayama Rika, cultural sociologist Mōri Yoshitaka argues that the move from "N" (or Nippon) to "J" is,

> in fact, a side-effect of globalization; it represents young peoples' ambiguous anxiety in the face of a crisis of national identity against globalization. It is an ironical attitude, because they project themselves as a homogeneous and unified entity in a nostalgic or even melancholic fantasy, although they already knew that they will not be able to be the same as in the past: they unconsciously recognize that their society and everyday life has become too fragmented and too destabilized to recover, [especially after the bubble economy burst in 1991]. It is a light, small, and "petty" nationalism.[56]

J-Pop came about at the height of the bubble economy, and later became a sort of fix for the deflation that followed and subsequent attempts to liberalize the economy. It thus provided reassurance that the contemporary Japanese culture that had arrived in the 1980s still had a place in the world in harder times and seemed to avoid becoming part of a harder neonationalism and historical revisionism that are also part of the 1990s.[57]

What was it about J-Pop, then, at its inception that allowed it to generate the possibility of globo-national imaginings? As mentioned, J-Pop initially was linked with the appearance of Shibuya-kei music, a term applied to bands that were reshaping accepted conventions in mainstream Japanese pop, such as the duo Flipper's Guitar, with its "happy"-sounding rock-dance music, and Pizzicato Five (P5), with its eclectic synthpop, dance, and retro-style music—artists systematically promoted by the buzzing Shibuya HMV store that opened in 1990.[58] The latter group "was to become the most iconic example of what *Shibuya-kei* was about," and as their music was able to gain international notice, examining this group allows us to see the cultural components that were set in play for J-Pop's "petty" nationalism.[59]

P5 was formed in 1985 and was known as Pizzicato V until 1987. Arguably, they came into their own in 1990, when the group consisted of Nomiya Maki (vocals), Konishi Yasuharu, and Takanami Keitarō (whose given name was stylized as "K-taro").[60] In 1991, they released the album *This Year's Girl*, which extensively relied on sampling—the use of preexisting music remixed into new forms—as the base for their music. The digital technology that enabled sampling only started developing in the late 1970s. So, P5 was innovative in creating a sound that sounded "indie" to Western ears but was actually closer to the commercial mainstream in Japan.

One of the best-known songs from *This Year's Girl* is "Twiggy Twiggy." It is typical of the knowing, ironic, yet light-handed use of 1960s pop-cultural references in the band's compositions, reinforced by clever visuals in their music videos and stage dress. The song was indicative of the cultural possibilities inherent in the rising "J" moment. The lyrics are simple and repetitive:

Sanjikan mo matte ita no yo
Watashi neko to issho ni

Sono toki denwa no beru ga
Watashi neko mitai ni shabetta

Terebi no volume sagete
Watashi uso mitai na koe de

Twiggy no mini skirt de
Twiggy mitai na pose de
Twiggy no mini skirt de
Twiggy mitai ni yassepochi no watashi

I was waiting for about three hours
My cat and I

At the time the phone rang
And I chatted away just like my cat

I turned down the TV and
Talked in a fake voice

In a Twiggy mini skirt
In a Twiggy-like pose
In a Twiggy mini skirt
Skinny like Twiggy, that's me[61]

The lyrics say nothing, and that may be part of the point. They reveal to us our reveling in leisure-time activity. As for the music itself, a large portion of it consists fundamentally of a loop dominated by jazzy percussion, with samples from the Ventures' theme for the TV series *Hawaii Five-O* (1968), Burt Bacharach and Hal David's "Another Night" (1966), and Argentinian composer Lalo Schifrin's "The Man from Thrush" (1965) and "The Cat" (1964). That piece is interposed with an electone-organ-type solo toward the end, and it all concludes with a keyboard solo featuring part of the James Bond theme composed by Monty Norman, first heard in *Dr. No* (1962).

The music video, directed by Konishi, reinforces the subtext that "Japanese" music and its take on leisure activity are now global and that this "arrival" can be taken in a relaxed manner. The music video was reedited and included in the release of P5's second American release by Matador Records, *Made in USA* (1994), a compilation album. The dominant image of the video is the three artists doing campy à go-go dance moves, although executed with restraint and with straight faces. Text is used in the video and new text is added for the US market.[62] The first text that appears proclaims "inside out with LES PIZZICATO FIVE." The video is largely in black and white, with one color section. We see Nomiya, Konishi, and Takanami performing primarily in a light-colored and airy studio space. Nomiya first appears in a fake fur hat, transparent rain jacket, and dark miniskirted dress with dark leggings and then, alternatively, in a light smock-like miniskirted dress with a dark choker for most of the rest of the video. The next set of text that appears references the title of the album and shamelessly flags the creativity of everything the viewer sees and hears: "pizzicato five; / the original artform / excerpt from this year's girl / in action."

Later on, "hello America" appears in outline text, with the three colors of the US flag filling in the text. References to pop figures and celebrities from the 1960s and from the late 1980s to theearly 1990s are made, in a minimalist, knowing manner: "twiggy [the model] / [author] jackie [Collins?] / cindy [Crawford the model?] /... [1960s British singers] sandie [Shaw] and petula [Clark]" are evoked and imposed onto a shot of Nomiya's face, this time in color. A TV set in the room is revealed, with images on it that monitor the three P5 members dancing behind the set, accompanied by the text: "the revolution *is* being televised." As "Twiggy Twiggy" concludes, with the James Bond theme, the last text appears in green and significantly advises the viewer, "buy japanese."

While "Twiggy, Twiggy" was released the year the bubble economy burst, the sampling, the music assembled and sung, and the video embody the confidence of a creative culture with an edge that rises to French cultural sophistication ("LES PIZZICATO FIVE") and counters American cultural dominance ("hello America," with the text in the red, white, and blue of the US flag) in a (seemingly) casual manner. After all, P5 seem to suggest, we know who "you" are fairly well—you are now part of "us," and the clichéd, Japanese occupation-era binary opposition of the West and the Rest no longer exists. We too can undertake wink-wink, nod-nod ironic approaches to stylish urban pop culture. We can be thin and dress like Twiggy and have fun, with no need to dragoon exotic symbols of Japan for your consumption of otherness. In fact, this is what you should do now: "buy japanese." This cultural transformation, this "revolution," can be broadcast by media everywhere. And herein, perhaps, is revealed at least a slight ambivalence—that the latest version of the new still needs to appeal for a fair hearing, even while advancing its case for equality and cultural quality, albeit in an understated way. If Shibuya-kei must be recognized as part of a "transnational soundscape [in the 1990s that was producing retro-oriented 'lounge music'], an ongoing international co-production involving both Japanese and non-Japanese musics and musicians," this does not mean that the specific Japanese context of its invention is inconsequential.[63] This music is an actively produced *local-yet-metropolitan* variant of a globalizing culture in which the "local is increasingly dissociated from specific social spaces and relations, as it is constituted through the process of commodification."[64] The achievement of this new J-culture continued on into the post-bubble 1990s, but with the "J" getting *repositioned* to represent "young peoples' ambiguous anxiety in the face of a crisis of national identity against globalization."[65]

J-Pop's larger impact, it could be said, receded by about 2004, with the release of Utada Hikaru's English-language album, *Exodus* (2004). This album was her debut in the American market, where it peaked at 160 (for one week) on the Billboard 200 chart and only sold some fifty-five thousand units, even though it reached number 1 on Japan's Oricon Weekly Albums chart and sold more than one million units.[66] Utada is significant in J-Pop's pantheon because, first, she is a bona fide singer-songwriter (and therefore "creative") rather than an idol singer and, second, she is bilingual and bicultural, having been born in Manhattan in 1983. These combined traits enabled Utada to be the pop icon who could front the cultural fantasy to "stand shoulder to shoulder" with pop music's origins—which is the "fantasy of globalized Japanese culture."[67] Her compositions and singing style were pop but modified with R&B and house/club music, which gave her an edge. Utada's debut album, *First Love* (1999), sold some nine million copies, mainly in Japan.[68] *Exodus* was a sophisticated, dance-oriented album that experimentally (and adventurously) incorporated a number of electronic genres, as well as R&B and hip-hop music. Its lyrical content dwelt on matters such as sexual relationships, which complicated Utada's reputation as a clean-cut J-Pop star.

In many ways, the cultural urges that fed into J-Pop nationalism were what gave J-Pop the luster that enabled regional prominence. However, Utada's difficulties in 2004 also indicated that paying too much attention to the United States/Japan binary and the subjectivity of Japanese youth, and not enough to the transformation of cultural subjectivity in Japan's regional backyard, meant that J-Pop could not take full advantage of emergent inter-Asian pop-cultural opportunities. Nor perhaps did it need to, given the size of its domestic market that, despite the decline in CD sales worldwide, has been the second-largest market for recorded music after the United States since the mid-1970s.[69]

K-Pop as Translocal Formation of the Contemporary

It is the expanding South Korean media and creative industries from the 1990s—first film and particularly television dramas, with pop music coming to the fore from the mid-2000s, "the so-called second stage of [the] Korean wave"—that firmly attempt to take advantage of debordered popular-cultural consumption, even while production remains national in origin.[70] Japanese pop culture, although without deliberate effort on its part, made its pre-K-Pop cultural presence felt in Korea in the 1980s and 1990s. This new Korean wave's uneven regional advent was unpredictable, as was the earlier Japanese wave, with different issues in the Korean market encouraging a more deliberate outward orientation for K-Pop when compared to J-Pop.

J-Pop's "petty" nationalism gave rise to a contradictory regional intake of a putative globo-national culture on offer that ignored its nationalism. K-Pop's version of pop-cultural glamor *furthers* that attempt to overcome the underclass status of nonmetropolitan pop-cultural creations that cannot be and is not interested in being labeled as exotic "world music" by leveraging a now-existing global sameness in the region that seems tolerant of national/ethnic/linguistic difference. The Korean wave's spectacular stature and keen interest in the actual effectiveness of the Korean state's intervention in the creative industry has generated prodigious scholarship that appears to exceed that of the Japanese wave.[71] I submit that K-Pop builds upon the possibilities that first arose with J-Pop in the region. K-Pop becomes a translocal formation of the contemporary, catering to the "localities" of established and ascending urban youth consumerist dreams of the regional middle class, ranging all the way from "advanced" (but post-bubble) Japan to South Korea's own more recently enfranchised "advanced" market status (having joined the Organization for Economic Cooperation and Development in 1996) to "lower-middle-income" Indonesia. As we know, exchange relations can serve to break down historically formed collective meanings, and K-Pop boy and girl "idol" bands are productive imaginative acts that performatively cross borders to project a fictive identity onto disjunctive spatial standpoints in Northeast and Southeast Asia.

To be sure, "fictive" does not mean "not really there." The region is standardized enough by market integration and social interconnectedness that Korean talent agencies can fulfill consumerist desires with empirical cultural content: capital allows the projection of utopian horizons in the form of a desire for metropolitan culture as a region-wide interconnectedness in the dystopian form of the market. In this regard, K-Pop fosters what Peter Osborne calls a "'distributive' unity," in which the different national "stages" of economic development and modernity from which the various pop consumers hail are enfolded into the stasis of the present moment of consumption.[72] The K-Pop industry, vitally, works at putting together fandoms.[73] Pop music performance and consumption become enabled as sites for the extraterritoriality of culture to manifest itself, as K-Pop groups traverse New Asia for live concerts—and with middle-class youth also crossing borders to attend these concerts. Such consumption indicates how existing national social forms have been transformed by economic exchange, but also that the *social* is not necessarily a collective form in any active practical or political sense. Korean pop culture's entanglements with pre–Cold War nationalisms are not surprising, and regionalizing inter-Asian pop's numerous fans are not proof against such entanglements.

Inter-Asian popular music flows did exist with Japan from the 1960s, before K-Pop's emergence from the mid-1990s, but the music forms circulating were not mainstream pop. The first relevant music form was *enka*, which included singers such as Kye Eunsook (b. 1961) and Kim Yonja (b. 1959); Kim moved to Japan in 1977 to further her career. Hyunjoon Shin observes that such singers were "an essential part of a 'postcolonial' networking between Japanese and Korean music industries. Korean *enka* singers stirred nostalgia for older forms of entertainment in Japan and East Asia."[74] This nostalgic orientation placed real limits on the ability to win full recognition for singers such as the versatile rock and pop star, Cho Yong-pil (b. 1950), known in Japan only for *enka*. The second relevant form is folk song (*p'ok'ŭsong*), which started as adaptations of Western modern folk and included such eclectic influences as Simon and Garfunkel, French *chanson*, and Italian *canzone*. Hyunjoon Shin contends that folk was taken to be the people's (or protest) song, raising questions "about the struggle for cultural nonalignment . . . in popular music," with music less commercial than *enka*.[75] Records by singers such as Kim Min-ki (b. 1951), who was part of a political "song movement," were distributed in Japan in the late 1970s.

The generally acknowledged point of origin for subsequent pop-music development was the iconic group Seo Taiji and Boys (Sŏ Taejiwa aidŭl), whose rise became conceivable thanks to the end of authoritarian military rule in the form of the Kim Young-sam government that came to power in 1993. As is well known, Kim created the Globalization Promotion Committee (*Segyehwa Ch'ujinwi Wŏnhoe*) in 1995 to implement structural reforms— and these reforms included a role for culture, especially culture with a less nationally autonomous agenda when compared with that of the 1960s.[76] That process gave the *sinsidae* (new generation) scope to invent and consume new pop-cultural productions in an economy that was benefiting from earlier developmentalist strategies—and development, after the Asian financial crisis in 1997, was transformed into a global rather than national project.[77]

Born Jung Hyun-chul, Seo Taiji formed his group in 1991 with two other young men who also sang and acted as backing dancers. He wrote his own songs and released his first single, "Nan arayo" (I know), a song about heading off a breakup, and first album the following year. The single created a template for later Korean pop music—hip-hop verses with guitars in the bridge, a melodic chorus, a dance orientation, and heightened image consciousness in the assemblage of then–unconventional urban, African American–inspired fashion.[78] Seo was an independent figure who dropped out of high school—nonconformism on palpable display—and "contested the [then-]hegemonic powers of the broadcasting system with their in-house star system and big band orchestra-centered TV shows."[79] The group helped to break the domination of bland pop ballads (*palladŭ kayo*), with their moderate tempos and safe sentimental themes, which had emerged in the 1970s and were deemed unthreatening to the military regime.[80] Seo's lyrics became more edgy as he developed, challenging, for example, the norms of the rigid examination system ("Kyosil idea" [Classroom ideology], 1994) or taking up the topic of national reunification ("Parhae rŭl kkumkkumyŏ" [Dreaming of Balhae], 1994). The pop-cultural libidinal energies of 1990s Korean youth certainly surfaced in a realm with clear sociopolitical implications, a contrast with that of post-bubble 1990s Japanese youth.

If Seo Taiji and Boys' innovations set the stage for the possibilities of expressive popular music, it was H.O.T. (High-five of Teenagers), assembled by the then–new talent agency SM Entertainment, who turned those innovations into a functioning, replicable, and domesticated expressive model for what would be called K-Pop across the region. The group was active from 1996 to 2001, almost literally picking up the slack from Seo Taiji and Boys, who disbanded in 1996. Eight hundred thousand copies of H.O.T.'s first album, *We Hate All Kinds of Violence* (1996), were sold within ten days of its release in South Korea, and the group would go on to record five studio albums before themselves disbanding.[81] H.O.T. sang a range of music, spanning from teen pop to ballads to rock—oftentimes with the genres mixed up and with hip-hop verses thrown into the resulting mix. Their first hit single, "Candy" (1996), was a piece of bubblegum pop, with lyrics about a boy needing individual space from the girl he loves. The music video, largely set against a merry-go-round in an amusement park, had the members in exaggerated hip-hop fashions using primary colors and oversized fuzzy mittens, accompanied by deliberately infantilized and "cute" campy choreography. By the time the single "I yah" (Dear child) was released in 1996, we find them offering a critical commentary on a society in which pupils are allowed to be locked in a kindergarten room, with disastrous consequences when a fire occurs. The style was harder-edged rock, and the accompanying music video showed them in slick, all-black Japanese-inspired Goth-*cum*-sci-fi looks. In 2000, band members appeared in Beijing in front of thirteen thousand fans, launching the export pop music component of the Korean wave, and yet while "China was the big goal, . . . the immediate market was Japan[,] . . . whose music market was twenty times larger than Korea's."[82]

The eclectic musical range and flexible (if not incoherent) dress styles of H.O.T. demonstrate that, like J-Pop, K-Pop is not a musical genre per se but describes a pop music that is teen-centric and star-centered, and with carefully nurtured performers who are managed by talent agencies. The best known of these are SM Entertainment (the pioneer, started in 1995), YG Entertainment (founded by a former member of Seo Taiji and Boys), and JYP Entertainment. The agencies are organized via an "'in-house' system," which "integrates 'production' and 'management' and all other necessary functions for developing and training talents."[83] This agency system is adapted at least partially from (and in terms of export-orientation, outdoes) the Japanese *jimusho* or "office" system—and in particular Johnny & Associates, established in 1962 and the most famous creator of idol boybands in Japan, including SMAP.[84] (In 2023, in the wake of charges of sexual abuse against the company's late founder, Johnny Kitagawa, that appeared in a March 2023 BBC documentary, the company was renamed as Smile-Up.[85]) K-Pop groups, broadly speaking, are marked by being mainly idol bands, by the use of English in the lyrics, by having differentiated roles for each band member (vocalists, rappers, dancers), and in general by being dance-pop and thus performance oriented, so that the dance routine rather than the melody shapes a song from the start.[86] The end result is a pop-cultural form that simultaneously uses the Korean language and tries to escape looking too "national" as a product.

It is revealing that "K-Pop" is not a term of Korean origin, as the more usual South Korean designation for popular song is *kayo* (a term that has historical links to the Japanese term *kayōkyoku*, discussed earlier in the chapter), but was a term first used by the Japanese media and then circulated in the region.[87] This explanation, in effect, makes K-Pop into J-Pop's successor. And that, in some respects, does not seem inaccurate. Hyunjoon Shin asks us to think of K-Pop as "a combination of heterogeneous elements" that is the result of, apart from the influence of US pop culture, cultural border crossings with South Korea's other, Japan.[88] Japanese popular music—including J-Pop—has a historical relationship with pre-K-Pop Korea. There was a hidden "presence" of Japanese popular music in South Korea in the years before 1998, when President Kim Dae-jung's administration (1998–2002) launched a gradual lifting of the Cold War–era ban on Japanese culture (film, video, manga, etc.), a process that reached its completion in 2004. Ironically, the banning of Japanese products facilitated the direct unattributed sampling of Japanese music, such as occurred with a song by hip-hop and dance group Roo'ra (Roots of reggae), "Chŏnsang yuae" (Love in heaven; 1996), which drew on the song "Omatsuri Ninja" (Ninja festival; 1990) by the Johnny & Associates' boyband, Ninja.[89] There were those such as the then-president of Line Records, Kim Chang-Hwan, who felt that the lifting of the ban would ultimately be for Korea's good: "Local 'pretty-face' singers who used to copy and plagiarize Japanese pop music will disappear, . . . which will help improve the quality of domestic music."[90] The adaptation of Japanese talent management approaches mentioned in the previous paragraph then became a part of K-Pop's translocal and specific inter-Asian formation. K-Pop thus is neither a "pure" nor purist cultural production—the latter intentionally so, of course—but exists in interconnection within the longer history of the reinvention of contemporary Northeast Asian culture out of older modern cultural forms dating from the early twentieth century, such as Japanese *enka* or Korean *yuhaengga* (song in fashion).

To talk about "inter-Asian pop" is not to suggest that any easy multiculturalism has been achieved in East Asia—but the current reality is that K-Pop needs East and Southeast Asia, and therefore K-Pop needs to be an Asian-global pop, despite the inevitable murkiness that results when any discussion of "Asianness" transpires. Despite an unsurprising postcolonial hope to compete in the homelands of pop music, as witnessed in the JYP Entertainment's star Rain's sold-out concerts in 2006 at Madison Square Garden, the US reviews that followed were withering. With tedious predictability, Asian cultural productions that could not be tagged as ethnically inflected "world music" were taken to be either unoriginal or behind the curve.[91] That is, K-Pop finds it hard to be taken as *true* or perhaps *authentic* global contemporary culture in the metropole, although at the same time it is apparent enough that distinct niche (and presumably expandable) cultures now exist for it in various non-East Asian locales.[92] In 2011, music exports to Japan—on the increase for a few years—were worth US$157.9 million (up significantly from US$21.6 million in 2009), those to Southeast Asia were worth US$25.6 million (up from US$6.4 million in 2009), and those to China, with all the challenges its difficult market poses, were worth US$6.8 million (up from US$2.4 million in 2009).[93] In contrast, exports to Europe were worth US$4.6 million (up from US$299,000 in 2009), and those to North America a miniscule US$587,000 (up from US$351,000 in 2009).[94] The 1997 Asian financial crisis saw the domestic music market contract, and export orientation became a necessity for survival for small- and medium-sized companies. The collapse of physical music sales between 2001 and 2005 in South Korea due to the Internet and illegal music downloading also spurred the need for overseas expansion. China, given its potential market size, will remain a "point of commercial cultural exchange."[95]

Two well-known and trailblazing cases of the advance into Japan are the SM Entertainment stars Kwon Boa, whose stage name is BoA, and TVXQ. With the opening up of cultural exchange between Korea and Japan in 1998, SM Entertainment's head Lee Soo-man arranged for a teen singer with moderate Korean success to move to Japan, where she learned Japanese, and he established a partnership with the major Japanese entertainment company Avex Group. The latter's Avex Trax label launched BoA's first Japanese-language album in 2002, *Listen to My Heart*—composed of R&B, dance pop, and ballad tracks written by mainly Japanese composers. It went on to sell more than one million units, and the album established, for the first time, that a non-Japanese singer could become a J-Pop star.[96] Although her ethnonational identity was not concealed, it was not dwelt upon. BoA thus became a simultaneous K-Pop/J-Pop star. The strategy of having K-Pop stars learn other languages—principally Japanese, Chinese, and English—is now generally practiced.

The five-man boyband, TVXQ, which launched in 2003 and signed with Avex in 2004, built upon BoA's success, although it was apparent from their Japanese television appearances that the group members were Koreans whose Japanese was improving rapidly. Dance-pop, rock with a heavy urban dance inflection, and R&B mark the overall musical output of TVXQ. At the start, SM had China as one of its overseas target markets for TVXQ. This resulted in a version of their first Korean album, *Tri-Angle* (2004), being released in China under the title *Dongfang Shenqi*, the group's Chinese name, by the CRC (China Record Corporation) label. This version had three of the songs appear twice, in Korean and in (slightly strained) Mandarin-Chinese. In Korea, TVXQ are known as Dong Bang Shin Ki, and in Mandarin-Chinese as Dongfang Shenqi, both meaning "gods rising in the east." They later appeared in Japan under the name Tōhōshinki, which has the same meaning as the Korean and Chinese names.[97] TVXQ's effective breakthrough came in 2008 when, over the course of the year, they had four singles reach the top of the Oricon charts and also had the distinction of being invited to national broadcaster NHK's still-prestigious Kōhaku Uta Gassen, the year-end song festival.[98] But despite such ongoing successes in Japan, Shin Hyunjoon rightly observes that inter-Asian pop production is an uneven field: "K-pop is 'localized' for Japan's markets, [but] J-pop is consumed in Korea in its original form, without its contents being altered. . . . An international imbalance of so-called soft power still persists in this phase of this transnational cultural flow."[99] While K-Pop itself is already created with the region in mind (excluding the specific case of Japan), what is seen and heard is the same inside and outside South Korea.

Despite creating and promoting an inter-Asian pop that aimed to affirm a more-confident New Asia, nationalist and racist responses occurred as early as 2006. In that year, both Taiwanese and mainland Chinese reacted to the increasing presence of Korean wave TV dramas, with Taipei's Government Information Office and CCTV saying they would restrict the time allocated to such dramas.[100] Similar reactions recurred: 2011 saw Taiwan's National Communications Commission request restraint in airing Korean dramas as well as protests against Korean programs in Japan. The Korean newspaper *Dong-A Ilbo* suggested that "the solution to these problems is for Korea to continue efforts to understand and accept cultures of other countries."[101] Cultural productions may be inter-Asian in production format, but was cultural dialogue adequately emphasized? A particularly notorious anti-*Hallyu* event took place in Japan with the 2005 publication of *Manga Kenkanryū* (Hating the Korean wave) by the pseudonymous Yamano Sharin. At that point, the Korean presence had been strongly apparent only since 2004 with the second-round broadcast by NHK of the regionally popular KBS drama *Winter Sonata* (*Gyeoul Yeonga*, 2002).[102] Yamano's comic depicts a freshman joining his university's "East Asia Investigation Committee," where he learns the "truth" about historical disputes between Japan and Korea, with pro-Korean Japanese and Korean students' ignorance of this joint history getting exposed in the process.[103] A crude binary of self/other is an inevitable part of the comic's rhetorical strategy. Nearly a decade later, in 2014, the *Korea Times* reported that although "experts and observers in Korea and Japan" said attendance at anti-Korean rallies "reportedly staged every weekend across Japan" were small, Korean culture content exports and even small shops in "Tokyo's Korea Town" "seem[ed] to face grave challenges sparked by right-wing politicians and activists in Japan whose voices against the boom . . . resonate widely amid a sluggish economy," as well as unresolved tensions over disputed islands and "comfort women" issues.[104] Political detritus from the Cold War and before made their presence felt in the unending post-bubble era.

The various negative reactions to cross-border pop culture in effect really serve to highlight an undeniable change in cultural subjectivity in the region—after all, the reactions are to a changed profile of pop music in the region. K-Pop, as the more *arriviste* contemporary pop culture that enjoyed state support, followed and exceeded many of the routes of circulation that J-Pop, with its domestic orientation, had unintentionally pioneered. We might then also inquire how we can *see* this translocal assortment of pop fans that, in its Japanese "branch," has provoked the right wing? To do this, we might go back to J-Pop as the accidental prototype because that may reveal to us this translocal "community" as it existed without the additional complexities produced by K-Pop's export-oriented glossiness.

We turn to the five-man group, Arashi (i.e., "storm"), which debuted in 1999. Its members—Ōno Satoshi (the leader), Sakurai Shō, Aiba Masaki, Ninomiya Kazunari, Matsumoto Jun—were born between 1980 and 1983, and they are managed by Johnny and Associates. They went into "indefinite hiatus" in January 2021. Their oeuvre largely consists of upbeat, cheerful pop with a tame hip-hop element, along with some bubblegum pop during the early part of their career. A chat session carried out with the audience in a concert at the Taipei Arena in Taiwan on August 17, 2006, is revealing. That is an apposite year, as by that time, the Korean wave (including K-Pop) had already started to overtake the 1990s Japanese wave—which meant that the audience that was present possessed a commitment that continued from the earlier fan-consumption impulses of inter-Asian pop. The K-Pop artists that might be mentioned as outstanding around the mid-2000s in Northeast and

Southeast Asia include R&B singers Rain and Se7en (pronounced "Seven"), along with dance-pop girl band Baby V.O.X.

Even as late as 2016, the Johnny & Associates' website directly stated that it did not allow fans not domiciled in Japan to join any of their groups' fan clubs—membership is the only way to receive priority for concert ticket purchases.[105] For a male idol group such as Arashi, arguably second in renown in Japan only to SMAP, concert tickets then become nearly impossible to purchase for overseas fans. This situation is compounded by the fact that Johnny's groups rarely tour outside Japan, as there is no need to cater to a larger market, whatever the real demand. The Taipei concert was part of Arashi's first-ever set of performances overseas. After Taipei, they traveled to represent Japan at Korea's 3rd Asia Song Festival in Gwangju—an ongoing Korean-organized festival that attempts to promote cultural dialogue by inviting singers from across the region and thus fending off the charge of cultural imperialism—and finally to Bangkok, where Arashi headlined a concert commemorating the 120th anniversary of the Declaration of Amity and Commerce between Thailand and Japan.[106] This tour with mixed commercial and semi-diplomatic goals was named "Arashi around Asia: Thailand—Taiwan—Korea."[107]

Inter-Asian pop concerts are characterized by a typical pattern that has evolved over the years, including an extended chat session with the audience to enable "bonding" with the fans. The Taipei concert was no exception. In the video of the event, a translator stands on the stage with Arashi facilitating the session. Matsumoto Jun mentions that Arashi started seven years ago, and Ninomiya Kazunari apologizes that it has taken the band so long to get to Taiwan, acknowledging that they do know that they have overseas fans. Ninomiya then proceeds to ask if anyone has been to Japan to watch their shows and gets positive shouts in return from the audience, eliciting the response from him, "*Sugoi ne!*" ("amazing" or "wow"). So, it seems "if the mountain won't come to Muhammed . . ." Soon after, Sakurai Shō—who notices that sections of the audience had been laughing at their jokes even before the translation to Mandarin-Chinese—makes a comment that it appears some in the audience know Japanese. There is again an affirmative audience response, and Ninomiya follows up soon by asking if they learned their Japanese in school or at home. The translator gives them the reply, "by themselves," leaving all of Arashi—surprisingly, given their long careers as pop singers—looking slightly taken aback, as if it is the first time they have heard that overseas audiences learn Japanese to follow the Japanese wave better. (Now, as we know, fans in the region learn Korean to follow the more recent wave.) Sakurai then observes that he sees fans from Hong Kong, Singapore, and Thailand (presumably from the placards that the fans hold up), and Ninomiya edges in saying that he was confused by a placard that said "Macau" (in Kanji or Chinese characters), thinking that it was a person's name. Aiba Masaki then spots the Macanese contingent and points at them, with Sakurai shouting out, "Hi, Macau!" (in English) at them. Soon after, the recording of the chat ends, and the concert resumes. While we can assume that the concertgoers are mainly Taiwanese, clearly youths from other countries are also in attendance and happy to proclaim their identities to the artists on the stage, if they will notice. If Arashi goes "around Asia," Asia is also willing to go to Arashi.

The regional contemporary pop concert becomes a productive imaginative event where a non-national unity is invoked, perhaps involuntarily, by the multinational audience. It could be said that the artists, their production team, and the audience performatively co-project a fiction of unity, a common (even if internally disjunctive) historical time. The subject of modernity tends to be singular—the nation-state, or national culture, both of which presuppose a "we" with some sort of dialectical unity. In contrast, in Taipei, the concert audience is multiple and multinational, enfolded within an immanently differential contemporary moment in which the desire for urbanized pop culture is fulfilled. Despite the disjunctive spatial and historical relations in the region, the modernity expressed is characterized by the desire for an increasingly regional cultural capital. If art, as it is claimed, is a privileged carrier of the contemporary, as it was of modernity, then pop culture, because it is more quotidian in its claims than high culture, has at least the same capacity to serve as a carrier of the contemporary and to assist in the imagining of a non-singular subjectivity.

The concluding question is, naturally, Where do we stand now? In 2018, the K-Pop idol band BTS (Bangtan Sonyeondan [Bulletproof Boy Scouts]), born between 1992 and 1997 and formed in 2013, broke into the metropolitan center of pop music, the United States, in a substantial manner. That year witnessed two of their singles, "IDOL" and "Fake Love," reach numbers 11 and 10, respectively, on the Billboard Hot 100 charts, and two of their albums, *Love Yourself: Tear* and *Love Yourself: Answer*, both reached number 1 on Billboard's Independent Albums charts in June and August, respectively, with each retaining that pole position for two weeks.[108] On October 9, 2018,

BTS performed on the American Music Awards show—their first outing on American network television. Their upbeat hip-hop, inflected with pop and R&B, along with their dynamic, precise, and mesmerizing dance choreography, seem to have propelled their Asian pop beyond the successes of early East Asian pretenders such as Japan's Sakamoto Kyū (1941–1985), whose "Sukiyaki" remained at number 1 for three weeks on the Billboard Hot 100 in 1963; K-Pop girl band Wonder Girl's "Nobody," which peaked at number 76 on the Billboard Hot 100 in 2009; and PSY's "Gangnam Style," which reached number 2 in 2012—the only three notable chart successes before BTS. Is this the moment Asian pop becomes, at last, global pop?[109] The breakthrough by BTS has allowed younger groups such as Tomorrow X Together (sometimes stylized as TXT), born between 1999 and 2002, to headline a major music festival—as TXT did for Lollapalooza in August 2023 in Chicago.[110]

In 2018—and in rapid succession—two controversies took the shine off BTS's potential moment of arrival on the global stage. In September, the boy band's Korean fans reacted negatively to news from the group's management agency, Big Hit Entertainment (now Big Hit Music), that the Japanese producer of the hugely popular Japanese girl band, AKB48, Akimoto Yasushi, would be writing a Japanese-language single, "Bird," for BTS. Akimoto had previously used the Rising Sun Flag (*Kyokujitsu-ki*)—which evoked memories of Japanese colonialism—on AKB48's costumes, and he was also accused of using misogynist lyrics in the girl group's songs. Around the same time, images appeared online of a BTS member wearing a T-shirt that had an image of an atomic bomb explosion and the text "Patriotism Our History Liberation Korea" printed repetitively on it. The furor that resulted in Japan led to TV Asahi canceling BTS's scheduled November 9 appearance on its long-running show *Music Station*.[111]

The appearance of a postwar global market in cultural commodities had allowed the construction of a world music (even if "experienced as a tide of 'Americanization'"), although that also "enclosed the cultural commons as all sorts of vernacular art forms that had circulated [previously] as common property, . . . were . . . copyrighted, and sold as commodities."[112] At the same time, world music becomes more complex as what I elsewhere have described as "the global and cultural dispersal of . . . the global West" is requisitioned to engender new forms of cultural difference that link various regional identities into a cosmopolitan-contemporary Asianness, although one unable to forswear modern nationalism.[113] The contemporary moment manifests an antagonistic unity within which the great modern ideology of nationalism lives, even if there is a vision of a regional market with a relatively newfound interdependence, where sameness and difference are no longer in an antinomian relationship. Pop culture is now part of a regionally affirmative culture in this inconclusive moment of the contemporary.

CODA: CONTEMPORARY CHINA AND ASIA

Literary-cultural critic Rey Chow has reflected upon a new visibility of the Orient for the times we live in. Amid the Cold War in the 1970s, there was a binary academic construction of the two major states in the so-called Far East: China and Japan. The latter reemerged after the disaster of the Pacific War and could offer "the quietist contemplation of the beauty of the natural world," but the People's Republic of China, behind the bamboo curtain from October 1, 1949, was thought of in the language of political economy and in regard to its difficult economic conditions. Its modern literature and culture existed in a spectral zone while, in the "respectable realm of sinology, . . . [traditional] poetry, fiction, art, music, and other types of cultural production [that] gained esteem on account of their remoteness from the present known as 'modernity.'"[1] All that has changed, and for Chow, the "fifth generation" mainland Chinese directors from the 1980s, such as Chen Kaige and Zhang Yimou, "carry the import of an exercise in cultural redemption, compelling reflection on [recent] Chinese history through a focus on the . . . often rural . . . masses . . . on the margins of twentieth-century Chinese society."[2] She appropriately asks, "What does it mean for Western knowledge production when China can no longer be imagined and approached with the line 'I am hungry'?"[3]

We have seen how, increasingly from the 1990s, the "new visibility of the Orient" has been further transforming. China's reform and opening have benefited and expanded urban constituencies.[4] As part of the turn away from "Mao-era anti-imperialism that demanded withdrawal from global capitalism," as historian Arif Dirlik explains, the "reform era 'opening' of the national economy has sought to turn the tables on imperialism by exploiting the global economy in the service of national ends."[5] The Communist Party leadership by and large wanted to participate in the global capitalist economy without giving up national autonomy and sovereignty.

How does the event of the PRC's rise and the factors of urbanization, urbanized culture, and a nationalist orientation toward globalized modernization require an extension to the argument that *A Regional Contemporary* has been making regarding rapid economic development and the enablement of cultural production and representation in relation to that problematic regionally shared space that is Asia? While it is not possible to offer a definitive statement, given the scale and the complexity of the question, it is possible at least to reflect on two indicative artistic-cultural events in the 2000s. This will allow a sense of some directions taken when China came into firm capitalist view in Northeast and Southeast Asia, or Eastern Asia, when admitted as the 143rd member of the World Trade Organization on December 11, 2001. Earlier, in 1986, the PRC had sought what, from its point of view, was a resumption of its status as a contracting party to the 1947 General Agreement on Trade and Tariffs (GATT), from when China was still the Republic of China run by the Guomindang (GMD, or Nationalist Party). The 1986 GATT application was transformed into a WTO accession application in 1995.[6] Cold War history, even amid an "opening up," cannot be ignored.

The two indicative artistic-cultural events are the Shanghai Biennale 2000: Shanghai Spirit (SB2000) and the coproduced 2007 Sino-Japanese film *The Longest Night in Shanghai* (*Yoru no Shanghai/Ye Shanghai*). Writing as the director of the Shanghai Art Museum—the biennale's host institution—and the director of SB2000's Artistic Committee, artist and educator Feng Zengxian describes how the theme of "Shanghai Spirit" served as SB2000's framing curatorial concept: "The changes Shanghai has been undergoing are typical of changes undergone by China in the past century.... Today's Shanghai, with its vigor and magnetism, gets increasingly involved in the trend of globalization and has successfully caught the focus of the world. To more and more foreigners, it exists no longer as a mere geographical concept. So 'Shanghai Spirit' is embodied in the eager readiness of this city to assimilate various elements and renovate its own cultural tradition."[7] Feng's framework of older urban space into significant remade place, we will see, will also be applicable to the making of *Longest Night*. We can also mention that the allowance for individual curation in an art museum itself was part of the biennale's innovation, given that Chinese state museums made collective curatorial decisions. While SB2000 commissioned four curators, the Artistic Committee that Feng chaired could temper proposed curatorial decisions regarding, say, the balance between Chinese and foreign artists.[8]

The urban culture of Republican-era, semicolonial Shanghai is to be re-trofitted to embrace the transition to capitalist-style modernization and even to "renovate its own cultural traditions." However—and quite apart from this renovation seeming to entail jettisoning revolutionary, national liberationist, and socialist/egalitarian goals, whatever may be said of "typical" changes in "the past century"—can the refitting operate in tandem with developments in the larger region to which the PRC was associated? Dirlik, for instance, notices "a remarkable 'forgetfulness' [in the PRC and even among foreign discussants] concerning the part that the Japanese, South Korean, Taiwanese, but especially the Singaporean 'models' played in inspiring policy in the initial phase of 'reform and opening' (*gaige kaifang*) in the 1980s and through the 1990s," when there is any discussion of a supposed "Chinese model" of development.[9] Will the various strands of cultural production that deploy Shanghai as presentist cultural place recognize and incorporate aspects of culturally imagined New Asia as a shared zone of contemporaneity? Or will the New China displace versions of New Asia?

SB2000 was the third edition of the Shanghai Biennale but its first fully-fledged international version, and it was flagged as being historically groundbreaking even as the exhibition started.[10] The biennale must be tied to Shanghai's efforts once again to assert itself as cosmopolitan—Deng Xiaoping called Shanghai the "Head of the Dragon" during his famed 1992 Chinese New Year tour of southern China.[11] Writing soon after the exhibition, art historian Wu Hung says that the claim for significance "becomes understandable when we realise that it relates particularly to officially sponsored exhibitions in China, which, before the 2000 Shanghai Biennale, were largely 'local'" and ambivalent about contemporary or more progressive art forms.[12] Contemporary artists from the PRC were already part of a global art scene from the early 1990s, but the National Art Gallery in Beijing had, up to 2000, refused to show installation, performance art, and multimedia work. SB2000, significantly, did exhibit such artwork and therefore can be taken as "reformist."[13]

The actual artwork selected, though, has been described as being an "eclectic pastiche" rather than possessing the appearance of contemporary "cultural hybridity." This was the result of a hesitant execution of the exhibition's theme, which was "Shanghai Spirit" in English and "Haishang, Shanghai" (Shanghai over the sea) in Chinese.[14] Wu Hung explains: "The Chinese title . . . relates to the ocean, marine culture and the outside world. Having pushed the idea of a Shanghai spirit this far, the exhibition's organisers had to stop and reassert the national identity of their project," given the organizers wish to firm up a Chinese interpretive system for art.[15] However, two curators from outside the PRC were involved: one a Chinese national based in Paris, the globetrotting Hou Hanru, and the other a Japanese curator, Shimizu Toshio. They offered a curatorial strand emphasizing a non-Eurocentric vision of cultural openness that the city of Shanghai could epitomize. We see here two inconsistent directions that the representation of the PRC's cultural transformation and production could take. Unfortunately, Wu Hung found the discussion that SB2000 generated to be mainly about the practical matters relating to the biennale's execution, and "the exhibition's content and contribution to art itself attracted much less attention."[16] That is, there was a moment of failed criticality to which we can turn in more detail.

The biennale catalogue has three essays by Chinese curator Zhang Qing, Hou, and Shimizu. Zhang Qing's essay leads in a direction that conflicts with that of Hou's and Shimizu's essays. The other Chinese curator, Li Xu, also wrote an essay, "Made in China," that "severely criticised Chinese contemporary artists for ingratiating themselves with Westerners"—a point that was also diplomatically made by Zhang Qing in his essay—but Li Xu's essay was left out apparently because of its "bluntness."[17] Between them, Hou and Shimizu make related arguments about artistic production and the question of transitional cultural norms in a more connected world but with differing emphases. For Hou, globalization has assisted an economic development that manifests "an active reaction and resistance" to Western economic and cultural forces that was less possible during its "semi-colonial history," and therefore Shanghai is now able to be a true global city that becomes "a[n experimental] laboratory for a new China" without the artistic and hallmarks of the "Oriental."[18] This, we can say, is a version of the post-exotic urban-modern. Hou is aware that "art experiments" in the PRC are "extremely complicated and difficult," but such artistic production is part of a liberating global modernity.[19] He does not invoke the nation-state and does not mention the region, remaining intent on discussing globalized contemporary art's potential.

Shimizu's accent is on the speed of information that facilitates a single or coeval time zone, bypassing any West/non-West binary. Shanghai "is starting to have the same kind of scent with other major cities of the world such as Tokyo, New York, Hong Kong . . . Singapore, Taipei or Seoul"—and so, each city can now create its own originality.[20] Therefore, flows of culture are no longer one way from "Western cities [that] are superior," and Shanghai and Chinese contemporary art "should share [and verily reflect] an expression of the time they are living in."[21] Like Hou, Shimizu desires that ordinary citizens may get used to attending museums and see in the biennale varieties of new cultural expression. We can note that although Asia is never directly brought up in either Hou's or Shimizu's essays, the exhibitions and general discourses on Asian contemporary art in the 1990s that they have been part of vitally feed into their curatorial outlines and contribute toward thinking on New China and the contemporary.

Zhang Qing's essay, "Beyond Left and Right: Transformation of the Shanghai Biennale," directly attacks the Western art market for undermining Chinese contemporary art's capacity for "intense observation and contemplation of their own conditions."[22] Therefore, SB2000 needs to "be taken as a scholastic pursuit of a uniquely Chinese contemporary art in a world characterized by accelerating internationalization and globalization," which he obviously finds to be less positive than Hou and Shimizu.[23] Western art markets' and curators' supposedly globalized/internationalized orientation really serves to direct PRC artists to issues that *seem* universal and plural—such as "Orientalism, race, history, class, identity, gender, finance, global capitalism, resource, super power, and regionalism"—but are really hegemonic attempts to advance a cultural agenda.[24] A Sinocentric defense of the local is required for national dignity. Zhang Qing, though, does try to break a nationalistic West/China binary by gesturing toward a larger Asian "Us," given China's geographical position adjacent to the "economic miracles of Japan . . . [and] south-east Asian countries" and their "flowering art scenes," as manifested in the region's many biennales and triennales.[25] The "Shanghai Biennale is making an effort to show the active role China plays on the Asian cultural stage," although quite what that role might be is not specified.[26] His position seems a Sinocentric one that he parlays onto a loose Asianism.[27]

While curator Mia Yu expresses skepticism regarding Zhang Qing's statement on supposedly redefining Asian culture for a mainstream discourse on art, seeing this as an attempt to give his Sinocentrism "a more international flavour," what perhaps matters is that this Asian "flavour" *is* articulated, offering an option for thinking China and Asia that could be picked up at some other moment.[28] Mia Yu herself offers such a moment pertinent to Zhang Qing's uneven thinking:

> Shortly after visiting SB2000, [curator and critic] Gao Shiming published an acerbic review in an art journal in Taiwan and bluntly criticised SB2000 . . . of lacking an understanding of China's historical and social complexities . . . [and]

called for "unweaving a binary based global-local" and reimagining a non-binary local. . . . Gao Shiming, [later] working within the institutional framework of China Art Academy, set out to investigate trans-Asian experiences through research initiatives such as [the exhibition] "Edges of the Earth: Migration of Contemporary Asian Art and Geopolitics" (2002–04).[29]

Gao has also worked within PRC institutional constraints and yet managed an exhibition just two years past SB2000 that tried to break out of Sinocentric artistic frameworks, applying the issue of China's adjacent position and geographical connection to its neighbors in a more concrete manner.

One of the projects Gao was involved with for "Rehearsal: 2010 Shanghai Biennale," the eighth edition for which he was also the executive curator, was the *Long March Project: Ho Chi Minh Trail* (2008–2010). During the Vietnam War, the Trail was a transportation and military supply route running from North Vietnam to Laos and Cambodia, and into South Vietnam. In Gao's words, "For this project we invited 25 people, including artists, scholars, and curators, to travel together for 22 days from . . . to revisit the Ho Chi Minh Trail. During this time, we re-examined our collective memories and historical narratives, to reflect on our own historical experience and political situation. We walked the Ho Chi Minh Trail for just six hours. It was a performative act."[30] The *Ho Chi Minh Trail* was an outgrowth of the *Long March Project* started in 2002 with Lu Jie as the chief curator. The project was conceived as a series of exhibitions, performances, and discussions exploring the relationship between contemporary art and the 10,000-kilometer Communist Chinese Long March (1934–1935). We might say that the newer project attempted an inter-Asian contemplation on painful Cold War experiences felt to be shared by Northeast and Southeast Asia. Gao therefore offers one artistic-cultural strategy to stitch Asia together beyond Zhang Qing's vague voicing on China and Asia.

Gao's approach to geographical adjacency and national borders and stance on the overtly local, we could say, is judicious for the idea of New Asia. To critic Lee Weng Choy, "'Adjacency' could be understood as a state of mutual coexistence between two or more proximate entities, whether creature, community or country," during which "art [can] develop dialogues with adjacent art—and non-art."[31] How Gao describes the *Long March Project: Ho Chi Minh Trail* fits such an understanding of adjacency. During a 2011 talk by him that brought up the *Ho Chi Minh Trail* project (HCMTP), philosopher John Rajchman asked what Asia is and whether China plays a specific role in

Asia. Gao's oblique yet pointed response was: "I [once] asked [curator] Alexandra Munroe about her understanding of Asia, and how it is different from the conception of Asia in the framework of [New York-based] Asia Society. It's very different. For we Asian people, maybe we can speak very roughly that there is no such thing as Asia, but only Asians. I think Asia is always inter-Asia, it's not a container for national states."[32] The conceptual step Gao makes is away from an Asia with national borders to an inter-Asia with historically interconnected and adjacent cultures and peoples. However, as we know, difficult political matters with thorny national and sometimes racially inflected provenances are not easily abrogated. We have already seen this in the films and pop music examined in chapters 4 and 5. I return to Lee Weng Choy: "Of course, the notion of adjacency as a happy coexistence amongst neighbours is an idealisation. . . . For Southeast Asia, China looms large and, sometimes, threateningly."[33] In place of adjacency, Lee mentions that there is also the prospect that, with SB2000, "Shanghai's insertion of China onto the global stage" in visual arts terms—whether intended or not—will for some make "China . . . [into] a metonym for Asia."[34]

As Lee submits, the full weight of China and its history are hard to avoid, even given the best of curatorial intentions. This became apparent during a public discussion held by the *Ho Chi Minh Trail* project organizers at the Himiko Visual Café in Ho Chi Minh city on June 19, 2010. Gao Shiming thanked Vietnamese participants for their presentations, and observed that if "thirty years ago, Vietnam, China, Cambodia, and Laos were connected because of a utopian [political] vision, then today the contemporary art that arises from that legacy needs to be discussed" via an understanding of contemporary time that should try to evade all "nation state categorization[s]" of art.[35] Curator Lu Jie reinforced Gao's stance by stating that "HCMTP history" will be written through discursive and artistic exchange and not by China or the project organizers: "We really do not represent Chinese art, and Chinese art does not represent China."[36] That is, they are not ethno-nationalistic, and they reject a domineering notion of Chinese national culture. He added that members of the Indian left whom he met at a conference in Delhi had extended an invitation to dialogue based on "a common historical thread" in Asia pertaining to postwar decolonization, "revolutionary narratives, [and] socialist thought."[37]

The response from Vietnamese American artist Dinh Q. Lê was immediate: "India and China are presently more equal powers. Vietnam and China have a long history that is very complicated."[38] Lê is probably referring to tensions that relate to the 1979 Sino-Vietnamese War, when Chinese troops entered northern Vietnam to punish the latter's incursions into Kampuchea to put down the genocidal but pro-Beijing Khmer Rouge regime.[39] While Lê proceeded to be conciliatory, stressing that discussion with people from the region who shared so much was good, "going deeper than . . . discussion[s] . . . with visiting Western critics, curators, or historians," it is evident that a plea for adjacency does not in itself overcome issues of divergent national-isms.[40] Art historian Pamela Corey notes that at another public discussion in Phnom Penh, Cambodia, in July 2010, the HCMTP group received questions that generated "the sense that the Long March artists were on a mission of knowledge-gathering rather than sharing, and [further indicated] their lack of sensitivity to specific national histories despite the desire for a romanti-cized notion of regional exchange."[41]

Adjacency as a notion in which cultural and global urban space can become worked into a representation of New China as a shareable place, even in multiracial or ethnic terms, takes on a rosy aspect in the upbeat 2007 romantic comedy *The Longest Night in Shanghai*. China's more pronounced global profile in the new millennium offered new market opportunities for coproduced films to take advantage of the PRC as both new market and loca-tion for production. The success in the early 2000s of Chinese-led, big-scale pan-Asian films such as Ang Lee's *Crouching Tiger, Hidden Dragon* (2000) and Zhang Yimou's *House of Flying Daggers* (2004) indicated to the Japanese, who were not leaders of coproduced media and film in the region, that "China was the marker of regional becoming at this moment," offering a geography of promise.[42] *Longest Night* was a coproduction with Shanghai Film Studios led by Japan's Movie Eye Entertainment, directed by Zhang Yibai, and made to capitalize on an understanding of the PRC's contemporary moment. Movie Eye had even set up shop in Shanghai to further their goals. To shoot a film in Shanghai was to participate *not* in some mythic Asia of *wuxia*, of martial arts heroes, but in "today's Shanghai, . . . increasingly involved in the trend of globalization."[43] Stephanie DeBoer posits that *Longest Night* tries to offer "Asia as a site of shared experience, encounter, and even proximity . . . [as part of] an assessment of the imagined [mainland Chinese and larger regional] market for the coproduction, whose very locations were intended to appeal to a wide transnational audience."[44] Shanghai is a venue for *Longest Night*'s confused lead characters, one where bewilderment can be alleviated by literal and cultural translation assisting new understandings of the self and culture. Shanghai joins the club of what literary-cultural critic Jini Kim Watson describes as "New Asian Cities," places for novel experience that may transcend national and racial/ethnic limitations.[45]

Celebrity hairdresser, makeup artist, and stylist Mizushima Naoki (Motoki Masahiro) goes to Shanghai to work with the performers and other participants in the Shanghai Music Awards, with attendees for the event expected from not only the PRC but also Hong Kong, Taiwan, Japan, and South Korea. Mizushima turns up in a rising world city where pop music has become inter-Asian and can draw a correspondingly multicultural regional audience. His girlfriend, personal assistant Takahashi Miho (Nishida Naomi), is with him. Their relationship is now stale, but being emotionally reserved, he is unable to face that reality.

At the venue for the awards in the futuristic Pudong New Area, Mizushima is confronted by an old but persistent suitor for his girlfriend, who has followed them from Tokyo. He walks out of the building into the plaza area, discomfited by the confrontation, and there that indexical Shanghai architectural item, the Oriental Pearl Radio and Television Tower, completed in 1994, looms up behind him in the night: it represents the city that, in his disappointment with love and life, he is about to be lost in. By the roadside, Mizushima literally runs into the vehicle of the harum-scarum but tomboyish and tough-talking taxi driver Lin Xi (singer Vicki Zhao/Zhao Wei), herself also confused and unable to tell her motor mechanic Tong Tong (Taiwanese Dylan Kuo) that she wants more than platonic friendship from him—and he is soon to be married.

To amend for her ramming Mizushima, Lin Xi offers to drive him around the city, and through force of her personality, she gets him into her taxi, even though they are incomprehensible to each other linguistically, even with his attempt at using English as a lingua franca. Much inevitable comic relief is made of the non- and miscommunication that occur. Mizushima is also unable to tell her where he is staying, as he had not bothered to find out the name of his hotel. Finally, after an extensive urban perambulation that touristically takes the viewer mainly to the newer Pudong and older colonial Bund areas, with some appearance of the French Concession, they end up in a quiet road. There, using Lin Xi's red lipstick, he writes in *kanji*—logographic Japanese characters taken from the Chinese script—and Lin Xi writes in Chinese: they communicate. Lipstick texts cover the taxi, the walls of the buildings next to them, and even the road; this becomes the most memorable scene in *Longest Night*. Communication runs into logocentric excess, and we learn that feeling, life situations, and even cultural difference need not get lost in translation—that textual and filmic signification are possible. Mizushima teaches her how to say, in Japanese, "I love you. Do you love me?"

When Tong Tong turns up to repair the taxi that Lin Xi has once again banged up, she finally tells him that she loves him but in Japanese. Looking on, Mizushima understands her present limits. Finally, the pair locate his hotel, where he is now able to face breaking up with Takahashi. After daybreak, he goes to Lin Xi's apartment to dress her for Tong Tong's wedding. A complete makeover is effected, with Mizushima even ripping up parts of her dress to make it more stylish—we understand that they have both been made over. The pair go to the mirror for the moment of self-realization. He says in Mandarin, "You are very beautiful"; in return, she asks in Japanese, "Do you love me?" The film ends.

While *Longest Night* hardly attempts to be profound—and it loses focus by having too many subplots distracting from the restrained yet warm bond developing between Mizushima and Lin Xi—it manages to get beyond the trite to represent the viability of "adjacency," as Lee Weng Choy defines it, as a state of mutual coexistence between two or more proximate entities, during which positive dialogue and even cultural translation transpires. The city—the "Shanghai Spirit" perhaps—is more than just the urban context that allows the renovation of selves, but the city is itself an embodiment of upbeat cultural renovation. The Japanese man and the Chinese woman find in Shanghai a shared regional place conducive for transethnic (or perhaps transracial, depending on the categories the pair think in) and transnational personal fulfillment.

The direction that *Longest Night* takes becomes more marked when we think of it against Sofia Coppola's slightly earlier and more melancholic *Lost in Translation* (2003). It seems probable that her film may have had some influence upon *Longest Night*, but the divergences in the handling of the East Asian metropolis—Tokyo for Coppola's film—and translation are revealing. *Lost in Translation* features two Americans who start to relate with each other emotionally partly because of their inability to comprehend frenetic Tokyo. Despite an affection for Tokyo that comes through in the film, the city with its unintelligible flashiness cannot foster connection: both the faded actor, Bob Harris (Bill Murray), and the young wife, Charlotte (Scarlett Johansson), must retreat into the hermetic confines of the Park Hyatt Tokyo. While Tokyo's neon-lit modernity seems to grant it a coeval temporality with the United States that Bob and Charlotte hail from—even if the city is also a place where exotic tradition resides, with Charlotte finding *ikebana* alienating—it offers no option for real cultural translation. The film, as has occurred in more colonial-era cultural production, "reproduces Japan as an enigma that can be deciphered only be recourse to broad generalization about 'Japanese culture.'"[46]

The PRC's rise and the significance of that for regional cultural representation and production remains an act in progress. Its contemporary art is now an accepted component of global art. Its contemporary art museums, both state-run and private, are to be found in Shanghai, Beijing, and other less major cities. Its popular culture has yet to have the same impact of Japanese and Korean popular culture, or the impact of an earlier popular culture hailing from Taiwan and Hong Kong, either in the region or in the Euro-American West. However, by 2022, the presence of TV dramas could be noticed. In that year, 714 drama series were exported, a number of them costume dramas, and "Southeast Asia is the core market for these dramas, accounting for one-third of the series . . . exported."[47] The moderate impact thus far is partly because the size of China's market allows its media and cultural industries to look within, and partly because of the strict control that the Communist Party of China imposes over its media.[48] For an example of the latter situation, the TV drama *Story of the Yanxi Palace* (*Yanxi gonglue*, 2018) was successful in the region and in China but was pulled from state-run TV channels in the PRC in 2019.[49]

The PRC's older media successes included serial costumed dramas from the 1980s that were exported to Taiwan and Hong Kong as central destinations, along with Singapore, Malaysia, Japan, Korea, the United States, Indonesia, and Thailand.[50] By about 2003, though, Korean drama exports competed effectively with dramas from China, although it is not that the PRC has no media and cultural industry ambitions.[51] On October 7–8, 2023, the National Conference on Propaganda, Ideology, and Cultural Work was held in Beijing, the third of a quinquennial series of conferences dedicated to such concerns. During the conference, Xi Jinping Thought on Culture was formally set out. Xinhua News Agency reported that Xi "called for efforts to continuously consolidate the common intellectual foundation for the whole Party and all Chinese people to strive in unity, and grow China's cultural soft power and the appeal of Chinese culture."[52]

Whatever nationalistic impulses exist in China, inter-Asian popular culture has made its presence palpably felt. While nationalism is able to stymie cross-border impulses, what has already come into existence cannot be ignored. China Global Television Network, the international wing of the state broadcaster CCTV, has acknowledged as much: "The spread of Asian popular culture highlights the changing attitudes of the younger generation of Asians to their neighbors. Through the shared interest in popular culture, those Asian countries effectively form positive relationships with one another since a common ground found in music and movies can certainly engender a sense of goodwill for one another."[53] Inter-Asian popular culture leads to motherhood statements on "positive relationships," if for no other reason than the pragmatic inclusion of the PRC's media and cultural industry products as participating in the burst of creativity. Will contemporary China join a cultural stage in Asia? Or will it be a metonym that will stand in for or displace an older New Asia?

More recently, the COVID pandemic from 2020 affected the economic globalization processes such as the long-term movement of people, goods, and services. However, supply-chain issues had already come to the fore with the heightened United States–PRC trade tensions that occurred during the days of the Trump administration of 2017–2021. Northeast and Southeast Asia assuredly cannot escape the consequences of such strain. The geopolitical stress has disrupted the attempts by the Association of Southeast Asian Nations to strengthen regionalism via their more-established means of engaging with an assertive China: "Southeast Asia's way to manage China's challenge was to enmesh it, socialise it and include and involve it with regional processes."[54] The strategic realignments that are still transpiring may be obsolescing the economic forces that supported regional cultural production and the cultural representation of the region in the 1990s to the 2000s. We will have to wait to witness how the existing forms of cross-border cultural production adapt.

The ongoing ascension of China has transformed the centrality of the United States–Japan partnership in the postwar power relation in Eastern Asia. "This transimperial moment," as it has been put, shows both the PRC's incorporation into global capitalism and speaks of a "shift of global hegemony," and the nature of such a shift is "always uneven, contradictory, and, at times, violent."[55] Such a change is transpiring at a point when cross-border cultural production and circulation have substantially increased—but also when cultural consumption, to varying degrees, can be both distinguished from and conflated with identity, whether multicultural, racial, or ethnonational. The disorderliness of a regional contemporary takes on new dimensions.

NOTES

Introduction

1. Henry Lau, "How Takuya Kimura Became One of East Asia's Best-Loved Stars: From Era-Defining Japanese Boy Band SMAP and Beloved TV Drama *Love Generation*, to Style Icon and Endorsement King," *South China Morning Post*, August 5, 2022, https://www.scmp.com/magazines/style/celebrity/article/3187709/how-takuya-kimura-became-one-east-asias-best-loved-stars, accessed July 19, 2023.

2. Levi Strauss and Company, "A Quick Q&A with Stars of Asia's Levi's® Engineered Jeans™ Campaign," https://www.levistrauss.com/2019/02/04/quick-qa-stars-asias-levis-engineered-jeans-campaign/, accessed July 19, 2023.

3. Yu-fen Ko, "The Desired Form: Japanese Idol Dramas in Taiwan," in *Feeling Asian Modernities: Transnational Consumption of Japanese TV Dramas*, ed. Kōichi Iwabuchi (Hong Kong: Hong Kong University Press, 2004), 123.

4. Yamamoto Atsuo, "From Dualism to Oneness: A Thought on the Potential of Asian Art," in Japan Foundation Asia Center and Tokyo Opera City Cultural Foundation, *Under Construction: New Dimensions of Asian Art*, ed. Kataoka Mami, exhibition catalogue (Tokyo: Japan Foundation Asia Center, 2002), 29.

5. Kamiya Yukie, "Communicative Approach, from Asia," in Japan Foundation Asia Center and Tokyo Opera City Cultural Foundation, *Under Construction: New Dimensions of Asian Art*, ed. Kataoka Mami, exhibition catalogue (Tokyo: Japan Foundation Asia Center, 2002), 136.

6. Gayatri Chakravorty Spivak, "Can the Subaltern Speak?" in *Marxism and the Interpretation of Culture*, ed. Cary Nelson and Lawrence Grossberg (Urbana, IL: University of Illinois Press, 1988).

7. Mahathir Mohamad and Ishihara Shintarō, *The Voice of Asia*, trans. Frank Baldwin (Tokyo: Kodansha International, 1995), 6, 31.

8. Fredric Jameson, "The Aesthetics of Singularity," *New Left Review* 92 (2015): 119. The enlarged region is therefore part of a larger story of capitalist subsumption since the 1980s, "in which different dimensions—dimensions not only quantitatively distinct

but qualitatively incommensurate . . . —are brought into relationship with each other, however fleetingly" (Jameson, "The Aesthetic of Singularity," 119).

9. Mahathir Mohamad, in Mahathir and Ishihara, *The Voice of Asia*, 13.

10. World Bank, *The East Asian Miracle: Economic Growth and Public Policy* (New York: Oxford University Press, 1993).

11. Michael K. Bourdaghs, Paola Iovene, and Kaley Mason, "Introduction," in *Sound Alignments: Popular Music in Asia's Cold Wars*, ed. Michael K. Bourdaghs, Paola Iovene, and Kaley Mason (Durham, NC: Duke University Press, 2021), 10.

12. Joan Kee, *The Geometries of Afro Asia: Art Beyond Solidarity* (Oakland: University of California Press, 2023), 10.

13. Jameson, "Aesthetics of Singularity," 120, 104.

14. On the Asian values discourse, see C. J. W.-L. Wee, *The Asian Modern: Culture, Capitalist Development, Singapore* (Hong Kong: Hong Kong University Press, 2007), 101–119; and Beng-Huat Chua, "Culture, Multiracialism, and National Identity in Singapore," in *Trajectories: Inter-Asia Cultural Studies*, ed. Kuan-Hsing Chen (London: Routledge, 1998), 166–193.

15. Amitav Acharya, "Asia Is Not One," *Journal of Asian Studies* 69, no. 4 (2010): 1,002.

16. Edwin O. Reischauer and John K. Fairbank, *East Asia: The Great Tradition* (Boston, MA: Houghton Mifflin, 1960), 3.

17. Arif Dirlik, *Complicities: The People's Republic of China in Global Capitalism* (Chicago, IL: Prickly Paradigm, 2017), 21.

18. Michael Schaller, "Securing the Great Crescent: Occupied Japan and the Origins of Containment in Southeast Asia," *Journal of American History* 69, no. 2 (1982): 414.

19. Wen-Qing Ngoei, *Arc of Containment: Britain, the United States, and Anticommunism in Southeast Asia* (Ithaca, NY: Cornell University Press, 2019).

20. Quoted by Schaller, "Securing the Great Crescent," 413.

21. See Naoki Sakai, "'You Asians': On the Historical Role of the West and Asia Binary," *South Atlantic Quarterly* 99, no. 4 (2000): 789–817, later included in his *The End of Pax Americana: The Loss of Empire and Hikikomori Nationalism* (Durham, NC: Duke University Press, 2022). Sakai's critique appeared first in a 2000 Singapore conference, published in *"We Asians": Between Past and Future: A Millennial Regional Conference*, ed. Kwok Kian-Woon, Indira Arumugam, Karen Chia, and Lee Chee Keng (Singapore: Singapore Heritage Society, 2000). Sakai criticized the phrase "we Asians"—even though used with ironized self-awareness in relation to the Asian values discourse of the 1980s–1990s— as reaffirming the historicity of colonial history, thereby keeping an Orientalized "you Asians" notion in play.

22. Slavoj Žižek, "Multiculturalism, or, the Cultural Logic of Multinational Capitalism," *New Left Review* no. 225 (1997): 43–44.

23. Leo Ching, "Globalizing the Regional, Regionalizing the Global: Mass Culture and Asianism in the Age of Late Capital," *Public Culture* 12, no. 1 (2000): 257.

24. "Editorial Statement," *Inter-Asia Cultural Studies* 1, no. 1 (2000): 5.

25. "Editorial Statement," 5.

26. "Editorial Statement," 5. Leo Ching argues, in his assessment of the journal's impact on its tenth anniversary, that "the 'shifting geography of knowledge' in the postcolonial condition . . . is no longer understood as universal, without location and without history"; "*Inter-Asia Cultural Studies* and the Decolonial-turn," *Inter-Asia Cultural Studies* 11, no. 2 (2010): 184.

27. Harry Harootunian, *Marx after Marx: History and Time in the Expansion of Capitalism* (New York: Columbia University Press, 2017), 236.

28. Ezra Vogel, *Japan as Number One: Lessons for America* (Cambridge, MA: Harvard University Press, 1979).

29. Vipan Chandra, "What Can Japan Teach Us?" *Christian Science Monitor*, February 11, 1980, https://www.csmonitor.com/1980/0211/021150.html, accessed March 18, 2022.

30. Edward W. Said, *Orientalism* (1978; New York: Vintage, 1979), 323. Later, Said goes on to add, "How does one *represent* other cultures? What is *another* culture? Is the notion of a distinct culture (or race, or religion, or civilization) a useful one, or does it always get involved either in self-congratulation (when one discusses one's own) or hostility and aggression (when one discusses the 'other')?" (325). Those indeed become both intellectual and practical questions for making art exhibitions, films, and pop music in Asia—when the other chooses to represent his or her own "selves."

31. Harry Harootunian, *Uneven Moments: Reflections on Japan's Modern History* (New York: Columbia University Press, 2019), 55.

32. Patrick D. Flores observes that "a delimitation [between curation as a subject and what is being curated] may prove to be useful in distinguishing the spheres of contemporary art, or declensions for purpose of study, or categories of analysis and materials: art and artist, curation, public, criticism and theory, aesthetics" (*Past Peripheral: Curation in Southeast Asia* [Singapore: NUS Museum, 2008], 30).

33. Paul O'Neil, "The Curatorial Turn: From Practice to Discourse," in *Issues in Curating Contemporary Art and Performance*, ed. Judith Rugg and Michèle Sedgwick (Bristol: Intellect, 2007), 16.

34. James Elkins, "Afterword," in *Art and Globalization*, ed. James Elkins, Zhivka Valaivicharska, and Alice Kim (University Park: Pennsylvania State University Press, 2010), 264.

35. Fredric Jameson, "Notes on Globalization as a Philosophical Issue," in *The Cultures of Globalization*, ed. Fredric Jameson and Masao Miyoshi (Durham, NC: Duke University Press, 1998), 54–77.

36. Andreas Huyssen, "Introduction: World Cultures, World Cities," in *Other Cities, Other Worlds: Urban Imaginaries in a Globalizing Age* (Durham, NC: Duke University Press, 2008), 14.

37. Other experiments in the representation of Asia existed. There were large-scale films from about 2000, sometimes coproduced by combinations of media companies from the People's Republic of China, Japan, South Korea, and Hong Kong that tried

to represent an "historical" Asia or East Asia using China as an indexical if sometimes deterritorialized location, such as *House of Flying Daggers* (2004), *The Promise* (2005), and *Battle of Wits* (2006). They are outside of the scope of this book; see Stephanie DeBoer, *Coproducing Asia: Locating Japanese–Chinese Regional Film and Media* (Minneapolis: University of Minnesota Press, 2014), 163–172.

38. Kōichi Iwabuchi, "East Asian Popular Culture and Inter-Asian Referencing," in *Routledge Handbook of East Asian Popular Culture*, ed. Kōichi Iwabuchi, Eva Tsai, and Chris Berry (Abingdon, UK: Routledge, 2016), 29.

39. See Nissim Otmazgin and Eyal Ben-Ari, eds., *Popular Culture Co-Productions and Collaborations in East and Southeast Asia* (Singapore: NUS Press and Kyoto: Kyoto University Press, 2012); Nissim Kadosh Otmazgin, *Regionalizing Culture: The Political Economy of Japanese Popular Culture in Asia* (Honolulu: University of Hawai'i Press, 2013); and Nissim Otmazgin, "A New Cultural Geography of East Asia: Imagining a 'Region' through Popular Culture," *Asia-Pacific Journal: Japan Focus* 14, issue 7, no. 5 (2016), https://apjjf.org/2016/07/Otmazgin.html, accessed April 14, 2022.

40. Thomas Crow, *Modern Art in the Common Culture* (New Haven, CT: Yale University Press, 1998), 37.

41. Clement Greenberg, "Avant-Garde and Kitsch" (1939), in *Art and Culture: Critical Essays* (Boston, MA: Beacon Press, 1961), 9.

42. Leo T. S. Ching, *Anti-Japan: The Politics of Sentiment in Postcolonial East Asia* (Durham, NC: Duke University Press, 2019), 133.

43. Andreas Huyssen, "High/Low in an Expanded Field," *Modernism/modernity* 9, no. 3 (2002): 370.

44. Okwui Enwezor, "Mega-exhibitions: The Antinomies of a Transnational Global Form," in *Other Cities, Other Worlds: Urban Imaginaries in a Globalizing Age*, ed. Andreas Huyssen (Durham, NC: Duke University Press, 2008), 177, n1.

45. Stuart Hall, "Notes on Deconstructing 'the Popular'" (1981), in *Essential Essays, Volume 1: Foundations of Cultural Studies*, ed. David Morley (Durham, NC: Duke University Press, 2019), 348. See also Devon Powers, "The Problem of Popular Culture," *Communication Theory*, 32, no. 4 (2022): 461–470.

46. Huyssen, "High/Low in an Expanded Field," 371.

47. Immanuel Wallerstein, *The Modern World System: Capitalist Agriculture and the Origins of the European World-Economy in the Sixteenth Century* (New York: Academic Press, 1974), 349.

48. Sandro Mezzadra and Brett Neilson, *Border as Method, Or, the Multiplication of Labor* (Durham, NC: Duke University Press, 2013), 73.

49. James E. Cronin, *The World the Cold War Made: Order, Chaos, and the Return of History* (New York: Routledge, 1996), 252.

50. Peter Osborne, *The Postconceptual Condition: Critical Essays* (London: Verso, 2018), 109.

51. Patrick D. Flores, personal e-mail communication to the author, April 21, 2007.

52. Faisal Devji, "The Turn to Empire," *Inter-Asia Cultural Studies* 21, no. 1 (2020): 112.

53. Patrick D. Flores, "Phases of Curatorial Passage," in *Art Studies 04: Condition Report: Shifting Perspectives in Asia—Curator's Book*, ed. Beverly Yong and Furuichi Yasuko (Tokyo: Japan Foundation Asia Center, 2018), 138.

54. Jameson, "Notes on Globalization," 55.

55. Harootunian, *Uneven Moments*, 64.

56. Dipesh Chakrabarty, "'Asia' and the Twentieth Century: What Is 'Asian Modernity'?" in *"We Asians": Between Past and Future: A Millennial Regional Conference*, ed. Kwok Kian-Woon, Indira Arumugam, Karen Chia, and Lee Chee Keng (Singapore: Singapore Heritage Society, 2000), 22.

57. Chakrabarty, "'Asia' and the Twentieth Century," 26.

58. Prasenjit Duara, *Sovereignty and Authenticity: Manchukuo and the East Asian Modern* (Lanham, MD: Rowman & Littlefield, 2003), 9.

59. Giovanni Arrighi, *The Long Twentieth Century: Money, Power, and the Origins of Our Times* (London: Verso, 1991), 59. The classic study of the imperialism of free trade is Ronald Robinson and John Andrew Gallagher with Alice Denny's *Africa and the Victorians: The Official Mind of Imperialism* (London: Macmillan, 1961).

60. Daniel Leese, "'Revolution': Conceptualizing Political and Social Change in the Late Qing Dynasty," *Oriens Extremus* 51 (2012): 30. For a related argument with the terms *guojia* (state), *minzu* (nation), and *shijie* (world), see Marc A. Matten, "'China Is the China of the Chinese': The Concept of Nation and Its Impact on Political Thinking in Modern China," *Oriens Extremus* 51 (2012): 63–106. A pioneering argument on how *modernity* becomes linguistically and culturally translated into May Fourth literary discourse in China is Lydia H. Liu's *Translingual Practice: Literature, National Culture, and Translated Modernity—China, 1900–1937* (Stanford, CA: Stanford University Press, 1995).

61. Duara, *Sovereignty and Authenticity*, 25. See also Harumi Befu, ed., *Cultural Nationalism in East Asia: Representation and Identity* (Berkeley: Institute of East Asian Studies, University of California, 1993).

62. Kakuzō Okakura, *Ideals of the East, with Special Reference to the Art of Japan* (London: J. Murray, 1903), 1, 8.

63. As Younjung Oh notes, "Meiji elites' ambitious vision [regarding Japanese guardianship of Asian arts and culture] had not yet led to popular interest in and mass consumption of Asian arts and culture within Japan at that time[, the start of the twentieth century]" ("Oriental Taste in Imperial Japan: The Exhibition and Sale of Asian Art and Artifacts by Japanese Department Stores from the 1920s through the Early 1940s," *Journal of Asian Studies* 78, no. 1 [2019]: 52).

64. Duara, *Sovereignty and Authenticity*, 89–123. Regarding the ambivalence toward Western civilization and the modernizing process in this period, see Sun Ge, "In Search of the Modern: Tracing Japanese Thought on 'Overcoming Modernity,'" in *Impacts of*

Modernities, ed. Thomas Lamarre and Kang Nae-hui (Hong Kong: Hong Kong University Press, 2004).

65. Cronin, *The World the Cold War Made*, 253.

66. See John Page, "The East Asian Miracle: Four Lessons for Development Policy," in *NBER Macroeconomics Annual 1994, Vol. 9*, ed. Stanley Fischer and Julio J. Rotemberg (Cambridge, MA: MIT Press, 1994). He does not argue for an easily transferrable model for development—the politics and the capitalist economics coincide, but they are never a complete fit: "Certainly geographical proximity plays an important role. Technological transfers, worker mobility, trade links, and political peer pressure may be important factors in regional development" (279). Page was part of the team who wrote the World Bank's policy report, *The East Asian Miracle*, in 1993.

67. Jini Kim Watson, *Cold War Reckonings: Authoritarianism and the Genres of Decolonization* (New York: Fordham University Press, 2021), 16.

68. For "the key years of the 1960s to the 1970s, . . . when communism was a clear and present danger in Southeast Asia, cultural identity—what your society was—was simply an absurd issue; what mattered was whose side you were on" (Wee, *Asian Modern*, 156).

69. Heonik Kwon, "The Transpacific Cold War," in *Transpacific Studies: From an Emerging Field*, ed. Janet Hoskins and Viet Thanh Nguyen (Honolulu: University of Hawai'i Press, 2014), 64–84.

70. Heonik Kwon, *The Other Cold War* (New York: Columbia University Press, 2010), 6.

71. Kuan-Hsing Chen, *Asia as Method: Toward Deimperialization* (Durham, NC: Duke University Press, 2010), 121.

72. Bourdaghs, Iovene, and Mason, "Introduction," 3.

73. Wang Hui, "The Idea of Asia and Its Ambiguities," *Journal of Asian Studies* 69, no. 4 (2010): 989.

74. Giorgio Agamben, "What Is the Contemporary?" in *What Is an Apparatus and Other Essays*, trans. David Kishit and Stefan Pedatella (Stanford, CA: Stanford University Press, 2009), 45.

75. Agamben, "What Is the Contemporary?" 50.

76. Agamben, "What Is the Contemporary?" 51.

77. Agamben, "What Is the Contemporary?" 53.

Chapter 1

1. J. Victor Koschmann, "Asianism's Legacy," in *Network Power: Japan and Asia*, ed. Peter J. Katzenstein and Takashi Shiraishi (Ithaca, NY: Cornell University Press, 1997), 87–95.

2. Harootunian, *Marx after Marx*, 237.

3. Kishore Mahbubani, *The New Asian Hemisphere: The Irresistible Shift of Global Power to the East* (New York: Public Affairs, 2008). Mahbubani was a noted "Asian values"

spokesman from Singapore and was called, satirically, "the scourge of the West"; "Asian Values: The Scourge of the West," *Economist*, April 22, 1995, 24.

4. Flores, *Past Peripheral*, 25.

5. See "Intersections: Issues in Contemporary Art," ed. Joan Kee, special issue, *positions: east asia cultures critique* 12, no. 3 (Winter 2004); and Caroline Turner, ed., *Tradition and Change: Contemporary Art of Asia and the Pacific* (St. Lucia, Australia: University of Queensland Press, 1993).

6. Apinan Poshyananda, "Asian Art and the New Millennium: From Glocalism to Techno-Shamanism," in *International Symposium 1999: "Asian Art: Prospects for the Future" Report*, ed. Furuichi Yasuko and Hoashi Aki (Tokyo: Japan Foundation Asia Center, 2000), 165, https://www.jpf.go.jp/e/publish/asia_exhibition_history/23_99_prospects.html, accessed December 22, 2019.

7. Kaname Akamatsu, "A Historical Pattern of Economic Growth in Developing Countries," *Journal of Developing Economies* 1, no. 1 (1962): 3–25.

8. For the claims made for Asian democracy, see Robert Bartley, Chan Heng Chee, Samuel P. Huntington, and Shijuro Ogata, *Democracy and Capitalism: Asian and American Perspectives* (Singapore: Institute of Southeast Asian Studies, 1993).

9. See Khoo Boo Teik, *Paradoxes of Mahathirism: An Intellectual Biography of Mahathir Mohamad* (Kuala Lumpur: Oxford University Press, 1995); and Wee, *Asian Modern*, 15–19.

10. Arif Dirlik, "Asia Pacific Studies in an Age of Global Modernity," *Inter-Asia Cultural Studies* 6, no. 2 (2005): 158.

11. Žižek, "Multiculturalism, or, the Cultural Logic," 44. One limitation to Žižek's formulation is that the argument does not to conceive that "natives" can create their own phantasmatic subjectivity to "speak back" and participate in capitalist universality.

12. Naoko Munakata, "Has Politics Caught Up with Markets? In Search of East Asian Regionalism," in *Beyond Japan: The Dynamics of East Asian Regionalism*, ed. Peter J. Katzenstein and Takashi Shiraishi (Ithaca, NY: Cornell University Press, 2006), 130–158.

13. See, for example, Ian Buruma, "What Happened to the Asian Century?" *New York Times*, December 29, 1999, https://www.nytimes.com/1999/12/29/opinion/what-happened -to-the-asian-century.html?pagewanted=1, accessed December 30, 1999. The misfortunes of the emerging Southeast Asian economies are more than balanced by the increased economic presence of China, and many observers replaced the little tigers, Indonesia, Malaysia, and Thailand, with China in their view of Asia. See Paul Keating, "The American Era Is Ending: The Asian Century Is Dawning," *The Age* (Melbourne), October 16, 2003, http:// www.theage.com.au/articles/2003/10/15/1065917476292.html?from=storyrhs, accessed October 18, 2003.

14. Wang Hui, "The Politics of Imagining Asia: A Genealogical Analysis," *Inter-Asia Cultural Studies* 8, no. 1 (2007): 14.

15. Kōichi Iwabuchi, *Recentering Globalization: Popular Culture and Japanese Transnationalism* (Durham, NC: Duke University Press, 2002), 1–50.

16. World Bank, "Urban Population (% of Total Population)—East Asia & Pacific," https://data.worldbank.org/indicator/SP.URB.TOTL.IN.ZS?locations=Z4, accessed December 24, 2021.

17. Shahid Yusuf and Kaoru Nabeshima, *Postindustrial East Asian Cities: Innovation for Growth* (Stanford, CA: Stanford University Press; Washington, DC: World Bank, 2006), 29.

18. Peter J. Taylor, D. R. F. Walker, and J. V. Beaverstock, "Firms and their Global Service Networks," in *Global Networks, Linked Cities*, ed. Saskia Sassen (New York: Routledge, 2002), 102.

19. Göran Therborn, "Asia and Europe in the World: Locations in the Global Dynamics," *Inter-Asia Cultural Studies* 3, no. 2 (2002): 287–307.

20. Nigel Harris, *The End of the Third World: Newly Industrializing Countries and the Decline of an Ideology* (London: I. B. Tauris, 1987); and Soogil Young, "East Asia as a Regional Force for Globalism," in *Regional Integration and the Global Trading System*, ed. Kym Anderson and Richard Blackhurst (New York: St. Martin's Press, 1993), 126–143. It was also conveniently ignored that industrial policy and state direction existed to varying degrees in the Asian newly industrialized countries, although the research shows that the key regional "integrators" have been corporations.

21. Cronin, *The World the Cold War Made*, 252.

22. Timothy Garton Ash, "Another 9/11 Isn't Our Worse Problem," *Guardian Weekly*, September 19, 2008, 20.

23. Dieter Ernst, "Searching for a New Role in East Asian Regionalization: Japanese Production Networks in the Electronic Industry," in *Beyond Japan: The Dynamics of East Asian Regionalism*, ed. Peter J. Katzenstein and Takashi Shiraishi (Ithaca, NY: Cornell University Press, 2006), 161–187.

24. Mike Douglass, "The 'New' Tokyo Story: Restructuring Space and the Struggle for Place in a World City," in *Japanese Cities in the World Economy*, ed. Kuniko Fujita and Richard Child Hill (Philadelphia, PA: Temple University Press, 1993), 83–119.

25. Yusuf and Nabeshima, *Postindustrial East Asian Cities*, 31.

26. Peter J. Katzenstein, "East Asia—Beyond Japan," in *Beyond Japan: The Dynamics of East Asian Regionalism*, ed. Peter J. Katzenstein and Takashi Shiraishi (Ithaca, NY: Cornell University Press, 2006), 33.

27. AMRO (ASEAN+3 Macroeconomic Research Office), "Saving Globalization? Global Value Chains in East Asia After the Pandemic," May 20, 2021, https://www.amro-asia.org/saving-globalization-global-value-chains-in-east-asia-after-the-pandemic/, accessed December 24, 2021.

28. Fredric Jameson, *A Singular Modernity: Essay on the Ontology of the Present* (London: Verso, 2002), 6.

29. Jameson, *A Singular Modernity*, 211.

30. Munakata, "Has Politics Caught Up," 157. Fredric Jameson sees the move from *modernization* to *globalization* as a significant change, indicating not only different

power and economic relations from an older colonial period but also a different politics; Jameson, "Notes on Globalization."

31. Fukuzawa Yukichi, "On De-Asianization by Fukuzawa Yukichi," trans. Okada Hidehiro, in *The Meiji Japan through Contemporary Sources*, vol. 3 (Tokyo: Centre for East Asian Cultural Studies, 1969–1972), 129.

32. "It is in Asia that the ethical world of political consciousness first arose. Asia is the continent of sunrise and of origins in general"; Georg Wilhelm Friedrich Hegel, *Lectures on the Philosophy of World History*, trans. H. B. Nisbet (Cambridge: Cambridge University Press, 1975), 190.

33. Sun Ge, "How Does Asia Mean? (Part II)," trans. Hui Shiu-Lun and Lau Kinchi, *Inter-Asia Cultural Studies* 1, no. 2 (2000): 326–327, 330–331; Iwabuchi, *Recentering Globalization*, 6–11.

34. Sun Ge, "How Does Asia Mean? (Part I)," trans. Hui Shiu-Lun and Lau Kinchi, *Inter-Asia Cultural Studies* 1, no. 1 (2000): 14. See also Peter J. Katzenstein and Takashi Shiraishi, eds., *Network Power: Japan and Asia* (Ithaca, NY: Cornell University Press, 1997).

35. Melissa Chiu, "Asian Contemporary Art: An Introduction," *Grove Art Online*, http://www.groveart.com/grove–owned/art/asiancontintro.htm, accessed January 19, 2008.

36. See George Yúdice, *The Expediency of Culture: Uses of Culture in the Global Era* (Durham, NC: Duke University Press, 2003); and Mark W. Rectanus, *Culture Incorporated: Museums, Artists, and Corporate Sponsorships* (Minneapolis: University of Minnesota Press, 2002).

37. Kobena Mercer, "Introduction," in *Cosmopolitan Modernism: Annotating Art's Histories*, ed. Kobena Mercer (London: Institute of International Visual Arts and MIT Press, 2005), 7.

38. Julian Stallabrass, *Art Incorporated: The Story of Contemporary Art* (Oxford: Oxford University Press, 2004), 11.

39. Quoted by Paloma Checa-Gismero, "Craft as Anti-Colonial Universalism in the Bienal de La Habana," *Third Text* 36, no. 3 (2022): 272, https://www.tandfonline.com/doi/abs/10.1080/09528822.2022.2052608. Checa-Gismero takes issue with Martin's claim, pointing out that two iterations of the Bienal de La Habana—the first in 1984 and the second in 1986—had been mounted by the time of *Magiciens*. Havana used an anticolonial strategy to weaken the museographic difference between art and craft. Significantly, the second iteration in 1986 saw artists from Africa, Asia, and the Middle East taking part. The third occurred in the same year as *Magiciens*. I address this matter in chapter 2.

40. Checa-Gismero, "Craft as Anti-Colonial Universalism," 272–277.

41. Jean-Hubert Martin, Préface to Centre Georges Pompidou, Musée national d'art moderne, [and] La Grand Halle, La Villette, *Magiciens de la Terre*, exhibition catalogue (Paris: Editions du Centre Pompidou, 1989), 8.

42. Tatehata Akira, "A Trojan Horse? Multiculturalism in International Art Exhibitions," in *International Symposium 2002: "Asia in Transition: Representation and Identity" Report*, ed. Furuichi Yasuko and Hoashi Aki (Tokyo: Japan Foundation Asia Center, 2003), 310.

43. Tatehata, "A Trojan Horse?" 312. Modernist art here repeats an anthropological phenomenon as examined by Johannes Fabian in his important *Time and the Other: How Anthropology Makes Its Object* (New York: Columbia University Press, 1983).

44. Tatehata, "A Trojan Horse?" 314.

45. Art historian Joan Kee observes that she is not sure "whether one [strictly speaking] can call the 1970s–80s a 'pre-biennial' culture if only for the fact that [East] Asia was biennale/triennale crazy throughout the 1960s and 1970s. Granted, many of these initiatives were dead upon arrival, holding just one version of the biennale (Saigon in 1962; Seoul in 1974). But people were obsessed with the topic"; personal e-mail communication to the author, November 15, 2008.

46. Alison Carroll, "The Political and the Personal: Australia's Experience in Visual Arts Exchange in Southeast Asia through the 1990s," in *Art Studies 02: The 1990s: The Making of Art with Contemporaries Report*, ed. Furuichi Yasuko and Hoashi Aki (Tokyo: Japan Foundation Asia Center, 2016), 69. For broader arguments on biennials at the "periphery" and the "decentralization of the West," see Oliver Marchart, "The Globalization of Art and the 'Biennials of Resistance[']: A History of the Biennials from the Periphery," *On Curating* 46 (2020), https://www.on-curating.org/issue-46-reader/the-globalization -of-art-and-the-biennials-of-resistance-a-history-of-the-biennials-from-the-periphery .html, accessed January 31, 2022; and Anthony Gardner and Charles Green, "Biennials of the South on the Edges of the Global," *Third Text* 27, no. 4 (2013): 442–455.

47. Ahmad Mashadi, "Contexts and Predicaments: Singapore 1996–2006," in *Art Studies 02: The 1990s: The Making of Art with Contemporaries Report*, ed. Furuichi Yasuko and Hoashi Aki (Tokyo: Japan Foundation Asia Center, 2016), 62–63.

48. Uchino Tadashi, "Presenter Interview: Connecting the Theater People of Asia: The Japan Foundation International Collaboration Program" (Interview of the Japan Foundation's Performing Arts Division coordinator, Hata Yuki), http://performingarts.jp/E /pre_interview/0711/1.html, accessed January 30, 2008. I will return to the symposia in chapter 3.

49. Takashi Shiraishi, "Japan and Southeast Asia," in *Network Power: Japan and Asia*, ed. Peter J. Katzenstein and Takashi Shiraishi (Ithaca, NY: Cornell University Press, 1997), 184–186.

50. Flores, *Past Peripheral*, 31, note 5.

51. Kishi Sayaka, "Cultural Diplomacy and Museum Management: Beyond an Imaginary Asia," trans. Andrew Maerkle, in *Art Studies 02: The 1990s: The Making of Art with Contemporaries Report*, ed. Furuichi Yasuko and Hoashi Aki (Tokyo: Japan Foundation Asia Center, 2016), 76.

52. "A Short Chronology of Modernism in East Asia," in "The Road to Venice: Asia-Pacific at the Biennale, special issue," *ART iT* (Spring/Summer 2007): 123.

53. See also Kamiya, "Communicative Approach, from Asia," 133. Kamiya's source is National Research Institute for Cultural Properties, *Kataru Genzai Katarareru Kako:*

Nihon no Bijutsushigaku 100-nen (The Present That Tells, the Past That Is Told Of: 100 Years of Art History in Japan), Report of the International Symposium on the Preservation of Cultural Property, Tokyo, Japan, 1997 (Tokyo: Heibonsha, 1999), 317.

54. Rasheed Araeen, "An Open Letter to African Thinkers, Theorists, and Art Historians," *Documenta Magazine* no. 1, "Modernity?" (2007): 129.

55. Jeannine Tang, "Spectacle's Politics and the Singapore Biennale," *Journal of Visual Culture* 6, no. 3 (2007): 365–377; and C. J. W.-L. Wee, "Global Art, Globalised Art and 'Belief,'" *Broadsheet: Contemporary Visual Arts and Culture* 35, no. 4 (2007): 214–219.

56. Iftikhar Dadi, "Globalization and Transnational Modernism," in *Globalization and Art*, ed. James Elkins, Alice Kim, and Zhivka Valiavicharska (University Park: Penn State University Press, 2010), 187.

57. Discussion, Sessions 1 and 2, in *Art Studies 02: The 1990s: The Making of Art with Contemporaries Report*, ed. Furuichi Yasuko and Hoashi Aki (Tokyo: Japan Foundation Asia Center, 2016), 51–52.

58. Toshihiro Kennoki, "Acknowledgement," in Fukuoka Art Museum, *Modern Asian Art: India, China & Japan*, exhibition catalogue (Fukuoka: Fukuoka Art Museum, 1979), 6.

59. Kazuma Shinto, "Acknowledgement," in Fukuoka Art Museum, *Modern Asian Art: India, China & Japan*, exhibition catalogue (Fukuoka: Fukuoka Art Museum, 1979), 4.

60. "The city has the geographical advantage of being close to the Korean Peninsula and the Chinese Continent and from the ancient times, has been serving as a gateway to import Asian culture"; *About Fukuoka City: A Quick Guide*, http://www.city.fukuoka.jp /profile/index_e.htm, accessed January 20, 2008.

61. Kay Itoi, "Mutual Feelings: Japan Falls for Asia," *Newsweek*, November 7, 1999, https://www.newsweek.com/mutual-feelings-japan-falls-asia-164142, accessed January 1, 2022.

62. Caroline A. Jones, *The Global Work of Art: World's Fairs, Biennials, and the Aesthetics of Experience* (Chicago, IL: University of Chicago Press, 2016), 154.

63. Laxmi P. Sihare, "100 Years of Modern Indian Art," in Fukuoka Art Museum, *Modern Asian Art: India, China & Japan*, exhibition catalogue (Fukuoka: Fukuoka Art Museum, 1979), 22, 23.

64. Sihare, "100 Years of Modern Indian Art," 25.

65. Michiaki Kawakita, "Modern Japanese Art," in Fukuoka Art Museum, *Modern Asian Art: India, China & Japan*, exhibition catalogue (Fukuoka: Fukuoka Art Museum, 1979), 38.

66. Kawakita, "Modern Japanese Art," 38.

67. Kawakita, "Modern Japanese Art," 38. Even in the 1960s, there were sympathetic views from unexpected quarters of the Japanese struggle with the modernization, such as this by a literary critic on nineteenth-century American literature: "Japan, the 'hermit empire,' which had thought of itself as the mightiest of nations, feeling a sudden humiliation as it

confronted the wonders of the West, went in for waltzing, mesmerism, cock-fighting, and planchette, while everything Japanese seemed on the point of being swept away. As foreign teachers and missionaries flocked into the country, the Japanese ceased to treasure their traditions and their heirlooms"; Van Wyck Brooks, "Ernest Fenollosa and Japan," *Proceedings of the American Philosophical Society* 106, no. 2 (1962): 107.

68. Exhibition Organization of the People's Republic of China, "Outline of the Development of Modern and Contemporary Art in the People's Republic of China," in Fukuoka Art Museum, *Modern Asian Art: India, China & Japan*, exhibition catalogue (Fukuoka: Fukuoka Art Museum, 1979), 33.

69. Exhibition Organization of the People's Republic of China, "Outline of the Development of Modern and Contemporary Art," 33.

70. Xu Hong, "Chinese Art," in *Art and Social Change: Contemporary Art in Asia and the Pacific*, ed. Caroline Turner (Canberra: Pandanus Books, 2005), 330–359.

71. Author's interview with Yasunaga Kōichi, Fukuoka Asian Art Museum, May 15, 2012.

72. Shinji Koike, "Asian Artists Exhibition Part I: 'Modern Asian Art—India, China & Japan,'" in Fukuoka Art Museum, *Modern Asian Art: India, China & Japan*, exhibition catalogue (Fukuoka: Fukuoka Art Museum, 1979), 11.

73. Koike, "Asian Artists Exhibition Part I," 11.

74. Koike, "Asian Artists Exhibition Part I," 11.

75. Koike, "Asian Artists Exhibition Part I," 11.

76. Okakura, *Ideals of the East*, 1.

77. Okakura Kakuzō, *The Heart of Heaven: Being a Collection of Writings Hitherto Unpublished in Book Form* (Tokyo: Nippon-Bijutsuin, 1922), 199.

78. Shigeru Aoki, "Acknowledgement," in Fukuoka Art Museum, *Festival: Contemporary Asian Art Show, 1980*, exhibition catalogue (Fukuoka: Fukuoka Art Museum, 1980), 7.

79. Aoki, "Acknowledgement," 7.

80. Aoki, "Acknowledgement," 7.

81. Author's interview with Yasunaga.

82. Kajiya Kenji, "Asian Contemporary Art in Japan and the Ghost of Modernity," in Japan Foundation, *Count 10 Before You Say Asia: Asian Art after Postmodernism: International Symposium 2008: Report*, ed. Furuichi Yasuko (Tokyo: Japan Foundation, 2009), 218. He adds, "In 2006 three international exhibitions including the Singapore Biennale, Shanghai Biennale, and Gwangju Biennale had a joint press conference in Tokyo. Emerging is the horizon of multilateral communication without any transcendent frame of reference. On that horizon, for example, it will not be unusual for a Japanese to think about 'Korean people's special interest in Indian culture'"; Kajiya "Asian Contemporary Art," 219. Kajiya is quoting Fukuoka-based curator Kuroda Raiji.

83. Furuichi was a member of the Visual Arts Division of the Japan Foundation and has since retired, and Kataoka has been the director of the Mori Art Museum, Tokyo, since 2020.

84. Furuichi Yasuko, "Asia: The Possibility of a Collaborative Space—Under Construction Project," in Japan Foundation Asia Center, *Under Construction: New Dimensions of Asian Art*, ed. Kataoka Mami, exhibition catalogue (Tokyo: Japan Foundation Asia Center, 2002), 14–15.

85. Furuichi, "Asia: The Possibility of a Collaborative Space," 13.

86. Furuichi, "Asia: The Possibility of a Collaborative Space," 14.

87. Kataoka Mami, "Asia's Art Map," in Japan Foundation Asia Center, *Under Construction: New Dimensions of Asian Art*, ed. Kataoka Mami, exhibition catalogue (Tokyo: Japan Foundation Asia Center, 2002), 20–21.

88. Furuichi, "Asia: The Possibility of a Collaborative Space," 14.

89. Furuichi, "Asia: The Possibility of a Collaborative Space," 15–16.

90. Kataoka, "Asia's Art Map," 21–22.

91. Kataoka, "Asia's Art Map," 20.

92. Kataoka, "Asia's Art Map," 23.

93. Kataoka, "Asia's Art Map," 21.

94. Edan Corkill, "Under Construction," *World Press Review* 50, no. 3 (2003), https://www.worldpress.org/Asia/941.cfm, accessed January 1, 2022. Corkill's review first appears in *Asahi Shimbun*, December 21, 2002.

95. Takeuchi Yoshimi, "Asia as Method," in *What is Modernity? Writings of Takeuchi Yoshimi*, ed. and trans. Richard F. Calichman (New York: Columbia University Press, 2005), 13.

96. Takeuchi, "Asia as Method," 155.

97. Takeuchi, "Asia as Method," 155.

98. Takeuchi, "Asia as Method," 156–157.

99. Takeuchi, "Asia as Method," 161. For the differences and disagreements between Takeuchi and other scholars, particularly the ethnologist and comparative civilizations scholar Umesao Tadao (1920–2010), see Sun Ge, "How Does Asia Mean? (Part I)," 36–42.

100. Takeuchi, "Asia as Method," 162.

101. Takeuchi, "Asia as Method," 164, 165.

102. Compare Dutch architect-critic Rem Koolhaas's put-down of the East Asian forms of urbanism he dislikes: "Maybe this lack of geometry is typically Asian: Tokyo is the eternal example"; Rem Koolhaas, "Singapore Songlines: Portrait of a Potemkin Metropolis . . . or Thirty Years of Tabula Rasa," in Rem Koolhaas and Bruce Mau, *Small, Medium, Large, Extra-Large*, ed. Jennifer Sigler (Rotterdam: 010 Publishers, 1995), 1975.

103. Pi Li, "Fantasia: An Imagination Toward the Daily Life," in Japan Foundation Asia Center, *Under Construction: New Dimensions of Asian Art*, ed. Kataoka Mami, exhibition catalogue (Tokyo: Japan Foundation Asia Center, 2002), 149, 150.

104. Kamiya, "Communicative Approach," 133.

105. Kamiya, "Communicative Approach," 135.

106. Asmudjo Jono Irianto, "Asia Now: Under Construction?" in Japan Foundation Asia Center, *Under Construction: New Dimensions of Asian Art*, ed. Kataoka Mami, exhibition catalogue (Tokyo: Japan Foundation Asia Center, 2002), 93.

107. Asmudjo, "Asia Now," 93.

108. Asmudjo, "Asia Now," 94.

109. Asmudjo, "Asia Now," 95. The quotation is from Hans Belting, "Art and Art History in the New Museum: The Search for a New Identity," in *Painting in the Age of Artificial Intelligence*, ed. David Moos (London: Academy Editions, 1996), 34.

110. Asmudjo, "Asia Now," 96.

111. Asmudjo, "Asia Now," 95.

112. Kamiya Yukie, "The 1990s: Building Platforms through Creative Thinking," trans. Andrew Maerkle, in *Art Studies 02: The 1990s: The Making of Art with Contemporaries Report*, ed. Furuichi Yasuko and Hoashi Aki (Tokyo: Japan Foundation Asia Center, 2016), 96.

Chapter 2

1. Andreas Huyssen, *After the Great Divide: Modernism, Mass Culture, Postmodernism* (Bloomington: Indiana University Press, 1986), vii–viii. If modernists such as Stravinsky and T. S. Eliot had interests in the primitive and tradition, it was also, as Huyssen later observes, still "their mission to salvage the purity of high art from the encroachments of urbanization, massification, technological modernization, in short, of modern mass culture"; Huyssen, *After the Great Divide*, 163. The popular culture examined in chapters 4 and 5 represents what such modernists would have seen as negative cultural encroachments.

2. Matei Calinescu, *Faces of Modernity: Avant-Garde, Decadence, Kitsch* (Bloomington: Indiana University Press, 1977), 140.

3. Peter Bürger, *Theory of the Avant-Garde* (Minneapolis: University of Minnesota Press, 1984).

4. Kawazoe Noburo, Kikutake Kiyonori, Ōtaka Masato, Maki Fumihiko, and Kurokawa Kishō, *Metabolism 1960: The Proposals for New Urbanism/Metaborizumu 1960: Toshi e no teian* (Tokyo: Bijutsu shuppansha, 1960).

5. Iftikhar Dadi, "Reflections on the First Decade," *Broadsheet: Contemporary Visual Arts and Culture* 41, no. 4 (2012): 267.

6. "Discussions, Sessions 1 and 2," in Japan Foundation Asia Center, *Art Studies 02: The 1990s: The Making of Art with Contemporaries Report*, ed. Furuichi Yasuko and Hoashi Aki (Tokyo: Japan Foundation Asia Center, 2016), 51, 51–52. See also Joan Kee, "The Scale Question in Contemporary Asian Art," in Japan Foundation Asia Center, *Art Studies 02: The 1990s: The Making of Art with Contemporaries Report*, ed. Furuichi Yasuko and Hoashi Aki (Tokyo: Japan Foundation Asia Center, 2016), 35–41.

7. "Early History of the Havana Biennial," *Havana Biennial 2019 Information*, http://biennialhavana.org/early-history-of-the-havana-biennial/465/465/, accessed May 31, 2020.

8. Jones, *The Global Work of Art*, 113–150.

9. Tatehata, "A Trojan Horse?" 314. *Magiciens* becomes recognized as groundbreaking, even though, as Annie Cohen-Solal points out, the catalogue was never translated into English and that fewer than three hundred thousand saw it in 1989 at both the Centre Pompidou and La Villette: "A great many were *discussing* it without actually having *seen* it"; "Revisiting *Magiciens de la Terre*," in "Collecting Geographies," *Stedelijk Studies* 1 (Fall 2014), (https://stedelijkstudies.com/journal/revisiting-magiciens-de-la-terre/, accessed April 11, 2024.

10. Pablo Lafuente, "Introduction: From the Outside In—'Magiciens de la Terre' and Two Histories of Exhibitions," in Lucy Steeds, Pablo Lafuente, Jean-Marc Poinsot, Jean-Hubert Martin, Benjamin H. D. Buchloh, Rasheed Araeen, Jean Fisher, Gayatri Chakravorty Spivak, and Thomas McEvilley, *Making Art Global (Part 2): "Magiciens de la Terre" 1989* (London: Afterall Books, 2013), 9.

11. Sean O'Toole, "The Context and Legacy of Jean-Hubert Martin's Contentious 1989 Exhibition, 'Magiciens de la Terre,'" *Frieze*, October 1, 2017, https://frieze.com/article/other-stories, accessed May 30, 2020.

12. Maureen Murphy, "From *Magiciens de la Terre* to the Globalization of the Art World: Going Back to a[n] Historic Exhibition," trans. Simon Pleasance, *Critique d'art* (online) 41 (2013), https://journals.openedition.org/critiquedart/8308?lang=en, accessed May 27, 2020.

13. Jean-Hubert Martin, Preface to Centre Georges Pompidou, Musée national d'art moderne, [and] La Grand Halle, La Villette. *Magiciens de la Terre*, exhibition catalogue (Paris: Editions du Centre Pompidou, 1989), n.p.

14. Checa-Gismero, "Craft as Anti-colonial Universalism," 12S. The late Jean Fisher commented on art as magic in 1989 in *ArtForum International*: "We should not be misled into believing that the 'aesthetic' and the 'magical' . . . are one and the same thing, and that (western) universal values govern both"; "Fictional Histories: 'Magiciens de la Terre'—The Invisible Labyrinth," *Jean Fisher*, https://www.jeanfisher.com/fictional-histories-magiciens-de-la-terre/, accessed June 6, 2020.

15. Apinan Poshyananda, "Asian Art in the Posthegemonic World," in Japan Foundation ASEAN Culture Center, *The Potential of Asian Thought Handout: Contemporary Art Symposium 1994 Handout*, ed. Furuichi Yasuko and Kobayashi Izumi (Tokyo: Japan

Foundation ASEAN Culture Center), 4, https://www.jpf.go.jp/e/publish/asia_exhibition
_history/15_94_potential.html, accessed May 14, 2015.

16. Lucy Steeds, "'Magiciens de la Terre' and the Development of Transnational Project-
based Curating," in Lucy Steeds, Pablo Lafuente, Jean-Marc Poinsot, Jean-Hubert Martin,
Benjamin H. D. Buchloh, Rasheed Araeen, Jean Fisher, Gayatri Chakravorty Spivak, and
Thomas McEvilley, *Making Art Global (Part 2): "Magiciens de la Terre" 1989* (London:
Afterall Books, 2013), 25.

17. Hou Hanru, "In Defense of Difference: Notes on *Magiciens de la Terre*, Twenty-Five
Years Later," *Yishu: Journal of Contemporary Chinese Art* 13, no. 3 (2014): 9.

18. Marian Pastor Roces, "Crystal Palace Exhibitions," in *The Biennial Reader: An
Anthology on Large-Scale Perennial Exhibitions of Contemporary Art*, ed. Elena Filipovic,
Merieke van Hal, and Solveig Øvstebø (Ostfildern: Hatje Cantz Verlag, 2010), 50–65.

19. "Evento: Bienal de La Habana," http://www.geifco.org/actionart/actionart02/eventos
/bienales/habana/intro-habana.htm, accessed May 31, 2020.

20. Rachel Weiss, "A Certain Place and a Certain Time: The Third Bienal de La Habana
and the Origins of the Global Exhibition," in Rachel Weiss, Charles Esche, Gerardo Mosquera, Mirko Lauer, Geeta Kapur, Coco Fusco, Luis Camnitzer, and Lucy Steeds, *Making
Art Global (Part 1): The Third Havana Biennial 1989* (London: Afterall Books, 2011), 14.

21. Weiss, "A Certain Place and a Certain Time," 65.

22. Caroline Turner, "Introduction—From Extraregionalism to Intraregionalism?" in
Queensland Art Gallery, *The First Asia-Pacific Triennial of Contemporary Art, Brisbane,
Australia, 1993*, exhibition catalogue (Brisbane: Queensland Art Gallery, 1993), 8.

23. See Steeds, "'Magiciens de la Terre' and the Development."

24. Clark Everling, *Social Economy: The Logic of Capitalist Development* (Abingdon:
Routledge, 1997).

25. Lilian Llanes, "La Bienal de La Habana," *Third Text* 6, no. 20 (1992): 9.

26. Jose Edgardo Campos and Hilton L. Root, *The Key to the Asian Miracle: Making
Shared Growth Credible* (Washington, DC: Brookings Institution Press, 2001).

27. Weiss, "A Certain Place and a Certain Time," 66. Weiss adds that complaints were
raised of "a 'Latinisation' of the concept Third World"; Weiss, "A Certain Place and a
Certain Time," 66.

28. E. Erinze [Emmanuel Arinze], Piedad Casas de Ballesteros, T. K. Sabapathy, G. Sheik
[Gulammohamed Sheikh], Apinan Poshyananda, Jim Supangkat, and A. D. Pirous, "Introduction," in Departemen Pendidikan dan Kebudayaan (Department of Education and
Culture), *Contemporary Art from the Non-Aligned Countries: Unity in Diversity in International Art: Post-Event Catalogue*, exhibition catalogue (Jakarta: Balai Pustaka, Project for
Development of Cultural Media, Directorate General for Culture, Department of Education and Culture, 1998), 3. Arinze's and Sheikh's names are wrongly rendered.

29. See, for example, Paul James, "Postdependency? The Third World in an Era of
Globalism and Late-Capitalism," *Alternatives: Global, Local, Political* 22, no. 2 (1997):

205–226; and Joan Kee, "Introduction: Contemporary Southeast Asia Art: The Right Kind of Trouble," *Third Text* 25, no. 4 (2011): 381: "The idea of contemporaneity could help us trace new patterns of affiliation that might directly link parts of the world formerly connected only through events, institutions or persons based in Euro-American metropolises."

30. Jim Supangkat, "'White Paper' on the Non-aligned Movement Exhibition," *Digital Archive of Indonesia Contemporary Art, @rsipIVAA*, 4, http://archive.ivaa-online.org /files/uploads/texts/[English]%201995_GNB_05-16.pdf, accessed June 6, 2020.

31. Supangkat, "'White Paper' on the Non-aligned Movement Exhibition," 4.

32. Supangkat, "'White Paper' on the Non-aligned Movement Exhibition," 5.

33. Supangkat, "'White Paper' on the Non-aligned Movement Exhibition," 5.

34. Checa-Gismero, "Craft as Anti-Colonial Universalism," 15.

35. Vijay Prashad, *The Darker Nations: A People's History of the Third World* (New York: New Press, 2007), 246.

36. Mikio Soejima, "Cultural Identities in Asian Art," in Fukuoka Art Museum, *2nd Asian Art Show, Fukuoka*, exhibition catalogue (Fukuoka: Fukuoka Art Museum, 1985), 9.

37. Soejima, "Cultural Identities," 9. The same framework would apply to the original 1979/1980 Asian art show. As contended in chapter 1, Fukuoka's initial shows are international-regional exhibitions displaying the artwork of distinct entities that had to relate to each other across borders made less porous by Cold War–era nationalisms.

38. Soejima, "Cultural Identities," 10.

39. Soejima, "Cultural Identities," 10. See Joan Kee, *Contemporary Korean Art: Tansaekhwa and the Urgency of Method* (Minneapolis: University of Minnesota Press, 2013).

40. Soejima, "Cultural Identities," 10.

41. Kuwahara Keiichi, "Foreword," in *4th Asian Art Show, Fukuoka: Realism as an Attitude*, exhibition catalogue (Fukuoka: Fukuoka Art Museum, 1989), 7. Kuwuhara was then the mayor of the city of Fukuoka.

42. Fukuoka Art Museum, *Symposium: "What Must be Done for the Future of Asian Tradition and Art Which Have Been Changed Under the Influence of Western Art?": Asian Artists Exhibition Part II: "Festival: Contemporary Asian Art Show, 1980,"* conference proceedings (Fukuoka: Fukuoka Art Museum, 1980), 41.

43. Fukuoka Art Museum, *Symposium*, 16.

44. Fukuoka Art Museum, *Symposium*, 27–28.

45. Fukuoka Art Museum, *Symposium*, 36.

46. Mikio Soejima, "In Pursuit of a Genuinely Asian World," in Fukuoka Art Museum, *3rd Asian Art Show, Fukuoka*, exhibition catalogue (Fukuoka: Fukuoka Art Museum, 1989), 28–29.

47. Soejima, "In Pursuit of a Genuinely Asian World," 27.

48. Soejima, "In Pursuit of a Genuinely Asian World," 28.

49. Soejima, "In Pursuit of a Genuinely Asian World," 27.

50. Soejima, "In Pursuit of a Genuinely Asian World," 28.

51. Soejima, "In Pursuit of a Genuinely Asian World," 28.

52. Soejima, "In Pursuit of a Genuinely Asian World," 28.

53. Soejima, "In Pursuit of a Genuinely Asian World," 29.

54. Soejima, "In Pursuit of a Genuinely Asian World," 29.

55. Reiko Tomii, *Radicalism in the Wilderness: International Contemporaneity and 1960s Art in Japan* (Cambridge, MA: MIT Press, 2016), 140.

56. Reiko Tomii, "Toward *Tokyo Biennale 1970*: Shapes of the International in the Age of 'International Contemporaneity,'" *Review of Japanese Culture and Society* 23 (2011): 195.

57. Soejima, "In Pursuit of a Genuinely Asian World," 29.

58. Kuroda joined the Fukuoka Asian Art Museum in 1985 and was later appointed as the director, stepping down in March 2021.

59. Kuroda Raiji, "Symbols Transgressing the Border," in Fukuoka Art Museum, *3rd Asian Art Show, Fukuoka*, exhibition catalogue (Fukuoka: Fukuoka Art Museum, 1989), 270.

60. Kuroda, "Symbols Transgressing the Border," 270–271.

61. Kuroda, "Symbols Transgressing the Border," 271.

62. Simon Avenell, "What Is Asia for Us and Can We Be Asians? The New Asianism in Contemporary Japan," *Modern Asian Studies* 48, no. 6 (2014): 1596. For an early assessment of Japan's reentry into Southeast Asia, see Peter Duus, "The 'New Asianism,'" in *Can Japan Globalize? Studies on Japan's Changing Political Economy and the Process of Globalization in Honour of Sung-Jo Park*, ed. Arne Holzhausen (Heidelberg: Physica-Verlag, 2001).

63. Kōichi Iwabuchi, "Return to Asia? Japan in the Global Audio-Visual Market," *Sojourn: Journal of Social Issues in Southeast Asia* 9, no. 2, special issue, "Mass Media: Local and Global Positions" (1994): 226–245.

64. Avenell, "What Is Asia for Us," 1629.

65. Ushiroshōji joined the Fukuoka Art Museum in 1978 and moved to the Fukuoka Asian Art Museum—the recipient museum of Fukuoka Art Museum's Asian collection—when it opened in 1999.

66. Ushiroshōji Masahiro, "Realism as an Attitude: Asian Art in the Nineties," in Fukuoka Art Museum, *4th Asian Art Show, Fukuoka: Realism as an Attitude*, exhibition catalogue (Fukuoka: Fukuoka Art Museum, 1994), 34.

67. Ushiroshōji, "Realism as an Attitude," 33.

68. Ushiroshōji, "Realism as an Attitude," 33.

69. Ushiroshōji, "Realism as an Attitude," 34. The essay in question is Ushiroshōji Masahiro, "The Labyrinthine Search for Self-Identity: The Art of Southeast Asia from the 1980s

to the 1990s," in Japan Foundation ASEAN Culture Center, *New Art from Southeast Asia*, exhibition catalogue (Tokyo: Japan Foundation ASEAN Culture Center, 1992), 21–24.

70. Ushiroshōji, "Realism as an Attitude," 34.

71. Ushiroshōji, "Realism as an Attitude," 34.

72. Ushiroshōji, "Realism as an Attitude," 35.

73. Ushiroshōji, "Realism as an Attitude," 35.

74. Ushiroshōji, "Realism as an Attitude," 35.

75. Ushiroshōji, "Realism as an Attitude," 35.

76. Ushiroshōji, "Realism as an Attitude," 35.

77. Tomii, *Radicalism in the Wilderness*, 13.

78. Ushiroshōji, "Realism as an Attitude," 37.

79. Julie Ewington, "In Time," in Queensland Art Gallery, *The Second Asia-Pacific Triennial of Contemporary Art, Brisbane, Australia, 1996*, ed. Caroline Turner and Rhana Devenport, exhibition catalogue (Brisbane: Queensland Art Gallery, 1996), 19.

80. Ewington, "In Time," 19. Discussion of "the enunciative present" occurs in Homi K. Bhabha, *The Location of Culture* (London: Routledge, 1994). A number of the curators discussed in this chapter also draw upon Bhabha for their understanding of cultural hybridity to think through the postmodern and cultural diversity in visual art.

81. Patrick D. Flores, "Moments of the Modern in Southeast Asia: Art, Region, Art History," in *Art Studies 03 Anthology: Shaping the History of Art in Southeast Asia*, guest ed. Patrick D. Flores and Kajiya Kenji (Tokyo: Japan Foundation Asia Center, 2017), 5.

82. Author's interview with Vishaka N. Desai, March 1, 2015.

83. Apinan quoted in Timothy Morrell, "Cultural Crossfire: The Curatorial Travels of Apinan Poshyananda," *Art Asia-Pacific* 3, no. 4 (1996): 44.

84. Vishaka Desai observes that "the first 1992 meeting [was] to make American colleagues aware of what they did not know" (author's interview with Vishaka N. Desai, March 1, 2015).

85. Nick Jose, "Over the Borders," *Australian Review of Books*, November 1996, 18.

86. Pat Hoffie, "The Irreverent Contemporary and Radical Tradition," in *Contemporary Asian Art and Exhibitions: Connectivities and World-Making*, ed. Caroline Turner and Michelle Antoinette (Canberra: ANU Press, 2014), 128.

87. Caroline Turner, "The Asia-Pacific Triennial," in *Contemporary Art from the Asia Pacific Region*, International Institute for Asian Studies, n.d., https://iias.asia/iiasn/iiasn8 /ascult/triennia.html, accessed October 12, 2017.

88. Masahiro Ushiroshōji, "Present Encounters: The Asia-Pacific Triennial," *ArtAsiaPacific* 15 (1997): 31.

89. Stuart Koop, "Asia-Pacific Triennial of Contemporary Art 2002: Free *Tai Chi* Classes with Green Tea," *Eyeline* 50 (2003): 31. For an extended consideration of the APT's

collaborative approach, see Lisa Chandler, "'Journey without Maps': Unsettling Curatorship in Cross-Cultural Contexts," *Museum and Society* 7, no. 2 (2009): 74–91.

90. Geeta Kapur, "Two or Three Things about Ourselves," in Queensland Art Gallery, *The Second Asia-Pacific Triennial of Contemporary Art, Brisbane, Australia, 1996*, ed. Caroline Turner and Rhana Devenport, exhibition catalogue (Brisbane: Queensland Art Gallery, 1996), 23.

91. Caroline Turner, "Mirror of the Future: Shadows Before," in *Present Encounters: Papers from the Conference of the Second Asia-Pacific Triennial of Contemporary Art, 1996*, ed. Caroline Turner and Rhana Devenport (Brisbane: Queensland Art Gallery, 1997), 19, 21.

92. Apinan Poshyananda, "Preface," in Asia Society Galleries, *Contemporary Art in Asia: Traditions/Tensions*, exhibition catalogue (New York: Asia Society Galleries, 1996), 13.

93. Apinan, "Preface," 16, 17.

94. Apinan Poshyananda, "Roaring Tigers, Desperate Dragons in Transition," in Asia Society Galleries, *Contemporary Art in Asia: Traditions/Tensions*, exhibition catalogue (New York: Asia Society Galleries, 1996), 25. The title of the chapter is a play on expressions current in the 1990s—"four little dragons" and "four Asian tigers"—and is not a reference to Ang Lee's film *Crouching Tiger, Hidden Dragon* (2000).

95. Apinan, "Roaring Tigers," 25.

96. Apinan, "Roaring Tigers," 26.

97. Apinan, "Roaring Tigers," 29.

98. Apinan Poshyananda, "Contemporary Thai Art: Nationalism and Sexuality à la Thai," in Asia Society Galleries, *Contemporary Art in Asia: Traditions/Tensions*, exhibition catalogue (New York: Asia Society Galleries, 1996), 105, 102.

99. Apinan, "Contemporary Thai Art," 107, 108.

100. Geeta Kapur, "Dismantling the Norm," in Asia Society Galleries, *Contemporary Art in Asia: Traditions/Tensions*, exhibition catalogue (New York: Asia Society Galleries, 1996), 60, 61.

101. Kapur, "Dismantling the Norm," 61.

102. On the use of hybridity, see Vishaka N. Desai, "Foreword," in Asia Society Galleries, *Contemporary Art in Asia: Traditions/Tensions*, exhibition catalogue (New York: Asia Society Galleries, 1996), 13–14; and Apinan Posyananda, "Preface," in *Contemporary Art in Asia: Traditions/Tensions*, exhibition catalogue (New York: Asia Society Galleries, 1996), 15–16.

103. Kapur, "Dismantling the Norm," 64.

104. Kapur, "Dismantling the Norm," 66.

105. Kapur, "Dismantling the Norm," 66.

106. Kapur, "Dismantling the Norm," 68.

107. Marian Pastor Roces, "Bodies of Fiction, Bodies of Desire," in Asia Society Galleries, *Contemporary Art in Asia: Traditions/Tensions*, exhibition catalogue (New York: Asia Society Galleries, 1996), 83, 87.

108. Roces, "Bodies of Fiction," 90.

109. Roces, "Bodies of Fiction," 90.

110. Roces, "Bodies of Fiction," 88.

111. Jae-Ryung Roe, "Encountering the World: The Past and the Present," in Asia Society Galleries, *Contemporary Art in Asia: Traditions/Tensions*, exhibition catalogue (New York: Asia Society Galleries, 1996), 100.

112. Roe, "Encountering the World," 94.

113. Roe, "Encountering the World," 95.

114. Roe, "Encountering the World," 97.

115. Roe, "Encountering the World," 98.

116. Soyeon Anh, "Korean Art and Its Identity in the International Context," in Queensland Art Gallery, *Present Encounters: Papers from the Conference of the Second Asia-Pacific Triennial of Contemporary Art, 1996*, ed. Caroline Turner and Rhana Devenport, exhibition catalogue (Brisbane: Queensland Art Gallery, 1997), 97.

117. Anh, "Korean Art," 99.

118. Fumio Nanjo, "The Present Situation of Japanese Art," in Queensland Art Gallery, *The Second Asia-Pacific Triennial of Contemporary Art, Brisbane, Australia, 1996* ed. Caroline Turner and Rhana Devenport, exhibition catalogue (Brisbane: Queensland Art Gallery, 1996), 36.

119. Nanjo, "The Present Situation," 37.

120. Kapur, "Two or Three Things," 22.

121. Kapur, "Two or Three Things," 23.

122. Kapur, "Two or Three Things," 23.

123. Kapur, "Two or Three Things," 23, 24.

124. Jose, "Over the Borders," 16.

125. David Elliott, "A Short Walk in the Hindu Kush," in Queensland Art Gallery, *The Second Asia-Pacific Triennial of Contemporary Art, Brisbane, Australia, 1996*, ed. Caroline Turner and Rhana Devenport, exhibition catalogue (Brisbane: Queensland Art Gallery, 1996), 21.

126. Elliott, "A Short Walk," 21.

127. Elliott, "A Short Walk," 21.

128. *Cities* appeared with varying artwork selections at: PS1, New York; capcMusée d'art contemporain de Bordeaux; Louisiana Museum of Modern Art, Humlebæk; Hayward Gallery, London; locations across Bangkok; and Kiasma Museum of Contemporary Art, Helsinki. Each rendition had individualized exhibition catalogues. The iteration in

Bordeaux did not have an architect due to tight timing issues, and PS1 had to resort to slides and projection for some of the work because of financial constraints (Kee, "Scale Question in Contemporary Asian Art," 36).

129. Hou Hanru and Lucy Steeds, "Exhibition Histories Talks: Hou Hanru—Video Online," *Afterall*, June 22, 2015, https://www.afterall.org/article/exhibition-histories-talks_hou-hanru-video-online, accessed August 7, 2021.

130. Wong Hoy Cheong, "Cities on the Move: Twenty Years On," in *Podium Issue 1: Visual Culture, M+ Stories*, November 8, 2017, https://stories.mplus.org.hk/en/podium/issue-1-visual-culture/cities-on-the-move-twenty-years-on/, accessed December 31, 2020.

131. Douglas Fogle, "Cities on the Move," *Flash Art*, November 29, 2016, https://flash---art.com/article/cities-on-the-move/, accessed August 7, 2021.

132. Different iterations of the exhibition featured their own catalogues. What follows only applies to the 1997 catalogue.

133. Hou Hanru and Hans Ulrich Obrist, "Cities on the Move," in Wiener Secession and capcMusée d'art contemporain de Bordeaux, *Cities on the Move*, ed. Hou Hanru and Hans Ulrich Obrist, exhibition catalogue (Ostfildern-Ruit: Hatje, 1997), section 1. The catalogue has no pagination. The curatorial essay is organized into sections.

134. Hou and Obrist, "Cities on the Move," sections 1 and 3.

135. Hou and Obrist, "Cities on the Move," section 1.

136. Hou and Obrist, "Cities on the Move," section 1. Recent political events that could have indicated democratic changes in the offing included, in 1985, Filipino President Ferdinand Marcos being voted out of power and, in 1997, Thailand receiving its first constitution drafted by an elected Constitutional Drafting Assembly.

137. Hou and Obrist, "Cities on the Move," section 4.

138. Hou and Obrist, "Cities on the Move," section 1. This is true, but it is also a reductive understanding of key aspects of the region's popular cultural production, which I will address in chapters 4 and 5.

139. Hou and Obrist, "Cities on the Move," section 9.

140. Hou and Obrist, "Cities on the Move," section 9.

141. Hou and Obrist, "Cities on the Move," section 8.

142. Hou and Obrist, "Cities on the Move," section 9.

143. Vanessa Couzens, "Ken Yeang and Bioclimatic Architecture," in *Australian Architecture Association*, "News," June 4, 2012, https://www.architecture.org.au/news/enews/354-ken-yeang-and-bioclimatic-architecture, accessed August 22, 2021.

144. Hou and Obrist, "Cities on the Move," section 9.

145. William O. Gardner, *The Metabolist Imagination: Visions of the City in Postwar Japanese Architecture and Science Fiction* (Minneapolis: University of Minnesota Press, 2020), 4. In 2011–2012, the Mori Art Museum mounted a major retrospective exhibition on Metabolism; see Mori Art Museum, International Union of Architects, and Nihon

Keizai Shinbunsha, *Metabolism, the City of the Future: Dreams and Visions of Reconstruction in Postwar and Present-day Japan*, ed. Hirose Mami, Maeda Naotake, Sasaki Hitomi, Tagomori Miho, Tamayama Ami, and Yoshida Yuri, exhibition catalogue (Tokyo: Mori Art Museum, 2011).

146. Hou and Obrist, "Cities on the Move," section 10.

147. Hou and Obrist, "Cities on the Move," section 10.

148. Michel Foucault, "Of Other Spaces," *Diacritics*, trans. Jay Miskowiec, 16, no. 1 (1986): 24.

149. For a pertinent discussion of the complexities of Foucault's heterotopia, see Lieven De Cauter and Michiel Dehaene, "The Space of Play: Towards a General Theory of Heterotopia," in *Heterotopia and the City: Public Space in a Postcivil Society*, ed. Michiel Dehaene and Lieven De Cauter (London: Routledge, 2008), 87–102.

150. Hou and Obrist, "Cities on the Move," section 12.

151. "01 Arahamaiani," in Wiener Secession and capcMusée d'art contemporain de Bordeaux, *Cities on the Move*, ed. Hou Hanru and Hans Ulrich Obrist, exhibition catalogue (Ostfildern-Ruit: Hatje, 1997), n.p.

152. Hou and Obrist, "Cities on the Move," section 1.

153. Hou and Obrist, "Cities on the Move," section 3.

154. This image was part of Cai's artwork for the "Mito Annual '94: Open System," titled *Proposal for Universal Design: Feng Shui Project for Mito: Dragon Meridian (Unrealized)* (1994).

155. "03 Cai Guo Qiang," in Wiener Secession and capcMusée d'art contemporain de Bordeaux, *Cities on the Move*, ed. Hou Hanru and Hans Ulrich Obrist, exhibition catalogue (Ostfildern-Ruit: Hatje, 1997), n.p.

156. Kee, "Scale Question in Contemporary Asian Art," 39.

Chapter 3

1. Hoashi Aki, "The 1990s: Asia as Medium," in *Art Studies 02: The 1990s: The Making of Art with Contemporaries Report*, eds. Furuichi Yasuko and Hoashi Aki (Tokyo: Japan Foundation Asia Center, 2016), 97.

2. Caroline Turner, "Internationalism and Regionalism: Paradoxes of Identity," in *Tradition and Change: Contemporary Art of Asia and the Pacific*, ed. Caroline Turner (St. Lucia, Australia: University of Queensland Press, 1994), xiv.

3. Okakura Kakuzō, *The Awakening of Japan* (New York: Century, 1904), 96.

4. Armand Mattelart, *Networking the World, 1794–2000* (Minneapolis: University of Minnesota Press, 2000).

5. Okakura, *Awakening of Japan*, 96–97, 197.

6. Okakura, *Awakening of Japan*, 218–219.

7. Caroline Turner, "Introduction Part 1—Critical Themes, Geopolitical Change and Global Contexts in Contemporary Asian Art," in *Contemporary Asian Art and Exhibitions: Connectivities and World-Making*, ed. Michelle Antoinette and Caroline Turner (Canberra: ANU Press, 2014), 12.

8. Hannah Appel, "Infrastructural Time," in *The Promise of Infrastructure*, ed. Nikhil Anand, Akhil Gupta, and Hannah Appel (Durham, NC: Duke University Press, 2018), 46.

9. Bruce Cumings, *Parallax Visions: Making Sense of American-East Asian Relations* (Durham, NC: Duke University Press, 1999).

10. Mezzadra and Neilson, *Border as Method*, 61.

11. See Francis Fukuyama, *The End of History and the Last Man* (New York: Free Press, 1992), and a recent critique of him by Louis Menand, "Francis Fukuyama Postpones the End of History," *New Yorker*, August 27, 2018, https://www.newyorker.com/magazine/2018/09/03/francis-fukuyama-postpones-the-end-of-history, accessed January 10, 2020.

12. "Connecting the Theater People of Asia: The Japan Foundation International Collaboration Program: Yuki Hata," Japan Foundation, *Performing Arts Network Japan*, December 28, 2007, https://performingarts.jp/E/pre_interview/0711/1.html, accessed March 15, 2015.

13. DeBoer, *Coproducing Asia*, 141.

14. Yamamoto Tadashi and Caroline Hernandez, "Social and Cultural Dimensions in East Asian Community Building," in *ASEAN-Japan Cooperation: A Foundation for East Asian Community*, ed. Japan Center for International Exchange (Tokyo: Japan Center for International Exchange, 2003), 172.

15. Ahmad Mashadi, "Moments of Regionality: Negotiating Southeast Asia," in *Art Studies 03: Shaping the History of Art in Southeast Asia*, ed. Patrick D. Flores and Kajiya Kenji (Tokyo: Japan Foundation Asia Center, 2017), 58.

16. Kajiya Kenji, "Learning from Modern and Contemporary Art in Southeast Asia," in *Art Studies 03: Shaping the History of Art in Southeast Asia*, ed. Patrick D. Flores and Kajiya Kenji (Tokyo: Japan Foundation Asia Center, 2017), 13.

17. Kajiya, "Learning from Modern and Contemporary Art," 13.

18. Kishi, "Cultural Diplomacy and Museum Management," 73.

19. Kishi, "Cultural Diplomacy and Museum Management," 74.

20. Kishi, "Cultural Diplomacy and Museum Management," 74n11.

21. Furuichi Yasuko, "The Construction of Collaborative Space and Its Possibilities 2000–2017: From 'Under Construction' to 'Condition Report,'" in *Art Studies 04: Condition Report: Shifting Perspectives in Asia—Curator's Book*, ed. Beverly Yong and Furuichi Yasuko (Tokyo: Japan Foundation Asia Center, 2018), 21.

22. Furuichi, "Construction of Collaborative Space," 21.

23. Furuichi, "Construction of Collaborative Space," 21.

24. Okakura, *Awakening of Japan*, 197.

25. Osborne, *Postconceptual Condition*, 37.

26. Irit Rogoff, "Smuggling: A Curatorial Model," in *Under Construction: Perspectives on Institutional Practice*, ed. Vanessa Müller and Nicolaus Schafhausen (Cologne: Walther König, 2006), 132.

27. Paul O'Neill, *The Culture of Curating and the Curating of Culture(s)* (Cambridge, MA: MIT Press, 2012), 5–6.

28. Shimizu Toshio, "Proposals from the Present," trans. Stanley N. Anderson, in *The Potential of Asian Thought: Contemporary Art Symposium 1994 Handout*, ed. Furuichi Yasuko and Kobayashi Izumi (Tokyo: Japan Foundation ASEAN Culture Center), 1, https://www.jpf.go.jp/e/publish/asia_exhibition_history/15_94_potential.html, accessed May 14, 2015.

29. Nakamura was later professor at the Nagoya Zokei University of Art and Design in Komaki, Aichi.

30. Nakamura Hideki, "Suggestions for the Symposium," trans. Stanley N. Anderson, in *The Potential of Asian Thought: Contemporary Art Symposium 1994 Handout*, ed. Furuichi Yasuko and Kobayashi Izumi (Tokyo: Japan Foundation ASEAN Culture Center, 1994), 4, https://www.jpf.go.jp/e/publish/asia_exhibition_history/15_94_potential.html, accessed May 14, 2015.

31. Nakamura, "Suggestions for the Symposium," 3.

32. Nakamura, "Suggestions for the Symposium," 4.

33. Nakamura, "Suggestions for the Symposium," 4.

34. Apinan, "Asian Art in the Posthegemonic World," 5, 4.

35. Apinan, "Asian Art in the Posthegemonic World," 10.

36. Apinan, "Asian Art in the Posthegemonic World," 6.

37. Apinan, "Asian Art in the Posthegemonic World," 11.

38. Apinan, "Asian Art in the Posthegemonic World," 12.

39. Apinan, "Asian Art in the Posthegemonic World," 12.

40. Kuroda Raiji, "The Other Side of the Other: Asian Artists in the West," trans. Stanley N. Anderson, In *The Potential of Asian Thought: Contemporary Art Symposium 1994 Handout*, ed. Furuichi Yasuko and Kobayashi Izumi (Tokyo: Japan Foundation ASEAN Culture Center, 1994), 1, https://www.jpf.go.jp/e/publish/asia_exhibition_history/15_94_potential.html, accessed May 14, 2015.

41. Kuroda, "Other Side of the Other," 1, 2–3.

42. Tani later was the commissioner of the Asian section at 2000 Gwangju Biennale and, from 1997 to 2017, the director of Utsunomiya Museum of Art.

43. Tani Arata, "History: Steps Towards the Present," in *The Potential of Asian Thought Handout: Contemporary Art Symposium 1994 Handout*, ed. Furuichi Yasuko and Kobayashi Izumi (Tokyo: Japan Foundation ASEAN Culture Center, 1994), 4, https://www.jpf.go.jp/e/publish/asia_exhibition_history/15_94_potential.html, accessed May 14, 2015.

44. Tani, "History: Steps Towards the Present," 4, 1.

45. Takeuchi, "Asia as Method," 13.

46. Furuichi Yasuko, "Conclusion," in Japan Foundation Asia Center, *Symposium: "Asian Contemporary Art Reconsidered" Report*, ed. Furuichi Yasuko and Hoashi Aki (Tokyo: Japan Foundation Asia Center, 1998), 221.

47. Noro Masahiko, "Foreword," in Japan Foundation Asia Center, *Symposium: "Asian Contemporary Art Reconsidered" Report*, ed. Furuichi Yasuko and Hoashi Aki (Tokyo: Japan Foundation Asia Center, 1998), 7.

48. Apinan Poshyananda, "Opening remarks, Session I," in Japan Foundation Asia Center, *Symposium: "Asian Contemporary Art Reconsidered" Report*, ed. Furuichi Yasuko and Hoashi Aki (Tokyo: Japan Foundation Asia Center, 1998), 137.

49. Apinan, "Opening remarks, Session I," 137.

50. Vishaka N. Desai, "East in the West: Presentations of Contemporary Asian Art in the US," in Japan Foundation Asia Center. *Symposium: "Asian Contemporary Art Reconsidered" Report*, ed. Furuichi Yasuko and Hoashi Aki (Tokyo: Japan Foundation Asia Center, 1998), 138.

51. Desai, "East in the West," 138.

52. Lisa Lowe, "Heterogeneity, Hybridity, Multiplicity: Marking Asian American Differences," *Diaspora: A Journal of Transnational Studies* 1, no. 1 (1991): 27.

53. Desai, "East in the West," 140.

54. Desai, "East in the West," 140. Desai quotes from the art critic Holland Cotter's summation of the criticism he had heard of *Traditions/Tensions*; Holland Cotter, "The Brave New Face of Art from the East," *New York Times*, September 29, 1996, H1.

55. Desai, "East in the West," 141.

56. Caroline Turner, "Enriching Encounters," in Japan Foundation Asia Center, *Symposium: "Asian Contemporary Art Reconsidered" Report*, ed. Furuichi Yasuko and Hoashi Aki (Tokyo: Japan Foundation Asia Center, 1998), 142–143.

57. Turner, "Enriching Encounters," 146, 144.

58. Ushiroshōji Masahiro, "Emergence of Asian Art Gallery," in Japan Foundation Asia Center, *Symposium: "Asian Contemporary Art Reconsidered" Report*, ed. Furuichi Yasuko and Hoashi Aki (Tokyo: Japan Foundation Asia Center, 1998), 156.

59. Ushiroshōji, "Emergence of Asian Art Gallery," 157.

60. Ushiroshōji, "Emergence of Asian Art Gallery," 157.

61. Ushiroshōji, "Emergence of Asian Art Gallery," 157.

62. Tatehata Akira, "A Trap in Multiculturalism," in Japan Foundation Asia Center, *Symposium: "Asian Contemporary Art Reconsidered" Report*, ed. Furuichi Yasuko and Hoashi Aki (Tokyo: Japan Foundation Asia Center, 1998), 172.

63. Tatehata, "A Trap in Multiculturalism," 170, 172.

64. Nakahara Yusuke, "General comments, Session III," in Japan Foundation Asia Center, *Symposium: "Asian Contemporary Art Reconsidered" Report*, ed. Furuichi Yasuko and Hoashi Aki (Tokyo: Japan Foundation Asia Center, 1998), 187.

65. Apinan Poshyananda, "Cultural Sentinels at the Crossroads," in Japan Foundation Asia Center, *Symposium: "Asian Contemporary Art Reconsidered" Report*, ed. Furuichi Yasuko and Hoashi Aki (Tokyo: Japan Foundation Asia Center, 1998), 180.

66. Japan Foundation Asia Center, "Foreword," in Japan Foundation Asia Center. *International Symposium 1999: "Asian Art: Prospects for the Future" Report*, ed. Furuichi Yasuko and Hoashi Aki (Tokyo: Japan Foundation Asia Center, 2000), n.p., https://www.jpf.go.jp /e/publish/asia_exhibition_history/23_99_prospects.html, accessed December 22, 2019.

67. David Elliott, "'Asia': Enduring Stereotype or Black Hole?" in Japan Foundation Asia Center, *International Symposium 1999: "Asian Art: Prospects for the Future" Report*, ed. Furuichi Yasuko and Hoashi Aki (Tokyo: Japan Foundation Asia Center, 2000), 137, https://www.jpf.go.jp/e/publish/asia_exhibition_history/23_99_prospects.html, accessed December 22, 2019. Regarding Asia's economic coherence in the 2000s, see Peter Drysdale, "Asia's Economic and Political Interdependence," *East Asia Forum*, May 28, 2012, http:// www.eastasiaforum.org/2012/05/28/asias-economic-and-political-interdependence/.

68. Elliott, "'Asia': Enduring Stereotype or Black Hole?" 138.

69. Elliott, "'Asia': Enduring Stereotype or Black Hole?" 139.

70. Elliott, "'Asia': Enduring Stereotype or Black Hole?" 139.

71. Elliott, "'Asia': Enduring Stereotype or Black Hole?" 139.

72. Elliott, "'Asia': Enduring Stereotype or Black Hole?" 139.

73. "Roundtable Discussion: Looking Back at Asian Contemporary Art during the 1990s," in Japan Foundation Asia Center. *International Symposium 1999: "Asian Art: Prospects for the Future" Report*, ed. Furuichi Yasuko and Hoashi Aki (Tokyo: Japan Foundation Asia Center, 2000), 196, https://www.jpf.go.jp/e/publish/asia_exhibition_history/23 _99_prospects.html, accessed December 22, 2019.

74. "Session II Discussion," in Japan Foundation Asia Center, *International Symposium 1999: "Asian Art: Prospects for the Future" Report*, ed. Furuichi Yasuko and Hoashi Aki (Tokyo: Japan Foundation Asia Center, 2000), 156, https://www.jpf.go.jp/e/publish/asia _exhibition_history/23_99_prospects.html, accessed December 22, 2019.

75. "Session II Discussion," 157.

76. "Session II Discussion," 158.

77. Nanjo Fumio, "The Sea of Diversity: Divisions and Syntheses," in Japan Foundation Asia Center, *International Symposium 1999: "Asian Art: Prospects for the Future" Report*, ed. Furuichi Yasuko and Hoashi Aki (Tokyo: Japan Foundation Asia Center, 2000), 162, https://www.jpf.go.jp/e/publish/asia_exhibition_history/23_99_prospects .html, accessed December 22, 2019.

78. Apinan, "Asian Art and the New Millennium," 165.

79. Apinan, "Asian Art and the New Millennium," 166.

80. Apinan, "Asian Art and the New Millennium," 166.

81. Apinan, "Asian Art and the New Millennium," 167.

82. Apinan, "Asian Art and the New Millennium," 165.

83. Apinan, "Asian Art and the New Millennium," 166.

84. Apinan, "Asian Art and the New Millennium," 166.

85. "Session III Discussion," in Japan Foundation Asia Center, *International Symposium 1999: "Asian Art: Prospects for the Future" Report*, ed. Furuichi Yasuko and Hoashi Aki, (Tokyo: Japan Foundation Asia Center, 2000), 176, https://www.jpf.go.jp/e/publish/asia_exhibition_history/23_99_prospects.html, accessed December 22, 2019.

86. "Session III Discussion," 180.

87. See Glenn Adamson, *The Invention of Craft* (London: Bloomsbury, 2017).

88. "Session III Discussion," 184. Shimizu's point related to how Japan tried "shedding Asia" (*Datsu-A Ron*), Meiji intellectual Fukuzawa Yukichi's infamous phrase from 1885. He was mentioned in chapter 1, and his conjuration is another repeated sign of the entrenched past.

89. "Session III Discussion," 184.

90. Mizusawa Tsutomu, "Toward an Anonymous Individuality," in Japan Foundation Asia Center, *International Symposium 1999: "Asian Art: Prospects for the Future" Report*, ed. Furuichi Yasuko and Hoashi Aki (Tokyo: Japan Foundation Asia Center, 2000), 188, https://www.jpf.go.jp/e/publish/asia_exhibition_history/23_99_prospects.html, accessed December 22, 2019.

91. Agamben, "What is the Contemporary?" 53.

92. Japan Foundation Asia Center, "Foreword," in Japan Foundation Asia Center, *International Symposium 2002: "Asia in Transition: Representation and Identity" Report: The Japan Foundation 30th Anniversary*, ed. Furichi Yasuko and Hoashi Aki (Tokyo: Japan Foundation Asia Center), n.p., https://www.jpf.go.jp/e/publish/asia_exhibition_history/29_02_transition.html, accessed April 10, 2019.

93. Jameson, "The Aesthetics of Singularity," 101–132.

94. Mizusawa Tsutomu. "Opening Comment for Session I," in Japan Foundation Asia Center, *International Symposium 2002: "Asia in Transition: Representation and Identity" Report: The Japan Foundation 30th Anniversary*, ed. Furichi Yasuko and Hoashi Aki (Tokyo: Japan Foundation Asia Center, 2003), 234–235, https://www.jpf.go.jp/e/publish/asia_exhibition_history/29_02_transition.html, accessed April 10, 2019.

95. "Session II Discussion," in Japan Foundation Asia Center, *International Symposium 2002: "Asia in Transition: Representation and Identity" Report: The Japan Foundation 30th Anniversary*, ed. Furuichi Yasuko and Hoashi Aki (Tokyo: Japan Foundation Asia Center, 2003), 342, https://www.jpf.go.jp/e/publish/asia_exhibition_history/29_02_transition.html, accessed April 10, 2019.

96. Sakai Naoki, "Asia: Co-figurative Identification," In Japan Foundation Asia Center, *International Symposium 2002: "Asia in Transition: Representation and Identity" Report: The Japan Foundation 30th Anniversary*, ed. Furuichi Yasuko and Hoashi Aki (Tokyo: Japan Foundation Asia Center, 2003), 224, https://www.jpf.go.jp/e/publish/asia_exhibition _history/29_02_transition.html, accessed April 10, 2019.

97. Sakai, "Asia: Co-figurative Identification," 224–225.

98. Sakai, "Asia: Co-figurative Identification," 227.

99. Sakai, "Asia: Co-figurative Identification," 230.

100. Sakai, "Asia: Co-figurative Identification," 231.

101. Sakai, "Asia: Co-figurative Identification," 224.

102. Wang Hui, "Imagining Asia: A Genealogical Analysis," in Japan Foundation Asia Center, *International Symposium 2002: "Asia in Transition: Representation and Identity" Report: The Japan Foundation 30th Anniversary*, ed. Furuichi Yasuko and Hoashi Aki, (Tokyo: Japan Foundation Asia Center, 2003), 245, https://www.jpf.go.jp/e/publish/asia _exhibition_history/29_02_transition.html, accessed April 10, 2019.

103. Wang Hui, "Imagining Asia," 259.

104. "Reflecting on the Symposium: Panelists' Comments," in Japan Foundation Asia Center, *International Symposium 2002: "Asia in Transition: Representation and Identity" Report: The Japan Foundation 30th Anniversary*, ed. Furichi Yasuko and Hoashi Aki (Tokyo: Japan Foundation Asia Center, 2003), 442, https://www.jpf.go.jp/e/publish/asia _exhibition_history/29_02_transition.html, accessed April 10, 2019.

105. "Session I Discussion," in Japan Foundation Asia Center, *International Sympo-sium 2002: "Asia in Transition: Representation and Identity" Report: The Japan Founda-tion 30th Anniversary*, ed. Furuichi Yasuko and Hoashi Aki (Tokyo: Japan Foundation Asia Center, 2003), 285, https://www.jpf.go.jp/e/publish/asia_exhibition_history/29_02 _transition.html, accessed April 10, 2019.

106. "Session I Discussion," 285.

107. Yoshimi Shunya, "Opening Comment for Session II," in Japan Foundation Asia Center, *International Symposium 2002: "Asia in Transition: Representation and Identity" Report: The Japan Foundation 30th Anniversary*, ed. Furuichi Yasuko and Hoashi Aki (Tokyo: Japan Foundation Asia Center, 2003), 290, https://www.jpf.go.jp/e/publish/asia _exhibition_history/29_02_transition.html, accessed April 10, 2019.

108. Turner, "Introduction Part 1," 12.

109. Lee Yong Woo, "Globalism and the Vanity of Its System," in Japan Foundation Asia Center, *International Symposium 2002: "Asia in Transition: Representation and Identity" Report: The Japan Foundation 30th Anniversary*, ed. Furichi Yasuko and Hoashi Aki (Tokyo: Japan Foundation Asia Center, 2003), 294, https://www.jpf.go.jp/e/publish/asia _exhibition_history/29_02_transition.html, accessed April 10, 2019. Subsequent refer-ences to this text are cited parenthetically by page number only.

110. Lee, "Globalism and the Vanity of Its System," 292.

111. Lee, "Globalism and the Vanity of Its System," 295.

112. "Session II Discussion," 342.

113. Lee, "Globalism and the Vanity of Its System," 294.

114. Lee, "Globalism and the Vanity of Its System," 300.

115. Lee, "Globalism and the Vanity of Its System," 300.

116. Lee, "Globalism and the Vanity of Its System," 302.

117. "Introduction: History of the Gwangju Biennale," *2018 Gwangju Biennale*, accessed November 24, 2018, https://www.gwangjubiennale.org/en/biennale/intro.do.

118. Lee, "Globalism and the Vanity of Its System," 303.

119. Lee, "Globalism and the Vanity of Its System," 296.

120. Jameson, "Notes on Globalization," 57.

121. Osborne, *Postconceptual Condition*, 34, 37.

Chapter 4

1. Henri Lefebvre, *State, Space, World: Selected Essays*, ed. Neil Brenner and Stuart Elden, and trans. Gerald Moore, Neil Brenner, and Stuart Elden (Minneapolis: University of Minnesota Press, 2009), 215.

2. Lefebvre, *State, Space, World*, 202.

3. Henri Lefebvre, *The Production of Space*, trans. Donald Nicholson-Smith (Malden, MA: Blackwell, 1991), 49.

4. Michel de Certeau, *The Practice of Everyday Life*, trans. Stephen Rendall (Berkeley: University of California Press, 1984), 117.

5. Harry Harootunian, "Ghostly Comparisons," in *Impacts of Modernities*, ed. Thomas Lamarre and Kang Nae-hui (Hong Kong: Hong Kong University Press, 2004), 39–52; Peter G. Rowe, *East Asia Modern: Shaping the Contemporary City* (London: Reaktion Books, 2005), 8.

6. Thomas Lamarre, "Introduction: The Impacts of Modernities," in *Impacts of Modernities*, ed. Thomas Lamarre and Kang Nae-hui (Hong Kong: Hong Kong University Press, 2004), 1–36.

7. Mezzadra and Neilson, *Border as Method*, 59.

8. Rumi Sakamoto, "Popular Culture and Historical Memories of War in Asia," in *Routledge Handbook of East Asian Popular Culture*, ed. Kōichi Iwabuchi, Eva Tsai, and Chris Berry (Abingdon, UK: Routledge, 2016), 254–264.

9. DeBoer, *Coproducing Asia*, 186–187.

10. Kōichi Iwabuchi, "Pop Culture's *Lingua Franca*: Language and Regional Popular Cultural Flows in East Asia," in *Babel or Behemoth: Language Trends in Asia*, ed. Jennifer

Lindsay and Tan Ying Ying (Singapore: Asia Research Institute, National University of Singapore, 2003), 171–172.

11. For an argument that emphasizes the former position, see Fredric Jameson, *The Geopolitical Aesthetic: Cinema and Space in the World System* (Bloomington: Indiana University Press, 1992), 115–155.

12. Jameson, "Notes on Globalization," 67.

13. J. S. Eades, "Economic Miracles and Megacities: The Japanese Model and Urbanization in East and Southeast Asia," in *Understanding the City: Contemporary and Future Perspectives*, ed. John Eade and Christopher Mele (Oxford: Blackwell, 2002), 222.

14. World Bank, *East Asian Miracle*.

15. Lefebvre, *State, Space, World*, 204.

16. Eades, "Economic Miracles and Megacities," 232. Of course, urbanization can occur without economic growth—Manila is one example.

17. Eades, "Economic Miracles and Megacities," 222.

18. Takashi Shiraishi, "The Third Wave: Southeast Asia and Middle-Class Formation in the Making of a Region," in *Beyond Japan: The Dynamics of East Asian Regionalism*, ed. Peter J. Katzenstein and Takashi Shiraishi (Ithaca, NY: Cornell University Press, 2006), 241.

19. Shiraishi, "Third Wave," 245.

20. Douglass, "The 'New' Tokyo Story," 83–119.

21. Yusuf and Nabeshima, *Postindustrial East Asian Cities*, 31.

22. Rowe, *East Asian Modern*, 191. Rowe, though, does step out of the realm of development and modernization issues to say that there is "the shared Confucian base of culture" among China, Hong Kong, Japan, South Korea, Taiwan, and Singapore, "quite apart from more recent manifestations of other kinds of belief and socio-political orientations"; Rowe, *East Asian Modern*, 9. With the qualification offered, Rowe just about moves away from implying some existence of some *genuine* Confucian modernity that is other to the West's version of modernity.

23. Rowe, *East Asian Modern*, 192.

24. Rowe, *East Asian Modern*, 34.

25. Koolhaas, "Singapore Songlines," 1017.

26. Laikwan Pang, "Postcolonial Hong Kong Cinema: Utilitarianism and Trans(Local)," *Postcolonial Studies* 10, no. 4 (2007): 413–430; Michael Curtin, *Playing to the World's Biggest Audience: The Globalization of Chinese Film and TV* (Berkeley: University of California Press, 2007).

27. Dirlik, *Complicities*, 15–44.

28. Jameson, "Notes on Globalization," 64.

29. Shunya Yoshimi and David Buist, "'America' as Desire and Violence: Americanization in Postwar Japan and Asia during the Cold War," *Inter-Asia Cultural Studies* 4, no. 3 (2003): 433–450.

30. See Kwai-Cheung Lo's "There Is No Such Thing as Asia: Racial Particularities in the 'Asian' Films of Hong Kong and Japan," *Modern Chinese Literature and Culture* 17, no. 1 (2005): 133–158, for an example of a study committed to denouncing any hint of an essentialized East Asia: "If Asia's heterogeneity is primordial and irreducible and if it designates a unity that can never be contained by any cinematic representation, should we understand those 'Asian' films of Japan and Hong Kong as tokens of presence for that which is absent?"; Lo, "There Is No Such Thing," 143. Lo's stance is understandable but does not account for why any media company should then attempt "Asian" films.

31. See Richard Robison and David S. G. Goodman, eds., *The New Rich in Asia: Mobile Phones, McDonald's and Middle Class Revolution* (London: Routledge, 1995); Beng-Huat Chua, ed., *Consumption in Asia: Lifestyle and Identities* (London: Routledge, 2000).

32. Jameson, *Geopolitical Aesthetic*, 4.

33. Huyssen, *After the Great Divide*, 20.

34. Huyssen, *After the Great Divide*, 19.

35. Powers, "Problem of Popular Culture," 468.

36. See Hsiao-peng Lu, *Transnational Chinese Cinemas: Identity, Nationhood, Gender* (Honolulu: University of Hawai'i Press, 1997); Meaghan Morris, Siu Leung Li, and Stephen Chan Ching-kiu, eds., *Hong Kong Connections: Transnational Imagination in Action Cinema* (Hong Kong: Hong Kong University Press, 2005); Anthony Fung and Alice Chik, eds., *Made in Hong Kong: Studies in Popular Music* (New York: Routledge, 2020); and Eva Tsai, Tung-Hung Ho, Miaoju Jian, eds., *Made in Taiwan: Studies in Popular Music* (New York: Routledge, 2019).

37. DeBoer, *Coproducing Asia*, 13.

38. Leo Ching writes, "mass cultural Asianism is a symptom of deeper structural and historical changes in the ways Asia is being perceived as both a mode of production and a regime of discursive practice in the Japanese [popular-cultural] imaginary. . . . [I]n today's Asianism . . . difference [between Asia and the West] itself exists only as a commodity, a spectacle to be consumed in a globalized capitalist system"; Leo Ching, "Globalizing the Regional, Regionalizing the Global: Mass Culture and Asianism in the Age of Late Capital," in *Globalization*, ed. Arjun Appadurai (Durham, NC: Duke University Press, 2001), 282.

39. Hyunjoon Shin, "Have You Ever Seen the Rain? And Who'll Stop the Rain?: The Globalizing Project of Korean Pop (K-Pop)," *Inter-Asia Cultural Studies*, 10, no. 4 (2009): 507–523.

40. Iwabuchi, *Recentering Globalization*, 123–136.

41. Hiroshi Shimizu, *Japanese Firms in Contemporary Singapore* (Singapore: NUS Press, 2008), 34–40, 184–217.

42. Kōichi Iwabuchi, ed., *Feeling Asian Modernities: Transnational Consumption of Japanese TV Dramas* (Hong Kong: Hong Kong University Press, 2004).

43. Douglas McGray, "Japanese Gross National Cool," *Foreign Policy* 130 (2002): 44–54, https://www.jstor.org/stable/3183487?origin=crossref, accessed April 25, 2014.

44. Mark James Russell, *POP Goes Korea: Behind the Revolution in Movies, Music, and the Internet Culture* (Berkeley, CA: Stone Bridge Press, 2008); Chua Beng Huat and Kōichi Iwabuchi, eds., *East Asian Pop Culture: Analysing the Korean Wave* (Hong Kong: Hong Kong University Press, 2008).

45. Law Kar, in *Border Crossings in Hong Kong Cinema: The 24th Hong Kong International Film Festival*, ed. Law Kar (Hong Kong: Leisure and Cultural Services Department, 2000), 105; cited by Meaghan Morris, "Transnational Imagination in Action Cinema: Hong Kong and the Making of a Global Popular Culture," *Inter-Asia Cultural Studies* 5, no. 2 (2004): 184–185. See also Yeh Yueh-Yu and Darrell William Davis, "Japan Hongscreen: Pan-Asian Cinemas and Flexible Accumulation," *Historical Journal of Film, Radio and Television* 22, no. 1 (2002): 61–82.

46. NHK, "One-off Productions and Serials, Foreign Dramas," n.d., https://www.nhk.or.jp/digitalmuseum/nhk50years_en/categories/p53/index.html, accessed July 4, 2022.

47. For a discussion of media and cultural productions made within the context of China–Japan relations, see Shuk-ting Kinnia Yau, "Japanese Media and China–Japan Relations: From the Normalization of Diplomatic Relations to the Second Abe Regime," *Asia-Pacific Journal: Japan Focus* 19, no. 14:4 (2021), https://apjjf.org/2021/14/yau, accessed April 16, 2024.

48. DeBoer, *Coproducing Asia*, 7.

49. Morris, "Transnational Imagination," 185.

50. Film versions of *Zatōichi* played by Katsu were produced from 1962 to 1973, with a final film in 1989. There were television series as well in 1974, 1976, 1978, and 1979. Sequels to *The One-Armed Swordsman* were made in 1969 and 1971.

51. DeBoer, *Coproducing Asia*, 84.

52. Laikwan Pang, "Masculinity in Crisis: Films of Milkyway Image and Post-1997 Hong Kong Cinema," *Feminist Media Studies* 2, no. 3 (2002): 325. See also Stephen Teo, "Local and Global Identity: Whither Hong Kong Cinema?," modified paper, Second International Conference on Chinese Cinema, Hong Kong Baptist University, Hong Kong, April 9, 2000, https://www.sensesofcinema.com/2000/asian-cinema/hongkong/, accessed April 16, 2024.

53. Yeh and Davis, "Japan Hongscreen," 64, 65.

54. The multilingual strategy also applied to commercial pop music. A representative example is Lee Soo Man's SM Entertainment Group, one of South Korea's leading production houses. Kwon Boa, known as BoA, who learned Japanese and English and was prepared for the Japanese market, was SM's first major overseas success. Lee's sights also turned to China. When queried as to why he was not thinking of the US market, Lee responded, "China will soon become the US; why waste energy by entering the US market? It's Asians after Whites, Blacks, and Hispanics. Even if I go there, it would be difficult to get out of minor market"; "Interview with Lee Soo Man," *BoAjjang Forums*, September 1, 2005, http://forums.boajjang.com/index.php?act=ST&f=1&t=34315, accessed September 26, 2006. SM's attention later moved back to Japan from China, given the latter's poor intellectual property protection.

55. For a discussion of cultural commonalities, see Chua Beng Huat, "Conceptualizing an East Asian Popular Culture," *Inter-Asia Cultural Studies* 5, no. 2 (2004): 200–221.

56. The obvious mistake in the film—the Wan Chai district where Suzie is to be found is actually Hollywood Road and Ladder Street in the Central District—manages not to detract from the film's overall representation of the then-colony's urbanscape.

57. Jonathan Clements and Motoko Tamamuro, *The Dorama Encyclopedia: A Guide to Japanese TV Drama Since 1953* (Berkeley, CA: Stone Bridge Press, 2003), xxvii. A fan in the PRC, though, recalls *Tokyo Love Story* being broadcast in 1995; see Ding Yu, "Follow the Steps of 'East Love,'" August 19, 2012, https://web.archive.org/web/20190513103252 /http://dingyu.me/blog/tokyo-love-story, accessed July 4, 2022.

58. See Yu-fen Ko: "Research on Japanese idol dramas in Taiwan point out that Taiwanese youths consider the urban Tokyo setting as the major reason for their popularity" ("The Desired Form," 118). In 1999, Liao Hsiang-siong, a deputy director of the Kuomintang's Department of Cultural Affairs, observed: "The Taiwanese can easily reflect upon their own lives while watching Japanese TV dramas. Yet, Japan is much more advanced and trendy, and they hope to become like the Japanese"; cited in Sayuri Daimon, "Taiwanese Youths Become Japan Freaks," *Japan Times*, September 13, 1999, https://www.japantimes.co.jp /news/1999/09/13/national/taiwanese-youths-becoming-japan-fans/, accessed April 25, 2024.

59. Eva Tsai, "Kaneshiro Takeshi: Transnational Stardom and the Media and Culture Industries in Asia's Global/Postcolonial Age," *Modern Chinese Literature and Culture* 17, no. 1 (2005): 100–132.

60. Janice Tong, "*Chungking Express*: Time and Its Displacements," in *Chinese Films in Focus II*, ed. Chris Berry (Houndmills, UK: Palgrave Macmillan, 2008), 67. On the film's feeling of *déjà disparu*, see Ackbar Abbas, *Hong Kong and the Culture of Disappearance* (Minneapolis: University of Minnesota Press, 1997), 25.

61. Gordon Matthews, "Chungking Mansions: A Center of 'Low-End Globalization,'" *Ethnology* 46, no. 2 (2007): 169–183.

62. Kamiya, "Communicative Approach, from Asia," 133.

63. Étienne Balibar, *Politics and the Other Scene* (London: Verso, 2002), 76.

64. *Sleepless Town* won Best Cinematography and Best Art Direction for the 18th Hong Kong Film Awards in 1999.

65. Tsai, "Kaneshiro Takeshi," 115. She later adds, "Japanese consumers, who consume mass cultural goods from Japan and the West, have both a nostalgic and a familiar feeling about Asia"; Tsai, "Kaneshiro Takeshi," 117.

66. Lo, "There Is No Such Thing," 146, 147. Lee Chi-Ngai is credited as a co-writer of the screenplay.

67. Shelley Kracer, "*Sleepless Town* Review," *Chinese Cinema Site*, 1998, http://www .chinesecinemas.org/sleeplesstown.html, accessed November 20, 2016.

68. This is the first film in what is called Miike's *Black Society Trilogy* (*Kuro-shakai San-busaku*), with films released later in 1997 (*Rainy Dog*/*Gokudō kuroshakai*) and 1999 (*Ley Lines*/*Nihon kuroshakai Rei Rainzu*), both of which have comparable border-crossing orientations.

69. Tim Larimer, "'There's No Need for an Apology': Tokyo's Boisterous Governor is Back in the Headlines," *Time Asia* 155, no. 16, April 24, 2000, https://web.archive.org/web/20130408091806/http://cgi.cnn.com/ASIANOW/time/magazine/2000/0424/int.ishihara.html, accessed July 11, 2022. For a discussion of Chinese gangs in Japan, see Andrew Rankin, "Recent Trends in Organized Crime in Japan: Yakuza vs. the Police, and Foreign Crime Gangs, Part 2," *Asia-Pacific Journal: Japan Focus* 10, no. 7:1 (2012): 9–13, https://apjjf.org/2012/10/7/Andrew-Rankin/3692/article.html, accessed July 1, 2022.

70. *Tokyo Raiders* grossed HK$28 million, then about US$3.5 million; Derek Elley, "*Tokyo Raiders*," *Variety*, October 23, 2000, http://www.variety.com/review/VE1117788435.html?categoryid=31&cs=1, accessed November 29, 2007. In July 2022, Netflix added *Tokyo Raiders* to their list of "international films," at least for the Singapore market; Netflix, *Tokyo Raiders*, n.d., https://www.netflix.com/sg/title/60020214, accessed July 13, 2022. Jingle Ma attempted a sequel in 2005, *Seoul Raiders*, that again featured Tony Leung in the lead role. This follow-up did not fare as well. Derek Elley writes that "from the thin script to the so-so action sequences, there's a general air of haste. . . . Clean-lined Seoul, here bathed in cold, wintry light, [also] isn't the most atmospheric of locations"; "*Seoul Raiders*," *Variety*, April 4, 2005, https://variety.com/2005/film/markets-festivals/seoul-raiders-1200526722/, accessed October 22, 2022. The last comment indicates, by implication, Tokyo's legibility internationally that Seoul at that moment did not quite possess.

71. David Bordwell, *Planet Hong Kong: Popular Cinema and the Art of Entertainment* (Cambridge, MA: Harvard University Press, 2000), 150; DeBoer, *Coproducing Asia*, 72–78.

72. Yeh and Davis, "Japan Hongscreen," 63.

73. Yeh and Davis, "Japan Hongscreen," 65.

74. Colin McCabe, Preface to Jameson, *Geopolitical Aesthetic*, xiv.

75. Quoted in Charles Leary, "Full Time Cinema: An Interview with Johnnie To," *Off-screen* 8, no. 6 (2004), https://offscreen.com/view/johnnie_to, accessed July 5, 2022.

76. Stephen Teo, "Author's Interview with Johnnie To," in Stephen Teo, *Director in Action: Johnnie To and the Hong Kong Action Film* (Hong Kong: Hong Kong University Press, 2007), 239.

77. Or, as Stephen Teo suggests, "The inconsistency of [multiple] language [usage] adds a jarring tone and rhythm to the narrative; language itself is a sign of the pathology of narrative and in a paradoxical way, it sustains one's interest in the [film's] narrative"; Teo, "Author's Interview with Johnnie To," 157.

78. The railway station scene was shot at the Tanjong Pagar railway station in Singapore.

79. Pang, "Masculinity in Crisis," 337.

80. Teo, *Director in Action*, 159.

81. References are made to other films such as Richard Donner's *Assassins* (1995) and John Ford's classic Western, *The Man Who Shot Liberty Valance* (1962). As has been noted, *Fulltime Killer* is a "transnational collage" of action film that "far exceeds any notion of Asia"; Lo, "There is No Such Thing," 150. However, it *is* an action film that deliberately engages with contemporary East Asian culture.

82. In 1988, Toei Animation adapted the manga series for an anime "original video animation" (OVA), meaning that it was a direct-to-video product.

83. Paul Gilroy, *Postcolonial Melancholia* (New York: Columbia University Press, 2006), 3.

84. Quotation from Leary, "Full Time Cinema."

85. Lefebvre, *State, Space, World*, 206.

86. Curtin, *Playing to the World's Biggest Audience*, 283–284.

87. Harootunian, "Ghostly Comparisons," 51.

88. Lefebvre, *State, Space, World*, 215.

Chapter 5

1. SMAP's management company made the surprising announcement in August 2016 that the group would break up at the end of the year.

2. "Wen 'Sincerely Welcomes' SMAP's Beijing Concert Fri.," *Kyodo News*, September 15, 2011, english.kyodonews.jp/news/2011/09/115129.html, accessed September 19, 2011.

3. "Japan Pop Band SMAP in Rare Beijing Concert," *BBC News Asia-Pacific*, September 16, 2011, www.bbc.co.uk/news/world-asia-pacific-1494563?print=true, accessed September 19, 2011.

4. Okakura, *Ideals of the East*, 1.

5. Cumings, *Parallax Visions*, 218.

6. See Jennifer Lindsay, "Musical Travels of the Coconut Isle and the Socialist Popular," in *Sound Alignments: Popular Music in Asia's Cold Wars*, ed. Michael K. Bourdaghs, Paola Iovene, and Kaley Mason (Durham, NC: Duke University Press, 2021), 43–67.

7. Wang Hui, *The Politics of Imagining Asia*, trans. Theodore Huters (Cambridge, MA: Harvard University Press, 2011), 62.

8. Sakai, "'You Asians,'" 789–818.

9. Cumings, *Parallax Visions*, 213. See also John W. Dower, *Empire and Aftermath: Yoshida Shigeru and the Japanese Experience, 1878–1954* (Cambridge, MA: Council on East Asian Studies, Harvard University, 1979).

10. Jung-en Woo, *Race to the Swift: State and Finance in Korean Industrialization* (New York: Columbia University Press, 1991).

11. Cumings, *Parallax Visions*, 213.

12. For an account of some Japanese attempts to open up non-neoliberal paths to development, see Vijay Prashad's chapter, "Tokyo's Road to Nowhere," in his *The Poorer Nations: A Possible History of the Global South* (London: Verso, 2012), 145–158.

13. Kevin Rudd, "Abe Shinzo Was the Most Important Japanese Leader in the Past 50 Years, says Kevin Rudd," *Economist*, July 11, 2022 (updated July 14, 2022), https://www.economist.com/by-invitation/2022/07/11/abe-shinzo-was-the-most-important-japanese-leader-in-the-past-50-years-says-kevin-rudd, accessed July 17, 2022.

14. Cumings, *Parallax Visions*, 216. According to Takashi Shiraishi, "the United States remained hegemonic [in East, including Southeast, Asia], casting a long shadow over the regional architecture. This is especially evident in security, and to a lesser extent in finance and trade" (Shiraishi, "Third Wave," 238).

15. Bonnie S. Glaser explains: "The risk of conflict in the South China Sea is significant. China, Taiwan, Vietnam, Malaysia, Brunei, and the Philippines have competing territorial and jurisdictional claims, particularly over rights to exploit the region's possibly extensive reserves of oil and gas. Freedom of navigation in the region is also a contentious issue, especially between the United States and China over the right of US military vessels to operate in China's two-hundred-mile exclusive economic zone (EEZ). These tensions are shaping—and being shaped by—rising apprehensions about the growth of China's military power and its regional intentions"; Bonnie S. Glaser, "Armed Clash in the South China Sea: Contingency Planning Memorandum No. 14," Council on Foreign Relations, April 11, 2012, https://www.cfr.org/report/armed-clash-south-china-sea, accessed April 25, 2024).

16. "South China Sea: Conflicting Claims and Tensions," Lowy Institute for International Policy, http://www.lowyinstitute.org/issues/south-china-sea, accessed September 19, 2015.

17. Evan A. Feigenbaum and Robert A. Manning, "A Tale of Two Asias: In the Battle for Asia's Soul, Which Side Will Win—Security or Economics?," *Foreign Policy*, October 31, 2012, https://foreignpolicy.com/2012/10/31/a-tale-of-two-asias/, accessed June 23, 2015.

18. Ian Storey and Malcolm Cook, "The Trump Administration and Southeast Asia: America's Asia Policy Crystalizes," *ISEAS Perspectives*, no. 77 (November 29, 2018), 6, https://www.academia.edu/36971997/The_Trump_Administration_and_Southeast_Asia_After_the_Singapore_Summit, accessed April 25, 2024.

19. Jameson, "Notes on Globalization," 55, 69; Peter Osborne, *Anywhere or Not at All: Philosophy of Contemporary Art* (London: Verso, 2013), 17.

20. Osborne, *Anywhere or Not at All*, 194.

21. Michael K. Bourdaghs, *Sayonara Amerika, Sayonara Nippon: A Geopolitical Prehistory of J-Pop* (New York: Columbia University Press, 2012), 128.

22. DeBoer, *Coproducing Asia*, 73.

23. Lu, *Transnational Chinese Cinemas*.

24. Chua Beng Huat, *Structure, Audience and Soft Power in East Asian Pop Culture* (Hong Kong: Hong Kong University Press, 2012), 5.

25. Kant Udornpim and Arvind Singhal, "*Oshin*, a Pro-Social Role Model, in Thailand," *Keio Communication Review* 21 (1999): 3–21.

26. On televisual dramas, see Iwabuchi, *Recentering Globalization*; and Iwabuchi, *Feeling Asian Modernities*. On pop music, see David Leheny, "A Narrow Place to Cross Swords: 'Soft Power' and the Politics of Japanese Popular Culture in East Asia," in *Beyond Japan: The Dynamics of East Asian Regionalism*, ed. Peter J. Katzenstein and Takashi Shiraishi (Ithaca, NY: Cornell University Press, 2006), 212–213. For possibly the earliest assessment of the Japanese Wave, see Honda Shiro, "The Spreading of Japan's Popular Culture in East Asia," *Japan Echo* 21, no. 4 (1994): 75–79. For an early critique, see C. J. W.-L. Wee, "Is Consumption-Oriented Popular Culture in Singapore Being 'Japanized'?" (in Japanese translation) *Gaiko Forum* 74 (1994): 66–68, in which this writer (wrongly) dismissed the strength of this wave in Singapore. On the liberalization of political life and the emergence of the Korean wave, see Russell, *POP Goes Korea*; Doobo Shim, *Waxing the Korean Wave*, ARI Working Paper 158 (Singapore: Asia Research Institute, National University of Singapore, 2011); and Chua and Iwabuchi, *East Asian Pop Culture*.

27. Shiraishi, "Third Wave."

28. Leheny, "A Narrow Place to Cross Swords." See also Yoshiko Nakano, "Who Initiates a Global Flow? Japanese Popular Culture in Asia," *Visual Communication* 1, no. 2 (2002): 229–253; and Hiro Katsumata, "Japanese Popular Culture in East Asia: A New Insight into Regional Community Building," *International Relations of the Asia-Pacific* 12, no. 1 (2011): 133–160.

29. See Hiroshi Aoyagi's chapter, "The Spread of Idol Performances in New Industrial Economies," in his *Island of Eight Million Smiles: Idol Performers and Symbolic Production in Contemporary Japan* (Cambridge, MA: Harvard University Asia Center, 2005), 232–258.

30. Yoshimi and Buist, "'America' as Desire and Violence," 433–450; Carolyn S. Stevens, *Japanese Popular Music: Culture, Authority, and Power* (Abingdon, UK: Routledge, 2008); Bourdaghs, *Sayonara Amerika*.

31. Jameson, "Notes on Globalization," 67.

32. Korean Culture and Information Service, *The Korean Wave: A New Pop Culture Phenomenon* (Seoul: Korean Culture and Information Service, Ministry of Culture, Sports, and Tourism, 2011), 20. The series' audience share was 16.6 percent; Sun Jung, *Korean Masculinities and Transcultural Consumption: Yonsama, Rain, Oldboy, K-Pop Idols* (Hong Kong: Hong Kong University Press, 2011), 1.

33. Cho Hae-Joang argues of Korean pop culture that "it appeals to a certain global middle and lower middle class by presenting upscale hyper-modern lifestyles. In a way, the Korean Wave plays a significant role in accelerating the transformation of global residents into neoliberal subjects in an era where all types of communities are being disintegrated and atomized"; Cho Hae-Joang, "Reading the 'Korean Wave' as a Sign of Global Shift," *Korea Journal* 45, no. 4 (2005): 176.

34. Fredric Jameson, "Reification and Utopia in Mass Culture (1979)," in *Signatures of the Visible* (New York: Routledge, 1990), 156.

35. Michael Denning, *Culture in the Age of Three Worlds* (London: Verso, 2004), 102–103.

36. Yoshitaka Mōri, "J-Pop: From the Ideology of Creativity to DiY Music Culture," *Inter-Asia Cultural Studies* 10, no. 4 (2009): 479.

37. Stevens, *Japanese Popular Music*, 10.

38. Japan Ministry of Posts and Telecommunications, *White Paper: Communications in Japan 1997*, http://www.mpt.go.jp/eng/Resources/top.html, accessed June 8, 2001.

39. Katsumata, "Japanese Popular Culture," 138.

40. Nakano, "Who Initiates a Global Flow?" 231. See also the essays in Iwabuchi, *Feeling Asian Modernities*.

41. Masashi Ogawa, "Japanese Popular Music in Hong Kong: What Does TK Present?," in *Refashioning Pop Music in Asia: Cosmopolitan Flows, Political Tempos, and Aesthetic Industries*, ed. Allen Chun, Ned Rossiter, and Brian Shoesmith (London: Routledge/Curzon, 2004), 146–147; Nakano, "Who Initiates a Global Flow?" 236–237.

42. On Bangkok, see Ubonrat Siriyusavak, "Popular Culture and Youth Consumption: Modernity, Identity and Social Transformation," in *Feeling Asian Modernities: Transnational Consumption of Japanese TV Dramas*, ed. Kōichi Iwabuchi (Hong Kong: Hong Kong University Press, 2004), 177–202.

43. Benjamin Wai-ming Ng, "Japanese Popular Music in Singapore and the Hybridization of Asian Music," *Asian Music* 34, no. 1 (2002): 4–5, 2–3.

44. Jon Herskovitz, "Top Japanese Girl Group Speed Coming to a Halt: Members to Pursue Solo Careers," *Variety*, October 11, 1999, https://variety.com/1999/music/news/top-japanese-girl-group-speed-coming-to-a-halt-1117756500/, accessed January 2, 2016.

45. Bonnie C. Wade, *Music in Japan: Experiencing Music, Expressing Culture* (Oxford: Oxford University Press, 2005).

46. Mōri, "J-Pop," 476. See also Stevens, *Japanese Popular Music*, 16, 106–107. Mōri and Stevens both draw from Ugaya Hiromichi, *J-Poppu to wa nani ka* [What is J-Pop?] (Tokyo: Iwanami Shoten, 2005), in their accounts of J-WAVE and the appearance of "J-pop." For a detailed examination of "English and English-like Japanese lyrics," see Stevens, *Japanese Popular Music*, 132–155.

47. Martin Roberts, "'A New Stereophonic Sound Spectacular': *Shibuya-kei* as Transnational Soundscape," *Popular Music* 32, no. 1 (2013): 111–123. See also Mōri, "J-Pop," 476.

48. Stevens, *Japanese Popular Music*, 16.

49. For example, the eighth album of the pop trio Dreams Come True, *Love Unlimited* (1996), sold more than two hundred thousand units in Taiwan; Steve McClure, *Nippon Pop* (Tokyo: Charles E. Tuttle, 1998), 153.

50. Stevens, *Japanese Popular Music*, 16–17.

51. Wade, *Music in Japan*, 134.

52. Yoshimi and Buist, "'America' as Desire and Violence," 434–444. See also Shunya Yoshimi, "Consuming 'America': From Symbol to System," in *Consumption in Asia: Lifestyle and Identities*, ed. Beng-Huat Chua (London: Routledge, 2000), 202–224.

53. As Kōichi Iwabuchi argues, "Japanese cultural products themselves have come to hold a certain symbolic appeal to other Asian nations—which can be conceived neither as merely 'odorless' [that is, without any marked 'Japanese' identity], nor as nonderivative of American cultural power, nor as comparable to the Americanization paradigm—in the context of the proliferation of non-Western indigenized modernities"; Iwabuchi, *Recentering Globalization*, 47.

54. Patrick W. Galbraith and Jason G. Karlin, "Introduction: The Mirror of Idols and Celebrity," in *Idols and Celebrity in Japanese Media Culture*, ed. Patrick W. Galbraith and Jason G. Karlin (Houndmills, UK: Palgrave Macmillan, 2012), 4. See also Stevens, *Japanese Popular Music*, 49–51.

55. According to Mōri, "Looking back to the age of the analogue record in the mid 1980s, Japanese audiences listened to western music much more than they do [around 2009]"; Mōri, "J-Pop," 477.

56. Mōri, "J-Pop," 477. For a critique of Asada, see Tomiko Yoda, "A Roadmap to Millennial Japan," *South Atlantic Quarterly* 99, no. 4 (2000): 659–662.

57. Rumi Sakamoto comments that the "recession and the subsequent neoliberal restructuring and precariatization of young people [that] destroyed the economic pride many had once felt . . . also coincided with an increase emphasis on Japan's war responsibility over issues such as the Yasukuni Shrine, 'comfort women,' and the Nanjing Massacre, as well as Chinese and Korean demands for apologies and reparations," with the result that "Japanese public discourse in the twenty-first century has shifted to the right"; Sakamoto, "Popular Culture and Historical Memories," 256.

58. W. David Marx writes, "The shop's real innovation . . . was the corner where the staff curated a selection of more interesting contemporary Japanese bands—ones that had strayed far from classic *kayōkyoku* conventions to sound like Japanese-language versions of modern Western music. At first, this focused around Flipper's Guitar, Love Tambourines, Pizzicato Five, and Scha Dara Parr"; W. David Marx, "R.I.P. Shibuya HMV," *Néojaponisme* Blog Archive, August 25, 2010, https://neojaponisme.com/2010/08/25/r-i-p-shibuya-hmv/, accessed January 10, 2016.

59. Roberts, "'A New Stereophonic Sound Spectacular,'" 113.

60. Takanami remained with the group until 1994.

61. "Twiggy Twiggy Lyrics," *AllTheLyrics.com*, https://www.allthelyrics.com/lyrics/pizzicato_five/twiggy_twiggy-lyrics-227513.html#ixzz3wre0s3wA, accessed January 11, 2016.

62. Pizzicato Five, "Twiggy Twiggy," directed by Konishi Yasuharu, track 7–21, Matador Promotional Video, 4:00, in *The Band of 20th Century: Pizzicato Five 6 DVD Set*, Bonus Disc: Trailers and Footages, Readymade Records XT-1544~1549, 2004, DVD.

63. Roberts, "'A New Stereophonic Sound Spectacular,'" 112.

64. Yoda, "A Roadmap," 661.

65. Mōri, "J-Pop," 478.

66. "Hikaru Utada: Chart History," *Billboard*, https://www.billboard.com/artist/303512 /hikaru-utada/chart, accessed January 13, 2016; Lars Brandle, "Utada's 'Exodus' Breaks Record in Japan," *BillboardBiz*, September 10, 2004, www.billboard.com/biz/articles /news/1428984/utadas-exodus-breaks-record-in-japan, accessed January 13, 2016.

67. Stevens, *Japanese Popular Music*, 146 (quoting Ugaya Hiromichi's critique of J-Pop); Mōri, "J-Pop," 478.

68. "Hikaru Utada—Biography," *Billboard*, www.billboard.com/artist/303512/hikaru -utada/biography, accessed January 13, 2016.

69. Kawabata Shigeru, "The Japanese Record Industry," *Popular Music* 10, no. 3 (1991): 327.

70. Ubonrat Siriyuvasak and Shin Hyunjoon, "Asianizing K-Pop: Production, Consumption and Identification Patterns among Thai Youth," *Inter-Asia Cultural Studies* 8, no. 1 (2007): 128n13.

71. Keith Negus, *The South Korean Music Industry: A Literature Review*, CREATe (Centre for Copyright and New Business Models in the Creative Economy) Working Paper Series (Glasgow: CREATe, 2015).

72. Osborne, *Anywhere or Not at All*, 25.

73. Haekyung Um, *K-Pop on the Global Platform: European Audience Reception and Contexts* (Seoul: KOFICE [Korean Foundation for International Cultural Exchange], 2014).

74. Hyunjoon Shin, "Reconsidering Transnational Cultural Flows of Popular Music in East Asia: Transbordering Musicians in Japan and Korea Searching for 'Asia,'" *Korean Studies* 33, no. 1 (2009): 109.

75. Hyunjoon Shin, "Searching for Youth, the People (*Minjung*), and 'Another' West While Living Through Anti-Communist Cold War Politics: South Korean 'Folk Song' in the 1970s," in *Sound Alignments: Popular Music in Asia's Cold Wars*, ed. Michael K. Bourdaghs, Paola Iovene, and Kaley Mason (Durham, NC: Duke University Press, 2021), 147.

76. Michael Fuhr, *Globalization and Popular Music in South Korea: Sounding Out K-Pop* (New York: Routledge, 2016), 133–149; Gi-Wook Shin and Joon Nak Choi, "Paradox or Paradigm? Making Sense of Korean Globalization," in *Korea Confronts Globalization*, ed. Chang Yun-Shik, Hyun-Ho Seok, and Donald L. Baker (London: Routledge, 2009), 250–272; Jung-Yup Lee, "Managing the Transnational, Governing the National: Cultural Policy and the Politics of 'the Cultural Archetype Project in South Korea,'" in *Popular Culture and the State in East and Southeast Asia*, ed. Nissim Otmazgin and Eyal Ben-Ari (London: Routledge, 2011), 123–143; Seung-Ho Kwon and Joseph Kim, "The Cultural Industry Policies of the Korean Government and the Korean Wave," *International Journal of Cultural Policy* 20, no. 4 (2014): 422–439.

77. Youna Kim, "Introduction: Korean Media in a Digital Cosmopolitan World," in *The Korean Wave: Korean Media Go Global*, ed. Youna Kim (Abingdon, UK: Routledge, 2013), 1–28.

78. On melodic chorus, see Eun-Young Jung, "Transnational Cultural Traffic in Northeast Asia: The 'Presence' of Japan in Korea's Popular Music Culture" (Ph.D. diss., University of Pittsburgh, PA, 2007), 70–73. See also Fuhr, *Globalization*, 52–54; and Russell, *POP Goes Korea*, 143–147.

79. Fuhr, *Globalization*, 53–54.

80. Eun-Young Jung, "The Place of Sentimental Song in Contemporary Korean Musical Life," *Korean Studies* 35 (2011): 71–92.

81. The album sold 1.5 million units; Keith Howard, "Exploding Ballads: The Transformation of Korean Pop Music," in *Global Goes Local: Popular Culture in Asia*, ed. Timothy I. Craig and Richard King (Honolulu: University of Hawai'i Press, 2002), 80–95.

82. Russell, *POP Goes Korea*, 156. See also Fuhr, *Globalization*, 75–76. Japanese pop music, as a point of comparison, began to have a notable presence in China from the early 1990s. For example, in 1992, the pop-rock band Southern All Stars had the first concert of any foreign group in China at the Beijing Capital Gymnasium; Amuse, Inc., "Corporate History," https://www.amuse.co.jp/en/corporate/history/, accessed June 27, 2016; Jung, *Transnational Cultural Traffic*, 238.

83. Shin, "Have You Ever Seen the Rain?" 510. Shin continues: "Although it would be controversial to say that this system has 'East Asian' characteristics, it is true that it cannot be easily found outside the [East Asia] region"; Shin, "Have You Ever Seen the Rain?" 510.

84. Natsuko Fukue, "Johnny's: So You Wanna Be a Johnny," *Japan Times*, April 14, 2009, www.japantimes.co.jp/news/2009/04/14/reference/so-you-wanna-be-a-johnny, accessed June 27, 2016; W. David Marx, "The *Jimusho* System: Understanding the Production Logic of the Japanese Entertainment Industry," in *Idols and Celebrity in Japanese Media Culture*, ed. Patrick W. Galbraith and Jason G. Karlin (Houndmills, UK: Palgrave Macmillan, 2012), 35–55.

85. Smile-Up, Inc., was set up for the purpose of compensating the abuse victims. The plan is also for separate a separate talent agency to be established to manage the performers of the former Johnny & Associates; "Johnny's Changes Name to Smile-Up in Wake of Sexual Abuse Scandal," *Kyōdō News Plus*, October 17, 2023, https://english.kyodonews.net/news/2023/10/047ecbeb7bfc-johnnys-changes-name-to-smile-up-in-wake-of-sexual-abuse-scandal.html, accessed November 4, 2023.

86. Dal Yong Jin and Woongjae Ryoo, "Critical Interpretation of Hybrid K-Pop: The Global-Local Paradigm of English Mixing in Lyrics," *Popular Music and Society* 37, no. 2 (2014): 113–131; Fuhr, *Globalization*, 59–124.

87. It has also been reported that a former journalist, Cho Hyun-jin, was the inventor of the term "K-Pop," when he wrote for *Billboard* from 1999 to 2002; Kim Hyung-eun, "Bringing US Music History to Korea," *Korea Joongang Daily*, December 29, 2015, https://koreajoongangdaily.joins.com/news/article/article.aspx?aid=3013294, accessed July 5, 2016.

88. Shin, "Reconsidering Transnational Cultural Flows," 107; Oliver Boyd-Barrett, "Reconfiguring Media and Empire," in *The Korean Wave: Korean Media Go Global*, ed. Youna Kim (Abingdon, UK: Routledge, 2013), 58–70.

89. Jung, *Transnational Cultural Traffic*, esp. 121–123; Keith Howard, "Coming of Age: Korean Pop in the 90s," in *Korean Pop Music: Riding the Wave*, ed. Keith Howard (Folkestone, UK: Global Orient, 2006), 96. Ninja's song was an update of "Omatsuri Mambo" (1952) by Misora Hibari (1937–1989), the famous postwar *enka* singer, who some said was *zainichi*, a Japanese of Korean descent (Bourdaghs, *Sayonara Amerika*, 79–83). An unintended echo of emotional, historically imbricated debates occurs here.

90. Quoted in Cho Hyun-jin, "S. Korea Braces for Japanese Pop: Lifting of Culture Ban Will Allow Imports for First Time," *Billboard*, July 25, 1998, 59.

91. Shin, "Have You Ever Seen the Rain?"; Jeroen de Kloet and Jaap Kooijman, "Karaoke Americanism Gangnam Styl [*sic*]: K-Pop, Wonder Girls, and the Asian Unpopular," in *Unpopular Culture*, ed. Martin Lüthe and Sascha Pöhlmann (Amsterdam: Amsterdam University Press, 2016), 113–128; Jeongmee Kim and Basil Glynn, "'Oppa'-tunity Knocks: PSY, 'Gangnam Style' and the Press Reception of K-Pop in Britain," *Situations: Cultural Studies in the Asian Context* 7, no. 1 (2013/2014): 1–20.

92. Christian Oliver, "South Korea's K-Pop Takes Off in the West," *Financial Times*, February 10, 2012, www.ft.com/cms/s/0/ddf11662-53c7-11e1-9eac-00144feabdc0.html #axzz4DY5wwcc8, accessed July 1, 2015.

93. On exports to Japan, see Patrick St. Michel, "How Korean Pop Conquered Japan," *Atlantic*, September 13, 2011, www.theatlantic.com/entertainment/archive/2011/09/how -korean-pop-conquered-japan/244712/, accessed May 27, 2016.

94. Fuhr, *Globalization*, 142. The figures in this paragraph are from Korean Creative Content Agency (KOCCA) publications.

95. Negus, *South Korean Music Industry*, 13.

96. Stevens, *Japanese Popular Music*, 32–33.

97. Despite their Japanese success, all activities by TVXQ in Korea ceased at the end of 2009 owing to contractual challenges from three of the singers. The revamped boyband that reappeared in 2010 consisted of only two of the original five members.

98. "NHK Sees Ratings for 'Kōhaku' Music Show Sink to Lowest Ever," *Japan Times*, January 2, 2016, www.japantimes.co.jp/news/2016/01/02/national/media-national/nhk -sees-ratings-for-kohaku-music-show-sink-to-lowest-ever/#.V3ncDmOP5a_, accessed July 4, 2016.

99. Shin, "Reconsidering Transnational Cultural Flows," 108.

100. "Taiwan, China United in Backlash Against Korean Wave," *Chosun Ilbo*, January 11, 2006, https://english.chosun.com/site/data/html_dir/2006/01/11/2006011161009.html, accessed July 1, 2016.

101. Hong Chan-sik, "Korean Wave Backlash in Taiwan," *Dong-A Ilbo*, January 2, 2012, https://www.donga.com/en/List/article/all/20120102/402867/1, accessed July 3, 2016.

102. Yoshitaka Mōri, "*Winter Sonata* and Cultural Practices of Active Fans in Japan: Considering Middle-Aged Women as Cultural Agents," in *East Asian Pop Culture: Analysing*

the Korean Wave, ed. Chua Beng Huat and Kōichi Iwabuchi (Hong Kong: Hong Kong University Press, 2008), 127–141.

103. Nicola Liscutin, "Surfing the Neo-Nationalist Wave: A Case Study of *Manga Kenkanryū*," in *Cultural Studies and Cultural Industries in Northeast Asia: What a Difference a Region Makes*, ed. Chris Berry, Nicola Liscutin, and Jonathan D. Mackintosh (Hong Kong: Hong Kong University Press, 2009), 171–189; Rumi Sakamoto and Matthew Allen, "Hating 'The Korean Wave' Comic Books: A Sign of a New Nationalism," *Asia Pacific Journal/Japan Focus* 5, no. 10 (2007), https://apjjf.org/-Rumi-SAKAMOTO /2535/article.html, accessed July 1, 2016.

104. Park Si-soo, "Anti-*Hallyu* Voices Growing in Japan," *Korea Times*, February 21, 2014, www.koreatimes.co.kr/www/news/culture/2014/02/386_152045.html, accessed July 3, 2016.

105. Johnny's Net, "Family Club," www.johnnys-net.jp/page?id=jfcJoin&lang=en_us, accessed July 4, 2016.

106. The festival is organized by the Korean Foundation for International Cultural Exchange (KOFICE). See Fuhr, *Globalization*, 143–149; and Gunjoo Jang and Won K. Paik, "Korean Wave as Tool for Korea's New Cultural Diplomacy," *Advances in Applied Sociology* 2, no. 3 (2012): 196–202.

107. A two- and three-DVD concert selection was released in 2007 by J Storm, Johnny's in-house music label. The fan-chat session is on the first disc of the three-DVD "limited" edition (JABA-5020–5022).

108. "BTS: Chart History: Hot 100," *Billboard*, www.billboard.com/music/bts, accessed February 16, 2019; "BTS: Chart History: Independent Albums," *Billboard*, www.billboard .com/music/bts/chart-history/independent-albums, accessed February 16, 2019.

109. See Hyunjoon Shin, "K-Pop, the Sound of Subaltern Cosmopolitanism?" in *Routledge Handbook of East Asian Popular Culture*, ed. Kōichi Iwabuchi, Eva Tsai, and Chris Berry (Abingdon, UK: Routledge, 2016), 116–123.

110. Eshita Srinivas, "Tomorrow X Together Set to be the First K-Pop Group to Headline Lollapalooza 2023," *Lifestyle Asia*, August 2, 2023, https://www.lifestyleasia.com/ind /whats-on/news-whats-on/tomorrow-x-together-k-pop-group-at-lollapalooza-2023/, accessed August 6, 2023. TXT share the same management agency as BTS.

111. Kwak Yeon-soo, "K-Pop Boy Band BTS Agency under Fire for Working with Japanese Producer Yasushi Akimoto," *South China Morning Post*, September 18, 2018, www.scmp .com/magazines/style/people-events/article/2164649/k-pop-boy-band-bts-agency-under -fire-working-japanese, accessed November 9, 2018; "BTS T-Shirt: Japanese TV Show Cancels BTS Appearance over Atomic Bomb Shirt," *BBC News*, November 9, 2018, www .bbc.com/news/world-asia-46147777, accessed February 16, 2018.

112. Denning, *Culture in the Age*, 30–31, 31.

113. C. J. W.-L. Wee, "Staging the Asian Modern: Cultural Fragments, the Singaporean Eunuch, and the Asian *Lear*," *Critical Inquiry* 30, no. 4 (2004): 772.

Coda

1. Rey Chow, "Framing the Orient: Toward a New Visibility of the Orient," *PMLA* 126, no. 3 (2011): 556.

2. Chow, "Framing the Orient," 556.

3. Chow, "Framing the Orient," 556.

4. In 1980, 19 percent of the PRC's population lived in cities, but by 2021, 63 percent of the population lived in cities; World Bank, "Urban Population [% of Total Population]—China," https://data.worldbank.org/indicator/SP.URB.TOTL.IN.ZS?locations=CN, accessed July 26, 2022.

5. Dirlik, *Complicities*, 31.

6. World Trade Organization, "Accessions: China," https://www.wto.org/english/thewto_e/acc_e/a1_chine_e.htm, accessed July 26, 2022. See the PDF of the PRC's GATT application L/6017, dated July 14, 1986, https://docs.wto.org/gattdocs/q/GG/L6199/6017.PDF, accessed July 26, 2022.

7. Feng Zengxian, "Preface," in Shanghai Art Museum, *Shanghai Biennale 2000: Shanghai Spirit*, exhibition catalogue (Shanghai: Shanghai Art Museum, 2000), n.p.

8. Mia Yu, "Manifolds of the Local: Tracing the Neglected Legacies of the Shanghai Biennale 2000," in Jane DeBevoise, John Tain, Liu Ding, Carol Yinghua Lu, Lee Weng Choy, Xu Hong, and Anthony Yung, *Uncooperative Contemporaries: Art Exhibitions in Shanghai in 2000* (London: Afterall Books, 2020), 65–69.

9. Dirlik, *Complicities*, 21.

10. The first and second editions were held in 1996 and 1998, respectively. The venue of the 2012 or the ninth biennale was changed to the then–new contemporary art museum, Power Station of Art—it was a former power station, the Nanshi Power Plant.

11. Thomas J. Campanella, *The Concrete Dragon: China's Urban Revolution and What It Means for the World* (New York: Princeton Architectural Press, 2008), 7.

12. Wu Hung, "The 2000 Shanghai Biennale: The Making of a Historical Event," *Art and AsiaPacific* no. 31 (2000): 45.

13. Wu, "2000 Shanghai Biennale," 45.

14. Mia, "Manifolds of the Local," 62.

15. Wu, "2000 Shanghai Biennale," 46.

16. Wu, "2000 Shanghai Biennale," 44. See also Xu Hong, "To Select, To Be Selected and Who Selects: The Shanghai Biennale in the Context of Globalisation," trans. Zhao Han, in Jane DeBevoise, John Tain, Liu Ding, Carol Yinghua Lu, Lee Weng Choy, Xu Hong, and Anthony Yung, *Uncooperative Contemporaries: Art Exhibitions in Shanghai in 2000* (London: Afterall Books, 2020), 236–241.

17. Mia, "Manifolds of the Local," 69.

18. Hou Hanru. "Shanghai Spirit: A Special Modernity," in Shanghai Art Museum, *Shanghai Biennale 2000: Shanghai Spirit*, exhibition catalogue (Shanghai: Shanghai Art Museum, 2000), n.p.

19. Hou, "Shanghai Spirit," n.p.

20. Toshio Shimizu, "Shanghai Biennial: A New Expression in a New Epoch," in Shanghai Art Museum, *Shanghai Biennale 2000: Shanghai Spirit*, exhibition catalogue (Shanghai: Shanghai Art Museum, 2000), n.p.

21. Shimizu, "Shanghai Biennial."

22. Zhang Qing, "Beyond Left and Right: Transformation of the Shanghai Biennale," in Shanghai Art Museum, *Shanghai Biennale 2000: Shanghai Spirit*, exhibition catalogue (Shanghai: Shanghai Art Museum, 2000), n.p.

23. Zhang, "Beyond Left and Right."

24. Zhang, "Beyond Left and Right." Zhang Qing does not or cannot engage with the difficulties then facing some versions of Chinese contemporary art: "The unexpected international success of contemporary Chinese art in the 1990s was problematic for the [Communist] Party. . . . The problem . . . was that the Western art world was more in favour of challenging and alternative voices and did not pay attention to artists who honoured the Party line"; Yao Yung-wen, "China's Modern Image—Contemporary Chinese Art," *Journal for Cultural Research* 21, no. 1 (2017): 55.

25. Zhang, "Beyond Left and Right."

26. Zhang, "Beyond Left and Right."

27. Curator Mia Yu is of the opinion that despite the disparate curatorial directions, there is a shared question in SB2000 is: "How might we construct the global terrain of the contemporary as 'coeval and in exchange with,' instead of simplistically emanating from, Euro-American contemporaneity?"; Mia, "Manifolds of the Local," 82.

28. Mia, "Manifolds of the Local," 69.

29. Mia, "Manifolds of the Local," 83.

30. Asia Art Archive in America, "Rehearsal, or, Art without Artwork: A Presentation by Gao Shiming with a Response by John Rajchman," December 14, 2011, https://www.aaa-a.org/programs/rehearsal-or-art-without-artwork, accessed July 29, 2022. A catalogue for the *Ho Chi Minh Trail* project was published separately from the 8th Shanghai Biennale; see Gao Shiming and Lu Jie, eds., *Long March Project: Ho Chi Minh Trail*, 2 volumes (Beijing: Long March Project, 2010).

31. Lee Weng Choy, "Coincidence and Re-collection; Lateness and Insight," in Jane DeBevoise, John Tain, Liu Ding, Carol Yinghua Lu, Lee Weng Choy, Xu Hong, and Anthony Yung , *Uncooperative Contemporaries: Art Exhibitions in Shanghai in 2000* (London: Afterall Books, 2020), 125, 124.

32. Asia Art Archive in America, "Rehearsal, or, Art without Artwork."

33. Lee, "Coincidence and Re-collection," 126.

34. Lee, "Coincidence and Re-collection," 124.

35. "Building a Yellow Light Commonwealth," *Yishu: Journal of Contemporary Chinese Art* 10, no. 2 (2011): 20.

36. "Building a Yellow Light Commonwealth," 21.

37. "Building a Yellow Light Commonwealth," 27.

38. "Building a Yellow Light Commonwealth," 27.

39. The reasons for the Sino-Vietnamese War and its consequences are more complex than can be addressed here. See Nguyen Minh Quang, "The Bitter Legacy of the 1979 China-Vietnam War," *The Diplomat*, February 23, 2017, https://thediplomat.com/2017 /02/the-bitter-legacy-of-the-1979-china-vietnam-war/, accessed September 14, 2022.

40. "Building a Yellow Light Commonwealth," 27.

41. Pamela N. Corey, "Metaphor as Method: Curating Regionalism in Mainland Southeast Asia," *Yishu: Journal of Contemporary Chinese Art* 13, no. 2 (2014): 81–82.

42. DeBoer, *Coproducing Asia*, 161, see also 155–162.

43. Feng, "Preface," n.p.

44. DeBoer, *Coproducing Asia*, 178.

45. Jini Kim Watson, *The New Asian City: Three-Dimensional Fictions of Space and Urban Form* (Minneapolis: University of Minnesota Press, 2011), 251–256.

46. T. Fujitani, *Race for Empire: Koreans as Japanese and Japanese as Americans During World War II* (Berkeley: University of California Press, 2011), 15.

47. "Hit Chinese Shows Gain Popularity in Overseas Markets," *Nation* (Bangkok), January 4, 2023, https://www.nationthailand.com/lifestyle/entertainment/40023699, accessed October 24, 2023. See also Elizabeth Law, "The Chinese Paradox: Hard Selling Culture to Gain Soft Power," *Straits Times* (Singapore), October 23, 2023, https://www .straitstimes.com/opinion/the-chinese-paradox-hard-selling-culture-to-gain-soft -power, accessed October 26, 2023.

48. Julie Hollingsworth, "Why the Past Decade Saw the Rise and Rise of East Asian Pop Culture," *CNN*, December 29, 2019, https://edition.cnn.com/2019/12/28/entertainment /east-asia-pop-culture-rise-intl-hnk/index.html, accessed July 30, 2022.

49. Andreas Illmer, "*Yanxi Palace*: Why China Turned Against its Most Popular Show," *BBC News*, February 8, 2019, https://www.bbc.com/news/world-asia-china-47084374, accessed August 1, 2022.

50. Michael Keane, "Keeping Up with the Neighbors: China's Soft Power Ambitions," *Cinema Journal* 49, no. 3 (2010): 134.

51. Keane, "Keeping Up with the Neighbors," 132–133. For studies on components of the PRC's media and cultural industries, see Michael Keane and Anthony Y. H. Fung, "Digital Platforms: Exerting China's New Cultural Power in the Asia-Pacific," *Media Industries* 5, no. 1 (2018): 47–50, https://doi.org/10.3998/mij.15031809.0005.103; and

Geng Song, *Televising Chineseness: Gender, Nation, and Subjectivity* (Ann Arbor, MI: University of Michigan Press, 2022). Song's study is largely restricted to the PRC.

52. "Xi Focus: Xi Jinping Thought on Culture Put Forward at National Meeting," *Xinhua*, October 8, 2023, https://english.news.cn/20231008/410cce50806443cda29227e6cf 0f6415/c.html, accessed October 26, 2023.

53. China Global Television Network, "How the Spread of Asian Popular Culture Contributed to a Positive Pan-Asian Identity," May 14, 2019, https://news.cgtn.com/news/3 d3d414f7a596a4e34457a6333566d54/index.html, accessed July 30, 2022.

54. Huong Le Thu, "The COVID-19 Pandemic and Geopolitics in Southeast Asia," Asia Society Policy Institute-Asia Society Australia, *Southeast Asia and COVID-19*, January 27, 2021, https://southeastasiacovid.asiasociety.org/the-covid-19-pandemic-and-geopolitics -in-southeast-asia/, accessed August 10, 2022.

55. Ching, *Anti-Japan*, x.

SELECT BIBLIOGRAPHY

Primary Material

Anh Soyeon. "Korean Art and Its Identity in the International ContextIn Queensland Art Gallery, *The Second Asia-Pacific Triennial of Contemporary Art: Brisbane Australia 1996: Present Encounters—Papers from the Conference*, edited by Caroline Turner and Rhana Devenport, 97–99. Brisbane: Queensland Art Gallery, 1997.

Apinan Poshyananda. "Asian Art and the New Millennium: From Glocalism to Techno-Shamanism." In Japan Foundation Asia Center, *International Symposium 1999: "Asian Art: Prospects for the Future" Report*, edited by Furuichi Yasuko and Hoashi Aki, 165–167. Tokyo: Japan Foundation Asia Center, 2000. Accessed December 22, 2019. https://www.jpf.go.jp/e/publish/asia_exhibition_history/23_99_prospects.html.

Apinan Poshyananda. "Asian Art in the Posthegemonic World." In Japan Foundation ASEAN Culture Center, *The Potential of Asian Thought Handout: Contemporary Art Symposium 1994 Handout*, edited by Furuichi Yasuko and Kobayashi Izumi, 1–13. Tokyo: Japan Foundation ASEAN Culture Center, 1994. Accessed May 14, 2015. https://www.jpf.go.jp/e/publish/asia_exhibition_history/15_94_potential.html.

Apinan Poshyananda. "Contemporary Thai Art: Nationalism and Sexuality à la Thai." In Asia Society Galleries, *Contemporary Art in Asia: Traditions/Tensions*, exhibition catalogue, 102–110. New York: Asia Society Galleries, 1996.

Apinan Poshyananda. "Cultural Sentinels at the Crossroads." In Japan Foundation Asia Center, *Symposium: "Asian Contemporary Art Reconsidered" Report*, edited by Furuichi Yasuko and Hoashi Aki, 177–181. Tokyo: Japan Foundation Asia Center, 1998.

Apinan Poshyananda. "Roaring Tigers, Desperate Dragons in Transition." In Asia Society Galleries, *Contemporary Art in Asia: Traditions/Tensions*, exhibition catalogue, 23–53. New York: Asia Society Galleries, 1996.

Asia Society Galleries. *Contemporary Art in Asia: Traditions/Tensions*, exhibition catalogue. New York: Asia Society Galleries, 1996.

Carroll, Alison. "Networks." In Queensland Art Gallery, *The Second Asia-Pacific Triennial of Contemporary Art, Brisbane, Australia, 1996*, exhibition catalogue, edited by Caroline Turner and Rhana Devenport, 30–31. Brisbane: Queensland Art Gallery, 1996.

Centre Georges Pompidou, Musée national d'art moderne, [and] La Grand Halle La Villette. *Magiciens de la Terre*, exhibition catalogue. Paris: Editions du Centre Pompidou, 1989.

Departemen Pendidikan dan Kebudayaan (Department of Education and Culture). *Contemporary Art from the Non-Aligned Countries: Unity in Diversity in International Art: Post-Event Catalogue*, exhibition catalogue. Jakarta: Balai Pustaka, Project for Development of Cultural Media, Directorate General for Culture, Department of Education and Culture: ,1998.

Desai, Vishakha N. "East in the West: Presentations of Contemporary Asian Art in the US." In Japan Foundation Asia Center, *Symposium: "Asian Contemporary Art Reconsidered" Report*, edited by Furuichi Yasuko and Hoashi Aki, 138–142. Tokyo: Japan Foundation Asia Center, 1998.

Elliott, David. "A Short Walk in the Hindu Kush." In Queensland Art Gallery, *The Second Asia-Pacific Triennial of Contemporary Art, Brisbane, Australia, 1996*, exhibition catalogue, edited by Caroline Turner and Rhana Devenport, 20–22. Brisbane: Queensland Art Gallery, 1996.

Elliott, David. "'Asia': Enduring Stereotype or Black Hole?" In Japan Foundation Asia Center, *International Symposium 1999: "Asian Art: Prospects for the Future" Report*, edited by Furuichi Yasuko and Hoashi Aki, 137–139. Tokyo: Japan Foundation Asia Center, 2000. Accessed December 22, 2019. https://www.jpf.go.jp/e/publish/asia_exhibition_hist ory/23_99_prospects.html.

Feng Zengxian. "Preface." In Shanghai Art Museum, *Shanghai Biennale 2000: Shanghai Spirit*, exhibition catalogue, edited by Chen Long, n.p. Shanghai: Shanghai Art Museum, 2000.

Fukuoka Art Museum. *Festival: Contemporary Asian Art Show, 1980*, exhibition catalogue. Fukuoka: Fukuoka Art Museum, 1980.

Fukuoka Art Museum. *4th Asian Art Show, Fukuoka: Realism as an Attitude*, exhibition catalogue. Fukuoka: Fukuoka Art Museum, 1994.

Fukuoka Art Museum. *Modern Asian Art: India, China & Japan*, exhibition catalogue. Fukuoka: Fukuoka Art Museum, 1979.

Fukuoka Art Museum. *2nd Asian Art Show, Fukuoka*, exhibition catalogue. Fukuoka: Fukuoka Art Museum, 1985.

Fukuoka Art Museum. *Symposium: "What Must be Done for the Future of Asian Tradition and Art Which Have Been Changed Under the Influence of Western Art?": Asian Artists Exhibition Part II: "Festival: Contemporary Asian Art Shows, 1980,"* conference proceedings. Fukuoka: Fukuoka Art Museum, 1980.

Fukuoka Art Museum. *3rd Asian Art Show, Fukuoka*, exhibition catalogue. Fukuoka: Fukuoka Art Museum, 1989.

Fukuoka Art Museum. *The Birth of Modern Art in Southeast Asia: Artists and Movements*. Fukuoka: Fukuoka Art Museum, 1997.

Furuichi Yasuko. "Conclusion." In Japan Foundation Asia Center, *Symposium: "Asian Contemporary Art Reconsidered" Report*, edited by Furuichi Yasuko and Hoashi Aki, 221. Tokyo: Japan Foundation Asia Center, 1998.

Hayward Gallery. *Cities on the Move: Urban Chaos and Global Change—East Asian Art, Architecture and Film Now*, exhibition catalogue. London: Hayward Gallery, 1999.

Hou Hanru. "Shanghai Spirit: A Special Modernity." In Shanghai Art Museum, *Shanghai Biennale 2000: Shanghai Spirit*, exhibition catalogue, edited by Chen Long, n.p. Shanghai: Shanghai Art Museum, 2000.

Hou Hanru, and Hans Ulrich Obrist. "Cities on the Move." In Wiener Secession and capcMusée d'art contemporain de Bordeaux, *Cities on the Move*, exhibition catalogue, edited by Hou Hanru and Hans Ulrich Obrist, n.p. Ostfildern-Ruit: Hatje, 1997.

Ishida Tetsuro, Shioda Junichi, Kumagi Isako, Fukunaga Osamu, and Okamoto Yoshie, eds. *Art in Southeast Asia 1997: Glimpses into the Future*, exhibition catalogue. Tokyo: Museum of Contemporary Art, Tokyo; Hiroshima: Hiroshima City Museum of Contemporary Art; Tokyo: Japan Foundation Asia Center, 1997.

Japan Foundation. *Count 10 Before You Say Asia: Asian Art after Postmodernism: International Symposium 2008: Report*. Edited by Furuichi Yasuko. Tokyo: Japan Foundation, 2009.

Japan Foundation ASEAN Culture Center. *The Potential of Asian Thought: Contemporary Art Symposium 1994 Handout*. Edited by Furuichi Yasuko and Kobayashi Izumi. Tokyo: Japan Foundation ASEAN Culture Center, 1994. Accessed April 10, 2015. https://www.jpf.go.jp/e/publish/asia_exhibition_history/15_94_potential.html.

Japan Foundation Asia Center. *International Symposium 1999: "Asian Art: Prospects for the Future" Report*. Edited by Furuichi Yasuko and Hoashi Aki. Tokyo: Japan Foundation Asia Center, 2000. Accessed December 22, 2019. https://www.jpf.go.jp/e/publish/asia_exhibition_history/23_99_prospects.html.

Japan Foundation Asia Center. *International Symposium 2002: "Asia in Transition: Representation and Identity" Report: The Japan Foundation 30th Anniversary*. Edited by Furuichi Yasuko and Hoashi Aki. Tokyo: Japan Foundation Asia Center, 2003. Accessed April 10, 2019. https://www.jpf.go.jp/e/publish/asia_exhibition_history/29_02_transition.html.

Japan Foundation Asia Center. *International Symposium 2005: "Cubism in Asia: Unbounded Dialogues" Report*. Edited by Furuichi Yasuko and Hoashi Aki. Tokyo: Japan Foundation Asia Center, 2006.

Japan Foundation Asia Center. *International Symposium 2008: "Count 10 Before You Say Asia—Asian Art after Postmodernism" Report*. Edited by Furuichi Yasuko. Tokyo: Japan Foundation, 2009.

Japan Foundation Asia Center. *Shaping the History of Art in Southeast Asia, Art Studies 03 Anthology*. Edited by Patrick D. Flores and Kajiya Kenji. Tokyo: Japan Foundation Asia Center, 2017.

Japan Foundation Asia Center. *Symposium: "Asian Contemporary Art Reconsidered" Report*. Edited by Furuichi Yasuko and Hoashi Aki. Tokyo: Japan Foundation Asia Center, 1998.

Japan Foundation Asia Center and Tokyo Opera City Cultural Foundation. *Under Construction: New Dimensions of Asian Art*. Edited by Kataoka Mami. Tokyo: Japan Foundation Asia Center, 2002.

Kapur, Geeta. "Dismantling the Norm." In Asia Society Galleries, *Contemporary Art in Asia: Traditions/Tensions*, exhibition catalogue, 60–69. New York: Asia Society Galleries, 1996.

Kapur, Geeta. "Two or Three Things about Ourselves." In Queensland Art Gallery, *The Second Asia-Pacific Triennial of Contemporary Art, Brisbane, Australia, 1996*, exhibition catalogue, edited by Caroline Turner and Rhana Devenport, 22. Brisbane: Queensland Art Gallery, 1996.

Kawazoe Noburo, Kikutake Kiyonori, Ōtaka Masato, Maki Fumihiko, and Kurokawa Kishō. *Metabolism 1960: The Proposals for New Urbanism/Metaborizumu 1960: Toshi e no teian*. Tokyo: Bijutsu shuppansha, 1960.

Kuroda Raiji. "The Other Side of the Other: Asian Artists in the West." In Japan Foundation ASEAN Culture Center, *The Potential of Asian Thought: Contemporary Art Symposium 1994 Handout*, edited by Furuichi Yasuko and Kobayashi Izumi, translated by Stanley N. Anderson, 1–12. Tokyo: Japan Foundation ASEAN Culture Center, 1994. Accessed May 14, 2015. https://www.jpf.go.jp/e/publish/asia_exhibition_history/15_94 _potential.html.

Lee Yong Woo. "Globalism and the Vanity of Its System." In Japan Foundation Asia Center, *International Symposium 2002: "Asia in Transition: Representation and Identity" Report: The Japan Foundation 30th Anniversary*, edited by Furichi Yasuko and Hoashi Aki, 292–308. Tokyo: Japan Foundation Asia Center, 2003. Accessed April 10, 2019. https://www.jpf .go.jp/e/publish/asia_exhibition_history/29_02_transition.html.

Martin, Jean-Hubert. "Preface." In Centre Georges Pompidou, Musée national d'art moderne, [and] La Grand Halle La Villette, *Magiciens de la Terre*, exhibition catalogue. 8–11. Paris: Editions du Centre Pompidou, 1989.

Mizusawa Tsutomu. "Opening Comment for Session I." In Japan Foundation Asia Center, *International Symposium 2002: "Asia in Transition: Representation and Identity" Report: The Japan Foundation 30th Anniversary*. edited by Furichi Yasuko and Hoashi Aki, 234–236. Tokyo: Japan Foundation Asia Center, 2003. Accessed April 10, 2019. https://www.jpf .go.jp/e/publish/asia_exhibition_history/29_02_transition.html.

Mizusawa Tsutomu. "Toward an Anonymous Individuality." In Japan Foundation Asia Center, *International Symposium 1999: "Asian Art: Prospects for the Future" Report*, edited by Furuichi Yasuko and Hoashi Aki, 187–188. Tokyo: Japan Foundation Asia Center, 2000. Accessed December 22, 2019. https://www.jpf.go.jp/e/publish/asia_exhibition_history/23 _99_prospects.html.

Museum of Contemporary Art, Tokyo, Hiroshima City Museum of Contemporary Art, and Japan Foundation Asia Center. *Art in Southeast Asia 1997: Glimpses into the Future*, exhibition catalogue. Edited by Tetsurō Ishida, Shioda Junichi, Kumagi Isako, Fukunaga

Osamu, and Okamoto Yoshieet al. Tokyo: Tōkyō-to Gendai Bijutsukan; Hiroshima: Hiroshima-shi Gendai Bijutsukan; and Tokyo: Japan Foundation Asia Center, 1997.

Nakahara Yusuke. "General comments, Session III." In Japan Foundation Asia Center, *Symposium: "Asian Contemporary Art Reconsidered" Report*, edited by Furuichi Yasuko and Hoashi Aki, 187–188. Tokyo: Japan Foundation Asia Center, 1998.

Nakamura Hideki. "Suggestions for the Symposium." In Japan Foundation ASEAN Culture Center, *The Potential of Asian Thought: Contemporary Art Symposium 1994 Handout*, edited by Furuichi Yasuko and Kobayashi Izumi, translated by Stanley N. Anderson, 1–4. Tokyo: Japan Foundation ASEAN Culture Center, 1994. Accessed May 14, 2015. https://www.jpf.go.jp/e/publish/asia_exhibition_history/15_94_potential.html.

Nanjo, Fumio. "The Present Situation of Japanese Art." In Queensland Art Gallery, *The Second Asia-Pacific Triennial of Contemporary Art, Brisbane, Australia, 1996*, exhibition catalogue, edited by Caroline Turner and Rhana Devenport, 36–38. Brisbane: Queensland Art Gallery, 1996.

Nanjo Fumio. "The Sea of Diversity: Divisions and Syntheses." In Japan Foundation Asia Center, *International Symposium 1999: "Asian Art: Prospects for the Future" Report*, edited by Furuichi Yasuko and Hoashi Aki, 161–162. Tokyo: Japan Foundation Asia Center, 2000. Accessed December 22, 2019. https://www.jpf.go.jp/e/publish/asia_exhibition_history/23_99_prospects.html.

National Museum of Modern Art, Tokyo and Japan Foundation. *Cubism in Asia: Unbounded Dialogues*, exhibition catalogue. Edited by Miwa Kenjin, Suzuki Katsuo, Matsumoto Tohru and Furuichi Yasuko. Tokyo: Tōkyō Kokuritsu Kindai Bijutsukan and Japan Foundation, 2005.

Noro Masahiko. "Foreword." In Japan Foundation Asia Center, *Symposium: "Asian Contemporary Art Reconsidered" Report*, edited by Furuichi Yasuko and Hoashi Aki, 7. Tokyo: Japan Foundation Asia Center, 1998.

Pastor Roces, Marian. "Bodies of Fiction, Bodies of Desire." In Asia Society Galleries, *Contemporary Art in Asia: Traditions/Tensions*, exhibition catalogue, 82–92. New York: Asia Society Galleries, 1996.

Queensland Art Gallery. *Beyond the Future: The Third Asia-Pacific Triennial of Contemporary Art*, exhibition catalogue. Edited by Jennifer Webb. Brisbane: Queensland Art Gallery, 1999.

Queensland Art Gallery. *The First Asia-Pacific Triennial of Contemporary Art, Brisbane, Australia, 1993*, exhibition catalogue. Edited by Suzanne Grano. Brisbane: Queensland Art Gallery, 1993.

Queensland Art Gallery. *The Second Asia-Pacific Triennial of Contemporary Art, Brisbane, Australia, 1996*, exhibition catalogue. Edited by Caroline Turner and Rhana Devenport. Brisbane: Queensland Art Gallery, 1996.

Queens Museum of Art. *Global Conceptualism: Points of Origin, 1950s–1980s*, exhibition catalogue. Edited by Philomena Mariani. New York: Queens Museum of Art, 1999.

"Reflecting on the Symposium: Panelists' Comments." In Japan Foundation Asia Center, *International Symposium 2002: "Asia in Transition: Representation and Identity" Report: The Japan Foundation 30th Anniversary*, edited by Furichi Yasuko and Hoashi Aki, 432–449. Tokyo: Japan Foundation Asia Center, 2003. Accessed April 10, 2019. https://www.jpf.go.jp/e/publish/asia_exhibition_history/29_02_transition.html.

Roe, Jae-Ryung. "Encountering the World: The Past and the Present." In Asia Society Galleries, *Contemporary Art in Asia: Traditions/Tensions*, exhibition catalogue, 93–101. New York: Asia Society Galleries, 1996.

"Roundtable Discussion: Looking Back at Asian Contemporary Art during the 1990s." In Japan Foundation Asia Center, *International Symposium 1999: "Asian Art: Prospects for the Future" Report*, edited by Furuichi Yasuko and Hoashi Aki, 195–198. Tokyo: Japan Foundation Asia Center, 2000. Accessed December 22, 2019. https://www.jpf.go.jp/e/publish/asia_exhibition_history/23_99_prospects.html.

Sakai Naoki. "Asia: Co-figurative Identification." In Japan Foundation Asia Center, *International Symposium 2002: "Asia in Transition: Representation and Identity" Report: The Japan Foundation 30th Anniversary*, edited by Furuichi Yasuko and Hoashi Aki, 222–231. Tokyo: Japan Foundation Asia Center, 2003. Accessed April 10, 2019. https://www.jpf.go.jp/e/publish/asia_exhibition_history/29_02_transition.html.

"Session I Discussion." In Japan Foundation Asia Center, *International Symposium 2002: "Asia in Transition: Representation and Identity" Report: The Japan Foundation 30th Anniversary*, edited by Furuichi Yasuko and Hoashi Aki, 273–286. Tokyo: Japan Foundation Asia Center, 2003. Accessed April 10, 2019. https://www.jpf.go.jp/e/publish/asia_exhibition_history/29_02_transition.html.

"Session II Discussion." In Japan Foundation Asia Center, *International Symposium 1999: "Asian Art: Prospects for the Future" Report*, edited by Furuichi Yasuko and Hoashi Aki, 152–160. Tokyo: Japan Foundation Asia Center, 2000. Accessed December 22, 2019. https://www.jpf.go.jp/e/publish/asia_exhibition_history/23_99_prospects.html.

"Session II Discussion." In Japan Foundation Asia Center, *International Symposium 2002: "Asia in Transition: Representation and Identity" Report: The Japan Foundation 30th Anniversary*, edited by Furuichi Yasuko and Hoashi Aki, 328–342. Tokyo: Japan Foundation Asia Center, 2003. Accessed April 10, 2019. https://www.jpf.go.jp/e/publish/asia_exhibition_history/29_02_transition.html.

"Session III Discussion." In Japan Foundation Asia Center, *International Symposium 1999: "Asian Art: Prospects for the Future" Report: The Japan Foundation 30th Anniversary*, edited by Furuichi Yasuko and Hoashi Aki, 173–186. Tokyo: Japan Foundation Asia Center, 2000. Accessed December 22, 2019. https://www.jpf.go.jp/e/publish/asia_exhibition_history/23_99_prospects.html.

Shanghai Art Museum. *Shanghai Biennale 2000: Shanghai Spirit*, exhibition catalogue. Shanghai: Shanghai Art Museum, 2000.

Shanghai Art Museum. *Shanghai Biennale 2002: Urban Creation*, exhibition catalogue. Shanghai: Shanghai Art Museum, 2002.

Shimizu Toshio. "Proposals from the Present," In Japan Foundation ASEAN Culture Center, *The Potential of Asian Thought: Contemporary Art Symposium 1994 Handout*, edited by Furuichi Yasuko and Kobayashi Izumi, translated by Stanley N. Anderson, 1–2. Tokyo: Japan Foundation ASEAN Culture Center, 1994. Accessed May 14, 2015. https://www.jpf.go.jp/e/publish/asia_exhibition_history/15_94_potential.html.

Shimizu, Toshio. "Shanghai Biennial: A New Expression in a New Epoch." In Shanghai Art Museum, *Shanghai Biennale 2000: Shanghai Spirit*, exhibition catalogue. edited by Chen Long, n.p. Shanghai: Shanghai Art Museum, 2000.

Singapore Art Museum. *Modernity and Beyond: Themes in Southeast Asian Art*, exhibition catalogue. Edited by T. K. Sabapathy. Singapore: Singapore Art Museum, 1996.

Supangkat, Jim. "Multiculturalism/Multimodernism." In Asia Society Galleries, *Contemporary Art in Asia: Traditions/Tensions*, exhibition catalogue, 70–81. New York: Asia Society Galleries, 1996.

Supangkat, Jim. "'White Paper' on the Non-aligned Movement Exhibition." *Digital Archive of Indonesia Contemporary Art*, @rsipIVAA, 4. Accessed June 6, 2020. http://archive.ivaa-online.org/files/uploads/texts/[English]%201995_GNB_05-16.pdf.

Tani Arata. "History: Steps Towards the Present." In Japan Foundation ASEAN Culture Center, *The Potential of Asian Thought: Contemporary Art Symposium 1994 Handout*, edited by Furuichi Yasuko and Kobayashi Izumi, translated by Stanley N. Anderson, 1–5. Tokyo: Japan Foundation ASEAN Culture Center, 1994. Accessed May 14, 2015. https://www.jpf.go.jp/e/publish/asia_exhibition_history/15_94_potential.html.

Tatehata Akira. "A Trap in Multiculturalism." In Japan Foundation Asia Center, *Symposium: "Asian Contemporary Art Reconsidered" Report*, edited by Furuichi Yasuko and Hoashi Aki, 170–173. Tokyo: Japan Foundation Asia Center, 1998.

Turner, Caroline. "Enriching Encounters." In Japan Foundation Asia Center, *Symposium: "Asian Contemporary Art Reconsidered" Report*, edited by Furuichi Yasuko and Hoashi Aki, 142–148. Tokyo: Japan Foundation Asia Center, 1998.

Turner, Caroline. "Introduction—From Extraregionalism to Intraregionalism?" In Queensland Art Gallery, *The First Asia-Pacific Triennial of Contemporary Art, Brisbane, Australia, 1993*, exhibition catalogue, edited by Suzanne Grano, 8–9. Brisbane: Queensland Art Gallery, 1993.

Turner, Caroline. "Mirror of the Future: Shadows Before." In *The Second Asia-Pacific Triennial of Contemporary Art: Brisbane Australia 1996: Present Encounters—Papers from the Conference*, edited by Caroline Turner and Rhana Devenport, 19–22. Brisbane: Queensland Art Gallery, 1997.

Turner, Caroline, ed. *Tradition and Change: Contemporary Art of Asia and the Pacific*. St. Lucia, Australia: University of Queensland Press, 1994.

Turner, Caroline, and Rhana Devenport, eds. *Present Encounters: Papers from the Conference of the Second Asia-Pacific Triennial of Contemporary Art*. Brisbane: Queensland Art Gallery, 1997.

Ushiroshōji Masahiro. "A Difficult Journey of Contemporary ASEAN Art." In Japan Foundation ASEAN Culture Center, *Narrative Visions in Contemporary ASEAN Art*, exhibition catalogue, 8–10. Tokyo: Japan Foundation ASEAN Culture Center, 1990.

Ushiroshōji Masahiro. "Emergence of Asian Art Gallery." In Japan Foundation Asia Center, *Symposium: "Asian Contemporary Art Reconsidered" Report*, edited by Furuichi Yasuko and Hoashi Aki, 155–159. Tokyo: Japan Foundation Asia Center, 1998.

Ushiroshōji Masahiro. "Realism as an Attitude: Asian Art in the Nineties." In Fukuoka Art Museum, *4th Asian Art Show, Fukuoka: Realism as an Attitude*, exhibition catalogue, 33–38. Fukuoka: Fukuoka Art Museum, 1994.

Ushiroshōji Masahiro. "The Labyrinthine Search for Self-Identity: The Art of Southeast Asia from the 1980s to the 1990s." In Japan Foundation ASEAN Culture Center, *New Art from Southeast Asia*, exhibition catalogue, edited by Furuichi Yasuko, Sakonaka Yoko, and Ushiroshōji Masahiro, 21–24. Tokyo: Japan Foundation ASEAN Culture Center, 1992.

Ushiroshōji Masahiro, and Toshiko Rawanchaikul, eds. *The Birth of Modern Art in Southeast Asia: Artists and Movements*, exhibition catalogue. Fukuoka: Fukuoka Art Museum; Hiroshima: Hiroshima Prefectural Art Museum; Shizuoka: Shizuoka Prefectural Museum of Art; Tokyo: Tokyo Metropolitan Foundation for History and Culture; Tokyo: Yomiuri Shimbun; and Tokyo: Japan Association of Art Museums, 1997.

Wang Hui. "Imagining Asia: A Genealogical Analysis." In Japan Foundation Asia Center, *International Symposium 2002: "Asia in Transition: Representation and Identity" Report: The Japan Foundation 30th Anniversary*, edited by Furuichi Yasuko and Hoashi Aki, 245–263. Tokyo: Japan Foundation Asia Center, 2003. Accessed April 10, 2019. https://www.jpf.go.jp/e/publish/asia_exhibition_history/29_02_transition.html.

Wiener Secession and capcMusée d'art contemporain de Bordeaux. *Cities on the Move*, exhibition catalogue. Edited by Hou Hanru and Hans Ulrich Obrist. Ostfildern-Ruit: Hatje, 1997.

Yoshimi Shunya. "Opening Comment for Session II." In Japan Foundation Asia Center, *International Symposium 2002: "Asia in Transition: Representation and Identity" Report: The Japan Foundation 30th Anniversary*, edited by Furuichi Yasuko and Hoashi Aki, 288–291. Tokyo: Japan Foundation Asia Center, 2003. Accessed April 10, 2019. https://www.jpf.go.jp/e/publish/asia_exhibition_history/29_02_transition.html.

Zhang Qing. "Beyond Left and Right: Transformation of the Shanghai Biennale." In Shanghai Art Museum, *Shanghai Biennale 2000: Shanghai Spirit*, exhibition catalogue. edited by Chen Long, n.p. Shanghai: Shanghai Art Museum, 2000.

Filmography

Chungking Express (*Chongqing senlin*), Wong Kar-wai. Hong Kong: Jet Tone Production, 1994.

Fulltime Killer (*Quanzhi shashou*), Johnnie To, Wai Ka-Fai. Hong Kong: Milkyway Image (HK) Ltd., 2001.

Lost in Translation, Sofia Coppola. United States: American Zoetrope, Elemental Films, 2003.

Shinjuku Triad Society (*Shinjuku kuroshakai: Chaina mafia sensō*), Miike Takashi. Japan: Daiei; Excellent Film, 1995.

Sleepless Town (*Fuyajo/Bu ye cheng*), Lee Chi-Ngai. Japan: Asmik Ace Entertainment, Kadokawa Publishing, Hakuhudo DY Media Partners, 1998.

The Longest Night in Shanghai (*Yoru no Shanghai/Ye Shanghai*), Zhang Yibai. Japan: Movie Eye Entertainment, Avex Entertainment; People's Republic of China: Shanghai Film Studios, 2007.

The World of Suzie Wong, Richard Quine. UK: World Enterprises, Inc.; Worldfilm Ltd.; Paramount British Pictures Ltd., 1960.

Tokyo Raiders (*Dongjing gonglue*), Jingle Ma. Hong Kong: Golden Harvest, 2000.

Zatōichi Meets the One Armed Swordsman (*Shin Zatōichi: Yabure! Tōjiken/Mangxia dazhan Dubei dao*), Yasuda Kimiyoshi, Hsu Chen-hung. Japan: Katsu Productions; Hong Kong: Wing Luen (Yonglian) Movie Film Company, 1971.

Secondary Material

Agamben, Giorgio. "What Is the Contemporary?" In *What Is an Apparatus and Other Essays*, translated by David Kishit and Stefan Pedatella, 39–54. Stanford, CA: Stanford University Press, 2009.

Ahmad Mashadi. "Contexts and Predicaments: Singapore 1996–2006." In *Art Studies 02: The 1990s: The Making of Art with Contemporaries Report*, edited by Furichi Yasuko and Hoashi Aki, 58–65. Tokyo: Japan Foundation Asia Center, 2016.

Ahmad Mashadi. "Moments of Regionality: Negotiating Southeast Asia." In *Art Studies 03 Anthology: Shaping the History of Art in Southeast Asia*, edited by Patrick D. Flores and Kajiya Kenji, 57–62. Tokyo: Japan Foundation Asia Center, 2017.

Antoinette, Michelle, and Caroline Turner, eds. *Contemporary Asian Art and Exhibitions: Connectivities and World-Making*. Canberra: ANU Press, 2014.

Appel, Hannah. "Infrastructural Time." In *The Promise of Infrastructure*, edited by Nikhil Anand, Akhil Gupta, and Hannah Appel, 41–61. Durham, NC: Duke University Press, 2018.

Arrighi, Giovanni. *The Long Twentieth Century: Money, Power, and the Origins of Our Times*. London: Verso, 1991.

Atkins, E. Taylor. *A History of Popular Culture in Japan: From the Seventeenth Century to the Present*. London: Bloomsbury, 2017.

Avenell, Simon. "What Is Asia for Us and Can We Be Asians? The New Asianism in Contemporary Japan." *Modern Asian Studies* 48, no. 6 (2014): 1594–1636.

Balibar, Étienne. *Politics and the Other Scene*. London: Verso, 2002.

Baumbach, Nico, Damon R. Young, and Genevieve Yu. "Revisiting Postmodernism: An Interview with Fredric Jameson." *Social Text* 34, no. 2 (2016): 143–160.

Befu, Harumi, ed. *Cultural Nationalism in East Asia: Representation and Identity*. Berkeley: Institute of East Asian Studies, University of California, 1993.

Bell, Daniel. *The Cultural Contradictions of Capitalism*. 1976; New York: Basic Books, 1996.

Bordwell, David. *Planet Hong Kong: Popular Cinema and the Art of Entertainment*. Cambridge, MA: Harvard University Press, 2000.

Bourdaghs, Michael K. *Sayonara Amerika, Sayonara Nippon: A Geopolitical Prehistory of J-Pop*. New York: Columbia University Press, 2012.

Bourdaghs, Michael K, Paola Iovene, and Kaley Mason. "Introduction." In *Sound Alignments: Popular Music in Asia's Cold Wars*, edited by Michael K. Bourdaghs, Paola Iovene, and Kaley Mason, 1–39. Durham, NC: Duke University Press, 2021.

Boyd-Barrett, Oliver. "Reconfiguring Media and Empire." In *The Korean Wave: Korean Media Go Global*, edited by Youna Kim, 58–70. Abingdon, UK: Routledge, 2013.

Brooks, Van Wyck. "Ernest Fenollosa and Japan." *Proceedings of the American Philosophical Society* 106, no. 2 (1962): 106–110.

Bruce, Amy. "International Contemporaneity and the Third Havana Bienal (1989)." *RACAR: revue d'art canadienne/Canadian Art Review* 43, no. 2, special issue on "What Is Critical Curating?" (2018): 25–33.

"Building a Yellow Light Commonwealth." *Yishu: Journal of Contemporary Chinese Art* 10, no. 2 (2011): 19–27.

Bürger, Peter. *Theory of the Avant-Garde*. Minneapolis: University of Minnesota Press, 1984.

Călinescu, Matei. *Five Faces of Modernity: Modernism, Avant-Garde, Decadence, Kitsch, Postmodernism*. Bloomington: Indiana University Press, 1977.

Carroll, Alison. "The Political and the Personal: Australia's Experience in Visual Arts Exchange in Southeast Asia through the 1990s." In *Art Studies 02: The 1990s: The Making of Art with Contemporaries Report*, edited by Furichi Yasuko and Hoashi Aki, 66–71. Tokyo: Japan Foundation Asia Center, 2016.

Chakrabarty, Dipesh. "'Asia' and the Twentieth Century: What Is 'Asian Modernity'?" In *"We Asians": Between Past and Future: A Millennial Regional Conference*, edited by Kwok Kian-Woon, Indira Arumugam, Karen Chia, and Lee Chee Keng, 15–32. Singapore: Singapore Heritage Society, 2000.

Chandler, Lisa. "'Journey without Maps: Unsettling Curatorship in Cross-Cultural Contexts." *Museum and Society* 7, no. 2 (2009): 74–91.

Checa-Gismero, Palomo. "Craft as Anti-Colonial Universalism in the Bienal de La Habana." *Third Text* 36, no. 3 (2022): 262–277. https://www.tandfonline.com/doi/abs/10.1080/09528822.2022.2052608.

Chen, Kuan-Hsing. *Asia as Method: Toward Deimperialization*. Durham, NC: Duke University Press, 2010.

Ching, Leo. "Globalizing the Regional, Regionalizing the Global: Mass Culture and Asianism in the Age of Late Capital." In *Globalization*, edited by Arjun Appadurai, 279–306. Durham, NC: Duke University Press, 2001.

Ching, Leo. "*Inter-Asia Cultural Studies* and the Decolonial-Turn." *Inter-Asia Cultural Studies* 11, no. 2 (2010): 184–187.

Ching, Leo T. S. *Anti-Japan: The Politics of Sentiment in Postcolonial East Asia*. Durham, NC: Duke University Press, 2019.

Chiu, Melissa, and Benjamin Genocchio, eds. *Contemporary Art in Asia: A Critical Reader*. Cambridge, MA: MIT Press, 2011.

Cho Hae-Joang. "Reading the 'Korean Wave' as a Sign of Global Shift." *Korea Journal* 45, no. 4 (2005): 147–182.

Chua Beng Huat. "Conceptualizing an East Asian Popular Culture." *Inter-Asia Cultural Studies* 5, no. 2 (2004): 200–221.

Chua Beng Huat. *Structure, Audience and Soft Power in East Asian Pop Culture*. Hong Kong: Hong Kong University Press, 2012.

Chua, Beng-Huat, ed. *Consumption in Asia: Lifestyle and Identities*. London: Routledge, 2000.

Chua, Beng Huat and Kōichi Iwabuchi, eds. *East Asian Pop Culture: Analysing the Korean Wave*. Hong Kong: Hong Kong University Press, 2008.

Clark, John. *Modern Asian Art*. Sydney: Craftsman House, 1998.

Clark, John, Maurizio Peleggi, and T. K. Sabapathy, eds. *Eye of the Beholder: Reception, Audience, and Practice of Modern Asian Art*. Sydney: Wild Peony, 2006.

Clements, Jonathan, and Motoko Tamamuro. *The Dorama Encyclopedia: A Guide to Japanese TV Drama Since 1953*. Berkeley, CA: Stone Bridge Press, 2003.

Corey, Pamela N. "Metaphor as Method: Curating Regionalism in Mainland Southeast Asia." *Yishu: Journal of Contemporary Chinese Art* 13, no. 2 (2014): 72–84.

Crow, Thomas. *Modern Art in the Common Culture*. New Haven, CT: Yale University Press, 1996.

Crow, Thomas. *The Long March of Pop: Art, Music, and Design, 1930–1995*. New Haven, CT: Yale University Press, 2014.

Crow, Thomas. *The Rise of the Sixties: American and European Art in the Era of Dissent*. London: Laurence King, 1996.

Cumings, Bruce. *Parallax Visions: Making Sense of American-East Asian Relations*. Durham, NC: Duke University Press, 1999.

Curtin, Michael. *Playing to the World's Biggest Audience: The Globalization of Chinese Film and TV*. Berkeley: University of California Press, 2007.

Dadi, Iftikhar. "Globalization and Transnational Modernism." In *Globalization and Art*, edited by James Elkins, Alice Kim, and Zhivka Valiavicharska, 183–187. University Park: Penn State University Press, 2010.

Dadi, Iftikhar. "Reflections on the First Decade." *Broadsheet: Contemporary Visual Arts and Culture* 41, no. 4 (2012): 266–267.

Dai Jinhua. *After the Post–Cold War: The Future of Chinese History*. Edited by Lisa Rofel. Durham, NC: Duke University Press, 2018.

DeBevoise, Jane, John Tain, Liu Ding, Carol Yinghua Lu, Lee Weng Choy, Xu Hong, and Anthony Yung. *Uncooperative Contemporaries: Art Exhibitions in Shanghai in 2000*. London: Afterall Books, 2020.

DeBoer, Stephanie. *Coproducing Asia: Locating Japanese–Chinese Regional Film and Media*. Minneapolis: University of Minnesota Press, 2014.

de Certeau, Michel. *The Practice of Everyday Life*. Translated by Stephen Rendall. Berkeley: University of California Press, 1984.

De Gennaro, Mara. *Modernism After Postcolonialism: Toward a Nonterritorial Comparative Literature*. Baltimore, MD: Johns Hopkins University Press, 2020.

de Kloet, Jeroen, and Jaap Kooijman. "Karaoke Americanism Gangnam Styl [*sic*]: K-pop, Wonder Girls, and the Asian Unpopular." In *Unpopular Culture*, edited by Martin Lüthe and Sascha Pöhlmann, 113–128. Amsterdam: Amsterdam University Press, 2016.

Denning, Michael. *Culture in the Age of Three Worlds*. London: Verso, 2004.

Desai, Vishaka N., ed. *Asian Art History in the Twenty-First Century*. Williamstown, MA: Sterling and Francine Clark Art Institute, 2007.

Devji, Faisal. "The Turn to Empire." *Inter-Asia Cultural Studies* 21, no. 1 (2020): 111–114.

Dirlik, Arif. "Architectures of Global Modernity, Colonialism, and Places." *Modern Chinese Literature and Culture* 17, no. 1, special issue on "Chinese Culture in Inter-Asia" (2005): 33–61.

Dirlik, Arif. "Asia Pacific Studies in an Age of Global Modernity." *Inter-Asia Cultural Studies* 6, no. 2 (2005): 158–170.

Dirlik, Arif. *Complicities: The People's Republic of China in Global Capitalism*. Chicago, IL: Prickly Paradigm, 2017.

"Discussions, Sessions 1 and 2." In Japan Foundation Asia Center, *Art Studies 02: The 1990s: The Making of Art with Contemporaries Report*, edited by Furuichi Yasuko and Hoashi Aki, 49–56. Tokyo: Japan Foundation Asia Center, 2016.

Douglass, Mike. "The 'New' Tokyo Story: Restructuring Space and the Struggle for Place in a World City." In *Japanese Cities in the World Economy*, edited by Kuniko Fujita and Richard Child Hill, 83–119. Philadelphia, PA: Temple University Press, 1993.

Duara, Prasenjit. *Sovereignty and Authenticity: Manchukuo and the East Asian Modern*. Lanham, MD: Rowman & Littlefield, 2003.

Duus, Peter. "The 'New Asianism.'" In *Can Japan Globalize? Studies on Japan's Changing Political Economy and the Process of Globalization in Honour of Sung-Jo Park*, edited by Anne Holzhausen, 245–256. Heidelberg: Physica-Verlag, 2001.

Eades, J. S. "Economic Miracles and Megacities: The Japanese Model and Urbanization in East and Southeast Asia." In *Understanding the City: Contemporary and Future Perspectives*, edited by John Eade and Christopher Mele, 222–243. Oxford: Blackwell, 2002.

Elkins, James. "Afterword." In *Art and Globalization*, edited by James Elkins, Zhivka Valaivicharska, and Alice Kim, 251–283. University Park: Pennsylvania State University Press, 2010.

Enwezor, Okwui. "Mega-Exhibitions: The Antinomies of a Transnational Global Form." In *Other Cities, Other Worlds: Urban Imaginaries in a Globalizing Age*, edited by Andreas Huyssen, 147–178. Durham, NC: Duke University Press, 2008.

Fabian, Johannes. *Time and the Other: How Anthropology Makes Its Object*. New York: Columbia University Press, 1983.

Feigenbaum, Evan A., and Robert A. Manning. "A Tale of Two Asias: In the Battle for Asia's Soul, Which Side Will Win—Security or Economics?" *Foreign Policy*, October 31, 2012. Accessed June 23, 2015. https://foreignpolicy.com/2012/10/31/a-tale-of-two-asias/.

Filipovic, Elena, Merieke van Hal, and Solveig Øvstebø, eds. *The Biennial Reader: An Anthology on Large-Scale Perennial Exhibitions of Contemporary Art*. Ostfildern: Hatje Cantz Verlag, 2010.

Flores, Patrick D. "Moments of the Modern in Southeast Asia: Art, Region, Art History." In *Art Studies 03 Anthology: Shaping the History of Art in Southeast Asia*, edited by Patrick D. Flores and Kajiya Kenji, 5–8. Tokyo: Japan Foundation Asia Center, 2017.

Flores, Patrick D. *Past Peripheral: Curation in Southeast Asia*. Singapore: NUS [National University of Singapore] Museum, 2008.

Flores, Patrick D. "Phases of Curatorial Passage." In *Art Studies 04: Condition Report: Shifting Perspectives in Asia—Curator's Book*, edited by Beverly Yong and Furuichi Yasuko, 137–141. Tokyo: Japan Foundation Asia Center, 2018.

Flores, Patrick D. "The Curatorial Turn in Southeast Asia and the Aftermath of the Modern." In Japan Foundation, *Count 10 Before You Say Asia: Asian Art after Postmodernism: International Symposium 2008: Report*, edited by Furuichi Yasuko, 222–230. Tokyo: Japan Foundation, 2009.

Flores, Patrick D., and Kajiya Kenji, eds. *Art Studies 03 Anthology: Shaping the History of Art in Southeast Asia*. Tokyo: Japan Foundation Asia Center, 2017.

Foucault, Michel. "Of Other Spaces," trans. Jay Miskowiec. *Diacritics* 16, no. 1 (1986): 22–27.

Fuhr, Michael. *Globalization and Popular Music in South Korea: Sounding Out K-Pop*. New York: Routledge, 2015.

Fukuzawa Yukichi. "On De-Asianization by Fukuzawa Yukichi." In *The Meiji Japan through Contemporary Sources*, translated by Okada Hidehiro, 129–133. Vol. 3. Tokyo: Centre for East Asian Cultural Studies, 1969–1972.

Fung Anthony, and Alice Chik, eds. *Made in Hong Kong: Studies in Popular Music*. New York: Routledge, 2020.

Furuichi Yasuko. "The Construction of Collaborative Space and Its Possibilities 2000–2017: From 'Under Construction' to 'Condition Report.'" In *Art Studies 04: Condition Report: Shifting Perspectives in Asia—Curator's Book*, edited by Beverly Yong and Furuichi Yasuko, 19–24. Tokyo: Japan Foundation Asia Center, 2018.

Furuichi Yasuko, and Hoashi Aki, eds. *Art Studies 02: The 1990s: The Making of Art with Contemporaries Report*. Tokyo: Japan Foundation Asia Center, 2016.

Galbraith, Patrick W., and Jason G. Karlin, eds. *Idols and Celebrity in Japanese Media Culture*. Houndmills, UK: Palgrave Macmillan, 2012.

Gao Shiming, and Lu Jie, eds. *Long March Project: Ho Chi Minh Trail*. Vol. 2. Beijing: Long March Project, 2010.

Gardner, Anthony, and Charles Green. "Biennials of the South on the Edges of the Global." *Third Text* 27, no. 4 (2013): 442–455.

Gardner, Anthony, and Charles Green. *Biennials, Triennials, and Documenta: The Exhibitions that Created Contemporary Art*. Malden, MA: Wiley-Blackwell, 2016.

Gardner, William O. *The Metabolist Imagination: Visions of the City in Postwar Japanese Architecture and Science Fiction*. Minneapolis: University of Minnesota Press, 2020.

Greenberg, Clement. "Avant-Garde and Kitsch" (1939). In *Art and Culture: Critical Essays*, 3–21. Boston, MA: Beacon Press, 1961.

Hall, Stuart. "Notes on Deconstructing 'the Popular'" (1981). In *Essential Essays, Volume 1: Foundations of Cultural Studies*, edited by David Morley, 347–361. Durham, NC: Duke University Press, 2019.

Harootunian, Harry. "Ghostly Comparisons." In *Impacts of Modernities*, edited by Thomas Lamarre and Kang Nae-hui, 39–52. Hong Kong: Hong Kong University Press, 2004.

Harootunian, Harry. *Marx after Marx: History and Time in the Expansion of Capitalism*. New York: Columbia University Press, 2017.

Harootunian, Harry. *Uneven Moments: Reflections on Japan's Modern History*. New York: Columbia University Press, 2019.

Hirose Mami, Maeda Naotake, Sasaki Hitomi, Tagomori Miho, Tamayama Ami, and Yoshida Yuri, eds. *Metabolism, the City of the Future: Dreams and Visions of Reconstruction in Postwar and Present-day Japan*, exhibition catalogue. Tokyo: Mori Art Museum, 2011.

Hjorth, Larissa, Natalie King, and Mami Kataoka, eds. *Art in the Asia-Pacific: Intimate Publics*. New York: Routledge, 2014.

Hoashi Aki. "The 1990s: Asia as Medium." In *Art Studies 02: The 1990s: The Making of Art with Contemporaries Report*, edited by Furuichi Yasuko and Hoashi Aki, 97–99. Tokyo: Japan Foundation Asia Center, 2016.

Hoffie, Pat. "The Irreverent Contemporary and Radical Tradition." In *Contemporary Asian Art and Exhibitions: Connectivities and World-Making*, edited by Caroline Turner and Michelle Antoinette, 109–128. Canberra: ANU Press, 2014.

Honda Shiro. "The Spreading of Japan's Popular Culture in East Asia." *Japan Echo* 21, no. 4 (1994): 75–79.

Hou Hanru. "In Defense of Difference: Notes on *Magiciens de la Terre*, Twenty-Five Years Later." *Yishu: Journal of Contemporary Chinese Art* 13, no. 3 (2014): 7–18.

Howard, Keith. "Coming of Age: Korean Pop in the 90s." In *Korean Pop Music: Riding the Wave*, edited by Keith Howard, 82–98. Folkestone, UK: Global Orient, 2006.

Howard, Keith, ed. *Korean Pop Music: Riding the Wave*. Folkestone, UK: Global Orient, 2006.

Huyssen, Andreas. *After the Great Divide: Modernism, Mass Culture, Postmodernism*. Bloomington: Indiana University Press, 1986.

Huyssen, Andreas. "High/Low in an Expanded Field." *Modernism/modernity* 9, no. 3 (2002): 363–374.

Huyssen, Andreas. "Introduction: World Cultures, World Cities." In *Other Cities, Other Worlds: Urban Imaginaries in a Globalizing Age*, edited by Andreas Huyssen, 1–23. Durham, NC: Duke University Press, 2008.

Iwabuchi Kōichi. "East Asian Popular Culture and Inter-Asian Referencing." In *Routledge Handbook of East Asian Popular Culture*, edited by Kōichi Iwabuchi, Eva Tsai, and Chris Berry, 24–33. Abingdon, UK: Routledge, 2016.

Iwabuchi Kōichi. "Pop Culture's *Lingua Franca*: Language and Regional Popular Cultural Flows in East Asia." In *Babel or Behemoth: Language Trends in Asia*, edited by Jennifer Lindsay and Tan Ying Ying, 161–174. Singapore: Asia Research Institute, National University of Singapore, 2003.

Iwabuchi Kōichi. *Recentering Globalization: Popular Culture and Japanese Transnationalism*. Durham, NC: Duke University Press, 2002.

Iwabuchi Kōichi. "Return to Asia? Japan in the Global Audio-Visual Market." *Sojourn: Journal of Social Issues in Southeast Asia* 9, no. 2, special issue, "Mass Media: Local and Global Positions" (1994): 226–245.

Iwabuchi Kōichi, ed. *Feeling Asian Modernities: Transnational Consumption of Japanese TV Dramas*. Hong Kong: Hong Kong University Press, 2004.

Jameson, Fredric. *A Singular Modernity: Essay on the Ontology of the Present*. London: Verso, 2002.

Jameson, Fredric. "Notes on Globalization as a Philosophical Issue." In *The Cultures of Globalization*, edited by Fredric Jameson and Masao Miyoshi, 54–77. Durham, NC: Duke University Press, 1998.

Jameson, Fredric. *Signatures of the Visible*. London: Routledge, 1990.

Jameson, Fredric. "The Aesthetics of Singularity." *New Left Review* 92 (2015): 101–132.

Jameson, Fredric. "The End of Temporality." *Critical Inquiry* 29, no. 4 (2003): 695–718.

Jameson, Fredric. *The Geopolitical Aesthetic: Cinema and Space in the World System.* Bloomington: Indiana University Press, 1992.

Jameson, Fredric, and Masao Miyoshi, eds. *The Cultures of Globalization.* Durham, NC: Duke University Press, 1998.

Jang, Gunjoo, and Won K. Paik. "Korean Wave as Tool for Korea's New Cultural Diplomacy." *Advances in Applied Sociology* 2, no. 3 (2012): 196–202.

Jones, Caroline A. *The Global Work of Art: World's Fairs, Biennials, and the Aesthetics of Experience.* Chicago, IL: University of Chicago Press, 2016.

Jung, Eun-Young. "The Place of Sentimental Song in Contemporary Korean Musical Life." *Korean Studies* 35 (2011): 71–92.

Jung, Eun-Young. "Transnational Cultural Traffic in Northeast Asia: The "Presence" of Japan in Korea's Popular Music Culture." PhD diss., University of Pittsburgh, PA, 2007.

Jung, Sun. *Korean Masculinities and Transcultural Consumption: Yonsama, Rain, Oldboy, K-Pop Idols.* Hong Kong: Hong Kong University Press, 2011.

Kajiya Kenji. "Asian Contemporary Art in Japan and the Ghost of Modernity." In Japan Foundation, *Count 10 Before You Say Asia: Asian Art after Postmodernism: International Symposium 2008: Report,* edited by Furuichi Yasuko, 208–220. Tokyo: Japan Foundation, 2009.

Kajiya Kenji. "Learning from Modern and Contemporary Art in Southeast Asia." In *Art Studies 03 Anthology: Shaping the History of Art in Southeast Asia,* edited by Patrick D. Flores and Kajiya Kenji, 9–13. Tokyo: Japan Foundation Asia Center, 2017.

Kamiya Yukie. "The 1990s: Building Platforms through Creative Thinking." In *Art Studies 02: The 1990s: The Making of Art with Contemporaries Report,* edited by Furichi Yasuko and Hoashi Aki, translated by Andrew Maerkle, 94–96. Tokyo: Japan Foundation Asia Center, 2016.

Katsumata, Hiro. "Japanese Popular Culture in East Asia: A New Insight into Regional Community Building." *International Relations of the Asia-Pacific* 12, no. 1 (2011): 133–160.

Katzenstein, Peter J. "East Asia—Beyond Japan." In *Beyond Japan: The Dynamics of East Asian Regionalism,* edited by Peter J. Katzenstein and Takashi Shiraishi, 1–34. Ithaca, NY: Cornell University Press, 2006.

Kawabata Shigeru. "The Japanese Record Industry," *Popular Music* 10, no. 3 (1991): 327–345.

Keane, Michael. "Keeping Up with the Neighbors: China's Soft Power Ambitions." *Cinema Journal* 49, no. 3 (2010): 130–135.

Keane, Michael, and Anthony Y. H. Fung. "Digital Platforms: Exerting China's New Cultural Power in the Asia-Pacific." *Media Industries* 5, no. 1 (2018): 47–50. https://doi.org/10.3998/mij.15031809.0005.103.

Kee, Joan. "Introduction: Contemporary Southeast Asian Art: The Right Kind of Trouble." *Third Text* 25, no. 4 (2011): 371–381.

Kee, Joan. *The Geometries of Afro Asia: Art Beyond Solidarity*. Oakland: University of California Press, 2023.

Kee, Joan. "The Scale Question in Contemporary Asian Art." In *Art Studies 02: The 1990s: The Making of Art with Contemporaries Report*, edited by Furuichi Yasuko and Hoashi Aki, 35–41. Tokyo: Japan Foundation Asia Center, 2016.

Kee, Joan, ed. "Intersections: Issues in Contemporary Art." Special issue, *positions: east asia cultures critique* 12, no. 3 (2004).

Kim, Jeongmee, and Basil Glynn. "'Oppa'-tunity Knocks: PSY, 'Gangnam Style' and the Press Reception of K-Pop in Britain." *Situations: Cultural Studies in the Asian Context* 7, no. 1 (2013/2014): 1–20.

Kishi Sayaka. "Cultural Diplomacy and Museum Management: Beyond an Imaginary Asia." In *Art Studies 02: The 1990s: The Making of Art with Contemporaries Report*, edited by Furichi Yasuko and Hoashi Aki, translated by Andrew Maerkle, 72–76. Tokyo: Japan Foundation Asia Center, 2016.

Ko, Yu-fen. "The Desired Form: Japanese Idol Dramas in Taiwan." In *Feeling Asian Modernities: Transnational Consumption of Japanese TV Dramas*, edited by Kōichi Iwabuchi, 107–128. Hong Kong: Hong Kong University Press, 2004.

Korean Culture and Information Service. *The Korean Wave: A New Pop Culture Phenomenon*. Seoul: Korean Culture and Information Service, Ministry of Culture, Sports, and Tourism, 2011.

Koschmann, J. Victor. "Asianism's Legacy." In *Network Power: Japan and Asia*, edited by Peter J. Katzenstein and Takashi Shiraishi, 87–95. Ithaca, NY: Cornell University Press, 1997.

Kwon, Heonik. *The Other Cold War*. New York: Columbia University Press, 2010.

Kwon, Heonik. "The Transpacific Cold War." In *Transpacific Studies: From an Emerging Field*, edited by Janet Hoskins and Viet Thanh Nguyen, 64–84. Honolulu: University of Hawai'i Press, 2014.

Kwon, Seung-Ho, and Joseph Kim. "The Cultural Industry Policies of the Korean Government and the Korean Wave." *International Journal of Cultural Policy* 20, no. 4 (2014): 422–439.

Lafuente, Pablo. "Introduction: From the Outside In—'Magiciens de la Terre' and Two Histories of Exhibitions." In Lucy Steeds, Pablo Lafuente, Jean-Marc Poinsot, Jean-Hubert Martin, Benjamin H. D. Buchloh, Rasheed Araeen, Jean Fisher, Gayatri Chakravorty Spivak, and Thomas McEvilley, *Making Art Global (Part 2): "Magiciens de la Terre" 1989*, 8–22. London: Afterall Books, 2013.

Lamarre, Thomas. "Introduction: The Impacts of Modernities." In *Impacts of Modernities*, edited by Thomas Lamarre and Kang Nae-hui, 1–36. Hong Kong: Hong Kong University Press, 2004.

Lefebvre, Henri. *State, Space, World: Selected Essays*. Edited by Neil Brenner and Stuart Elden, and translated by Gerald Moore, Neil Brenner, and Stuart Elden. Minneapolis: University of Minnesota Press, 2009.

Lefebvre, Henri. *The Production of Space*. Translated by Donald Nicholson-Smith. Malden, MA: Blackwell, 1991.

Lie, John. *The Dream of East Asia: The Rise of China, Nationalism, Popular Memory, and Regional Dynamics in Northeast Asia*. Ann Arbor, MI: Association of Asian Studies, 2018.

Lindsay, Jennifer. "Musical Travels of the Coconut Isle and the Socialist Popular." In *Sound Alignments: Popular Music in Asia's Cold Wars*, edited by Michael K. Bourdaghs, Paola Iovene, and Kaley Mason, 43–67. Durham, NC: Duke University Press, 2021.

Lee, Jung-Yup. "Managing the Transnational, Governing the National: Cultural Policy and the Politics of 'the Cultural Archetype Project in South Korea.'" In *Popular Culture and the State in East and Southeast Asia*, edited by Nissim Otmazgin and Eyal Ben-Ari, 123–143. London: Routledge, 2011.

Lee, Vivian P. Y., ed. *East Asian Cinemas: Regional Flows and Global Transformations*. Houndmills, UK: Palgrave-Macmillan, 2011.Lee Weng Choy. "Coincidence and Recollection; Lateness and Insight." In Jane DeBevoise, John Tain, Liu Ding, Carol Yinghua Lu, Lee Weng Choy, Xu Hong, and Anthony Yung, *Uncooperative Contemporaries: Art Exhibitions in Shanghai in 2000*, 120–131. London: Afterall Books, 2020.

Liscutin, Nicola. "Surfing the Neo-Nationalist Wave: A Case Study of *Manga Kenkanryū*." In *Cultural Studies and Cultural Industries in Northeast Asia: What a Difference a Region Makes*, edited by Chris Berry, Nicola Liscutin, and Jonathan D. Mackintosh, 171–189. Hong Kong: Hong Kong University Press, 2009.

Liu Ding, and Carol Yinghua Lu. "'Fuck Off': Search for the Way in Which Art Lives as 'Wildfire.'" In Jane DeBevoise, John Tain, Liu Ding, Carol Yinghua Lu, Lee Weng Choy, Xu Hong, and Anthony Yung, *Uncooperative Contemporaries: Art Exhibitions in Shanghai in 2000*, 98–115. London: Afterall Books, 2020.

Llanes Godoy, Lilian. "La Bienal de La Habana." *Third Text* 6, no. 20 (1992): 5–12.

Lo, Kwai-Cheung. "There Is No Such Thing as Asia: Racial Particularities in the 'Asian' Films of Hong Kong and Japan." *Modern Chinese Literature and Culture* 17, no. 1 (2005): 133–158.

Lu, Sheldon Hsiao-peng. *Transnational Chinese Cinemas: Identity, Nationhood, Gender*. Honolulu: University of Hawai'i Press, 1997.

Mahathir Mohamad and Ishihara Shintarō. *The Voice of Asia*. Translated by Frank Baldwin. Tokyo: Kodansha International, 1995.

Marchart, Oliver. "The Globalization of Art and the 'Biennials of Resistance[']: A History of the Biennials from the Periphery." *On Curating* 46 (2020). Accessed January 31, 2022. https://www.on-curating.org/issue-46-reader/the-globalization-of-art-and-the-biennials -of-resistance-a-history-of-the-biennials-from-the-periphery.html.

Marks, Ethan. "'Asia's' Transwar Lineage: Nationalism, Marxism, and 'Greater Asia' in an Indonesian Inflection." *Journal of Asian Studies* 65, no. 3 (2006): 461–493.

Marx, W. David. "The *Jimusho* System: Understanding the Production Logic of the Japanese Entertainment Industry." In *Idols and Celebrity in Japanese Media Culture*, edited by Patrick W. Galbraith and Jason G. Karlin, 35–55. Houndmills, UK: Palgrave Macmillan, 2012.

Matsue, Jennifer Milioto. "Stars to the State and Beyond: Globalization, Identity, and Asian Popular Music." *Journal of Asian Studies* 72, no. 1 (2013): 5–20.

Mattelart, Armand. *Networking the World, 1794–2000*. Minneapolis: University of Minnesota Press, 2000.

McCabe, Colin. "Preface to Fredric Jameson." In Fredric Jameson, *The Geopolitical Aesthetic: Cinema and Space in the World System*, ix–xx. Bloomington: Indiana University Press, 1992.

McClure, Steve. *Nippon Pop*. Tokyo: Charles E. Tuttle, 1998.

McGray. Douglas. "Japanese Gross National Cool." *Foreign Policy* no. 130 (2002): 44–54. Accessed April 25, 2014. https://www.jstor.org/stable/3183487?origin=crossref.

Mezzadra, Sandro, and Brett Neilson. *Border as Method, Or, the Multiplication of Labor*. Durham, NC: Duke University Press, 2013.

Mia Yu. "Manifolds of the Local: Tracing the Neglected Legacies of the Shanghai Biennale 2000." In Jane DeBevoise, John Tain, Liu Ding, Carol Yinghua Lu, Lee Weng Choy, Xu Hong, and Anthony Yung, *Uncooperative Contemporaries: Art Exhibitions in Shanghai in 2000*, 62–86. London: Afterall Books, 2020.

Mignolo, Walter D., and Catherine E. Walsh. *On Decoloniality: Concepts, Analytics, Praxis*. Durham, NC: Duke University Press, 2018.

Mori Art Museum. *Metabolism, the City of the Future: Dreams and Visions of Reconstruction in Postwar and Present-day Japan*, exhibition catalogue. Tokyo: Mori Art Museum, 2011.

Mōri, Yoshitaka. "J-Pop: From the Ideology of Creativity to DiY Music Culture." *Inter-Asia Cultural Studies* 10, no. 4 (2009): 474–488.

Mōri, Yoshitaka. "Winter Sonata and Cultural Practices of Active Fans in Japan: Considering Middle-Aged Women as Cultural Agents." In *East Asian Pop Culture: Analysing the Korean Wave*, edited by Chua Beng Huat and Kōichi Iwabuchi, 127–141. Hong Kong: Hong Kong University Press, 2008.

Morrell, Timothy. "Cultural Crossfire: The Curatorial Travels of Apinan Poshyananda." *Art Asia-Pacific* 3, no. 4 (1996): 42–47.

Morris, Meaghan. "Transnational Imagination in Action Cinema: Hong Kong and the Making of a Global Popular Culture." *Inter-Asia Cultural Studies* 5, no. 2 (2004): 181–199.

Morris, Meaghan, Siu Leung Li, and Stephen Chan Ching-kiu, eds. *Hong Kong Connections: Transnational Imagination in Action Cinema*. Hong Kong: Hong Kong University Press, 2005.

Nakano, Yoshiko. "Who Initiates a Global Flow? Japanese Popular Culture in Asia." *Visual Communication* 1, no. 2 (2002): 229–253.

Negus, Keith. *The South Korean Music Industry: A Literature Review*. CREATe (Centre for Copyright and New Business Models in the Creative Economy) Working Paper Series. Glasgow: CREATe, 2015.

Ng, Benjamin Wai-ming. "Japanese Popular Music in Singapore and the Hybridization of Asian Music." *Asian Music* 34, no. 1 (2002): 1–18.

Ogawa, Masashi. "Japanese Popular Music in Hong Kong: What Does TK Present?" In *Refashioning Pop Music in Asia: Cosmopolitan Flows, Political Tempos, and Aesthetic Industries*, edited by Allen Chun, Ned Rossiter, and Brian Shoesmith, 144–156. London: Routledge/Curzon, 2004.

Oh, Younjung. "Oriental Taste in Imperial Japan: The Exhibition and Sale of Asian Art and Artifacts by Japanese Department Stores from the 1920s through the Early 1940s." *Journal of Asian Studies* 78, no. 1 (2019): 45–74.

Okakura, Kakuzō. *Ideals of the East, with Special Reference to the Art of Japan*. London: J. Murray, 1903.

Okakura-Kakuzō. *The Awakening of Japan*. New York: Century, 1904.

Okakura Kakuzō. *The Heart of Heaven: Being a Collection of Writings Hitherto Unpublished in Book Form*. Tokyo: Nippon-Bijutsuin, 1922.

O'Neill, Paul. *The Culture of Curating and the Curating of Culture(s)*. Cambridge, MA: MIT Press, 2012.

O'Neil, Paul. "The Curatorial Turn: From Practice to Discourse." In *Issues in Curating Contemporary Art and Performance*, edited by Judith Rugg and Michèle Sedgwick, 13–28. Bristol: Intellect, 2007.

Osborne, Peter. *Anywhere or Not at All: Philosophy of Contemporary Art*. London: Verso, 2013.

Osborne, Peter. *The Postconceptual Condition: Critical Essays*. London: Verso, 2018.

Otmazgin, Nissim. "A New Cultural Geography of East Asia: Imagining a 'Region' through Popular Culture." *Asia-Pacific Journal: Japan Focus* 14, no. 5–7 (2016). Accessed April 14, 2022. https://apjjf.org/2016/07/Otmazgin.html.

Otmazgin, Nissim Kadosh. *Regionalizing Culture: The Political Economy of Japanese Popular Culture in Asia*. Honolulu: University of Hawai'i Press, 2013.

Otmazgin, Nissim, and Eyal Ben-Ari, eds. *Popular Culture Co-Productions and Collaborations in East and Southeast Asia*. Singapore: NUS Press and Kyoto: Kyoto University Press, 2012.

Pang, Laikwan. "Masculinity in Crisis: Films of Milkyway Image and Post-1997 Hong Kong Cinema." *Feminist Media Studies* 2, no. 3 (2002): 325–340.

Pang, Laikwan. "Postcolonial Hong Kong Cinema: Utilitarianism and Trans(Local)." *Postcolonial Studies* 10, no. 4 (2007): 413–430.

Pastor Roces, Marian. "Crystal Palace Exhibitions." In *The Biennial Reader: An Anthology on Large-Scale Perennial Exhibitions of Contemporary Art*, edited by Elena Filipovic, Merieke van Hal, and Solveig Øvstebø, 50–65. Ostfildern: Hatje Cantz Verlag, 2010.

Powers, Devon. "The Problem of Popular Culture." *Communication Theory* 32, no. 4 (2022): 461–470.

Prashad, Vijay. *The Darker Nations: A People's History of the Third World*. New York: New Press, 2007.

Reischauer, Edwin O., and John K. Fairbank. *East Asia: The Great Tradition*. Boston, MA: Houghton Mifflin, 1960.

Roberts, Martin. "'A New Stereophonic Sound Spectacular': *Shibuya-kei* as Transnational Soundscape." *Popular Music* 32, no. 1 (2013): 111–123.

Robison, Richard, and David S. G. Goodman, eds. *The New Rich in Asia: Mobile Phones, McDonald's and Middle Class Revolution*. London: Routledge, 1995.

Rogoff, Irit. "Smuggling: A Curatorial Model." In *Under Construction: Perspectives on Institutional Practice*, edited by Vanessa Müller and Nicolaus Schafhausen, 132–135. Cologne: Walther König, 2006.

Rowe, Peter G. *East Asia Modern: Shaping the Contemporary City*. London: Reaktion Books, 2005.

Russell, Mark James. *POP Goes Korea: Behind the Revolution in Movies, Music, and the Internet Culture*. Berkeley, CA: Stone Bridge Press, 2008.

Sakai, Naoki. "'You Asians': On the Historical Role of the West and Asia Binary." *South Atlantic Quarterly* 99, no. 4 (2000): 789–817.

Sakamoto, Rumi. "Popular Culture and Historical Memories of War in Asia." In *Routledge Handbook of East Asian Popular Culture*, edited by Kōichi Iwabuchi, Eva Tsai, and Chris Berry, 254–264. Abingdon, UK: Routledge, 2016.

Schaller, Michael. "Securing the Great Crescent: Occupied Japan and the Origins of Containment in Southeast Asia." *Journal of American History* 69, no. 2 (1982): 391–414.

Shea, Timothy. "Where There Are No Art Circles: The *Long March Project* and New Geographies of Contemporary Chinese Art." *Yishu: Journal of Contemporary Chinese Art* 16, no. 6 (2017): 77–83.

Shin, Hyunjoon. "Have You Ever Seen the Rain? And Who'll Stop the Rain?: The Globalizing Project of Korean Pop (K-Pop)." *Inter-Asia Cultural Studies* 10, no. 4 (2009): 507–523.

Shin, Hyunjoon. "K-Pop, the Sound of Subaltern Cosmopolitanism?" In *Routledge Handbook of East Asian Popular Culture*, edited by Kōichi Iwabuchi, Eva Tsai, and Chris Berry, 116–123. Abingdon, UK: Routledge, 2016.

Shin, Hyunjoon. "Reconsidering Transnational Cultural Flows of Popular Music in East Asia: Transbordering Musicians in Japan and Korea Searching for 'Asia.'" *Korean Studies* 33, no. 1 (2009): 101–123.

Shin, Hyunjoon. "Searching for Youth, the People (*Minjung*), and 'Another' West While Living Through Anti-Communist Cold War Politics: South Korean 'Folk Song' in the 1970s." In *Sound Alignments: Popular Music in Asia's Cold Wars*, edited by Michael K. Bourdaghs, Paola Iovene, and Kaley Mason, 131–152. Durham, NC: Duke University Press, 2021.

Shiraishi, Takashi. "The Third Wave: Southeast Asia and Middle-Class Formation in the Making of a Region." In *Beyond Japan: The Dynamics of East Asian Regionalism*, edited by Peter J. Katzenstein and Takashi Shiraishi, 237–271. Ithaca, NY: Cornell University Press, 2006.

Smith, Terry, Okwui Enwezor, and Nancy Condee, eds. *Antinomies of Art and Culture: Modernity, Postmodernity, Contemporaneity*. Durham, NC: Duke University Press, 2008.

Stallybrass, Julian. *Art Incorporated: The Story of Contemporary Art*. Oxford: Oxford University Press, 2004.

Steeds, Lucy. "'Magiciens de la Terre' and the Development of Transnational Project-based Curating." In Lucy Steeds, Pablo Lafuente, Jean-Marc Poinsot, Jean-Hubert Martin, Benjamin H. D. Buchloh, Rasheed Araeen, Jean Fisher, Gayatri Chakravorty Spivak, and Thomas McEvilley, *Making Art Global (Part 2): "Magiciens de la Terre" 1989*, 24–92. London: Afterall Books, 2013.

Steeds, Lucy, Pablo Lafuente, Jean-Marc Poinsot, Jean-Hubert Martin, Benjamin H. D. Buchloh, Rasheed Araeen, Jean Fisher, Gayatri Chakravorty Spivak, and Thomas McEvilley. *Making Art Global (Part 2): "Magiciens de la Terre" 1989*. London: Afterall Books, 2013.

Stevens, Carolyn S. *Japanese Popular Music: Culture, Authority, and Power*. Abingdon, UK: Routledge, 2008.

Sun Ge. "How Does Asia Mean? (Part I)." *Inter-Asia Cultural Studies* 1, no. 1 (2000): 13–47.

Sun Ge. "In Search of the Modern: Tracing Japanese Thought on 'Overcoming Modernity.'" In *Impacts of Modernities*, edited by Thomas Lamarre and Kang Nae-hui, 53–75. Hong Kong: Hong Kong University Press, 2004.

Takeuchi Yoshimi. *What Is Modernity? Writings of Takeuchi Yoshimi*, edited by and translated by Richard Calichman. New York: Columbia University Press, 2005.

Taylor, Nora A., and Boreth Ly, eds. *Modern and Contemporary Southeast Asian Art: An Anthology*. Ithaca, NY: Cornell Southeast Asia Program, 2012.

Teo, Stephen. *Director in Action: Johnnie To and the Hong Kong Action Film*. Hong Kong: Hong Kong University Press, 2007.

Therborn, Göran. "Asia and Europe in the World: Locations in the Global Dynamics." *Inter-Asia Cultural Studies* 3, no. 2 (2002): 287–307.

Tomii, Reiko. *Radicalism in the Wilderness: International Contemporaneity and 1960s Art in Japan*. Cambridge, MA: MIT Press, 2016.

Tomii, Reiko. "Toward Tokyo Biennale 1970: Shapes of the International in the Age of 'International Contemporaneity.'" *Review of Japanese Culture and Society* 23 (2011): 191–210.

Tong, Janice. "*Chungking Express*: Time and Its Displacements." In *Chinese Films in Focus II*, edited by Chris Berry, 64–72. Houndmills, UK: Palgrave Macmillan, 2008.

Tsai, Eva. "Kaneshiro Takeshi: Transnational Stardom and the Media and Culture Industries in Asia's Global/Postcolonial Age." *Modern Chinese Literature and Culture* 17, no. 1 (2005): 100–132.

Turner, Caroline. "The Asia-Pacific Triennial." In *Contemporary Art from the Asia Pacific Region*, International Institute for Asian Studies, n.d. Accessed October 12, 2017. https://iias.asia/iiasn/iiasn8/ascult/triennia.html.

Turner, Caroline, and Michelle Antoinette, ed. *Contemporary Asian Art and Exhibitions: Connectivities and World-Making*. Canberra: ANU Press, 2014.

Ubonrat Siriyuvasak and Shin Hyunjoon. "Asianizing K-Pop: Production, Consumption and Identification Patterns among Thai Youth." *Inter-Asia Cultural Studies* 8, no. 1 (2007): 109–136.

Udornpim, Kant, and Arvind Singhal. "*Oshin*, a Pro-Social Role Model, in Thailand." *Keio Communication Review* 21 (1999): 3–21.

Um, Haekyung. *K-Pop on the Global Platform: European Audience Reception and Contexts*. Seoul: KOFICE (Korean Foundation for International Cultural Exchange), 2014.

Ushiroshōji, Masahiro. "Present Encounters: The Asia-Pacific Triennial." *ArtAsiaPacific* no. 15 (1997), 30–31.

Vogel, Ezra. *Japan as Number One: Lessons for America*. Cambridge, MA: Harvard University Press, 1979.

Wade, Bonnie C. *Music in Japan: Experiencing Music, Expressing Culture*. Oxford: Oxford University Press, 2005.

Wang Hui. "The Idea of Asia and Its Ambiguities." *Journal of Asian Studies* 69, no. 4 (2010): 985–989.

Wang Hui. *The Politics of Imagining Asia*. Translated by Theodore Huters. Cambridge, MA: Harvard University Press, 2011.

Wang, Xiaoming. "The Concept of 'Asia' in Modern China: Some Reflections Starting with the 2007 Shanghai Conference." Translated by Petrus Liu. *Inter-Asia Cultural Studies* 11, no. 2 (2010): 197–201.

Watson, Jini Kim. *Cold War Reckonings: Authoritarianism and the Genres of Decolonization*. New York: Fordham University Press, 2021.

Watson, Jini Kim. *The New Asian City: Three-Dimensional Fictions of Space and Urban Form*. Minneapolis: University of Minnesota Press, 2011.

Wee, C. J. W.-L. "Speaking of Modern and Contemporary Asian Art." In *Art and Globalization*, edited by James Elkins, Zhivka Valiacharska, and Alice Kim, 176–180. University Park: Pennsylvania State University Press, 2010.

Wee, C. J. W.-L. "Staging the Asian Modern: Cultural Fragments, the Singaporean Eunuch, and the Asian *Lear*." *Critical Inquiry* 30, no. 4 (2004): 771–799.

Wee, C. J. W.-L. *The Asian Modern: Culture, Capitalist Development, Singapore*. Hong Kong: Hong Kong University Press, 2007.

Weiss, Rachel. "A Certain Place and a Certain Time: The Third Bienal de La Habana and the Origins of the Global Exhibition." In Rachel Weiss, Charles Esche, Gerardo Mosquera, Mirko Lauer, Geeta Kapur, Coco Fusco, Luis Camnitzer, and Lucy Steeds, *Making Art Global (Part 1): The Third Havana Biennial 1989*, 14–69. London: Afterall Books, 2011.

Weiss, Rachel, Charles Esche, Gerardo Mosquera, Mirko Lauer, Geeta Kapur, Coco Fusco, Luis Camnitzer, and Lucy Steeds. *Making Art Global (Part 1): The Third Havana Biennial 1989*. London: Afterall Books, 2011.

World Bank. *The East Asian Miracle: Economic Growth and Public Policy*. New York: Oxford University Press, 1993.

Wu Hung. "The 2000 Shanghai Biennale: The Making of a Historical Event." *Art and AsiaPacific* no. 31 (2000), 42–49.

Xu Hong. "To Select, to be Selected and Who Selects: The Shanghai Biennale in the Context of Globalisation." In *Uncooperative Contemporaries: Art Exhibitions in Shanghai in 2000*, edited by Jane DeBevoise and other authors, translated by Zhao Han, 236–241. London: Afterall Books, 2020.

Yao Yung-wen. "China's Modern Image—Contemporary Chinese Art." *Journal for Cultural Research* 21, no. 1 (2017): 51–75.

Yeh, Yueh-Yu, and Darrell William Davis. "Japan Hongscreen: Pan-Asian Cinemas and Flexible Accumulation." *Historical Journal of Film, Radio and Television* 22, no. 1 (2002): 61–82.

Yong, Beverly, and Furuichi Yasuko, eds. *Art Studies 04: Condition Report: Shifting Perspectives in Asia—Curator's Book*. Tokyo: Japan Foundation Asia Center, 2018.

Yoshimi, Shunya. "Consuming 'America': From Symbol to System." In *Consumption in Asia: Lifestyle and Identities*, edited by Beng-Huat Chua, 202–224. London: Routledge, 2000.

Yoshimi, Shunya, and David Buist. "'America' as Desire and Violence: Americanization in Postwar Japan and Asia during the Cold War." *Inter-Asia Cultural Studies* 4, no. 3 (2003): 433–450.

Yusuf, Shahid, and Kaoru Nabeshima. *Postindustrial East Asian Cities: Innovation for Growth*. Stanford, CA: Stanford University Press; Washington, DC: World Bank, 2006.

Žižek, Slavoj. "Multiculturalism, or, the Cultural Logic of Multinational Capitalism." *New Left Review* no. 225 (1997): 28–51.

INDEX

valences contained in capitalist
entrenchment in, 17, 29, 128; film
and media culture industries in, 134;
as producers of their own representational space, culturally and artistically, 15, 127

Chakrabarty, Dipesh, 17

Chen, Kuan-Hsing, 8

China/Avant-Garde Exhibition (Beijing,
1989), 89

China Central Television (CCTV): *Back
to the Steppes* coproduced with NHK,
136; positive relationships fostered by
the spread of Asian popular culture
acknowledged by, 198; restrictions
imposed on Korean wave TV dramas,
181; *Son of the Good Earth* (*Daichi no
Ko*) coproduced with NHK, 136, 144

Ching, Leo T. S.: on how Asia popular
culture fosters sociopolitical relationships, 14; on the impact of *Inter-Asia
Cultural Studies*, 201n26; on mass
cultural Asianism, 230n38

Chong, Doryun: on the cultural category
of "contemporary Asian art," 42, 64

Chow, Rey, 187

Chua Beng Huat: on the circulation of
Pop Culture China, 163, 164; rhetoric
of the "rise of Asia" criticized by, 8

Chungking Express (*Chongqing senlin*,
Wong Kar-wai, 1994): Hong Kong's
urbanism depicted in, 54–55, 140;
urbanism of New Asia depicted in,
55–56

*Cities on the Move—Urban Chaos and
Global Change, East Asian Art, Architecture and Film Now* (1997–1999):
cocuration by Hou Hanru and Hans-
Ulrich Obrist, 12, 22; criticized by
Apinan Poshyananda as presenting
updated clichés of chaotic Asia, 116,
117; locations of with individualized
catalogues, 219–220n128; the "real

feeling and experiences" of ultra-
modernizing and urbanizing Asia
represented by, 115–116; speed as a
theme of the cocurators' catalogue
discourse, 90, 91; urban-presentist
bias and commitment to exhibition space design, 12, 90–91; at the
Vienna Secession (1997), 12, 22, 90

Cold War era: ban on Japanese culture
in South Korea during, 179; impact
on "East Asia" in the 1980s, 32–33;
importance of Third World futurity
and temporality to understanding
decolonization during, 19–20; role of
pop culture in overcoming of oppositional politics of economic regionalism, 4–5, 24, 159; as a subject of the
Ho Chi Minh Trail project, 192

Confucianism and Confucian values:
discourse on its impact on economic growth in East Asia, 6; non-
Confucian societies contrasted with,
27; shared Confucian heritage in
Asia, 158, 229n22

contemporaneity: Agamben on the
contemporary, 20–21; "global contemporary" described by Peter
Osborne, 105; identification of
present artistic practice by curators
and thought leaders, 23, 214–215n29;
impact on Shanghai discussed at
SB2000, 188–191; impact on the
inter-Asian flow of popular culture,
162–163, 179–180; as the temporality of global unity, 15–16; *tradición
y contemporaneidad* (tradition and
contemporaneity) as a theme of
Tercera Bienal de La Habana (Third
Havana Biennial, 1989), 64, 66–67

*Contemporary Art from the Non-Aligned
Countries*: Supangkat's rejection of
the need for a theoretical position in
his curation of, 68–70

East Asian miracle: recognition by the World Bank, 4; revivification of the idea of "Asia" by, 27

Elkins, James: on belatedness, 11

Elliott, David: on clichéd notions of Asia in curation, 115–116; conceptual topography of Asia presented in "A Short Walk in the Hindu Kush," 89, 90; on the need to integrate culture with a discussion of economics, 122; on the pluralism of contemporary art, 118

Enwezor, Okwui, 14

Ewington, Julie, 80

exhibitionary imaginary and curatorial imagination: engagement with alternative discourse and knowledge creation relating to culture and art, 10, 62, 67, 82, 105; incommensurate cultural, local-national, and historical components brought into relationship by, 13, 22–23, 28, 43, 114–114, 125

Fenollosa, Ernest, 46–47, 209–210n67

Flores, Patrick D.: on critiques of the universalized Western norm as applied to Southeast Asian art from the 2000s, 80; on delimiting between curation as a subject and what is being curated, 201n32; participation in *Under Construction*, 50; on "What is Asia?" as an unnerving proposition, 16

Fogle, Douglas, 91

Foucault, Michel: on heterotopias, 94

four mini dragons: middle-class formation in, 164; pursuit of economic and monetary power following the economic successes of, 78, 91–92; South Korea, Taiwan, Hong Kong, and Singapore identified as, 78

Fuji Television (Fuji TV): *Long Vacation (Rongu bakēshon)* drama series, 1;

Tokyo Love Story (Tōkyō Rabusutōrī), 139, 232n57

Fukuoka Art Museum: tradition addressed against the backdrop of regional economic development (1979/1980 to 1994), 70

Fukuoka Art Museum—*Asian Artists Exhibition* (1979–1980): Koike Shinji as the chief project officer for the curatorial process, 46; role in setting the pace for 1990s self-representation of Asian Art, 21, 29–30; twofold goals of, 43

Fukuoka Art Museum—*Asian Artists Exhibition—Festival: Contemporary Asian Art Show* (1980): global regionalism reflected in its representation of countries and presentation of present-day artwork, 48

Fukuoka Art Museum—*Asian Artists Exhibition—Modern Asian Art* (1979): common cultural essence(s) defining Asia as its focus, 42

Fukuoka Art Museum—*2nd Asian Art Show* (1985), 72, 113

Fukuoka Art Museum—*3rd Asian Art Show* (1989): arrangement of pictures of artwork in the catalogue for, 77; art selected for regional exhibitions, 73–74; Kuroda Raiji on economic logic behind the exhibition's Japanese selection, 75–76; preparatory meetings for, 72; "Symbolic Visions in Contemporary Asian Life" as the theme of, 49, 73

Fukuoka Art Museum—*4th Asian Art Show* (1994). *See also* Ushiroshōji Masahiro: pioneering reconstitution of tradition by, 71–72; "Realism as an Attitude" as the theme of, 77–78

Fulltime Killer (Quanzhi shashou): *Crying Freeman* referenced in, 153–154; multilingual features of,

Fulltime Killer (*Quanzhi shashou*) (cont.) 149–150; multitiered cultural reflection of, 149; plot summary, 150–151; as a "transnational collage," 151–152, 234n81; urban spaces presented as not quite national and not quite transnational, 24, 130, 148; violent cartographic imaginary of the New Asia presented in, 151

Furuichi Yasuko: on the central goal of *Under Construction*, 50–51; on understanding of social and cultural contexts informing art as the focus of JFAC's exhibition projects, 103

Gao Shiming: criticism of SB2000, 191–192; *Ho Chi Minh Trail* project (HCMTP), 192–193, 194, 244n30

Gen-X Cops (*Te jing xin ren lei*, 1999), 138

Glaser, Bonnie, 235n15

globalization—cultural: contradiction entailed in globalized modernity, 41–42; cultural pluralism of contemporary pop culture enabled by the Asian miracle economies, 166; globalizing Asia as the context for and vexed theme in the reimagining of Asia, 11, 87; "global-region" curatorial framework of 2002 contrasted with the "international-regional" framework of 1979–1980, 21–22, 30; inclusivity of its promotion in *Magiciens*, 65; inter-Asian flow of popular culture before the 1990s, 162–164; Iwabuchi Kōichi on a cultural economy that crosses borders, 139; mass cultural Asianism, 135, 230n38; new artistic options for Asian contemporary art created by, 117; overcoming of oppositional politics of economic regionalism and the not-quite post–Cold War nationalisms by pop culture, 24, 159

globalization—economic: circulation and consumption of regionalizing inter-Asian pop culture transformed by, 159; Japan as an economic force, 160–161; regional relations produced via trade, 32, 238n53

Greenberg, Clement, 13

Gu Wenda, 65

Gwangju: 3rd Asia Song Festival, 183

Gwangju Biennale (1995): curation by Lee Yong Woo, 120, 122–124

Gwangju Biennale (2000): Tani Arata as commissioner of the Asian section of, 223n43

Hall, Stuart, 14

Harootunian, Harry: call for Asian cultural and capitalist exceptionalism by, 9; on spatializing, 128

Havana Biennial, 1989. *See* Tercera Bienal de La Habana (Third Havana Biennial, 1989)

Hegel, G. W. F.: on human freedom, 27; universalist history and teleology of progress transmitted by, 28, 101, 114

Hoffie, Pat, 81–82

Hong Kong: Hong Kong's urbanism depicted in *Chungking Express* (1994), 54–55; identified as a mini-dragon economy, 78; identified as a tiger economy, 32

Hong Kong cinema: impact of the Asian economic crisis of 1997 on, 12, 24, 137–138; mixed depictions of the urban-modern, 141; multilingualism of 1990s Hong Kong films, 4, 12, 24, 27, 127–128, 129, 138, 141, 144, 146; urbanized "cosmopolitan fantasy" strain in, 138, 145

Hou Hanru: cocuration of *Cities on the Move*, 12, 22; at SB2000, 190; on cultural decentering evidenced in *Magiciens*, 66

Huyssen, Andreas: on the culture industry, 134; on how cultural circulation is linked to political and social discourse, 15; on the mission of modernists to salvage the purity of high art, 212n1

India: Asian contemporary art market in, 40; *4th Asian Art Show* (1994) presented in, 77; impact of the Asian financial crisis of 1997 on, 225; inclusion in *Festival: Contemporary Asian Art Show* (1980), 48; inclusion in *Traditions/Tensions*, 80, 83; Mumbai/Bombay as an alternative space of exchange and dialogue in contemporary art and culture, 83; Mumbai/Bombay exhibition of *Under Construction: New Dimensions of Asian Art* (2002), 2, 51; participants from India at the JFAC symposia, 104; *3rd Asian Art Show* (1989) presented in, 74; Triennale in New Delhi (1968), 38

Indonesia: Asmudjo on the absence of contemporary art in large cities of Indonesia, 56–58; Bandung exhibition of *Dream Project: Under Construction* (2002), 2, 51, 56–57; *Fabriek* (Dutch: factory) *Gallery*, by Jakarta based artist designer Sofwan, 57; *4th Asian Art Show* (1994) presented in, 77; inclusion in *Festival: Contemporary Asian Art Show* (1980), 48; inclusion in *Traditions/Tensions*, 80; Jakarta as an alternative space of exchange and dialogue in contemporary art and culture, 83; as a second-tier newly industrializing economy, 19, 57, 131; *3rd Asian Art Show* (1989) presented in, 75

Inter-Asia Cultural Studies: emergence as part of movement for the ongoing construction and reconstruction of Inter-Asian subjectivities, 8–9; Leo Ching on the impact of, 201n26

Ishihara Shintarō: on East Asia in light of nationalist concerns, 3, 31; on "violent crimes by *sangokujin*," 145

Iwabuchi Kōichi: on a cultural economy that crosses borders, 129; on the symbolic appeal to other Asian nations of Japanese cultural products, 139 232n57

Jameson, Fredric: assessment of Japanese cultural power in the 1990s, 165; on the move from *modernization* to *globalization*, 34, 165–166, 206–207n30; on the narrativizing of social worlds by film and the media and culture industries, 134; on synchronic heterogeneity and New Asia, 4, 124, 199–200n8

Japan: emergence of Asian tiger economies in the 1980s as a reflection of, 19, 131, 132; founding of Tokyo Fine Arts School (now Tokyo University of Fine Arts and Music), 41; *4th Asian Art Show* (1994) presented in, 77; "free and open Indo-Pacific" promoted by Abe Shinzo, 161; impact of "Americanization" on Japanese cultural products, 164–165, 248n53; inclusion in *Festival: Contemporary Asian Art Show* (1980), 48; Japanese viewed as the Other by many Asians, 108; normalization of diplomatic relations with the PRC (1972), 136; participation in the Vienna Expo (1873), 41; postwar economic recovery and industrialization, 7, 93; rebuilding in the postwar years, 19; struggle with modernization, 34–35, 46–47, 209–210n67; *3rd Asian Art Show* (1989) presented in, 73–74;

Japan Foundation Asia Center (JFAC)—
Symposium 1999: "*Asian Art:
Prospects for the Future*": Apinan
Poshyananda, "Asian Art and the
New Millennium: From Glocalism to
Techno-Shamanism," 116–117; what
it means to represent of the region's
contemporary art addressed at, 104
Japan Foundation Asia Center (JFAC)—
Symposium 2002: "*Asia in Transition*": the issue of Japan's struggle to
become a great power that resulted
in the Japanese Empire addressed
at, 104
Johnny & Associates: DVD concert
selection released by J Storm, 183,
242n107; idol boybands in Japan
created by, 178; renaming as Smile-
Up, 178, 240n85
J-Pop: acceleration of urbanization
associated with, 12; idol music
as part of a "Japanese-made" pop
music, 168, 170; Japanese audiences'
interest in Western music in the
mid-1980s compared with the 2000s,
170, 238n55; progressive translocal
change in cultural subjectivity testi-
fied by, 24; soft power of the transnational cultural flow of, 164–165,
181; spread to regional audiences
in the 1990s, 12; valorization of the
Anglocentric prefix "J," 170

Kajiya Kenji, 50, 102, 210n82
Kamiya Yukie: on art as a medium for
transnational dialogue, 59; cocuration of local shows in Seoul and
Beijing for *Under Construction*, 2, 50,
55; on the need for younger Asian
artists to have a platform, 56; on the
urbanism of New Asia depicted by
Wong Kar-wai in *Chungking Express*
(1994), 55–56

Kapur, Geeta: catalogue essay for *Tradi-
tions/Tensions*, 84–85; civilizational-
aesthetic framework of, 89; impact of
the May 1996 Indian general election
on her views, 88–89; tradition-in-
the-contemporary standpoint of,
87–88
Kataoka Mami: "Asia's Art Map" written
for *Under Construction*, 51, 52–53; as
chief curator of the Tokyo Opera City
Art Gallery, 50
kayōkyoku (Western-style pop songs that
did not deploy stylized pronunciations based on the English language):
Shibuya-kei (Shibuya-style) music
contrasted with, 168; the South
Korean term *kayo* link with, 179
Kee, Joan: on biennial/triennales in East
Asia in the 1960s and 1970s, 208n45;
on contemporary Asia art as a social-
political intervention, 96
Kim Soo-Ja, 83
Kimura Takuya: Levi's jeans promoted
by, 2; as a member of SMAP (Sports,
Music Assemble People), 1, 157; role
of Sena played in *Long Vacation*, 1
Kishi Sayaka: on *New Art from Southeast
Asia*, 40, 103; on protests directed
at the JFAC exhibition *Works of
Japanese Traditional Craft* (Seoul,
1994), 103
Ko, Yu-fen, 232n58
Koike Shinji, 46, 48
Koolhaas, Rem: gallery for the London
version of *Cities on the Move*
designed by, 115–116; put-down
of East Asian forms of urbanism,
115–116, 132, 211n102
Korea. *See* South Korea
Korean wave (*Hallyu*): anti-*Hallyu* event
in Japan, 181–182; emergence in the
late 1990s, 136, 164; initiation by
What is Love? (*Sarangi mwŏgillae*)

Pakistan: *4th Asian Art Show* (1994)
presented in, 77; Ghulam Rasul on
Pakistani art by the 1970s, 72; inclu-
sion in *Festival: Contemporary Asian
Art Show* (1980), 48; *3rd Asian Art
Show* (1989) presented in, 74

Pastor Roces, Marian: on Bienal de
La Habana (1984), 66; "Bodies of
Fiction, Bodies of Desire" for *Tradi-
tions/Tensions*, 84, 85, 92

People's Republic of China (PRC):
Beijing exhibition of *Under Construction: New Dimensions of Asian Art*
(2002), 2, 51, 55, 57; Chinese artists
included in the 45th Venice Biennale
(1993), 65; competing territorial and
jurisdictional claims in the South
China Sea, 161, 235n15; *4th Asian
Art Show* (1994) presented in, 77;
Huang Yong Ping as one of three
artists included in *Magiciens*, 65;
inclusion in *Festival: Contemporary
Asian Art Show* (1980), 48; as a
metonym that will stand in for New
Asia, 197–198; normalization of
diplomatic relations with the PRC
(1972), 136; participation in global
capitalism, 187, 198; shared Confucian base of culture among China,
Hong Kong, Japan, South Korea,
Taiwan, and Singapore, 229n22; strict
media control in, 197; *3rd Asian
Art Show* (1989) presented in, 73;
unexpected international success of
Chinese art in the 1990s, 244n24;
urban constituencies of, 187, 243n4;
Xi Jinping Thought on Culture set
out at the National Conference on
Propaganda, Ideology, and Cultural
Work, 197

People's Republic of China (PRC)—
reform and opening (*gaige kaifang*):
exploitation of the global economy in
the service of national ends, 7, 187;
forgetfulness of the role of models
from Japan, South Korea, Taiwan,
and Singapore, 189

Philippines: competing territorial and
jurisdictional claims in the South
China Sea, 235n15; *4th Asian Art
Show* (1994) presented in, 77; inclusion in *Festival: Contemporary Asian
Art Show* (1980), 48; inclusion in
Traditions/Tensions, 80; Manila as
an alternative space of exchange and
dialogue in contemporary art and
culture, 83; Manila exhibition of
*Under Construction: New Dimensions
of Asian Art* (2002), 2, 51; Raymundo
Albano on "borrowing" as a creative
act in '80s Philippine art, 72–73;
3rd Asian Art Show (1989) presented
in, 73

Pizzicato Five, 171–174

popular culture: and cultural consumption, 8, 12, 132, 133–135,
158–159, 166–167, 174–175;
historico-aesthetic associations about
it, 13; impact of Douglas McGray's
"Japanese Gross National Cool" on
its "soft power," 136; lack of a static
binary of high art *versus* the market
and popular culture, 8, 14–15

Powers, Devon, 134–135

Prashad, Vijay, 70

Realism as an Attitude. See Fukuoka Art
Museum—*4th Asian Art Show* (1994)

regional contemporary: fictive but
shared identity projected on East
Asia in by cultural expression, 2;
impact of the logic of cultural circulation on, 14–15; impact of the PRC's
rise on, 197; as a term, 5–6

Reischauer, Edwin O., and John K.
Fairbank, 6

Rimzon, N. N.: *The Inner Voice* (1992), 83

Rising Sun Flag (*Kyokujitsu-ki*): on AKB48 costumes, 185

Rising Sun (1992 novel by Michael Crichton; 1993 film starring Sean Connery), 16

Rostow, W. W., 101

Rowe, Peter G., 128, 229n22

Sabapathy, T. K., 68, 81

Said, Edward: on the production of knowledge and representation of other cultures, 9, 201n30

Sakai, Naoki, 121, 122

Sakamoto Kyū, 185

Sakamoto, Rumi: on neoliberal restructuring and precariatization of young people in twenty-first century Japan, 238n57

Sassen, Saskia, 95, 112

semiperiphery. *See* center/periphery model of knowledge and modern cultural production—semiperiphery

Seo Taiji and Boys (Sŏ Taejiwa aidŭl): impact on Korean pop-music development, 176–177; YG Entertainment founded by a former member of, 178

Shanghai: as a center for jazz, 162–163; identified as the "Head of the Dragon" by Deng Xiaoping, 189; Shanghai identified as a New Asian City, 195

Shanghai Biennale 2000: Shanghai Spirit (SB2000): criticism of, 189–190; impact of contemporaneity on Shanghai discussed at, 188–191; Shanghai's efforts to assert it as cosmopolitan, 189

Shaw Brothers: *King Drummer* (*Qing chun gu wang*, 1967), 163; *Princess Yang Kwei Fei* (*Yōkihi/Joeng Gwaifei*, 1955), 136

Shibuya HMV store, 171, 238n58

Shimizu Toshio, 106, 118–119, 190–191, 226n88

Shin, Hyunjoon, 176, 179, 181

Shiraishi, Takashi: on harmonizing internationalism and Asianism, 76; on the hegemony of the United States in East Asia, 235n14; on the middle class as a crucial engine of East Asian region-making, 131

Sihare, Laxmi Prasad, 45, 46

Singapore Art Museum: *Modernity and Beyond: Themes in Southeast Asian Art* (1996), 38, 39, 97

Singapore: biennial-type museum events in the 1990s, 10; broadcasting of the Japanese television drama *Oshin* (1984), 164; *4th Asian Art Show* (1994) presented in, 77; identified as a mini-dragon economy, 78; identified as a tiger economy, 32; inclusion in *Festival: Contemporary Asian Art Show* (1980), 48; Japanese television programs available in, 135; Singapore Biennale of 2006, 41, 210n82; *3rd Asian Art Show* (1989) presented in, 74

Sleepless Town (*Fuyajo/Bu ye cheng*, Lee Chi Ngai, 1998): awards earned at the 18th Hong Kong Film Awards (1999), 232n64; cross-border casting and multilingual screenplays featured in, 129, 145; ethnonational tensions reflected on, 144–145; *Fulltime Killer* compared with, 149; passive reproduction of audience expectations and of a fractured modernity, 130, 142, 144, 148; plot summary, 129, 142–144; *Tokyo Raiders* compared with, 141, 146; urban spaces presented as not quite national and not quite transnational, 24, 130, 145

SMAP (Sports, Music Assemble People):
break up announced in August 2016,
234n1; creation by Johnny & Associates, 178; invitation to perform in the
PRC by Wen Jiabao, 157; Japanese
wave of pop-cultural flows lead by,
157; Kimura Takuya as a member of,
1, 157
SM Entertainment Group: multilingual
strategy of, 180, 231n54; 1995 starting of, 178
Soejima, Mikio, 70–71, 73–75
soft power—cultural: impact of Douglas
McGray's "Japanese Gross National
Cool" on, 136; of the transnational
cultural flow of J-Pop, 164–165, 181;
of the transnational cultural flow of
K-Pop, 181; Xi Jinping's efforts to
grow China's cultural soft power, 197
South Korea: emergence of a capitalist
economy in, 9; *4th Asian Art Show*
(1994) presented in, 77; identified as
a mini-dragon economy, 32; identified as a tiger economy, 32; inclusion
in *Festival: Contemporary Asian Art
Show* (1980), 48; inclusion in *Tradi-
tions/Tensions*, 80, 81, 83; protests
directed at the JFAC exhibition
Works of Japanese Traditional Craft
(Seoul, 1994): 103; Seoul biennale
(1974), 208n45; Seoul exhibition of
*Under Construction: New Dimensions
of Asian Art* (2002), 2, 51, 55, 57;
Seoul Raiders (Jingle Ma, 2002), 233;
3rd Asian Art Show (1989) presented
in, 73; urbanization of Seoul, 131,
132, 190
Sri Lanka: inclusion in *Festival: Contemporary Asian Art Show* (1980), 48;
3rd Asian Art Show (1989) presented
in, 74
Story of the Yanxi Palace (*Yanxi gonglue*)
TV drama, 197

Sun Ge, 35
Supangkat, Jim: "Multiculturalism/
Multimodernism" (catalogue essay
for *Traditions/Tensions*), 84, 85–86;
participation in the 1992 planning
meeting for *Traditions/Tensions*, 81;
rejection of the need for a theoretical
position in his curation of *Contemporary Art from the Non-Aligned
Countries*, 68–70

Taiwan: competing territorial and jurisdictional claims in the South China
Sea, 161, 235n15; identified as a
mini-dragon economy, 32; identified
as a tiger economy, 32; shared Confucian base of culture among China,
Hong Kong, Japan, South Korea,
Taiwan, and Singapore, 229n22
Takeuchi Yoshimi—"Asia as Method"
("Hoho to Shite no Ajia"): differences
and disagreements with other scholars, 211n99; as the major intellectual
authority invoked in *Under Construction*, 53–55; on thinking of Asia as
the "formation of an interdependent
structure," 53, 109
Tani Arata, 109, 223n42
Tatehata Akira: on discussing indigeneity as relative rather than reduced to
a postcolonial gesture, 113–114; on
Magiciens, 37–38, 65
Tercera Bienal de La Habana (Third
Havana Biennial, 1989): Cuba
presented as a Third World cultural
leader, 22, 66–67; its display of
artworks viewed as an extension of
its critical framework, 69–70, 66;
Magiciens de la Terre (Magicians of
the Earth) compared with, 64
Thailand: Bangkok as an alternative
space of exchange and dialogue in
contemporary art and culture, 83;

urbanization (cont.)
modernization and modern culture
in New Asia associated with, 32;
Metabolism movement: art exhibitions with the theme of dynamically
expanding and unstable Asian cities,
11–12; new cultural consumption
patterns associated with the acceleration of, 12, 62, 131; Rem Koolhaas's
put-down of East Asian forms of,
115–116, 132, 211n102; revision of
formerly colonized and semicolonized zones into aspirational metropolitan zones, 8; world cities as assets
in attracting flows of capital, 132
Ushiroshōji Masahiro: on the role of
temporality in interpreting Asian art,
113; "realism" discussed in relation to
stances toward "everyday reality" of
political-economic events, 77–78
Utada Hikaru, 174

Venice: *Art iT* on the 2007 Venice Biennale, 41; Chinese artists included in
the 45th Venice Biennale (1993), 65;
Japan's unofficial participation in the
(2nd) Venice Biennale (1897), 41
Vienna: *Cities on the Move* at the Vienna
Secession (1997), 12, 22, 90; Japan's
participation in the Vienna Expo, 41
Vietnam: competing territorial and
jurisdictional claims in the South
China Sea, 235n15; discussed as part
of the *Ho Chi Minh Trail* project, 192,
193–194; *4th Asian Art Show* (1994)
presented in, 77
Vogel, Ezra, 9

Wallerstein, Immanuel, 15
Wang Hui: European characterization of
Asia questioned by, 121–122; on the
impact of the Cold War on the commonality of Asian imaginaries, 159

Watson, Jini Kim: on Cold War decolonization, 18–19; on New Asian Cities
that may transcend national and
racial/ethnic limitations, 195
Weiss, Rachel, 67–68
Wong Hoy Cheong: on *Cities on the
Move*, 90; *Sook Ching* (1989), 103
The World of Suzie Wong (Richard
Quine, 1960), 139, 147
Wu Hung, 189–190

Xu Bing, 66

Yasunaga Kōichi: as a member of the
curatorial team for the *Asian Artists
Exhibition*, 43, 46, 49
Yoshimi, Shunya: on American popular
culture in Japan, 169

Zatōichi Meets the One Armed Swordsman (*Shin Zatōichi: Yabure! Tōjiken/
Mangxia dazhan Dubei dao*), 137,
231n50
Zhang Qing: criticism of Chinese contemporary artists that ingratiated
themselves with Westerners, 190,
191, 244n24; effort to break a nationalistic West/China binary, 191, 192
Žižek, Slavoj, 8